JOHN ROSEMOND'S

❖ *NEW* ❖

PARENT POWER!

JOHN ROSEMOND'S

❖ *NEW* ❖

PARENT
POWER!

Andrews McMeel
Publishing®

Kansas City • Sydney • London

14 RR2 10 9

Library of Congress Cataloging-in-Publication Data

Rosemond, John K., 1947–
    John Rosemond's NEW parent power / by John Rosemond.
      p. cm.
    ISBN 10: 0-7407-1415-5
    ISBN 13: 978-0-7407-1415-3
    1. Child-rearing—United States. 2. Parenting—United States.
    3. Child development—United States. I. Title: NEW parent power.
    II. Title.
      HQ769.R7135   2001
      649'.1—dc21
                                                    2001022351

BOOK DESIGN AND COMPOSITION BY KELLY & COMPANY

*On behalf of Willie and myself, this book
is dedicated to our children, Eric and Amy,
and their spouses, Nancy and Marshall, for our
wonderful grandchildren—Jack Henry, Patrick,
Thomas, Connor, the* one who is currently
in the "oven," *and those who are yet to come.
Don't stop now, kids! This is too good!*

About the Author

JOHN ROSEMOND is a family psychologist, a syndicated columnist whose weekly parenting column runs in two hundred newspapers across the United States (including Alaska and Hawaii), the author of nine critically acclaimed parenting best-sellers, and one of America's busiest and most popular public speakers. In a typical eight-month speaking season, John is on the road almost constantly, delivering more than two-hundred presentations and workshops to audiences of parents, teachers, businesspeople, physicians, and other professionals.

John Rosemond's real qualifications, however, are that he and his wife, Willie, have been married for thirty-three years; they have two children, Eric and Amy, both of whom are married; and they are grandparents to five children, ranging in ages from six months to six years. John and Willie live in Gastonia, North Carolina.

John is executive Director of the Center for Affirmative Parenting, which provides resources for parents who want to raise their children in accord with traditional precepts. At his Internet site, www.rosemond.com, one can find a wide variety of parenting resources, including information about the Center's magazine, *Traditional Parent,* which features articles by John and other family-living experts and reaches some twenty thousand subscribers. Parents who become members of his site can actually ask John questions on-line.

For information on John's books, *Traditional Parent,* and a full list of parenting materials as well as for information on securing John as a public speaker or attending one of his parenting retreats, see the Web site or call 1-317-575-8050.

Contents

Contents

Contents

Acknowledgments

MY THANKS, AS ALWAYS, to all the good folks at Andrews McMeel, especially Tom Thornton and Chris Schillig for their unwavering support and patience over the years. Also to my copy editor, Janet Baker, who did a fabulous job with the raw material for this book.

To my darlin' Willie for putting up with the preoccupation that often envelops one who is absorbed in a major writing project: I love you for all time, Babes.

To my editors at the *Charlotte Observer,* most recently Kelvin Hart, for their support and encouragement, and to all the editors at all the newspapers who have stood by me in the face of the perennial firestorms my column evokes. To those editors who have not stood by, but have sought secure shelter from the storms, I understand. I've had to struggle not to do the same, many times. Finally . . .

It never fails that at the Academy Awards, one of the recipients will thank God for the honor he or she is receiving. That's always struck me as rather, I don't know, self-conscious. Nonetheless, because there is nothing I have ever said that does not have root in His Word, it would be dishonest of me not to do the same. Thank you, Lord, for the many blessings of this most rewarding ministry. I pray that my work on behalf of children and families is acceptable in thy sight.

Preface

My FIRST BOOK WAS PUBLISHED in 1981 by East Woods Press, a small house in Charlotte that was known for providing launching pads to fledgling Southern authors. At the suggestion of my editor, I titled it *Parent Power!* In 1981, the title alone amounted to throwing down the gauntlet, especially as regarded my colleagues in the mental-health professions who had succeeded at convincing the average American parent that children should be reared in "democratic" families so as to imbue them with high self-esteem. I decided that *Parent Power!* was appropriate to my emerging iconoclasm regarding mainstream psychology, especially as it concerns children and child-rearing. I was beginning to take up a position of strong opposition to what I now refer to as "psychological correctness," a force every bit as insidious and suffocating as political correctness.

My rebellion against the psychological powers-that-be had been conceived in the titanic struggles my wife, Willie, and I had experienced with our first child, Eric. Those problems had nothing to do with Eric and everything to do with our conscious decision to raise our children in the "new" way as opposed to the way of our ancestors. Having learned my parenting lessons through trial and much error, I was determined to do whatever I could to help other American parents avoid the same mistakes. In my newspaper columns and public presentations, I began telling parents that most mental-health professionals (and keep in mind, I *am* a psychologist) do not know what they are talking about when it comes to kids and their upbringing. They are intoxicated with the arrogant delusion that the profession has discovered something new under the sun. I know this all too well, because I was once similarly afflicted. In the process of putting my thoughts down on paper, that first book was born.

Predictably, its publication caused no small controversy. In fact, a fellow psychologist subsequently told me that he had been privy to conversations in which other members of the profession were actually plotting to strip me of my license to practice. My message, which recognizes the simple fact that the so-called old-fashioned methods of parenting still work, was and is still highly threatening to latter-day bandits who base their standards of living on persuading people otherwise. You read that right: Bandits. Con artists.

The first edition of *Parent Power!* sold reasonably well, but in the late '80s East Woods Press was purchased by another publishing company that had no interest in parenting books, so the publishing rights were returned to me. In the meantime, Andrews McMeel asked me if I was interested in writing books for them, and I happily agreed. Out of that arrangement came *John Rosemond's Six-Point Plan for Raising Happy, Healthy Children* in 1989. A year or so later, my editor informed me that I had written a parenting bestseller, not to be confused with a book that appears on the *New York Times* best-seller list, but no small achievement nonetheless.

My iconoclasm had by now mutated into out-and-out heresy, and my colleagues went apoplectic. I soon found myself the target of an ethics investigation, brought on because I had the temerity to tell parents the truth: that a child of eighteen months had no long-term memory, even for a traumatic event. Although my licensing board finally agreed that I was probably right (Note: I was right, but my board would only go so far as *probably*), my advice might have prevented some parents from paying a psychologist to either tell them the same thing or lie to them for the purpose of transferring money from their bank account to his or hers, so I was slapped on the wrist and told never to do it again. In spite of the perpetual threat, I continue to do all I can to cancel the power of psychology in contemporary American culture. America would be a better place if by some supernatural means all mental-health professionals, the good and the bad, were suddenly to disappear.

In 1991 Andrews McMeel published a revised, updated edition of *Parent Power!,* and it too became a parenting best-seller. Along the way, my activities as a public speaker had increased to the point where I could retire from private practice. I am now one of America's busiest public speakers, certainly the busiest in my field, which is a testament to the neurotic anxiety that drives American parenting today. In a typical eight-month speaking period, I give more than two hundred presentations, mostly in churches and schools. I sell my books at these events, and I stand behind the table, answering questions.

People often approach the book table and ask, "Which book should I buy?" I then ask the age(s) of their child(ren). If I'm dealing with a relatively "new" parent, I recommend what I term my "starter kit," consisting of *Parent Power!* and *John Rosemond's Six-Point Plan for Raising Happy, Healthy Children.* "This one," I say, pointing to the latter, "is my blueprint, while this one (now pointing to the former) is the details."

After saying that 4,260,733 times, it occurred to me that if the two books were indeed a "set," common sense dictated that they be contained in one volume. I approached Andrews McMeel with this idea and they agreed. So, here it is. In putting the two books together, I have revised and updated them by deleting outdated material and adding new information where "holes" existed in the original editions. For every page deleted, two new pages have been added. In short, the book is new and not new at the same time. I have not tried to "fix" the books, because they were not broken, but simply made them better, as when someone adds new memory software to a computer.

In the organization of the new book, I did what was simplest and most logical: I started with the blueprint and followed it with the details. *The Six-Point Plan* sets the stage in part 1; *Parent Power!* fleshes out the plot in parts 2 and 3. Part 1 lays out an approach to family making that is based on traditional precepts and understandings. As I said, there is nothing new under the sun. I tell my audiences, "I've never had an original thought in my life. I am the Great Parenting Plagiarist. I don't need any original ideas where

children are concerned because the 'old' ones still work just fine."
In part 2, I trace the development of the child in body, mind, and
spirit, from birth through the teen years. The purpose is to help
parents anticipate the problems that are typical to each of a child's
"seasons." Part 3 offers practical, nonpsychological approaches to
many of those problems. In no case have I offered a solution to a
problem without having first made sure it worked by testing it. I
can say with confidence that the approaches I put forth work, the
caveat being *if one works at them.*

I'm at the age when people begin looking for the easiest way to
do whatever it is they want or have to do. The fact that two books
are now one book suits that need quite nicely, because from now
on when someone asks, "Which of your books do you recommend
for parents of younger children?" I will have to point to only one
book and say, "This one." Maybe I'll live longer as a consequence.
I'd like that because the older I get, the more I'm aware of, and
therefore able to enjoy, the many blessings of life.

PART 1

The Six-Point Plan for Raising Happy Healthy Children

1

POINT ONE

The Parent-Centered Family

BECAUSE I'M REGARDED as an expert on parenting, people are forever asking me questions about raising children. These questions vary tremendously. On the other hand, despite the variety, all parents really seem to be asking one fundamental thing: "John, what's the secret, the key to raising a happy, healthy child?"

The question sounds as if it requires a long and complex answer. Quite a number of books have been written on the subject, and we certainly haven't seen the last of them. But during thirty-two years of being a husband and thirty-one years of being a father and six of being a grandfather, I came to the conclusion that "the secret" is not all that complicated.

Actually, there are two equally simple ways of answering the question. The choice depends on whether I'm talking to a parent who is married or a parent who is single. I'm going to take first things first and reserve my discussion of single parenting until later. In any case, most of what I have to say about being married and raising children has its parallel in single parenthood.

For those of you who are married, then, the secret to raising happy, healthy children is to give more attention to the marriage than you give to the children. If you succeed at that, your children will turn out just fine.

That answer often surprises people because it isn't what they're expecting. They're set up to hear me say something about building a child's self-esteem by giving praise or quality time or something equally child-centered. Instead, my answer has more to do with the health of the family as a *unit* than with any particular person in it. What I'm saying is that by ordering priorities properly within your family, you give your children the greatest possible guarantee of happiness.

"My Children Come First!"

A number of years ago, I conducted a series of parenting workshops for working mothers. I began each series by walking into the room and writing *In my family, my children come first* on the blackboard. Turning around, I would then ask for a show of hands from those women who subscribed to that principle. Hands would shoot up everywhere, and many of the women would turn to one another and smile and nod as if to say, Why, of course! We all know that, don't we? To me, however, those hands and those unspoken exchanges of consensus reflected the degree to which we, as a culture, have misplaced our family priorities.

In the years since World War II, we have become increasingly and neurotically obsessed with the raising of children. Something that used to be a fairly commonsense responsibility has taken on the trappings of science. Along the way, child-rearing has become "parenting," with all its high-pressure implications. In the process, we have elevated children to a position of prominence within families that they do not warrant, have certainly not earned, and definitely do not benefit from. Within the child-centered family, the implicit understanding is that the children are its most important members, and the parent–child relationship is the most important relationship. The more child-centered the American family has become, the more demandingly self-centered American children have become. And the more demanding the children, the more demanding the task of raising them.

In order to justify the frustrations inherent in this upside-down state of affairs, we've invented the idea that raising children is necessarily difficult. Time and again, I hear parents complain that it's the hardest thing they've ever done. But underneath the complaint I sense a feeling of pride, as if they *need* raising children to be difficult in order to feel that they're doing a good job.

Well, if you want raising children to be difficult, you need only to put them first. By putting your children first in your family, you guarantee they will become manipulative, demanding, and unappreciative of anything and everything you do for them. You guarantee they will grow up believing they can do as they please, that it's unfair of you to expect them to take on any responsibilities around the home, and that it's your bounden duty to give them everything they want and serve them in every conceivable way. Putting children first in the family further guarantees that you will experience parenthood as one of the most frustrating and unrewarding things you've ever done. Worst of all, it guarantees the ultimate unhappiness of your children, because happiness is achieved only by accepting responsibility for oneself, not by being led to believe that someone else is responsible for you.

Again, it's a question of priorities. In a two-parent family, the marriage must come first. After all, the marriage created the family, and the marriage sustains it. The marriage *preceded* the children and is meant to *succeed* them. If you don't put your marriage first and keep it there, it's likely to become a mirage instead.

The Life of a Cell

I describe the marriage-centered/parent-centered family in much the same way a biologist describes a cell. The biologist defines a cell as the basic building block of biological life. At the functional center of any particular cell, there is a nucleus that runs the show, so to speak. It is the executive authority within that cell. As such, it regulates the cell's metabolism, reproduction, and other essential functions. It also mediates that cell's relationship to its neighbor cells and determines what role the cell is going to perform within the larger organism of which it is a part. Furthermore, the biologist knows that if the nucleus of the cell is healthy and performing its role properly, the cell itself will be healthy and capable of making a positive contribution to its host organism. On the other hand, if the nucleus is not healthy, if it has been disturbed by disease or the invasion of foreign matter, it becomes less capable of performing its role, and the cell begins to deteriorate.

In a similar way, the family is the basic unit of social life. It is a social cell within a larger social organism called society. A family has a nucleus too. In a two-parent family, the nucleus is the marriage. In a single-parent family, the nucleus is the single parent. If the needs of the marriage or the single parent are being met, the family as a system will be healthy, and each individual within it will be healthy as well. In other words, if the marriage is being taken care of, or if the single parent is taking care of her- or himself, the children will, in all likelihood, be fine. They will feel protected. They will feel secure. They will have a clear sense of identity, and they will therefore have a foundation upon which to build good self-esteem.

This means that in a two-parent family, the marriage must be held in the highest regard. It must be the most important relationship within the family, and it must be more important than any single individual in the family. All too often, however, people give lip service to that idea but then turn around and *behave* as if the parent–child relationship is the most significant one. At the heart of that inconsistency lies the most destructive myth ever manufactured and sold to parents. It is the completely untrue but almost universally subscribed-to idea, that children need a lot of attention.

Myth? That's right, as in make-believe, not true. At best, it's a misunderstanding, born of misguided idealism. At worst, and especially when handed down from on high by a so-called parenting expert, it's a lie. In the last forty years or so, the "children-need-lots-of-attention" myth has exerted tremendous influence on our child-rearing practices, with absolutely disastrous results for children, their parents, and families as a whole.

Attention: The First Addiction

Children do *not* require a lot of attention. Children need very little attention, in fact. Let me help you digest this hard-to-swallow tidbit of news by talking, for a moment, about children and food.

Children need food. But they don't need a lot of it. If you persist in giving a child more food than he or she needs, that child will become dependent upon continuing to receive excessive amounts. If you continue to feed that dependency, it will grow into an obsession that will function as a powerful, driving force in that child's life. The child's sense of well-being will be based increasingly on the idea that, in order to feel secure, there must be ready access to food. Eventually, the child will become a food addict, and that addiction will hang like a stone around the youngster's neck, encumbering the growth of self-esteem.

Now go back and reread the previous paragraph, substituting the word *attention* wherever you see the word *food*. Go ahead, I'll wait.

Done? Quite revealing, isn't it? You see, it is as absurd to say that children need a lot of attention as it is to say that children need a lot of food. Too much attention is every bit as damaging as too much food. No one would argue that it is part of our job as parents to set limits on how much food a child may consume. It follows, therefore, that it's also part of our job to set limits on how much attention a child is allowed to consume within the family. But many, if not most, parents fail to set adequate limits on the amount of attention their children can expect to receive. So in many, if not most, families, you find a child or children who can't seem to get enough attention.

You probably know one: A child who constantly interrupts adult conversations, wants in on the action when the parents are being affectionate toward each other, talks incessantly (and loudly), acts silly, as if all of life is a performance, and, given the choice, would rather be inside with a group of adults than outside playing with a group of other children.

We're talking about an addict. And the child who develops an addiction to attention stands a better-than-average likelihood of some day transferring that dependency to drugs, alcohol, or some other form of self-destructive, high-risk behavior. At the very least, the attention-addicted child may never really grow up, may never truly attain emotional emancipation.

Earlier, I compared a family to a cell. A family is also structured somewhat like a solar system—which is, come to think of it, a galactic cell. At the center of a solar system, there is a source of energy that nurtures and stabilizes the system. Around this central core revolve a number of planets in various stages of maturity.

Likewise, a family needs a powerful, stabilizing, and nurturing source of energy at its center. The only people who are qualified to sit in that position of power and responsibility are parents. Their job is to define, organize, lead, nurture, and sustain the family.

Children are the planets in this system. When they are very young, they orbit close to the parent sun because they needs lots of nurturing and guidance. As they grow, their orbits increase steadily in circumference, so that by their late teens or early twenties they should be capable of escaping the pull of their parents' gravity and embarking on lives of their own. Our children's ultimate task is to move away from us, and our task is to help them. Allowing a child to bask in the spotlight of attention, however, encumbers the child's ability to establish greater and greater degrees of independence. A child cannot be the center of attention in a family and move away from that center at the same time. It's either one or the other.

If you put a child in the family spotlight, you create the illusion that he or she is the most important person. That center-stage position is cozy, warm, and comfortable, and the child who sits there will naturally want to stay, basking in the warm glow as long as possible.

Over the past thirty years, the percentage of twenty-two-year-olds still living with their parents (that is, freeloading) has more than doubled, during a time when the U.S. economy has never been better. This tells us that today's children are having increasingly serious difficulty emancipating themselves. Either we are clinging to them or they are clinging to us—or both.

Growing Up

For most of the first seven years of my life, my mother was a single parent. During this time, she and I lived with my grandmother in a small apartment in what is now the historic district of Charleston, South Carolina. In those days, it was just "the old part of town."

During the day, Grandma worked and Mom attended classes at the College of Charleston, working toward her degree in biology. At night and on weekends, she worked part-time at the post office, sorting mail. For several years, I was cared for in our home by a woman named Gertie Mae. The year before I started school, I attended a preschool program. My mother was a busy person in those days. She had to be, what with college, a job, and a child. There were many nights when she wasn't at home to tuck me in, so Grandma did it instead, always reading to me from classics such as Grahame's *Wind in the Willows* and Kipling's *Just So Stories*.

When Mom *was* home, she was often studying. She didn't spend much time with me as a child because she didn't have much time to spend. In fact, she discouraged me from even hanging around her much. When I did, she would look at me sternly and say something like, "You're underfoot. You should be outside, finding something to do." With that, she would usher me outdoors, where I'd find myself sharing the sidewalk with other children who'd also been kicked out of their houses. But we would be happy together, just being kids. Even though Mom had relatively little time for me and expected me to be fairly independent, I never felt unloved or rejected or uncared for. Quite the contrary. I felt *very* loved but very independent at the same time. Mom was always there when I needed her, but she was also quick to tell me when my need was not need at all, but simply unnecessary *want*.

In retrospect, I now realize that shooing me out from underfoot was simply Mom's way of letting me know she had a life of her own, separate from being my mother, and I had a life of my own as well. By not allowing me to become overly dependent on her presence and attention, Mom gave me permission to grow up and away from her.

That's exactly what the job of parent is all about. It's about helping our children get out of our lives. When I say that to an audience, some people laugh and some look shocked, as if I've just said something sacrilegious or obscene. But it's no joke, and I don't say it for shock value. It's the truth. When you strip away all the intellectual rhetoric and the flowery sentiment, you realize that the purpose of raising children is simply to help them out of our lives and into successful lives of their own. It's called emancipation. But emancipation is not an *event* that takes place at age twenty or thereabouts. It's a *process* that takes twenty or so years to unfold and come to fruition. And it's not that complicated, or even that difficult. It simply means doing for your child what my mother did for me.

Out of practical necessity, Mom became an expert at defining for me the difference between my needs and my wants. If I truly needed her, she was always there. On the other hand, if I wanted her to do something for me that I could do for myself or do without, she was quick to instruct me accordingly. I was not the center of attention in her life, and she made sure that, as I grew, she became less and less the center of attention in mine. I had growing up to do. She pointed the way.

Making that distinction is a parent's most *essential* responsibility. At first, the parent makes it for the child. Eventually, the child becomes capable of making it independently. That's called growing up, and *that,* not getting lots of attention, is what being a child is all about.

This is why it's so important for parents to realize that the amount of attention given a child very quickly reaches the point of diminishing returns. Once that point is reached, attention is more detrimental than beneficial to the emancipation process. As that process unfolds, so does a child's capacity for initiative, resourcefulness, creativity, self-sufficiency, achievement, and, therefore, self-esteem. So when I tell parents to pay more attention to their marriages than they do their children, I'm not advocating selfish neglect. You pay more attention to the marriage for the child's sake as well as your own.

The Games People Play

For the marriage to come first in a family means, among other things, that the man and the woman function primarily in the roles of husband and wife. Those are, after all, the roles they committed themselves to on the day they were married. All too often, however, when a couple begins having children, the roles of husband and wife begin receding into the background. Slowly but surely, the female stops functioning primarily in the role of wife and, instead, begins functioning primarily in the role of mother, even if she works outside the home. Simultaneously, the male shifts from his role as husband into the role of primary breadwinner. This process happens unconsciously. It's as if the birth of a child activates cultural programming that says, "Wife, your primary obligation is now to your children," and "Husband, your primary obligation is now to ensure permanent financial security for your family." And with that, the original contract—the commitment to each other as husband and wife—begins breaking down. As this insidious shift in roles takes place, the wife (now mother) begins to measure her self-esteem against how well behaved her children are and how well they perform academically, socially, and in the various activities to which she feels obligated to chauffeur them. Likewise, the husband (now breadwinner) begins to measure his self-esteem against how much money he makes, how quickly he climbs the career ladder, and how much social prestige he secures for himself and his family.

Unbeknownst to them, these two people are now moving in opposite and noncomplementary directions. The wife becomes increasingly involved with her children, increasingly obsessed with and consumed by the concerns and responsibilities of parenthood. Likewise, the husband becomes increasingly immersed in his career.

He begins spending more and more time at the office. When he comes home, he often brings the office with him—if not physically, in the form of a bulging briefcase, then mentally, in the form of headaches, worries, and other forms of stress. If his wife wants a relationship with him, she finds she has to maneuver around his preoccupation with work. On the other hand, if the husband comes home looking for a relationship with his wife, he discovers that, in order to have one, he must maneuver around her preoccupations with raising their children.

As this divergence takes place, resentment begins to build in the relationship. The husband begins to feel increasingly angry over the fact that his wife gives more time to the children than she does to him, even when he is at home. The wife becomes increasingly angry at the fact that her husband gives more time to his career than he does to her. The wife sees her half of the picture; the husband, his. But neither is able to see the whole and, with it, their own part in the process. Instead, each defines the situation in terms of the other person's "fault."

Now, in our culture we don't do a very good job of preparing people for relationship problems of this sort. So instead of putting their cards on the table, these two people begin playing games to express and deal with their pent-up resentments. These games are always variations on the theme of Guess What's on My Mind.

One of the most typical versions of Guess What's on My Mind that two people are likely to play is a game you may recognize. It's called Who Had the Worst Day? If you don't recognize it, or you need your memory refreshed, here's a description.

Who Had the Worst Day? begins around five-thirty in the afternoon, when Dad arrives home from work. (I'm going to describe the game in terms of the way it might be played in a more or less traditional American family—one in which Dad works at making a living, and Mom works at raising the children—but variations can be played even if both people have outside jobs.

Dad pulls into the driveway, and the news travels throughout the house: "Dad's home!" Immediately, the children begin bouncing around wildly, so as to greet Dad properly when he walks through the door. Dad parks the car, gets out, and immediately assumes his slumped and crumpled I've Had a Bad Day position.

Dad the Downtrodden shuffles up to the house, dragging his briefcase behind him. As he opens the door, he's met by a stampede of children, each of them wanting his attention. Each wants to tell Dad what he or she did that day. They want to tell on each other. They're yelling things at him, like "Did you bring me anything?" and "Take us to the store, please, Daddy, please, will you, Daddy, please, huh?"

Let's not forget Mom. She's standing in the background, viewing this chaos from the shadows. Her I've Had a Bad Day position, however, is quite different from her husband's.

Mom's pupils are dilated, her nostrils are flared, and every vein in her neck is taut. She doesn't have to say anything, because every nuance of her body language screams, *I've had it!* If she says anything at all, it's something along the lines of, "Well, it's about time you got home from your eight-hour vacation, Big Guy! Now it's time for *you* to find out what it's like to be a parent. From this moment on, they're all yours!"

And the game is on. Occasionally, the husband "wins." He persuades his wife to sympathize with what a bad day he's had, how rotten his boss is, how hard he works, *blah-blah-blah,* and his wife cooperates by allowing him to collapse in his favorite easy chair and zonk out behind the paper or in front of the television, while she keeps the kids occupied in another room.

Sometimes the wife "wins." Her hangdog husband takes the kids out for a ride to let her relax, he picks up supper at a Chinese restaurant so she doesn't have to cook, and he might even—if Mom's *real* lucky—put the kids to bed that night.

In the final analysis, however, Who Had the Worst Day? is a game with no winners. It's a game people play because they've already *lost* something, and that something is a proper sense of their priorities. Somewhere, back down the line, they misplaced the fact that the marriage is the most important commitment in their lives. Until they rediscover it, they will continue to become increasingly isolated in roles that do not complement one another and increasingly distant in terms of communication and intimacy.

It should come as no surprise to hear that the divorce rate among people forty-five and older has been accelerating faster than the divorce rate for any other age group. In the last fifty years or so, we've done such a good job of training wives to be mothers and husbands to be breadwinners that by the time their children leave home, they've forgotten how to be partners.

By no means am I ignoring realities. Children must be attended to and money must be made. I'm simply saying that wives can and should remain wives first and foremost, even after they become mothers. Likewise, husbands can and should remain husbands first and foremost, regardless of the demands of their careers. Mother, father, breadwinner—these are all secondary roles. Husband and wife are the primary adult roles in the family. If all this is somewhat difficult to accept, it's only because the cultural program to which I referred earlier is so demanding and insistent, so powerful and persuasive, that we succumb to it without thinking through the consequences.

The bad news is that many American families are in trouble because husbands and wives have lost touch with their primary commitment. The good news is that this problem is easier to fix than it is to live with. You can begin by giving your marriage some quality time.

The Real Meaning of Quality Time

The concept of quality time was coined in the early 1970s to address the anxieties of mothers who feared they were doing their children harm by entering or reentering the workplace.

"Not so!" announced the purveyors of quality time. "It isn't necessary to spend a lot of time with your children, as long as the time you spend is of good quality."

True enough, but your average American working mom takes that to mean she's obliged to spend every free moment giving her children large compensatory doses of positive attention. So after picking up the children from the day-care center, she goes home and flogs herself with the quality-time whip until the children go to bed, by which point Mom's too burned out to put anything of quality into the marriage. If Dad joined in the fun, he's burned out too. If he didn't, he's either too numb from watching television or too stressed out from working on stuff he brought home from the office to be much of a husband.

The fact is, leaving a child in someone else's care for significant periods of time isn't inherently bad unless you leave the child with the wrong people or in the wrong kind of place. For this reason, it's important that parents research their child-care options thoroughly and choose on the basis of quality, rather than hype, convenience, or cost.

If, while you work, your child is being taken good care of by big people who are trained to take good care of little people and who understand their needs, you have nothing for which to feel guilty and nothing for which to compensate. If, from Monday through Friday, you have only three or four hours a day in which to be a family, that's all the more reason to keep your family priorities in clear focus during that time.

I'm thinking about a young couple whom I once saw concerning their four-year-old daughter's apparent need always to be the center of attention. These parents were besieged by a steady stream of disruptions and interruptions, all of which were variations on the theme of "Look at me!" If they didn't immediately attend to their daughter's demands, she began whining. If that didn't bring results, she'd begin jumping up and down, flapping her hands, and crying. An absolutely ludicrous sight, to be sure, but one that can be frightening, especially for inexperienced parents.

These parents, both of whom worked, felt trapped between a rock and a hard place. On the one hand, even though their daughter was in one of the best day-care programs in the city, they felt their dual careers were depriving her of much-needed time and attention. Her constant demands for attention, they theorized, were expressions of insecurity. Unfortunately, dual careers were not a luxury.

At this point in the life of the family, they were an economic necessity. "What can we do?" they asked.

"First," I said, "tell me what you're already doing."

"Well," said the wife, "when we get home, we more or less devote ourselves to our daughter. We play with her, we read to her, we take her for walks. After being away from us all day, we feel she deserves to have us all to herself. "

"Stop right there," I said. "I think we've located the problem."

I proceeded to tell this young couple about some friends of mine, both of whom have careers. They also have two school-age children. After school, the kids are transported to a day-care center, where they stay until shortly after five o'clock, when their father picks them up and brings them home.

Several years ago, my friends created a rather unusual rule: For thirty minutes after everyone gets home, the children are not allowed in the den, kitchen, or any other room where their parents happen to be. They can play in their rooms or, weather permitting, go outside. The parents take this time to unwind and talk as they prepare the evening meal.

Until they created the thirty-minute rule, my friends had felt obliged to devote themselves to their children throughout the entire evening. The more attention they gave the children, however, the more demanding, self-centered, and disobedient the children became. Eventually, and not a moment too soon, my friends realized that the kids had taken over the family. In pursuit of good parenting, they'd created a monster!

Realizing that their relationship with each other was more important than their relationship with their children, they moved their marriage back to center stage in the family. The thirty-minute rule was one of many major policy changes. Here's how it worked: After everyone had arrived home in the evening, my friends set the stove time for thirty minutes and directed the children to find things to do. When the children tested the new rule, the parents refused their requests and sent them packing, firmly but gently. For the first few weeks, as soon as the kids heard the timer go off, they'd come racing into the kitchen, eager to get some parental attention.

As time passed, the interval between the buzzer and the children's appearance began to lengthen. Eventually, setting the timer became unnecessary. The children came home and found things to do until supper. After the meal, they'd return to their play until nearly bedtime, when they'd ask for a story and a proper tucking-in.

I would describe these children as independent, secure, outgoing, happy, mature, playful, obedient, polite . . . need I go on? Their parents cured them of their addiction to attention by putting the marriage first. In so doing, they defied a whole set of *shoulds* that operate in many if not most two-career families.

The little girl's parents were sufficiently impressed by my story to try my friends' technique for themselves. I lost touch with them for about six months and then happened to run into them one day in a store. They apologized for not having gotten back in touch with me but said there hadn't been a need. As we exchanged pleasantries, I could tell that things were different in their family. For one thing, the little girl stood quietly next to her parents without interrupting our conversation.

"We tried the thirty-minute rule," they said, "and it worked! These days, after we all get home, Julie takes responsibility for entertaining herself. We talk during dinner, but afterward she finds things to do until it's time for bed. At that point, we spend about thirty minutes reading and talking until lights out. We're all a lot happier these days." Looking down at her daughter, this young mother asked, "Aren't we, Julie?" Julie looked up, first at her mother, then at me. Smiling, she nodded and gave me a great big hug.

I love happy endings, don't you?

More Quality Time

Here are several more ways of making quality time for the marriage as well as helping children understand that Mom and Dad's relationship is numero uno. Single parents: These apply to you, too!

- Don't allow children to interrupt your conversations. Make them wait their turn, preferably in another room. Say, "We'll let you know when we're finished talking." A child who simply "can't wait" probably needs five minutes of cool-down time in his or her room.

- Create a weekly "Parents' Night Out" and don't let anything except acts of God interfere with the commitment. Every now and then, go off for a weekend without the kids. They need to realize that the marriage is a separate and autonomous entity within the family with a life and needs of its own.

- Put the children to bed early. Remember that your children's bedtime is for *your* benefit. In other words, determine how much down time you need in the evening during which you have no child-rearing responsibilities and set bedtimes accordingly. Instead of putting children to bed when *they're* ready, put them to bed when *you're* ready; then hang up your roles as mom and dad and just be husband and wife. I've always felt that eight is late enough for preschoolers; eight-thirty for children of grade-school age. I recommend that older children be in their rooms no later than nine, particularly on school nights. If children are willing to "make themselves invisible," it's all right if they read or work on hobbies until a slightly later lights-out.

- Once the kids are in bed, reduce distractions that interfere with communication and intimacy. Agree not to do either housework or office work after the kids' bedtime. Spend this time getting back in touch with the feelings that led to your original commitment. In this regard, the worst possible, and least creative thing you can do is get in the habit of centering your time together in the evenings around television.

Watching Television Alone

Since the early 1950s, the divorce rate in the United States has climbed steadily. Interestingly enough, it was in the early fifties that television invaded the American home and began dominating the life of the American family, especially in the evening. In your average American family, the television is on six hours a day, or forty-two hours a week. In a recent poll, couples married for one year were asked to identify their most prized household possession. Not surprisingly, most of the people in the survey named their TV sets. These couples were also asked what single aspect of their marriage needed the greatest amount of improvement. Ironically and sadly, the majority answered, "Communication."

A study found that the average American couple engages in less than thirty minutes of meaningful one-to-one conversation in a week's time. Each of those two people, however, is likely to spend more than twenty hours a week staring at a TV set.

The language of television watching conceals its reality. People talk about watching television "together," but the two things—watching television and togetherness—are mutually exclusive. When a family gathers in front of a TV set, each individual becomes isolated in a private audiovisual tunnel. You may as well be twenty miles away from the person sitting next to you if you're both staring at what is deservedly referred to as the boob tube. You can't watch television and truly communicate or be intimate at the same time. It's either one or the other. Ask yourselves. What's more important?

Questions?

Q: *I'm a single mother with two children. How does what you've said about putting the marriage first apply to single parents like myself?*

A: The situation may be different, but the priorities aren't. In a two-parent family, the needs of the marriage must come first. In a single-parent family, the needs of the single parent must come first.

The single-parent trap is more likely to snare single mothers than single fathers. For a number of reasons, mothers are more likely than fathers to neglect their own needs in the course of meeting their children's. Mothers also have more difficulty making the distinction between what their children need and what they simply want. When single mothers have primary custody of their children, which is most often the case, they usually feel that they need to compensate for the absence of a father in the home. In the process, they fall into the trap of overindulging and overprotecting the children and wind up stretching their emotional resources to the breaking point.

Look at it this way: You can't supply anyone else's warehouse unless your own is fully stocked. But instead of taking care of themselves well enough to keep their emotional warehouses full, single mothers often feel compelled to forgo their own needs in favor of their children's. They give and give—both emotionally and materially—to children who begin to take their giving for granted and appreciate it less and less. In no time at all, the children are likely to begin acting like demanding, ungrateful brats. Eventually and inevitably, the single mother's ability to go on giving collapses, and she vents her frustration on her children. Then guilt sets in.

"I shouldn't have gotten so mad at the kids. It's not *their* fault there's only one parent in the home."

At this point, our single mother feels compelled to do something special for her children in order to make up for having lost her temper with them. And it's back to business as usual.

In this continuing soap opera, the children are victims of circumstance and Mom does penance through self-sacrifice. Every time she gets angry at her kids, she ends up feeling like a bad parent. If I could only control my temper, she thinks, everything would be okay. But her temper's not the problem. It's her *lack* of tempering. To solve the problem, she has to learn to temper her own needs with those of her children. She must temper her giving to her children and begin getting for herself.

Compensations never work. Instead of solving problems, they eventually become part of them. As a single mother, you must establish an identify for yourself that has nothing to do with your kids. You must allow the adult woman in you to separate herself from her role as Mom and get her needs met—social, vocational, recreational, and sexual. For your children's sake as well as your own, you must give yourself permission to be creatively selfish. Only then will you have inventory enough to share freely with your kids.

Q: *I'm a single mother with two children, ages six and four. Their father and I have been divorced for over a year, and I've been involved in a serious relationship for the last six months. Unfortunately, the children don't seem to like my boyfriend. He has bent over backward to win them over, but the harder he tries, the less they seem to care. On more than one occasion, they've made it clear they don't want him over. The four-year-old has even told him, "It's time for you to go home now." I couldn't believe it! We're talking about marriage, but the children's attitude toward him gives me doubts. How should I handle this? Also, when is it all right to begin showing affection to each other around them?*

A: Actually, although "It's time for you to go home now" was a fairly outrageous statement, it's typical of the things kids say under circumstances such as these. Not having learned the art of social diplomacy, young children can be rudely candid when things don't suit them.

Keep in mind that their dislike of your boyfriend isn't really personal. In their eyes, Dad has a continuing interest in the family. Your boyfriend's presence, therefore, evokes a strong protective response from the kids.

Consider, also, that from Dad's leaving to the time your boyfriend arrived on the scene, the children enjoyed your undivided attention. They're probably having difficulty accepting the fact that some of those goodies are now going to someone else. This doesn't mean, however, that you should give them *more* attention. It means they need to adjust to getting *less*.

Talk to them about their feelings. Acknowledge that what they're experiencing is normal and help them understand that it's the situation and not really your boyfriend they don't like. Ask for their cooperation in extending hospitality and courtesy to any and all of your guests. An open discussion of this sort, in which you give the children an opportunity to express themselves and are accepting of their feelings, may or may not solve the problem. If it doesn't, you'll have to get more assertive.

Confront any further displays of rudeness on the spot. Tell the children, in no uncertain terms, that they do not have permission to be rude. Then banish them to their rooms until they decide to apologize. If you're consistent with this, the problem should disappear from view in fairly short order.

To help the kids adjust to seeing you and your boyfriend be affectionate toward one another, take things one step at a time. First, let them see you holding hands. If they try to break you apart, put them in their place and go on holding. When they seem to accept hand-holding, you can go public with hugging and kissing.

It would also help if your boyfriend made gestures of affection toward the children. He might, for instance, offer to read to them. If you're on an outing and one of them gets tired, he might offer to carry the youngster. Eventually, he can help you put the kids to bed. Again, don't rush it. Be sensitive to the children's comfort zone. If your boyfriend extends an invitation to the kids and they turn him down, he shouldn't take it personally. He should just step back, regroup, and try again later. Patience is the most important factor here.

If you and your boyfriend are hugging and the kids try to get in on the act, let them know it's not their turn. This says that your relationship with your boyfriend is, at times, exclusive. If you eventually decide to get married, this precedent will help you put the marriage at the center of the family.

Q: *I'm a married working woman with a six-week-old baby girl. Before she was born, I had planned to return to work after three months. Now that she's here, however, I'm beginning to feel I should be with her more than my job will allow. Is it psychologically damaging for a baby to be separated from her mother for long periods of time? When is the ideal time for a mother to return to work if her job isn't financially necessary?*

A: Bonding studies suggest that lots of parent–child interaction during infancy is necessary to healthy development, psychological and otherwise. Burton White, author of *The First Three Years of Life*, contends that children should, for the most part, be taken care of by their parents until age three. He recommends against full-time day care until then. Other developmental psychologists agree there is no truly adequate parent substitute during the first few months of life, but they don't feel there's any real danger to leaving older babies and toddlers with competent and attentive secondary care-givers, such as in-home sitters and trained day-care staff.

Ideally, parents should take primary care of their children for at least the first year of their children's lives. Realistically, however, if that's not possible because of economic pressures, or you truly feel your own mental health is at stake, stay home for at least six weeks and then go back to work. Regardless of when you decide to return to your job, it's important that you choose quality care. For example, a day-care center's child-to-staff ratio should be low enough to ensure each child adequate individual attention. For infants, the ratio should be no greater than five babies to one staff person.

Some of the questions parents should ask when shopping for child care are: Does the center require prior formal training and certification of key staff persons, or are they hired off the street? Does the center have enough play materials to go around, and are they of sufficient variety? Does it have a safe, interesting outdoor play area? What are its discipline policies?

Most states have an office within the Department of Human Services that oversees the delivery of child-care services. They will be glad to provide parents with information and referral concerning child-care resources.

Q: *Is it true, as many people seem to feel, that mothers are more important than fathers to the child-rearing process?*

A: We fathers are *just* as important as mothers in the raising of children. Unfortunately, the average American father still acts as if child-rearing is primarily "woman's work." As a result, there is a general tendency to ignore or minimize the strengths fathers can and do bring to the parenting process.

The result of this lopsided state of affairs is that mothers tend to feel more responsible for their children than they actually are, while fathers often feel insignificant and even excluded. Worse yet, some fathers use this myth as a convenient excuse to exclude themselves.

In effect, many American mothers, even though married and living with their spouses, function as single parents.

To be sure, there are predictable differences in the ways mothers and fathers relate to and interact with their children. These differences have to do with biology, psychology, cultural expectations, and practical considerations. For example, in all cultures and in all times, mothers have occupied the role of primary parent during infancy and early childhood. This arrangement makes sense from several perspectives, including the fact that women have the built-in ability to feed their babies while fathers do not.

But *primary* need not and should not mean *exclusive*. Even during the early years, fathers are important. Studies have shown, for example, that preschoolers whose fathers are actively involved in their upbringing tend to be more outgoing, adaptable, and accepting of challenge. Other research indicates that children with involved fathers do better in school, get along better with peers, and have better self-esteem. Children of actively involved and interested fathers are also less likely, during their teens, to become pregnant or develop problems with drugs or alcohol.

In *Never Cry Wolf,* naturalist and author Farley Mowat gives an insightful look at the wolf family, one of the few monogamous family units in the animal kingdom. Wolf cubs are never far from their mother. She protects and nurtures them until they reach adolescence, at which point the male wolf takes over as primary parent. He teaches his offspring to hunt and kill and survive in an often hostile environment. In other words, the wolf father endows his children with the skills they will need for self-sufficiency.

Reading Mowat's book, the thought struck me that perhaps we humans would do well to take a lesson from the wolf. I'm convinced, in fact, that children need more "mothering" than "fathering" during infancy and early childhood. I'm equally convinced that as children grow and their needs for autonomy increase, fathers become increasingly important.

I can already hear the outcry: "Rosemond's a chauvinist! He's saying that women aren't capable of raising successful children by themselves!"

No, I'm not a chauvinist, I'm a realist. I'm saying that women are inherently better suited to certain aspects of parenting than fathers and vice versa. I'm saying that their respective strengths are better suited to certain areas and times of a child's development than others. In the real world, mothers and fathers contribute differently, but equally, to their children's wholeness. I'm saying children fare better with two parents working together than with one of either sex working alone. This is not to say that single parents can't do a good job of raising children. And please note that I didn't merely say "two parents," but "two parents *working together*."

Nor am I saying that all fathers would be wonderful dads if only given the chance. It's a father's responsibility to create opportunities for creative relationships with his children. If he doesn't, it sure as shootin' isn't their momma's fault.

Q: *My husband and I were both married in our mid-thirties and now, five years later, have a two-year-old boy. We've tentatively decided not to have any more children. To be perfectly frank, we just don't have the energy for another baby at this stage of the game. We'd like to know whether you have any particular concerns or recommendations regarding only children.*

A: There are several caution flags I raise with parents of only children.

First, because all the parents' eggs, so to speak, are in one basket, the only child tends to receive more attention and more things than does the child in a family of two or more children. If the attention is excessive, it is to the disadvantage of all concerned, but particularly to the child. As I pointed out earlier, too much attention is addictive and detrimental to the growth of independence and self-esteem.

Overindulgence also leads to behaviors typically associated with the "spoiled" child: making unreasonable demands, acting starved for attention, throwing tantrums, being disrespectful and disobedient.

We have seen that the prevailing child-rearing myth of the sixties and seventies was that children need a lot of attention from parents. Except for the first few years of life, this simply isn't true. Children need attention, but too much can create a dependency that stifles emotional growth and development.

A second caution addresses something I've often heard from parents of only children: "It was just easier to take Bobby with us everywhere we went." On the surface of things, this degree of parent–child closeness may look desirable, but in the final analysis it is not. As a result of being included in so many adult activities, Bobby begins to perceive the marriage as a threesome, centered around him. This family dynamic makes it difficult, if not impossible, for Bobby to outgrow his infantile self-centeredness. Also, to the degree that the only child is treated and regards himself as an equal, parents will have a difficult time establishing themselves as authority figures. Furthermore, because the boundary between the child and the marriage is blurred, the child may fail to develop a clear sense of his own identity.

The only-child syndrome breeds its share of behavior problems. They typically include interrupting adult conversations, demanding to be included in adult activities, having problems in separating from parents, wanting to be included any time parents show affection toward each other, showing disobedience and disrespect, and wanting constantly to be the center of attention.

Despite the bickering that often characterizes sibling relationships, siblings help one another learn to share and resolve conflict. Only children sometimes have problems in both these areas. With other children, they tend to be possessive of their belongings and want everything to go their way. These potential problems are made worse by the fact that, by virtue of being included in so many adult activities, the only child is often better socialized to adults than to peers. Consequently, the only child is often perceived by peers as having a superior "know-it-all" attitude.

A little foresight can prevent these problems from ever developing:

- Center the family around the marriage, not the child.

- Limit the child's inclusion in adult activities.

- Enroll the child in day care no later than age three.

- Avoid indulging the child with either too much attention or too many things.

Q: *What suggestions do you have for the parents of a five-year-old only child who is addicted to attention, television, and toys? Our son is very demanding and easily bored. Instead of playing with other children in the neighborhood, he either wants us to play with him or wants to watch television. If we go somewhere, he either goes with us or stays with his grandparents. We want to undo the damage we've done but aren't sure where to begin, what to do, or how quickly to go about doing it.*

A: To begin with, you haven't done any permanent damage. You've simply set certain precedents that aren't working to anyone's advantage. You need to dismantle and replace them with more workable ones. Making major changes of this sort demands a well-organized and strategic approach. If you're ready, here are some tips on getting started.

First, limit your son's TV watching to no more than thirty minutes a day. The more time children spend occupied with television, the less able they are to find creative ways of occupying themselves. By turning the TV set off, you force him to find other ways of using his time.

Of course he'll want you to occupy it for him, so, second, limit the amount of time you spend playing with him to two fifteen-minute periods a day, once in the morning and once in the afternoon. When he asks you to play with him, set the kitchen timer for fifteen minutes. When it rings, excuse yourself and go back to what you were doing. This doesn't mean you're at his beck and call twice daily. If he asks you at an inconvenient time, tell him he's going to have to wait. If he pesters or whines, send him to his room for fifteen minutes.

Third, stop taking him with you everywhere you go. When you go out, leave him with baby-sitters instead of always with relatives. Hire a teenager in your neighborhood who relates well to children to come into your home one night a week while you and your husband go out to dinner or a movie. The understanding that he isn't a member of the marriage will help your son develop independence and a clear sense of personal identity. In the long run, it is also a prerequisite to successful emancipation.

Fourth, reduce his toy inventory. A child of five should have very few store-bought toys, and those should consist primarily of flexible toy sets such as Lincoln Logs, Tinker Toys, and Legos. Where toys are concerned, I often tell parents that if the toy wasn't in production before 1955, it's probably not worth buying. The right toys, in small numbers, encourage initiative, resourcefulness, and creativity.

Prepare him for all this by sitting him down one evening and telling him, in a gentle but straightforward manner, about the changes you're about to make. If he asks why, just say, "This is what happens when children are five years old." A more involved explanation will only confuse him or make him feel there's something wrong with him.

Later, if he balks at some new way of doing things, you can simply say, "Remember the talk we had? This is one of the changes we were talking about."

By the way, it's really not necessary that you do this one step at a time. In fact, your son will adjust more quickly to the changes if you implement them all at once.

Q: *I am a single mother with a nine-year-old son. My ex-husband and I divorced when Teddy was three. I've recently decided to get married again. My fiancé, who has been married before but has no children, and I have been seeing each other for almost two years. He and Teddy have a good relationship, which was one of the things I considered before saying yes. What are some of the problems we may face in our new family?*

A: You and your husband-to-be are creating what's known as a stepfamily, a family in which one parent is a stepparent.

The stepfamily is the most rapidly growing family type in America, representing 25 percent of our nation's families. At the millennium, nearly thirty million children were living in stepfamilies, and another million are added every year. At this rate, the stepfamily will eventually replace the traditional family as the dominant American family type.

There are actually two types of stepfamilies, the primary stepfamily and the secondary stepfamily. The primary stepfamily includes the parent who has primary custody of the children. The children visit with, but do not reside with, the secondary stepfamily. Since most mothers retain custody of their children after divorce, most primary stepfamilies are headed by a mother and stepfather.

The primary stepfamily faces a set of problems that are different from those faced by the traditional family. The two biggest hurdles involve, first, the need to establish the marriage at the center of the family and, second, the need to establish the stepfather as an authority figure.

Unfortunately, in many if not most stepfamily situations, certain precedents were set before the remarriage that interfere with the accomplishment of these goals.

The first of these involves the fact that, following a divorce, a mother becomes a single parent. Because she has no spouse, her relationship with her children may become the most important relationship in her life. Increasingly, the single mother devotes herself to the raising of her children, and her children become increasingly dependent on her attention. In effect, an unwritten pact evolves that reads essentially, "You meet my needs, and I'll meet yours."

Enter boyfriend, who quickly perceives the strength of the mother–child relationship and adopts an "If you can't beat 'em, join 'em" attitude. Wittingly or unwittingly, he begins to court not only the mother but her children as well. He tries to become their friend, a good buddy. He correctly realizes that he must, in effect, obtain the children's approval if he stands a chance of having their mother accept his proposal of marriage.

After the remarriage takes place, everyone continues to cling to old habits which, unfortunately, no longer work. The mother has difficulty moving out of a primary relationship with her children and into a primary relationship with her spouse. As a result, the stepfather begins to feel like a third wheel.

Making matters worse is the fact that the stepfather's need to shift gears from good buddy to parent causes everyone anxiety, confusion, and even anger. He attempts to discipline them, and the children run to their mother, complaining that he's being "mean." She responds protectively, accusing him of overreacting or taking his "jealousy" out on the kids. Round and round they go, and where they stop, heaven only knows.

All this can be avoided, or at least minimized, if people planning stepfamilies will, above all else, remember two things:

1. The marriage must be the most important relationship in the family. Stepfamilies are no different from other families in this respect.

2. The stepparent must assume authority equal to that of the natural parent. This means that the natural parent must be willing to share authority equally with his or her new spouse.

An ounce of prevention is always better than a pound of cure. Take the time to discuss just exactly what you're going to do to avoid these problems and how you're going to handle them when and if they do come up.

Q: *How should a husband and wife handle arguments between them when the children are around? We do our best not to argue in front of our two children, ages seven and four, but occasionally we let something slip when they're within earshot. It always seems to bother them, which makes us feel guilty. In fact, the younger one has sometimes told us point-blank: "Stop!" When this happens, which isn't often, we stop and apologize to them. Since neither of us ever heard our parents argue, we don't feel secure in this area of our relationship with our children. Do you have any suggestions?*

A: First of all, I suggest you start letting your children hear some of your arguments. Second, *never* allow them to interrupt while you're in the midst of one.

Disagreement is a natural and inevitable aspect of human relationships. As intimacy within a relationship increases, so does the
likelihood of disagreement. You can't have marriage without disagreement, but you *can* have marriage without *argument*, which is
the confrontation and working through of disagreement. Unfortunately, when two people don't confront the disagreements they
inevitably face once they're married, their relationship stands a
good chance of never growing. It's too bad your parents never
taught you the facts of being married. Don't make the same mistake.

Your children need to learn, first, that arguments come with
marriage. Then they need to learn that arguments don't destroy
people. Finally, they need to learn how to engage in constructive
disagreement with other people. If they don't learn these things
from you, how are they going to learn them?

I said your children should hear *some* of your arguments. Obviously, there are certain topics children should *not* overhear their
parents discussing, whether they're arguing or not. If you want
them to learn that arguments aren't necessarily destructive, you are
responsible for conducting your disagreements in a civilized, constructive manner. This doesn't mean you can't raise your voices,
but it does mean you should not slander or belittle each other. You
show respect for each other's point of view through active listening, making an attempt to consider points of view other than the
two you brought to the discussion, and trying to reach a win-win
resolution.

There will undoubtedly be times when you will want to save
your disagreements for after the children are asleep. But there are
probably more times when you want to have your disagreements
when they're awake and perhaps even in the same room. If you
choose to have an argument in front of them and they attempt to
interrupt you, you should say something like, "We are simply dis-
agreeing with each other. If you don't like it, you may leave the
room. If you stay, you may not interrupt us or cry. If you do, we'll
send you to your rooms until our discussion is over."

If you start arguing and the children suddenly appear in the
room with you, it's because they want to make sure everything is

going to be all right. Reassure them that you're both alive and well and intend to stay that way and send them from the room.

Q: *My husband and I are expecting our first child in November and are already having a disagreement over names—ours, not the baby's. My husband's older brother—whom he hero-worships—and sister-in-law allow their two children to call them by their first names and now my husband wants our child to do this too. I simply cannot envision our son or daughter calling us Jim and Liza, but my husband says "Mom" and "Dad" are roles that prevent give-and-take in the parent–child relationship and get in the way of open communication.*

A: This disagreement over what your child will call you is more significant than it may sound. It says that the two of you are on completely different wavelengths regarding your attitudes toward parenthood.

Furthermore, since your attitudes and conduct as parents will have great influence on your relationship as husband and wife, your marriage stands a good chance of ending up on the rocks if you don't do something now to get your act together. For that reason, I think the two of you would be wise to consider some marriage counseling before the baby comes.

Your husband's reluctance (and that of his brother) to accept without reservation the role of "Dad" suggests that perhaps there were serious problems in the relationship with his parents, particularly his father. Were his parents rigid and unaffectionate? Were they abusive, emotionally or otherwise? Did one or both of his parents have a drinking problem? During his childhood, was the older brother more of a father than the father actually was?

If the answer to any of these questions is yes, I'd also recommend that your husband find a therapist who can help him work through the confusion and hurt of his childhood. He needs to realize that having your child call him *Jim* as opposed to *Dad* is a compensation, not a solution, for problems he experienced with his parents. As such, it could have disastrous results.

As parents, the two of you will be responsible for giving your child a balance of love and firm discipline. In so doing, you guarantee your child's security and self-esteem, not to mention his or her love and respect for you. Your husband's belief that "Mom" and "Dad" are roles that prevent give-and-take and interfere with communication needs to be addressed now.

Mom and *Dad* are terms that should embody both endearment and respect. By contrast, *Jim* and *Liza* convey neither endearment nor respect. For a child to call his parents by their first names implies that the relationship is democratic. This is fine between friends, but the parent–child relationship is not and cannot be democratic. When parents attempt, through obvious or subtle means, to create the illusion of democracy in the family, the outcome is chaos.

Mom and *Dad* are also associated, almost automatically, with emotional responses—trust, belongingness, and the like—that are valuable, even essential, to a healthy parent–child relationship, one that fosters security and good self-esteem.

I would guess that herein lies part of the problem. *Mom* and *Dad* evoke painful rather than nurturing memories for your husband, memories he would prefer to avoid. I heartily encourage him to explore his feelings in more detail and in more depth, preferably with a qualified therapist.

Q: *What do you think about letting children sleep with their parents?*

A: Generally speaking, children should sleep in their own rooms, in their own beds, but I would bend this rule under certain circumstances. For example, there's no harm in having *infants* sleep in the same room with their parents. No harm, either, in letting children come temporarily into their parents' beds during illness or periods of extreme stress, such as might follow a significant death or a house fire. But aside from exceptions such as these, I say, "Children to their own beds at a reasonably early hour!"

Sleeping in his or her own bed helps establish that the child is an independent, autonomous individual, with a clearly separate identity. In addition, parents sleeping together and separate from the child enhances the child's view of the marriage as not only a separate entity within the family but also the most important relationship within it. A child who sleeps with his or her parents is in danger of never reaching this understanding, of feeling wrongly that the marriage is a threesome.

Separate sleeping arrangements also set an important precedent regarding separation. Children who separate from their parents at bedtime are better prepared to separate from them under other circumstances—when sitters come, at day care, the first day of school, for swimming lessons, and so on.

Q: *Isn't it true that the custom of having children sleep separate from their parents only began around the turn of this century? Isn't it also true that before this, and since prehistoric times, children were kept in bed with, or at least in another bed beside, their parents? If so, it would then seem that, whether society condones it or not, letting children sleep with parents is more natural than making children sleep alone.*

A: I'm absolutely certain that my position rests on firm clinical and developmental ground, as opposed to simply being an extension of societal expectations and prejudices.

Regarding the historical antecedents of this issue, I think I'm correct in saying that in other cultures and in other times, children have slept with their parents only when there were no other options. For instance, it would have been impractical, perhaps even deadly, for our prehistoric ancestors to hold out for nothing less than a two-bedroom cave. Nor does it make sense for nomadic people to lug two-bedroom tents from site to site, or Eskimos to waste valuable time and energy building two-bedroom igloos. In this and other countries, where you find parents and children sleeping together, it's usually out of necessity rather than choice.

Furthermore, the fact that a certain child-rearing practice is or was common to more primitive cultures may qualify it as more *natural,* but *natural* and healthy are not necessarily one and the same.

I'm sure that the characteristics of the particular culture dictate how this issue will be handled. In cultures where children usually sleep with their parents, other ways of cutting the cord have no doubt evolved. The adolescent puberty rites of some native cultures would be a prime example. In Western cultures, however, the separation of child and parents at bedtime is, I'm convinced, crucial to the development of autonomy—the child's *and* the parents'.

Q: *I'm thirty-eight and have been happily married for five years. I'm undecided over whether or not to have children. At times, I think it would be wonderful, especially in our later years. On the other hand, I have no overwhelming desire to spend the next eighteen years raising a child. What questions should my husband and I ask ourselves to help us reach this decision?*

A: Your dilemma is becoming increasingly commonplace. More and more people are putting off marriage as well as the decision of whether or not to have children. Considering that this is an extremely emotional issue, it's admirable that you're taking the time to weigh the pros and cons patiently and rationally.

It's unfortunate that our culture continues to communicate to women that they are in some way incomplete unless they opt for motherhood. Instead of enjoying the process of raising children, many women pressure themselves to *perform* at it. In order to demonstrate what good and conscientious mothers they are, they wind up devoting themselves body and soul to self-centered children who don't know their limits, never learn to accept *no* for an answer, and take everything they get for granted.

So just because two married people are capable of having children doesn't mean they should. The beauty of being human is that each of us is gifted with a broad range of capabilities. If you feel inspired to raise children, by all means raise children. If you'd rather raise sheep, raise sheep.

Ask yourselves these questions:

- Are we both in favor of having children or does one of us harbor reservations? When the decision to have children is made for the sake of one of the two adults involved, instead of being mutually arrived at, the eventual toll on the marriage can be enough to destroy it.

- Do we want to be just finishing our child-rearing responsibilities around age sixty, or would we rather spend our middle years together, relatively free to come, go, and do as we please?

- Do we feel emotionally up to dealing with the loss of freedom and the long-term obligations, financial and otherwise, that come with raising children?

- Do we enjoy being around other people's children or do they tend to annoy us?

- Did we have happy childhoods? I find that people tend to enjoy raising children to about the same extent they enjoyed *being* children. A happy childhood is perhaps the best guarantee of a happy parenthood.

You should also consider that the potential for certain genetic problems increases with the ages of the parents. Are you willing to take the higher risk of having a handicapped child? If you want more information about these dangers, ask your gynecologist to refer you to a genetic counselor.

A Final Word

Healing and strengthening the nucleus of your family, your marriage—or, if single, your own life—is something you can start doing right now. And once you've started, it's something you'll need to keep doing every day. Put your marriage first, and it's more likely to last. If you're a single parent, put *yourself* first, and you'll soon find you have far more of yourself to give to your children.

2

POINT TWO

The Voice of Authority

I'M OFTEN ASKED BY PARENTS, "John, how can we get our children to obey us?"

My answer is simple and direct: "If you expect your children to obey, they will."

At this, parents will often look puzzled and then say something like, "But, John, we do expect our children to obey us, but they *don't!* Instead, they complain and argue. Getting them to do anything is a major hassle. How can you tell us that if we simply expect obedience, it will magically happen?"

I'm sure most American parents would say that they expect their children to obey. I'm equally sure that most American children are not truly obedient. When told to do something by parents, the typical American child does not display a willing, cooperative attitude. Instead, he or she ignores, whines, argues, gets mad, or talks back.

The once-upon-a-time "yes, sir . . . no, sir" obedient child has become virtually extinct. But this sorry state of affairs is not the fault of children. It's the fault of parents who beat forever around the bush of obedience, afraid to disturb any leaves lest they damage the child's supposedly fragile psyche. It's the fault of parents who, instead of truly expecting children to obey, only go so far as wishing they would.

The distinction between expecting and wishing is found in the way parents communicate with children. When parents plead with children, they are wishing for obedience. When they complain to children about their behavior, they are wishing for obedience. When they bargain, bribe, threaten, give second chances, and "reason," they are wishing for obedience. These are all relatively passive forms of wishing, but there are more active and therefore less obvious forms as well. For example, the parent who pounds on the table, gets red in the face, and threatens the recalcitrant child with bodily harm, is—appearances aside—actually *wishing* for obedience. You see, this parent is in a snit precisely because his or her wishes haven't come true.

By far the most common form of wishing takes place when parents argue with children. All arguments with children get started in one of two ways. In the first, the parent makes a decision that the child doesn't like, and the child strains forward, grimaces, and in a voice that sounds like fingernails being dragged across a chalkboard, screeches, *Why!* In the second, parents make a decision that the child doesn't like and the child strains forward, grimaces, and, in a voice that sounds like fingernails being dragged across a chalkboard, screeches, *Why not!* Arguments start because parents make the mistake of thinking these are questions. They aren't! They are invitations to do battle. By accepting the invitation, you step squarely into quicksand. And the harder you struggle to be understood, the faster and farther you will sink.

A question is a request for information. If *"why!"* and *"why not!"* were truly questions, two things would occur. First, the child would listen to your answer. Second, after having listened, the child would at least occasionally agree. Now think about it. When is the last time your child, after listening to your most eloquent, honest, sincere explanation, looked at you and said, "Well, gosh, Mom! Since you put it *that* way, I have to agree. And gee, thanks for being my mom!"

What's that? It's never happened? Right! And it's never going to happen. Parents *cannot* win an argument with children. Winning an argument with someone means you change the person's way of thinking. As a result of the information or point of view you share, that person adopts a new and probably more mature point of view. Children don't have what it takes to appreciate and participate in this process. To compensate, they adopt an irrational position and hold on to it for dear life. So no matter how eloquent or how correct, parents cannot win because children can see only one point of view: their own.

Discussion requires the participation of two people who are as willing to listen as they are in wanting to be heard. Children want to be heard, but they rarely want to listen. As the parent explains, the child waits for an opportunity to interrupt. But despite the obvious fact that attempting to explain the *why* or *why not* of a parental decision serves no purpose except the child's need to argue, parents continue to do it.

This is why I believe in the power of four particular words. As a child, I couldn't stand to hear these four words. They made me so mad, I promised myself I would *never* say them to my children. When I became a parent, I kept this promise for several years. Then, having brought myself to the brink of disaster, I woke up to reality and broke it. *Because I said so* because part of my parenting vocabulary.

Some people say that children have a right to know the reasons behind the decisions we make. I agree, but with certain amendments. These are: First, they have a right to know in terms they can understand. Second, they have a right to know only if they are willing to listen. And third, if the truth is "Because I said so," they have a right to know that, too.

Save Your Breath

I have a two-part rule governing the giving of explanations to children. It's called the Save-Your-Breath Principle. Part One: Until children are mature enough to understand a certain explanation, no amount of words will successfully convey that understanding. In that case, it is in the child's best interest for the parent to say "Because I said so" or words to that effect. Part Two: When children are old enough to understand the explanation, they're also old enough to figure it out for themselves.

My two very strong-willed children frequently threw down the gauntlets of *why* and *why not*. When they were young, and after I had recovered from my idealistic naîveté, I often answered them with "Because I said so." I didn't bark or sound exasperated. I simply looked them in the eye and said it, without hint of threat or apology. As they approached their teens, I switched over to something along the lines of "You know me well enough to answer that question on your own." In reply, they would scowl and sigh and say, "Oh, sure, you probably think that" *blah-blah-blah*. Almost always, the *blah-blah-blah* was right on target, proving my point. It also proved that, regardless, they weren't about to agree.

There were times when I did explain myself to my children, but only if they were willing to listen. If they weren't—which was often, especially during their early years—I would say, "I don't talk when people don't listen." With that, the explanation was either put on hold or permanently canceled. If they protested loudly, I sent them to their rooms to cool down. Over the years, they learned that if they wanted to talk, they also had to listen. If they listened, I almost always ended up meeting them halfway. In this manner, I tried to teach them that discussion, not argument, is the way to get things accomplished.

Some people don't like the idea of saying "Because I said so" to a child. They argue that it isn't a reason. I disagree. Not only is it a reason, it's often the *only* reason. Let's face it, most of the decisions parents make are arbitrary. They are matters of personal preference, not universal absolutes. Why, for example, must your son go to bed at eight o'clock when the neighbor's boy, a year younger, is allowed to stay up until nine o'clock? Any and all attempts at explaining this inconsistency come down simply to: "That's the way I want it." Why don't you allow your daughter to ride her bike past the corner, when her best friend can ride three blocks to the convenience store? Again, any and all explanations boil down to "That's how I want it." In other words, "Because I said so."

If those four words stick in your throat, try "Because this decision belongs to me" or "Because I'm the parent, and making decisions of this sort is my responsibility." If you feel you simply must give some manner of "correct" explanation, save your breath by trimming it to twenty-five words or less. Remember, however, that regardless of how carefully you phrase your answer, the child is not likely to agree. In fact, you just might want to preface your answer with, "Okay, I'll pretend you're really asking me a question, and I'll give you an answer. But I don't expect you to agree. On the other hand, don't expect me to change my mind." When the inevitable happens, say, "That's all right. As I said, I didn't expect you to agree. I'm also not changing my mind."

Games Parents Play

Another common form of wishing children would obey is a game called Please? or Okay? that many of today's parents play with their children.

Please? begins when a parent wants a child to do something. It's usually something simple, such as wanting a child who is too big for a car seat to sit in the back. But parents have the darnedest ways of making simple things complicated and even confusing.

To play Please? the parent acts indecisive, as though not knowing exactly what the child is to do. Therefore, he or she makes no imperative, commanding statements. Instead, all statements are phrased as questions and asked in a small, pleasing voice.

For example, rather than "You are going to sit in the backseat" or "I want you in the backseat," a mother says, "Wouldn't you rather sit in the backseat so Mommy can sit up here?" This form and tone tells the child that Mommy needs help in making this difficult decision. The child is glad to provide it: "No! I want to sit in front. You sit in the back."

At this point, it's a jump ball, up for grabs to the quicker player. Often the parent commits a technical foul by changing the rules and becoming angry: "Look, I told you to sit in the backseat, now get there!" This is not true, since the parent never told the child anything. But the foul never gets called, unless the other parent is playing the role of referee.

More often, "Please?" does not come to that abrupt an end. The parent usually negotiates a compromise. For example, the child gets in back but Mommy sits in back too.

Parents play "Please?" to avoid confrontations, showdowns, and embarrassment. And it works! But what they get in the bargain is no bowl of cherries. Children are quick to learn when their parents are afraid to assert their authority and can be relied upon to give in. When it comes to a question of who's the boss, if parents won't run with the ball, children will.

There should never be any question about who's running the show. It is a child's inalienable right and privilege to be informed early in life that the parent is boss. Confucius say, "When parent at loss, child make bad boss."

Parents need to tell children what to do and then stand prepared to enforce their authority. Don't ask questions if you don't really intend the child to have a choice.

Children need to be told what to do by parents who aren't afraid or embarrassed by an occasional showdown. Children feel more secure and comfortable with parents who know where they stand (and where they want to sit).

Count the times you play "Please?" or "Okay?" with your child today. Once is too many.

Family Government

Since the late sixties, a number of books have been written on the subject of self-esteem in children. Several became the child-rearing bibles of their day. Their authors maintain that children develop self-esteem only if their parents show respect for them. Parents demonstrate respect for children by treating them as equals. This means that parents are supposed to give children an equal voice in determining rules, chores, privileges, and so on. Compromise is the prescribed way of settling any and all differences of opinion. When a child misbehaves, parents should appeal to the child's intellect and sense of responsibility by explaining the difference between right and wrong. Under no circumstances are parents ever actually to punish a child for misbehavior, because punishment violates the fundamental premise of equality.

These authors maintain that the only psychologically healthy family is a democratic family. In a democratic family, they say, no one is more powerful than anyone else. They market what is called "the art of active listening," which essentially prohibits parents from telling children what to do. Instead, parents should listen non-judgmentally to a child's point of view, calmly communicate their opinions, and leave it to the child to assume responsibility for his or her own actions.

As nice as it sounds, the democratic family is, was, and always will be fiction. You can, if it makes you feel better, *pretend* to have a democratic family, but pretense is as far as it ever will go. The illusion of democracy in a so-called democratic family is created and maintained with lots of words, lots of discussions, explanations, and lots of asking the children for their opinions. But if you sift through the rhetoric and finally get to the bottom of things, you will discover an incontrovertible truth: In this so-called democratic family, *someone* always has the final say. That simple fact strips away any and all illusions of democracy. Furthermore, that someone better be an adult, or everyone in the family is in trouble.

In the real world, there is no possibility of a truly democratic relationship between parents and children—not, at least, as long as the children live at home and rely on parents for emotional, social, and economic protections. Until a child leaves home, there can only be exercises in democracy, and these exercises must be carefully orchestrated by the child's parents, lest they get out of control.

If we're going to draw analogies between families and political systems, the most ideal form of family government—the one that works best for both parents *and* children—is a benevolent dictatorship.

In 1976, when I first began using that term, the reaction I often received indicated that people were only hearing the second word. Consequently, they thought I was giving parents permission to be rigidly, even punitively, authoritarian. Not true.

A benevolent dictatorship is a form of family government in which parents act on the recognition that their most fundamental obligation is to provide a balance of love (benevolence) and authority (dictation) to their children. This is not tyranny. Benevolent dictators are *authoritative*, not authoritarian. They do not demand unquestioning obedience. Quite the contrary, they encourage discussion (as opposed to argument), but they make the final decisions. They create rules that are fair and enforce them firmly but gently. Benevolent dictators don't derive sadistic pleasure out of bossing children around. They govern because they must. They recognize that it's a child's right to be governed well, and is every parent's responsibility to provide good government. Beyond all else, they prepare their children for the time when they must govern themselves and *their* children.

In a benevolent dictatorship, children experience increasing responsibility and privilege as they grow. This ensures that by the time they reach their late teens or early twenties, they are ready for self-government. Having experienced the model in their lives, they know how it works. Within the framework of discipline created for them by benevolently dictatorial parents, children learn the value of independence. They learn it is not something to be taken for granted but something to be worked for and, therefore, something worth taking care of.

There is a widespread tendency to regard love as a positive force and authority, or discipline, as a negative and potentially destructive one. This notion that love is somehow more valuable to a child's upbringing than discipline is what I term "the great misunderstanding." The facts are: First, you cannot effectively communicate your love to a child unless you are also a source of effective authority. Second, you cannot effectively discipline unless you are also a source of genuine love.

Authority strengthens parental love. Without that strengthening agent, love becomes indulgent and possessive, overly protective. Likewise, without the tempering effect of love, parental authority becomes overbearing. Love provides meaning and a sense of belonging to a child. Love gives a child reason to strive. Authority provides direction to the child's strivings. Love and authority are not opposite poles but two sides of the same coin. To be authoritatively loving and lovingly authoritative—*that's* the balancing act parents must master. Achieving that balance is not only essential to a child's security and self-esteem, it's also the key to a parent's sense of self-confidence. That's what being a benevolent dictator is all about.

Actually, whether they are willing to admit it or not, all parents are dictators of one sort or another. Some are more benevolent than others, and some are benevolent to a fault.

This idea may be somewhat difficult to accept, because we usually associate dictatorships with oppression and torture and people disappearing in the night. But a dictatorship is simply a system of government where one person is in control and is responsible for making decisions for a group of people who count on him or her to make good ones. And that's what parents do, isn't it? Like it or not, parents are dictators, preferably dictators of a benevolent nature.

Some time back, I was speaking to a group of physicians, explaining my concept of the family as a "benevolent dictatorship." One of the group, looking disturbed, raised a challenge.

"I think you're throwing this idea out in too general a fashion. Your 'benevolent dictatorship' may work quite well when children are very young, but we must give older children, especially teenagers, more freedom and more opportunities for making their own decisions."

"Yes!" I replied. "What you are saying is absolutely true and dovetails perfectly with my 'benevolent dictatorship.'

"You see," I went on, "the key in what you said was your use of the word *give*. And I agree! Parents must be willing to give their children greater freedom and more choices as they grow older—

even the freedom at selected times to make mistakes. But we must always retain control of the decision to give. We must never, as long as our children are dependent on us, hand complete control of their lives over to them."

There is no possibility of a democratic relationship between parents and children as long as children live at home and reply upon parents for legal protection and economic support. Until a child leaves home, there can only be *exercises* in democracy, which are carefully orchestrated by the parents. Yes, increasing degrees of independence must be given as the child matures, but given from a secure position of authority.

It is the parents' *right* to give the privilege and, likewise, their *right* to take it away. Within that framework, children learn the value of independence, not as something to be taken for granted but as something to be worked for—and therefore something worth taking care of. You are the boss. For *their* sake.

Respect: A Two-Way Street

In the past thirty-five years or so, we have grown increasingly dependent on experts to tell us how to raise our children. In the process, we have become more childlike in our unquestioning attitude toward their "expertness." Unfortunately, some of their advice has been more harmful than helpful.

Many parents were led to believe, for example, that obedient children were robots whose personalities and self-esteem had been squelched by parental heavy-handedness. That simply isn't so. While it's true that parents can frighten a child into cooperating, that child is also likely to look for opportunities to disobey whenever there stands to be a good chance of not getting caught. Fear does not teach obedience. It teaches a child to be cunning.

On the other hand, truly obedient children—that is, children who have invested great amounts of security in—and therefore respect—their parents' authority—are also the world's most outgoing, happiest, and creative kids. It's interesting and unfortunate that some parenting experts overlooked this connection and dealt in rhetoric rather than reality. It's unfortunate for the millions of American parents who were seduced into subscribing to their nonsensical philosophy that these authors failed, and still fail, to see the connection between parental authority and a child's self-esteem. It's even more unfortunate for the millions of directionless children who were the real victims of this oversight.

These experts make a big deal of the need for parents to respect children, pointing out that respect is a two-way street. As they use the term, "respecting your child" implies that parents should treat their children democratically, as equals. Most of us agree that every human being is worthy of respect. Parents *should* respect their children—for what they are and are becoming—but *not* as equals.

Respect between parent and child is indeed a two-way street, but the traffic going in each direction is different in every way. Children respect their parents by obeying them. Parents, on the other hand, respect their children by insisting that they obey. Parents who enforce obedience are caring for one of their children's most basic needs.

Unfortunately, many parents equate obedience with passivity. Not wanting to raise passive children, they find ways to avoid making them obey. These parents often fear that making children obey will stifle their independence.

The opposite is true. Learning obedience *enhances* a child's independence. Obedient children have parents who effectively describe and enforce limits. Within that clear framework, obedient children are free to be curious, to explore, and to invent—in short, to be as independent as their maturity allows.

Contrast this type of respect with the "respect" demanded by the authoritarian parent, who usually equates respect with fear. Children who fear their parents don't obey—they submit. Children who are truly obedient are not fearful. They are self-confident and secure. They are even secure enough to indulge in a certain amount of rebellion.

Children who fear their parents often become deceptive—they learn to lie in order to escape their restrictions. Children who are obedient are more likely to be honest and forthright, because they have been treated honestly and in accord with what they truly need.

At the opposite extreme from authoritarian parents are those who require no respect. Children whose parents do not require obedience live in a world of constantly shifting limits. Now they see them, now they don't. Their parents' agendas are hidden, and the children are forced to search for them. Their searching is usually frantic and attracts disapproval. Consequently, they are called "disobedient." I maintain, however, that there are no disobedient children; there are only parents who fail to accept their responsibilities and children who are scapegoats.

Children who don't know their limits must depend on their parents to reward them whenever they discover part of their parents' secret. Obedience, however, is its own reward. To the extent that children accept and function responsibly within the limits their parents define, those limits should steadily expand. Eventually, children no longer need someone else to define their limits for them.

Obedience, then, paves the road to maturity.

Parent Power!

Children need to become convinced at an early age that there are virtually no limits to their parents' capabilities. A toddler's sense of security rests upon the belief that mother and dad are capable of protecting, providing for, and preserving their children under any and all circumstances. This requires that parents convey to children an unquestionable sense of personal power—what I call Parent Power. Developmental psychologists have long recognized that young children believe, or want to believe, in their parents' infallibility. This belief is called the "omnipotency myth."

The infant's view of the world is egocentric, self-centered. Infants believe that all things exist for them and because of them. Parents exist because infants are hungry or uncomfortable or want to be held. For the first eighteen months or so of their baby's life, parents cooperate with this upside-down conception of how the world works. They cooperate because they must. When babies are hungry, they are fed. When diapers are messy, they are changed. Tired babies are soothed to sleep. Crying babies are held. Under the circumstances, it's no wonder that young children believe their parents were put here to serve them.

Sometime during the child's second year of life, however, parents begin the socialization process. They begin establishing limits and saying *no* to certain demands. This turnabout contradicts the infant's egocentric view of how the world works. The child whose sense of security is thus threatened struggles to keep things the way they were. This is the essence of the so-called terrible twos. That period from eighteen to thirty-six months is the single most misunderstood and maligned stage of human development. To be sure, it's a stressful, frustrating, and sometimes even confusing time in the parent–child relationship. But the conflict between parent and child that characterizes this stage is not only unavoidable but absolutely necessary.

The paradox is this: In order for a young child to develop an enduring, stable sense of *security,* the parents must first make their child temporarily *insecure.* They do this by firmly but gently dismantling the egocentric viewpoint of infancy and building, in its place, one based on the premise that *they* run the show. If they are successful in replacing egocentricity with "parent centricity," the child develops a respect for them that goes beyond what they are truly capable of. In the child's eyes, the parents now become omnipotent. This perception reflects the child's *need* to see parents as all-knowing, all-capable people. It follows that parents have a responsibility to present themselves to their children in precisely that light. The idea is not to make the child subservient but to create a nonthreatening authority upon which the child can rely.

Parent centricity, the young child's feeling that parents are safely controlling his or her world, forms the foundation of a new, more functional sense of security. Upon this solid foundation, the child can begin building creative competency in three realms: intellectual, social, and emotional. The establishment of parent centricity frees the child to go about the business of growing up without always having to worry about what unpredictable thing is going to happen next.

Spare the Rod, but Not the Rule

Rules are social boundaries. They outline the limits of acceptable behavior and preserve the stability of human environments. Rules knit society together; they are as essential to our survival as water is for the life of a fish.

For children, rules are an extension of parental authority. Rules are as necessary to healthy development as are stimulation, good nutrition, and sunshine. Rods can be spared; rules cannot.

Rules can be communicated to children in a number of ways. A direction or instruction is a rule. A task assigned to a child is a rule. Any decision defining what a child may or may not do or have is a rule.

When the rules of a game are clear, the player knows what moves are available and can predict with some degree of certainty what moves the other players will make. Rules organize the game. They reduce uncertainty and anxiety.

And so it is with children. When rules are present, a child knows what is and is not allowed and is able to predict parental behavior. Rules are fundamental to feelings of security. When rules are unclear or enforced sporadically, children can't predict what their parents will do next. Under these circumstances, children become anxious, insecure, and sometimes even physically sick. I do not advocate rules for the sake of rules. Bad rules or too many rules can be as detrimental to a child's well-being as poor nutrition.

Good rules should meet four basic requirements: They should be stated clearly, defined specifically, selected reasonably, and enforced consistently.

Rules should be stated clearly. Avoid dressings, garnishes, and complicated explanations. Preschool children will have difficulty understanding even the best reason for why a rule is necessary. If you must explain, make the explanation brief and to the point: twenty-five words or less.

Older children understand reasons and like to argue about them. If parents argue back, the basic issue—that parents set rules and children abide by them—becomes confused. If a child wants to argue, say, "I will not argue. You will have to do as you are told."

Some parents feel guilty about making straightforward demands on their children. So they disguise their demands as requests which require "yes" as the only acceptable answer. "Will you take out the garbage?" is really a rule if the child has no choice but to take out the garbage. Phrased as a question, however, the rule is unclear. The garbage sits in the kitchen, the parent becomes upset, and the child gets increasingly confused.

Rules should be clearly defined. What is meant by "Clean up your room"? Parents think their children know, but a child's idea of clean is never the same as as an adult's. Only Sylvia's mother knows exactly what she wants when she tells five-year-old Sylvia to clean up her room. To reduce uncertainty and confusion, define tasks specifically. "You must make your bed, fold your clothes and put them in your dresser, and put your books back on the shelf before you can go outside." If a chore must be done every day, making a list of the steps involved will eliminate many unnecessary arguments. When a rule is defined clearly, it is easier to enforce.

Rules should be reasonable, especially when they refer to chores. A child's day should not be filled with chores. Allow plenty of time for rest, study, and play. Before assigning a chore, be sure the child is able to do it. If initial guidance is required, break the task down into small steps and teach one step at a time.

For instance, most five-year-olds don't know how to make beds, but they can be taught. If Sylvia first watches her mother make the bed while each step is described, and then helps her mother, over several days, she will do more and more of the job until she is doing it alone.

Rules should be enforced consistently. When rules are made, children will break them. That is a rule too. Children *must* break new rules to be sure that they *are* rules. If their parents fail to enforce them, they are not rules at all. If this happens enough, the relationship between parent and child becomes tense and uncomfortable. Parents often become angry at children for breaking rules, not realizing that every child breaks every rule that is ever made. When parents say, "I've tried everything and nothing works," they really mean their rules have not been enforced.

Some parents attempt to enforce too many rules. These parents are usually found in hectic pursuit of their children, making up "don'ts" while the child tries desperately to escape.

Don't invent rules on the run. Concentrate on enforcing only two or three at a time. You will be surprised at how quickly other things seem to fall into place once this is accomplished.

We live by rules because without them there would be no freedom. When parents make good rules and enforce them, they create a relaxed emotional climate in which their children are free to be okay.

"Strict" Is Not the Sound of a Whip

I receive a fair number of letters and e-mails from people who are writing to affirm my belief that discipline is best when discipline is strict. Sometimes, someone will approach me at a speaking engagement to announce his or her membership in the Society for Disciplinary Strictness.

"I'm very strict," a mother will say with obvious pride, telling me about the many positive comments she receives from other often amazed people concerning her children's good behavior.

Unfortunately, however, I've recently discovered that what some people think is strict isn't strict at all. It's silly, obsessive, and exhausting (to engage in, to be the recipient of, to witness), but it isn't strict.

A number of times, I've had occasion to watch some of these pretenders be "strict" with their children. Here's a composite example of how they corrupt the term.

"Rambo! Give me that!"

Rambo, age seven, acts oblivious.

"Rambo! Did you hear me?"

"Yes."

"Well?"

"I'm just playing with it."

"I don't care. Give it to me. It's not a toy."

"But Mom!"

"No! Give it to me."

"Just let me play with it for a while. Please."

"No! Now!" Mom holds her hand out expectantly.

Rambo jerks the "toy" back, away from Mom's hand.

"Rambo! Give me that! Now!"

I think you get the picture. This game of Here We Go Round the Mulberry Bush may go on for two or three minutes before Mom wins, Rambo succeeds in persuading her to let him play with the object a little longer, or Dad intervenes (upon which Rambo immediately hands it over). I don't mean to imply, by the way, that the so-called "strict" parent is always Mom. It might be Dad. It might be both Mom and Dad.

In a time not so long ago, parents of the above sort were known as nags. Other parents—truly strict ones—rolled their eyes at them. In those days, however, most parents *were* strict. Today, most parents are anything but strict. In addition to nags, today's parents are wimps, bullies, soul mates, playmates, bedmates, servants, absents, and codependents. There are very few true stricts.

To illustrate truly strict, I'll return to my example, giving it a new outcome:

"Rambo, please hand that over to me. It isn't a toy."

Rambo acts oblivious.

Without any show of anger, Mom takes Rambo by the hand, leads him to his bedroom, and says, "You're going to be in here for one hour, young man. Furthermore, I'm calling off your spend-the-night with Freddy. Maybe some other time."

"Mom!"

"Rambo, you're a very smart fella, smart enough to figure out that when I talk to you I mean business. I'm certainly not going to insult your intelligence by repeating myself. Now, I'll let you know when your hour is up." And Mom walks away.

That's that. I think you get the picture, but just in case: Strict is letting a child know that words are not simply exhalations of hot air. Rather, they mean somethng. Strict isn't mean (although children sometimes think it is), loud, threatening, or even punitive. In fact, my consistent personal and professional experience is that strict parents, because they convince their children that words mean something, punish less and enjoy their children more.

Consistency

Consistency is an integral part of expecting children to obey. Consistency makes it possible for a child to predict the consequences of his or her behavior. The ability to anticipate consequences and adjust behavior accordingly is essential to the development of self-discipline, which is the ultimate goal of parental discipline. Without consistency, therefore, discipline isn't discipline. It's confusion.

Discipline is more than just an occasional act. It's a theme that should run through every aspect of the parent–child relationship. To be an effective disciplinarian, you must be a model of *self-discipline*. Consistency is the standard against which that self-discipline is measured. The inconsistent parent is, in effect, undisciplined. This parent's attempts at discipline are like the blind trying to lead the blind.

Parents create rules and children test them. Testing is, after all, a child's only way of discovering whether, in fact, a rule truly exists. Telling a child "This is a rule" isn't convincing enough. Children are concrete thinkers. They must be *shown*.

So when a child breaks a rule, parents have an obligation to impose some form of discipline. This gets the child's attention and says, "See, we were telling you the truth." Consistency, therefore, is a demonstration of reliability. The more children feel they can rely on—believe in—his parents, the more secure they feel. If, however, the child breaks a stated rule and instead of enforcing, parents threaten or talk themselves blue in the face or get excited but don't do anything, the child is forced to test the rule, again and again and again. Testing of this sort spins the child's wheels. It wastes time and energy that the child could otherwise be spending in creative, constructive, growth-producing activities. Because consistency frees children from the burden of having to repeat the testing of rules, it helps children become all they are capable of becoming.

Children who can predict consequences are in the driver's seat of their own discipline. They know what's going to happen if they do this or that, so they quickly learn how to maneuver through traffic. Inconsistency is like a traffic signal that switches unpredictably from red to green, from right turn to left turn, and so on. Inconsistency causes children to have disciplinary "accidents." Consistency, on the other hand, helps them learn to take responsible control of their own lives.

Self-discipline, security, capability, responsibility. They add up to self-esteem. That's why consistency is so important.

Children whose parents are inconsistent live in a world of constantly shifting limits, so these children must test their limits just as constantly. This constant testing is what we call "disobedience." If the parents' actions are inconsistent with their words, a child learns that parents are unreliable and incapable of controlling the child's world. As a result, in an attempt to reduce insecurity, the child attempts to control the world independently, in the process becoming self-conscious (and therefore self-centered), demanding, disrespectful, disruptive, and so on. This quickly becomes a vicious circle from which a child cannot escape without help. The more inconsistent the parents are toward this misbehavior, the more they demonstrate their lack of control. In turn, the child becomes even more insecure, and the behavior becomes increasingly agitated and inappropriate. As the behavior worsens, so does the parents' inconsistency. And round and round they go, until that child's parents learn the art of benevolent dictation. When previously inconsistent parents finally take control away from a misbehaving child, that child experiences an immense sense of relief and security. But the trick to never having to wrestle control away from a misbehaving child is truly to *expect* obedience in the first place.

To illustrate the importance of consistency, consider the job of basketball referee. The referee's job is simply to enforce the rules, consistently and dispassionately. Imagine the chaos that would result if nearly every time a rule was broken, the referee complained, threatened, gave second chances, and, every so often, vented his self-imposed frustrations by launching into a red-faced emotional tirade. Let's join just such a game in progress.

A player on the Red team takes a pass from one of his teammates and drives toward the basket for a layup. As he nears the goal, a Blue player sticks out a foot and sends the Red player sprawling unceremoniously across the floor. Immediately, the referee blows his whistle. As play stops, he points an accusing finger at the offender.

"Was that an accident, or did you trip him on purpose?" the referee demands. Looking sheepish, the Blue player answers, "It was just an accident, honest. I didn't mean to."

"Well, okay," the referee says. "I'll let it go this time, but don't let it happen again."

The next incident occurs as a Blue player sets up to take a shot from the corner. Before he can release the ball, a Red player leaps up from behind and grabs his arm, preventing the shot. Again, the referee blows his whistle, stops play, and confronts the guilty player.

"How many times have I told you not to do that?" he asks, exasperated. "You let me tell you something! I'm about to run out of patience with you! The next time you do something like that, you'll be sorry, believe me!"

Soon, another infraction occurs and another confrontation. "Why did you *do* that?" the referee pleads.

The player shrugs his shoulders and looks down at the floor. "I don't know," he replies.

"What in God's name am I going to do with you?" the referee shrieks, holding his head in his hands.

As the clock ticks on, fouls become more frequent and obvious. With nearly every one, the referee's reaction is the same: reprimand, threat, complaint. Occasionally, he actually follows through with a penalty, but only after putting on a great display of verbal and physical histrionics.

Eventually, the game is in shambles, a virtual free-for-all. Players push, trip, and even hit one another for control of the ball. All the while, the referee runs around red-faced and sweating, looking increasingly distraught. Finally, as the melee reaches peak intensity, he suddenly shouts, "I've had it!" and looks pleadingly toward the heavens. We'll leave the referee there, petitioning the powers that be for relief from his terrible burden.

This description may sound familiar, since it typifies the disciplinary tone of many an American family. Children test rules, and parents threaten, berate, plead, and complain, all the while becoming increasingly frustrated. Finally, they melt down in a spasm of exasperation. For a while, all is quiet. Then, slowly, the children come out of hiding, and once again the snowball begins its downhill descent.

Inconsistency causes children to play at misbehavior in much the same way compulsive gamblers play at games of chance. Compulsive gamblers keep gambling, even when they're losing their shirts, precisely because they can never predict when they're going to win. This randomness fuels the perpetual fantasy that Lady Luck might be just one more throw of the dice away. In the same manner, unpredictable discipline causes children to keep throwing the dice of misbehavior. The only difference between compulsive gamblers and children is that while gamblers eventually run out of money, children never run out of energy!

Parents who truly expect obedience from children discipline consistently and dispassionately. Consequently, discipline never becomes a big deal, something parents find themselves constantly stumbling over. A matter-of-fact attitude toward discipline creates a calm, relaxed atmosphere in which everyone's place is clear. This allows life within a family to be simple, as it should be.

Before I leave this topic, however, I need to answer an important question: "Is it absolutely necessary that the two parents, Mom and Dad, always agree on how to discipline a child?"

The answer—and it may surprise you—is no. Parents need to agree on the rules and expectations, but they do *not* have to agree on how those rules are enforced. To the extent that parents feel they must be in agreement, they will have problems.

It is unrealistic to expect two fundamentally different people, who come into a marriage with different ideas about children, to agree on a single set of tools with which to regulate a child's behavior.

Each parent's toolbox is different, and each feels familiar and skilled with his or her own methods. Mom is inclined to sit Junior on his least-favorite chair when he disobeys, while Dad is likely to whack Junior's behind. So what? There is no conflict here, and there need not be disagreement. That Mom and Dad use different means of enforcing the rule is only superficially relevant.

What counts in maintaining harmony in the family is that Mom and Dad agree on the importance of the rule itself—Do What We Tell You to Do—and are equally quick to act when Junior gets out of line. Mom and Dad are acting consistently, even though *differently*, to reinforce the rule.

But parents can get so hung up on the need to be consistent that they begin fighting over stylistic differences. Meanwhile, as the forest is increasingly obscured by the trees, the rule itself begins to gather dust, and it dawns on Junior that there is no rule at all— sometimes he can disobey and sometimes he can't.

It isn't even necessary for either parent, acting alone, to respond in the same manner every time a rule is violated.

Mom *prefers* to put Junior in the thinking chair when he's a rebel without a cause, but she is not required to do that every time. Sometimes she says he can't go outside, sometimes she sends him to his room, sometimes she simply repeats herself with more emphasis, and sometimes she reaches over into Dad's toolbox and pops Junior's behind.

And Dad may not always spank. There are times when he has a man-to-man talk with Junior. Sometimes he takes something away, and sometimes he sits him on the chair Mom uses.

But no matter what Mom and Dad do when Junior disobeys, the *rule* is there. It is being consistently enforced by a variety of means, but the end is the same. Furthermore, Mom and Dad's reactions are consistent with how each feels at the moment a transgression occurs.

There is even something to be said for being unpredictable in the way you enforce rules. Messages lose their impact when they are stated repetitiously. Being too consistent can evolve into boredom and rigidity.

Too much consistency also prevents parents from seeing changes in their children and adapting to those changes. Too much consistency promotes a simplistic view of life. Too much consistency restricts growth.

It's How You Say It!

Expecting children to obey has a lot to do with how parents communicate instructions to children. As I pointed out earlier, many parents communicate instructions in a wishful, wishy-washy manner. They plead, bargain, argue, threaten, and then—when they've finally reached the end of their rope—they lower the boom. This sort of disciplinary style creates and perpetuates an atmosphere of uncertainty and tension within the parent–child relationship.

When giving instructions to children, parents should be commanding, concise, and concrete. These are the Three C's of good communication.

1. Be commanding. Speak directly to the child and preface instructions with authoritative statements, such as "I want you to" or "It's time for you to" or "You need to." In other words, don't beat around the bush. If you want a child to do something, you must say so in no uncertain terms. The more uncertain your terms, the more uncertain the outcome.

2. Be concise: Don't use fifty words when five will do. Almost all of us were lectured as children, and we all remember hating it. We learned then that as soon as the lecturer gets going, a fuse blows somewhere between the child's ears and brain.

3. Be concrete: Speak in terms that are down-to-earth rather than abstract. Use language that refers to the specific *behavior* you expect, as opposed to the *attitude*. "I want you to be good in church this morning" is vague, abstract. "While we're in church I want you to sit quietly next to me" is clear and concrete. When parents leave doubt in a child's mind as to just exactly what they expect, the child can be counted on to appropriate the benefit of that doubt.

Some of the more common errors of communication parents commit include:

Phrasing instructions as if they were questions. This implies choice, when no choice actually exists.

WRONG: "How about picking up these toys so we can start getting ready for bed?"

RIGHT: "It's almost time for bed. You need to pick up your toys and put them away."

Phrasing expectations in abstract rather than concrete terms. Using words like *good, responsible,* and *nice* leaves the parent's actual meaning open to interpretation.

WRONG: "I want you to be *good* while we're in the store."

RIGHT:"While we're in the store, I want you to walk next to me and ask permission before touching anything."

Stringing instructions together. The mind of a child younger than five has difficulty holding more than one instruction at a time. With children older than five but younger than twelve, it's best to give no more than two instructions at a time. If it's not convenient to hand out chores in this patient fashion, give the child a list. If he or she can't read yet, use drawings.

WRONG: "Today, I want you to clean your room, take out the garbage, feed the dog, pick up the toys in the den, and help me move these boxes into the attic."

RIGHT: "The first thing I want you to do today is clean your room. When you finish, let me know, and I'll tell you what comes next."

Preceding instructions with Let's . . . This is another passive, non-authoritative form of communication. When you expect a child to do a chore on his or her own, say so. Don't confuse the issue and open the door for resistance by implying that you're willing to pitch in.

WRONG: "Let's set the table, okay?"

RIGHT: "It's time for you to set the table."

Following instructions with reasons or explanations. Putting the reason last attracts the child's attention to *it* rather than to the instruction itself. This makes argument more likely.

WRONG: "It's time to get off the swing so we can go home."

RIGHT: "It's time for us to go home now. Get off the swing and come with me."

Making an instruction into a sales pitch. This might work with small children, but a child of four or five is wise to ploys of this sort, and the chance of noncompliance increases.

WRONG: "Hey, Sissy! Guess what? Mom's cooked a really great supper tonight! Let's say goodbye to Sally and go see Mom's surprise!"

RIGHT: "It's time for supper, Sissy. You need to say goodbye to Sally and come inside."

Giving instructions with an open-ended time frame.

WRONG: "Billy, I need you to mow the lawn sometime today, when you get a chance."

RIGHT: "Billy, I want you to mow the lawn today, and I want you to be finished by the time I get home at six o'clock."

Expressing instructions in the form of wishes. This amounts to nothing more than passive complaint about the child's behavior. Children don't grant wishes, genies do.

WRONG: "I wish you'd stop chewing with your mouth open."

RIGHT: "Stop chewing with your mouth open."

Have a Plan!

Expecting children to obey also involves having a plan for what you are going to do if they don't. In fact, the secret to virtually frustration-free discipline is first to have a plan and then to carry it through consistently.

Most parents discipline by the seat of their pants. Consequently, when misbehavior occurs, they respond emotionally rather than with common sense. If businesses were run in this absurd manner, they would all be bankrupt in no time. To make a profit, a business must operate according to a plan. Its managers must anticipate potential problems and develop strategies for dealing with them, if and when they occur. The same goes for parents who value effective discipline. They too must anticipate potential problems and be ready to deal authoritatively with them. I call this "striking while the iron is cold." The most effective time for dealing with misbehavior is before it occurs.

Striking while the iron is cold is a three-step process:

1. *Anticipate the problem,* based on your knowledge either of the child or of children in general.

2. *Develop a strategy* for dealing with the problem.

3. *Talk with the child* about the problem, defining it and letting the child in on the strategy (but not asking permission to use it!).

By striking while the iron is cold, you put yourself in the most effective position possible for striking when the iron gets hot. When the heat is on, implement your strategy, following through as promised, and continue to follow through as needed until the problem is solved.

In the language of the business world, striking while the iron is cold is *pro*-active as opposed to *re*-active. In parenting, as in business, to deal with problems proactively is to control them rather than let them control you.

Let's see how this strategic process can be applied to a typical behavior problem. Take five-year-old Rodney, who persists in getting out of bed to ask unnecessary questions and make inappropriate requests. To make him stay in bed, Rodney's parents have threatened, bribed, spanked, and screamed—all examples of ineffective knee-jerk (reactive) emotional responses.

Finally, Rodney's parents wisely decide to strike while the iron is cold. They have no trouble anticipating the problem, since it's happened every night for the past two years, so they go straight to the planning stage. They decide Rodney will be allowed out of bed one time, and one time only, to ask a question or make a request. When they tuck him in, they'll give him a ticket, a small rectangle of colored cardboard. Rodney can use this one ticket to purchase the privilege of getting out of bed.

When he gets out of bed, as he surely will, he hands his parents the ticket. In return, they let him ask a question or tell them something. Then they put him back to bed. If, for whatever reason (including "needing" to go to the bathroom), he gets up again, his parents keep him indoors the next day and put him to bed one hour early (again with one ticket).

Having made their plans, his parents calmly communicate their decision to Rodney at five o'clock one afternoon. As they're preparing him for bed, they remind him of the new deal. Then they tuck him in, give him his ticket, and turn out the lights.

Does Rodney get out of bed? Of course! Does he get out of bed more than once? Of course! Rodney must test the rule in order to find out if it really exists.

The next day, Rodney's parents deliver his punishment as promised. That night, he gets out of bed twice. The next day, his parents again keep him indoors and put him to bed early. The third night, Rodney gets out of bed ten times. He's trying to find out if his parents will stick to the plan if he acts oblivious to it. The next day, his parents stick to the plan. That night, Rodney gets out of bed one time and no more.

Over the next few weeks, Rodney tests on several more occasions. Each time, he finds out that his parents are still sticking to the plan. At last, Rodney stops testing. In fact, he eventually stops getting out of bed altogether! And Rodney sleeps easier, knowing his parents mean what they say.

As this example points out, good discipline doesn't have to be complicated. Rather, it must be well organized, easily communicated, and easily dispensed. The simpler, the better!

Keep It Simple, Stupid!

Nothing will kill a discipline plan quicker than weighing it down with dozens of unnecessary if–then considerations. For example: "If you clean your room, you get a star. If you don't, you get a check. At the end of the week, we subtract checks from stars, and that determines your allowance. If there are more checks than stars, however, you owe us money, which we take off the top of *next week's* allowance. If there are no checks, you get a bonus. If, however, you owe us more than the bonus, the bonus is applied to the debt." See what I mean? Einstein couldn't have kept all that straight.

Another way of dooming discipline to failure is to bite off more than you can chew. Let's take, for example, a child who is destructive, disobedient, irresponsible, unmotivated, aggressive, disrespectful, bossy, and loud. Instead of tackling all the problems at once, which would be like wrestling with an octopus, you would do better to concentrate your energies on just one of them. Solving one problem puts you in position to solve another, and then another, and so on.

The parents of two children, ages five and two, were having the usual problems that come with children of those ages—they sassed, squabbled, screamed, jumped on furniture, wrote on walls, got into everything, and created general bedlam. These parents spent lots of time and energy racing from one child to the other, from one thing to the next, driving themselves bananas in the process. They reminded me of the plate spinners who used to appear on *The Ed Sullivan Show*. The more these parents tried to accomplish, the less successful they were.

"Pick three problems," I told them.

They picked sassing, squabbling, and screaming. Neither child could read, so we drew a picture for each problem. Screaming was represented by a stick child with mouth wide open; squabbling by two children with mouths wide open; sassing by one stick child sticking tongue out at stick parents. Artists, we weren't.

The pictures were posted on the refrigerator, and the children were told what each one meant. The parents bought a timer and kept it handy to the children's rooms. When one of the targeted behaviors occurred, the parent closer to the scene would identify the behavior ("That's sassing") and say, "That's on one of your pictures and means you have to go to your room." A squabble sent both children to their respective rooms, regardless of who "started" it.

The parent would take each offending child to his or her room, set the timer for ten minutes, and walk away. When the bell rang, the kids could come out of their neutral corners.

Talking with these parents, I stressed the importance of adhering to what I call the Referee's Rule: no threats, second chances, or deals.

"When you see an infraction," I said, speaking figuratively, "blow the whistle and assess the penalty. In hesitation or indecision, all is lost!"

I saw them again three weeks later. The mother started off by telling me she finally found a whistle at a sporting goods store.

"Wait a minute," I said. "You mean you actually went out and bought a real whistle?"

"Sure did!" she said. "It sounded like a good idea to me. When we're home, I wear it around my neck. When I blow the whistle, the kids march to their rooms. I don't even have to tell them to go. Better yet, they set the timer themselves."

I asked how she felt about the plan, and here's what she told me, word for word.

"I feel more confident in my parenting skills and more in control of the kids. Furthermore, the kids are reacting in a way that tells me *they're* more confident of my authority. They've learned my limits. Before, it seemed we were always in a frenzy. Now, the household is calm. It's a very organized feeling, and everyone is happier."

Strike another blow for simplicity.

Rewards and Incentives

"Okay, Junior, I know you don't want to take out the trash, but if you do I'll give you a dime. How's that sound?" Sounds pretty good, right?

The notion that children need to be rewarded for obedience has become popular, with some unfortunate consequences. Foremost among these is the idea that children perform better when they are promised tangible rewards, such as candy, a toy, or a special privilege.

In part, this is true. If you want Junior to do something mundane, such as cleaning up his room, offer him a piece of his favorite candy, a new toy, or a trip to the neighborhood ice-cream parlor. And then, the next time you want him to clean up his room, be prepared to make the same offer. If you're lucky, the child will only expect more of the same. If luck isn't standing on your side of the street that day, however, he'll want something even better. Yesterday, an ice-cream cone; tomorrow, a super-deluxe bicentennial hot-marshmallow-cream sundae!

Children are impressionable, and nothing impresses them more than stuff for their mouths or hands. (Unfortunately, many adults have the same trait.) It's the "What's in it for me?" syndrome, as much the new American way as Mom's factory-made frozen apple pie.

Accuse me of being an adult chauvinist swine, but I subscribe to a double standard: What's tolerable in an adult is not always tolerable in a child.

When Junior learns to expect something in return every time he puts out a little effort for someone besides himself, it's obnoxious but it's not his fault. The child is the addict, but we big people are the pushers. We adults tend to look for the most expedient way to accomplish things, the shortest distance between two points. When we want cooperation from a child, we know that offering some goody is likely to get the job done fast. In the child's mind, however, cooperation and the performance of certain tasks or chores become hooked to the promise of special rewards.

This can quickly become a revolving-door situation that traps both parent and child. The parent wants the work done without having to deal with the child's excuses; the child wants the handout and has learned that, after enough stalling, the parent will come through with the goods.

Children need certain tools to meet the challenges of adult life. Extremely important among these are the virtues of industry, initiative, and responsibility. All three involve being willing to work, even when the payoff may be intangible or in the uncertain future. Feelings of pride and a sense of accomplishment are the best rewards of all.

"All right, then, I won't ever again offer my child a bribe to get cooperation with one of my requests. And my child won't ever again lift a finger around here to help me! Now whose move is it?"

Well, I'm glad you asked. It's *your* move, and the sooner you make it, the better. You must play Br'er Rabbit and outfox your young Br'er Fox.

Begin by listing some privileges your child now enjoys and takes for granted. Any activity that is regularly available but has not been earned can be defined as a privilege. The list might include having friends over, riding a bicycle, going out to play after supper, or being allowed to stay up later than usual.

Make another list of the chores and responsibilities Br'er Fox avoids so cleverly. This list might include putting toys away, taking a bath, doing homework, emptying the trash, and walking the dog.

Now you have made two lists, and Br'er Fox still hasn't lifted a finger. Don't get excited. The next step is to look at each item on the lists and ask yourself the musical question, "When?" For the first list, for example, ask, "When does he like to ride his bike?" For the second list, ask, "When do I want him to take his bath?"

Put the two lists side by side and there you have it! By connecting the items, you can make rules such as, "Before you can play your stereo [List 1] in the evening, you must take your bath [List 2]." Or,

"Before you can ride your bicycle after school, you must change your clothes and take the dog out for a walk." Put only one item from the list of privileges into each rule. You can include more than one item from your second list if that seems reasonable. For instance, one rule at our house when Eric was twelve years old was that he had to take a bath, do his homework, and straighten his room before he worked on his models in the evening. It didn't matter to us exactly when he did the chores or in what order. We didn't remind him, but we checked to see that his chores were done and sometimes applied a little "quality control" before he was allowed to play.

So make some rules, because rules are a parent's most indispensable tools. This is also known as the Godfather Principle, because you are making Br'er Fox an offer he can't refuse.

Or, can he? Sure he can, and he *will*. Every child will test every rule you ever made. Like chemists trying to discover what solution a substance will dissolve in, children will put rules to every conceivable test, but there is one substance in which no rule will dissolve, and that is consistency.

By consistency I mean enforcing rules under all but the most unusual circumstances. I do not mean that a rule must be enforced in the same way every time (*see* my defense of inconsistency, page 58). If a rule has many exceptions, if a child discovers that a rule does not withstand the stress tests, it is not a rule but simply a wish. Also involved here is the issue of trust. If you establish rules and then fail to enforce them, can you be depended on in other ways?

These methods may not yield the kind of instant results that bribes do, and they require patience, a rather old-fashioned virtue. But, as Br'er Rabbit might say, "I never promised you a briar patch."

Commitment: More Than Just a Try

Not long ago, a young woman asked me about a problem she had with her five-year-old daughter. The problem was not an unusual one, but it had hung on in this family for two years, draining lots of energy and wasting everyone's time.

After I listened to this mother's exasperated description of the goings-on and asked a few questions, I told her what I thought could be done to settle the issue once and for all.

When I finished, she gave a slight shrug and said, "Well, I'll give it a try."

"Well," I replied, "giving it a try won't work."

"What do you mean?" she asked, coming to life again.

"Excuse me for being so frank, but at best the most watertight of all possible solutions to your problem won't make change happen if all you're going to do is give it"—and I shrugged—"a try."

She is by no means alone. Plenty of parents never get past trying. And that is why so many of them lose control of their children—and themselves in the process.

"I'll give it a try" is another way of saying "I can't." It is a statement of defeat, surrender, and personal ineffectiveness.

That brings us to the point: When you deal with a problem involving a child, more important than *what* you do is the act of *doing*.

Because of my professional credentials and my reputation, parents ask me a lot of questions. Most of them begin with the phrase, "*What* should I do when . . ." This manner of asking a question (the italics are mine) reflects a fundamental, widely held misunderstanding: that for every specific problem, there is one equally specific best solution.

Not so. For every specific problem there are countless effective solutions. It doesn't matter which one you select—you can even invent a new one—because for *any* and *all* problems the *real* solution has nothing to do with technique or method.

It's called commitment, or determination, or resolve. It's the sense of purpose you invest in the method of your choice (or invention). The difference between method and commitment, the *what* and the *doing*, is the difference between form and substance. Method is nothing more than a vehicle. Without commitment, that vehicle is doomed to stall. Without commitment your method is impotent.

The difference between method and commitment is the difference between saying "I'll give it a try" and "This is the way it's going to be." Commitment is the backbone of whatever you do.

Commitment is the energy of change. Believe me, your children will know immediately when you are "giving it a try." They will sense your ambivalence and your lack of determination, and they will not cooperate with you *because you will have given them no substantial reason to do so.*

When a child tests you, that is precisely what is happening—the child is testing *you.* Not the form but the substance. And when, in response, you demonstrate your own sense of purpose in what you are doing, you also demonstrate your commitment to *the child.* Only when convinced of your *commitment* will the child cooperate with you.

No question about it.

Negotiating from a Position of Power

Because I often speak and write about the power of "Because I said so," I am frequently asked whether Willie and I ever gave Eric and Amy reasons or permitted discussion of rules and such. On both counts, the answer is, "Yes, we did." We *always* gave our children reasons for our decisions. One of those reasons was "Because I said so" or a variation on that theme. We gave other reasons only when they were more honest than "Because I said so"—which is, as I've already said, the most honest answer more often than not.

When we gave reasons other than "Because I said so," we never expected the children to agree, and they never disappointed us. Nor did we try to persuade them to our point of view. After all, our points of view had been many years in the making. We're not foolish enough to think we can rush Mother Nature! As Orson Welles once said, "No mind before its time." Or was that Groucho Marx?

Although we refused to waste time, ours and theirs, by getting into arguments with them, we taught them how to get their way. A typical exchange went something like this:

A much-younger Eric comes to me with a request, to which I say *no.* He becomes visibly agitated, throws his arms out to his sides, strains forward, and yells, *"Why not?"*

"Wrong, Eric," I say. "That's not the way to do it. If you want me to give you an explanation, you must ask for it properly. By that I mean you must compose yourself and ask in a manner that's not irritating. So try again, from the top."

He stands for a moment, looking slightly disgusted, then makes his request a second time. Again, I say *no*. He takes a deep breath and says, "Would you mind telling me why?"

"Good job," I say. "No, Eric, I don't mind telling you why." With that, I begin explaining myself. Before I finish my first sentence, however, Eric interrupts with, "But, Dad!"

"No, Eric," I say, "you've blown it again. When you ask someone for an explanation, you have an obligation to listen, whether you agree or not. After I give my reason, it's your turn to tell me why you disagree. Got that?"

Eric nods, with a heavy sign.

"Good! Let's take it from the top again."

"Aw, Dad!" he complains, "you've got to be kidding."

"No, I'm not kidding. We're going to stand here together until you get the whole thing right. Unless, that is, you want to stop right here. In that case, you're going to have to live with my original answer. What'll it be?"

Begrudgingly, he starts over. Eventually, after much trial and error, he finally gets it right. When he does, I reward his efforts by meeting him halfway. This teaches him to negotiate, rather than argue and complain, for what he wants.

Some people might say this sounds like a lot of trouble, but it really isn't. Especially not when you consider the payoff. Besides, it was my responsibility to teach Eric the skills he would need to live a successful life.

What I did with Eric was no different from what a supervisor does when teaching an employee a new job. The supervisor teaches the task one step at a time. If the employee makes a mistake at some point in the sequence, the supervisor corrects it and has the employee start over from the top. In that manner, the employee eventually learns the entire sequence.

As I said, it was my responsibility to teach Eric the art of negotiation; it was Eric's responsibility to use it to his advantage. And use it he did, to create more freedom for himself during his high school years than most youngsters enjoy until they're in college. Now in his thirties, a pilot, married with three children, he's one of the most responsible people I know.

And it all goes back to "Because I said so."

Decision-Making

Decisions, decisions. Raising a child certainly involves its share. From the moment of birth through eighteen or more years of gradual emancipation, decisions never stop taking up a parent's time. No sooner have you made one than you must make another, and then another, and so on.

To complicate matters, there are not only those decisions *you* have to make but also the decisions you must help your *child* make: what to wear to school, whom to invite over to spend the night, how to handle conflicts with other children, and so on.

It's enough to drive a parent nuts, and indeed we all veer off in that direction every once in a while. Most of us return from these little side trips with only minor scars, but some of us become lost forever. Some parents drive themselves to distraction simply because they get hung up on the details. To them, every decision seems momentous, from whether teeth are brushed before or after breakfast to whether or not the child should be retained in the third grade. Believing that any wrong decision has the potential of ruining the child's future, these parents become obsessed with always making right ones.

This raises an interesting question: "What is a *right* decision?"

Many parents mistakenly think that for any given child-rearing situation there is only one *correct* course of action. That's like believing that of the forty or so items on a restaurant menu, just *one* is perfectly suited to your taste. The fact is, the *way* in which parents make decisions is far more important than the content of the decisions themselves.

The same applies to managing a business. Effective managers are decisive. They don't waste time and energy obsessing over details. They trust their intuition and common sense. More than anything else, good managers realize it's less important to always be "right" than to always inspire confidence and a sense of purpose in those they manage. Wrong decisions are less harmful to an organization than a faulty decision-making style. To the degree that a manager is obsessive or indecisive, that manager promotes distrust, insecurity, and conflict in the workplace. Indecisive parents create similar problems in the home.

Do you see yourself in the following description?

- You dwell on making decisions rather than trusting your feelings and your common sense and just snapping them off. Obsessing over every decision, large or small, wastes time, invites arguments, and is a sign to children that they can probably get their way by pushing harder.

- You include your children in too many decisions. Asking a child's opinion about some things has its place, but when that's the rule rather than the exception, the likelihood of conflict between parent and child increases.

- If your child dislikes a decision you've made, you're almost certain to compromise, if not give in. Parents give in to avoid conflict. Unfortunately, the more conflict they avoid, the more they ultimately have to deal with.

- You constantly explain yourself to your child. As I've previously said, children don't really want explanations, they want arguments. Requesting the explanation is nothing more than a means to that end.

If that shoe fits, you need to stop making your life—as well as your child's—so complicated. Start trusting your feelings. Stop worrying that you're going to traumatize your child for life if you make a bad decision. Bad decisions don't do long-term damage. Bad *people* do.

What's "Fair"?

"It's not fair!"

I heard that a lot in my day. In fact, I listened to variations on the same theme, delivered in sundry ways, from statement to scream, for most of Amy's childhood.

Poor Amy, she must have arrived before her appointed time, because the world was not prepared. The news of her arrival didn't even make a big splash in the media—just a blurred picture and two or three lines to distinguish her from the other infant mug shots in the lineup.

From birth, Amy tried to convince us that a mistake was made. This time around, she was scheduled to be a princess. She had, no doubt, paid her dues as a serving wench, a peasant—you know, the usual stuff we all endure before getting to the big time. This fling was to have been different. But something went wrong. What a disappointment it must have been!

Her mother and I couldn't even buy her everything she wanted. She didn't understand about mortgages and car payments. After all, the castle was supposed to have been paid for, along with a villa on the Mediterranean.

But the worst, the supreme insult, was that there was another child in the family before her: Eric.

The problem, as Amy saw it, was that Eric was sometimes given things before she was, or that he got something bigger or two of something to her one. Dad might have even taken Eric to the store and bought him something and come home empty-handed for Amy.

"It's not fair!"

"But Amy," I would say, "sometimes you and I go to the store and get something just for you. Why, don't you remember: Just yesterday we bought you a new coat and a pair of shoes. Eric didn't get anything then."

"It's not fair!"

Come to think of it, she was right. "What is fair?" I ask myself. It's a vague concept that is nothing short of impossible to achieve.

What would satisfy children is not for us to be "fair" but for us to give them everything they want. "Fair" means "me first" with the biggest and the best.

When there is more than one child in the family, there is no avoiding explosions over who gets what, and whose is the best and the brightest, and on and on.

So what are we to do? Should we try to spend the same amount of money on both children or buy the same number of things for each? Should we have bought Amy something whenever we took Eric to the store?

No. It would not have been in Amy's best interests for us to encourage the idea that the world can be relied upon to deliver to her an equal measure of whatever she sees someone else getting. Children with this idea are popularly called "spoiled," and spoiled children, when they grow up, are likely to be extremely frustrated and unhappy because the fairy tale *never* comes true.

I usually tried something like this:

"It may not seem fair that Mommy and Daddy have given something to Eric and not to you. But you and Eric are different people, and we treat you differently. You will have trips to the store of your very own."

Sometimes the explanation didn't sit well, and she went into her dying swan routine. I would walk away, refusing to get involved in the drama. Eventually she got over it.

It's not a question of fair. It's a question of balance.

The Pitfalls of Praise

Beware of truisms. Often enough, truisms turn out to be false-isms, and this is particularly the case within the pseudoscience of parenting.

Most people, for example, think children need a lot of praise, and praise builds self-esteem. Both statements are false. The facts are that children need little praise, and the effects of praise on a child's self-esteem can be either constructive or destructive. The turning point is also, as we shall see, the reference point.

A team of researchers once divided twenty five-year-old children into two groups of ten. Each group was taken separately into a large activity area staffed by several teachers. In the middle of the room stood a table overflowing with art supplies of every sort: colored paper, clay, crayons, paints, and scissors. After a brief get-acquainted period, the children were directed to sit down and make something.

With the first group, the teachers moved around the table giving lots of praise, holding each project up for everyone to see, and generally effervescing with enthusiasm for what the children were doing.

These same teachers were considerably more reserved with children in the second group. Instead of hovering, they stayed back from the table, involved in tasks of their own. Occasionally, one of them would ask if anyone needed help or more supplies. If a child showed his project to a teacher, obviously seeking praise, the teacher would respond with a few warm words.

The next day, the teachers brought the children back to the room. This time, they were allowed one hour of free play. The researchers kept track of the time children in each of the groups spent playing with the art material.

Lo and behold! Children in the first group avoided the art table as if it were contaminated; children in the second spent little time anywhere else. This tells us that too much praise is negative and causes children to actually avoid the activities, people, and places associated with it.

Psychologists make a distinction between evaluative and descriptive praise. Evaluative praise is judgmental and personal. For instance, when Johnny brings his teacher a leaf collection, the teacher exclaims, "Oh, Johnny, you're such a hard worker and a joy to teach. If it wasn't for you, this year would have been terribly routine for me."

By implication, evaluative praise takes away the child's right to be imperfect. As a result, Johnny may begin to internalize an unreasonably high standard of excellence for himself and may eventually begin feeling that he can't measure up. The end results of evaluative praise are feelings of inadequacy and discouragement, quite the opposite of what was intended.

Descriptive praise has no such built-in dangers. It is, as the name implies, simply a description, an acknowledgment of accomplishment. In the case of Johnny and his leaf collection, the teacher could have said, "You obviously put a lot of time and effort into this collection, Johnny. Thank you for sharing this with the class."

Like sugar, praise can be habit-forming. Children who are praised either excessively or evaluatively often develop a dependence on outside approval. Children so hooked are like tires with a slow leak: Every so often, they must be pumped up or they'll go flat.

Sometimes, adults praise things that shouldn't be praised, like using the toilet properly. We need not and should not praise children for growing up. A simple acknowledgment will suffice, because growth is its own reward. The adult who praises for an act of self-sufficiency is, in effect, appropriating the inherent pleasure of the event—stealing the child's thunder.

Praise can also backfire, particularly in the case of a child with low self-esteem. Praise is inconsistent with this child's self-image, particularly if the praise is evaluative. The mismatch between message and image generates anxiety, which the child may attempt to reduce by misbehaving—setting the record straight.

In other words, praise is not something to be tossed out carelessly. Be conservative and thoughtful about it. Above all else, with praise as with punishment, take aim at the act, *not* the child.

Worry: The Future Game

We influence the future in the way we anticipate it. In this respect, we are all, to some degree, fortune-tellers. This is not whimsy but a documented principle of human psychology called "the self-fulfilling prophecy." It's the lesson we learned as children from the story of the Little Engine That Could: If you *think* you can, you probably *will*. If you think you *can't*, you probably *won't*.

We not only affect our own future in the way we anticipate it but, in like manner, we influence the lives of others. The stronger the bond between two people, the stronger the potential effect. Between parents and children, parents wield the most potent influence. On the constructive side are influences such as commitment and optimism. Optimistic parents, who are not only hopeful but *certain* that their children will be all right, seem blessed with children who, by and large, turn out well.

On the destructive side are guilt and worry. Both are forms of negative energy that not only prevent parents from paying adequate attention to the here-and-now but also are self-fulfilling. Parents who worry about their children always seem to have something to worry about.

Bobby is three years old. He has been tossed out of two preschool programs and is working on being expelled from a third. Few children in his neighborhood are allowed to play with him. Bobby bites.

Bobby is an only child whose middle-class parents want him to grow up without any emotional problems. They have read countless books and articles about raising children. They want desperately to do it right, but something has gone wrong.

They search the past for a reason for Bobby's biting. "What did we do to cause it?" they ask, needing a hook on which to hang their guilt. The more they search, the more they ask, the more Bobby bites.

Bobby bit his mother when he was thirteen months old. He was in the throes of a tantrum that began when his mother took a photograph away from him. The bite set off a guilt-quake inside his mother. It was so big, even Bobby knew something extraordinary had happened. So he bit her again.

Three months later, after sufficient practice on his mother, he bit the next-door neighbor's child. When he was eighteen months old, his parents enrolled him in a day-care program, hoping that being around more children would help. He lasted two months.

Bobby's parents worry so much about what he will be like in ten minutes, ten days, or ten years that they don't notice what he's doing *right now*. Whenever he's around other children, they are consumed with anxiety. Bobby can feel their tension and knows what he's expected to do, so he does. And the more he bites, the more his parents worry.

It's usually impossible to determine, in such situations, whether the worry or the subject being worried about came first. The more parents worry, the more the subject comes up, the bigger it gets, and the more they worry. Until the cycle is broken, there is no resolution, only repetition. And the more the cycle is repeated, the more indelible its imprint on the family.

Worriers cannot be spontaneous, because they are not dealing with things as they happen. Their concerns are scattered somewhere up ahead, in the future, where they will *never* be. The more parents worry, the more they ignore the real problem. Meanwhile, the child bears the present-tense weight of the issue on *his* shoulders.

When, and if, Bobby's parents decide to do something about his biting, they might begin by telling him, "Bobby, you have been biting other children, and now you are going to stop. We are going to help you stop, because that's what mommies and daddies are for. Whenever you forget and bite someone, here's what's going to happen, every single time."

It won't matter much *what* they do. What will matter is that his parents will be doing *something*.

Bobby will be *very* relieved, believe me.

Questions?

Q: *My five-year-old son has difficulty making decisions. He starts the day unable to decide what he wants for breakfast. The more things I suggest, the more confused he becomes. During the day, he agonizes over everything from what friend to invite over to what toy to play with. At bedtime, he can't decide what book he wants read to him. Then he can't decide what clothes he wants to wear the following day. Since both my mother and I have problems making decisions, I'm beginning to wonder whether his problem might be genetic. Any ideas?*

A: Your son is having problems making decisions because you're giving him too many decisions to make. A problem doesn't have to be genetic in order for it to get handed down from one generation to the next. Indecisive people try to get other people to make decisions for them. When you were a child, your mother probably dealt with her indecisiveness by asking you to make not only too many decisions but also decisions you weren't capable of making. In so doing, she overloaded your decision-making capacity, and you eventually became indecisive too. Now that you have a child of your own, you're passing that indecisiveness along by asking *him* to make too many decisions. And round and round you go, and where you stop . . . nobody can decide.

The solution is obvious. You must stop expecting your son to make so many decisions. But wait, that means *you're* going to have to start making more decisions yourself. We need, therefore, to take a closer look at your own indecisiveness.

Indecisive parents are usually afraid of making mistakes. They think bad decisions scar children for life, so they end up making no firm decisions at all, which is one of the biggest mistakes a parent can *ever* make. The fact is, 'tis better for a parent to make a mistake every day than to be generally indecisive. Bad decisions can either be shrugged off, with an "Oh, well," or corrected. A faulty decision-making style, however, can spell long-term trouble.

A child's sense of security is founded upon paternal love and authority. A parent's indecisiveness causes children to feel insecure. That insecurity is likely to be expressed in the form of behavior problems. So you see? The more you try to avoid making mistakes that could cause problems, the more problems you cause.

So, get decisive! Time's a-wastin'!

Tonight, while you're preparing your son for bed, go stand in front of the bookshelf and, with your eyes closed, pick out a book. Say, "This is the book I'm reading to you tonight." *Don't* say, "Is this one okay?" That's not decisive! If he says the book you picked isn't the one he wants, say, "Well, it's the one I want to read, so lie down and enjoy."

When you finish the book, pick an outfit, any outfit, for him to wear the next day. Say, "Put these on when you wake up." Don't ask if he approves, and if he questions your selection, say, "Because it's what I've decided." Then tuck him in and say good night.

The next morning, when he gets up, blow his young mind by fixing a breakfast and putting it in front of him with, "Here's your breakfast." If he says it's not what he wants, tell him he doesn't have to eat it. Then go sit down and read the paper. You see how simple this is?

Anytime you see him becoming indecisive, either walk away (if you have the time) or take over (if you don't). If you show him how decisions are made, it shouldn't be long before he begins following your lead and taking better control of his life.

Q: *Our son, Ernie, recently decided to become a truly "terrible" two-year-old. My husband thinks Ernie is old enough to be spanked, but I'm not so sure. What do you think?*

A: That depends on your definition of spankings, as well as when and how you plan to use them. In my view, a spanking is a spanking only if the following conditions are adhered to:

- The parent administers it with his or her hand only.

- The parent's hand makes contact with the child's rear end only.

- The hand strikes the rear no more than three times.

Anything else is a beating. I also recommend that if parents are going to spank, they do so as a *first* resort. The more parents threaten, the more frustration they build and the more likely it is they will spank in a rage.

Contrary to accepted wisdom, parents should *always* spank in anger. If the parent isn't angry, a spanking isn't justified. A first-resort spanking delivered in anger is over quickly. The child isn't likely to feel resentment, and the parent isn't likely to feel guilt.

Some people think spankings of any sort constitute child abuse. I don't. Some parents *do* spank abusively, but then any form of discipline, even talking to a child, can be delivered destructively.

Other people think that spankings are the most effective form of discipline there is. I don't agree with that either. In and of themselves, spankings do not motivate appropriate behavior. A spanking accompanied by a period of restriction or a brief reprimand will have a much greater positive effect than a spanking alone. Furthermore, children who receive many spankings often become immune to them. The less parents spank, therefore, the more effective each spanking will be.

A spanking is really nothing more than a form of nonverbal communication. It's an exclamation point of sorts, placed in *front* of a verbal message. It says, "Now hear this!" A spanking serves as a reminder of authority and a demonstration of disapproval. But it's no substitute for more effective forms of discipline, verbal or otherwise.

There are some who use biblical references to the "rod" to justify using spankings as a primary and frequent form of discipline. I would simply point out that the rod was a symbol of authority in ancient times. Those passages, therefore, are more accurately interpreted to mean that parents who spare their authority will certainly spoil their children.

As a rule, spankings are not effective with two-year-olds. In the first place, twos are decidedly determined little people, and spankings often provoke even greater determination. Furthermore, a child of Ernie's age quickly forgets a spanking. Two minutes later, he's back doing the same thing. A firm but gentle approach to discipline, involving lots of Grandma's Rule—children can do or have what they want when they're done what their parents want—is much more effective than spankings.

Q: *Our five-year-old daughter, Margo, demands attention constantly. If we're in public, she asks for everything that catches her fancy and cries if we say no. At home, if we have guests, she interrupts conversations and is loud and sassy. When one of us tells her to do something, she ignores* *us. If we press the point, she either cries or complains or becomes down-right defiant. Nearly every request, even a simple one, turns into a confrontation. In every other respect, she is delightful. How can we control her without repressing her personality?*

A: I have an idea, and I guarantee it will not harm Margo's personality. First, make a list of the behaviors you want your daughter to eliminate, starting with problems that take place at home. For example, the list might read:

1. When we tell Margo to do something (or stop doing something), she pretends not to hear us, cries, complains, or says, "I won't!"

2. When we have company, Margo is loud.

3. Margo interrupts people when they are talking.

4. When Margo doesn't get her way, she cries.

Next, buy a portable kitchen timer and select an isolated place in your house where Margo can sit for five minutes at a time.

With everything in place, sit down and explain the program to Margo. Go over the problem behavior list with her, giving examples to make the descriptions clear.

"Margo, these are things we want you to stop doing. In the past, we have ranted and raved and gone blue in the face when you did these things. We are putting this list on the refrigerator. When you do something on it, we are going to take you to the downstairs bathroom and set this timer for five minutes. When the bell rings, you can come out."

To make this work, you must not make threats or give second chances. In other words, if Margo displays one of the behaviors on the problem-behavior list, don't threaten her with the bathroom. Just put her there, set the timer, and walk away. Upon telling Margo she's headed for the bathroom, she may suddenly decide to cooperate and say, "I'll be good!" or words to that effect. If so, just say,

"You can be good when you come out of the bathroom," and follow through with the plan.

It may take only a week or so before you see a change in Margo's behavior, but it will take at least three to six months of following through before good habits completely replace the bad ones.

Q: *Our eight-year-old son is a "forgetter." He can't seem to remember anything we tell him. Assign him a chore, he forgets. Give him a message for someone, it never gets there. If we tell him to do two things, one might get done. As he gets older, he seems to be getting worse. What, if anything, can we do to help improve his memory?*

A: Take heart! After being lost for nearly a generation, the secret to improving your son's memory has been found, and, lucky for you, it works just as well as ever. Not only that, but it doesn't cost a penny and comes with a guarantee of satisfaction. It's called *discipline.*

You can call your son *forgetful* if it makes you feel better. I'd call him disobedient. "I forgot" is an evasive way of saying "I didn't want to" or something equally noncompliant.

Consider the fact that "forgetting" is always so suspiciously selective. The same child who almost always "forgets" to feed the dogs, or to come in when the streetlights go on, never forgets things like ice cream in the refrigerator or the casual mention his parents made, several weeks ago, of a possible trip to the zoo. I'll just bet your son remembers things he wants to remember and "forgets" those things he would rather do without, like chores.

To improve his memory, first make a list of his privileges, such as:

Ride your bike
Go outside
Have a friend over
Watch television

Put the list on the refrigerator and every time he "forgets" something, cross off the highest remaining privilege, starting with Ride your bike. Every privilege crossed off is lost until the following Monday. After you've tucked your son into bed on Sunday, wipe the slate clean by taking the old list down and posting a new one.

By taxing his so-called forgetfulness in this painless manner, you make him responsible for the problem. If you're consistent, I can virtually guarantee that over the next few months you'll see an amazing improvement in his memory!

Q: *We have two sons, ages nine and seven. Except for an occasional spat, they get along just fine. Too fine, in fact. Whenever we discipline one of them, the other jumps in to tell us we're not being fair. They've occasionally flustered us into backing down altogether. We've talked ourselves blue in the face, but to no avail. What can we say to keep them from interfering in each other's discipline?*

A: You needn't do any more talking than you've already done. If talking is going to solve a problem, parents won't have to talk more than once, maybe twice. Your boys aren't stupid. They both know you don't want them interfering in your discipline. As it stands, you've said all you possibly can say on the subject. In fact, you've probably repeated yourself time and time again. More talking will only bring the same results: none.

Your problem isn't that you haven't made yourself clear. It's that you've failed to convince the boys you mean business. Up to now, you've given them every reason to believe you don't mean what you say. You said it yourself: When one of them interferes, you sometimes back down. And as you've discovered, you don't have to back down often to keep the problem alive.

Like compulsive gamblers pushing quarters into a slot machine, children don't have to be rewarded often for misbehavior to keep on misbehaving. If you punish a certain misbehavior forty-nine times and reward it once, that one reward is more powerful and motivating than the forty-nine previous punishments.

Here's how to cure your boys of "gambling." The next time you begin disciplining one of them and the other complains that you're not being fair, say, "Come to think of it, you're right. Fair means treating both of you the same. Therefore, since you decided to interfere, you'll receive the same punishment as your brother."

In this case, don't spoil your fun by warning them in advance that this is what you're going to do. Surprise them with your fairness. That should give them something to think about!

Q: *Our eight-year-old son has recently started lying to us. For example, when we questioned him about a bathroom drain that became mysteriously plugged with bubble gum, he swore he had nothing to do with it. After giving him the third degree, he finally admitted to it but was unable to tell us why he had lied. That's just one of several times we've caught him lying in the past few weeks. We've let him know that his punishment will always be worse if he lies, but that hasn't proven to be an effective deterrent. What does this mean and what should we do about it?*

A: It means he's a typical eight-year-old who, like most other children his age or thereabouts, is trying his hand at various forms of relatively harmless mischief, including the mischief of trying everything he can think of to throw the bloodhounds off his trail when he's done something wrong.

Why now? Good question. Up until age eight or nine, children tend to hold their parents in great awe. They think we big people can do just about anything: read minds, see through walls, and stuff like that. This perception of parents as powerful and all-knowing is, in fact, fairly essential to the young child's sense of security.

As the single-digit years draw to a close, however, children begin to realize we aren't quite as smart as they thought. They begin trying to expose the full extent of our stupidity by misbehaving and then playing innocent when confronted with circumstantial evidence of their guilt.

When these things began happening with our children, Willie and I applied the "Ask them no questions, they'll tell you no lies" rule. If, for instance, I was fairly certain that number-one son had put a hole in the wall, I might say, "Eric, for putting a hole in the wall, you are grounded for a week."

In other words, instead of asking the foolish question, I would make a statement. More often than not, the statement would include a consequence. Statements are assertive. As such, they are highly effective at preventing games of cat and mouse.

"Did you do this?" questions, because they are passive in nature, invite denial. And once the chase is on, the child is squarely in control of how long the chase lasts. This introduces a second, highly reinforcing element into the scenario—power.

So, going back to your question, you made your first mistake when you asked your son, "Did you put bubble gum in the drain?" You could have saved lots of time and energy by saying something like, "You're going to live in the bathroom until you figure out a way of getting the bubble gum out of the drain."

If he had protested his innocence, you could have simply said, "This isn't a court of law. It's a family and we're not going to waste everyone's time with a trial. I've made a decision and you're going to do as you're told."

Sure, you might be wrong, but in all likelihood you're right. As a parent, I found that my first intuitions about who-done-it were correct at least 90 percent of the time. The way I figure it, being wrong 10 percent of the time was less harmful to my children than giving them opportunity after opportunity to practice pulling the wool over people's eyes.

Q: *At a recent talk that I attended, you said that when children misbehave they should learn that misbehavior is not "free"—it should cost them something. I get frustrated because when one of my children misbehaves, I usually can't think of an appropriate consequence. The author of one parenting book I read says consequences should be either "natural" or "logical." That just confuses me further. Help!*

A: Yes, we parenting "experts" do seem to have an unwitting knack for making simple things confusing. One such area of confusion, even misinformation, concerns the dispensation of consequences for misbehavior. We've convinced parents that when a child misbehaves, the consequence must be delivered immediately, lest the child not make the connection. Indeed, that is true for children younger than three (because long-term memory does not begin to form until that age). Past that point, it is less and less necessary to deliver consequences immediately. A child of three and one half, for example, can make the connection between a misbehavior and a consequence that is delivered the *next day!* By age four, the delay can be upwards of several days, and by age six, the delay can be as much as a week. The mistaken belief that consequences must be delivered on the spot causes parents to become frustrated, yell, threaten, and do other things they later regret.

Now, here's a fact: More often than not, when a child misbehaves, an appropriate consequence is not immediately available.

I'd say that's true at least 75 percent of the time. Not a problem. In the first place, if the misbehavior in question is not chronic and the child in question is generally well behaved, the parent need do nothing more than simply say "I don't like that" or words to that effect. By definition, the well-behaved child values parental approval; therefore, parental disapproval will be sufficiently corrective, generally speaking.

When a consequence is clearly in order, as when a child is disrespectful or defiant, and one is not immediately available—as will usually be the case—the parent should shrug and walk away. That's right, just bide your time, relax, or, as my daughter used to say, chill. Within a suitable period of time, a consequence will present itself. I call this "waiting for a strategic opportunity."

Let's say a five-year-old boy, upon being told to pick up his toys, says, "I don't want to." Mom, having assessed the situation and come up empty-handed (and knowing that 99 percent of threats can't be followed through with), simply shrugs her shoulders and picks up the toys herself. The next day, this same child asks permission to go over to a friend's house, at which point Mom says, "Under normal circumstances, you could go, but not today because *yesterday*, when I told you to pick up your toys, you refused to obey." The child, of course, will fall into a swoon, complaining that Mom isn't being "fair" and perhaps even disavowing his love for her. Mom, unmoved, just walks away, letting her young rebel stew in his own juices.

In the real world, when a person misbehaves, the consequence is rarely experienced immediately. Parents need to portray the workings of the real world as early in their children's lives as those workings can be revealed. Therefore, parents need not—should not, even—deliver consequences immediately (except with very young children).

To the business of "natural" and "logical" consequences: The concept is, I agree, confusing. Furthermore, the real world does not operate according to this rule, What, pray tell, is "logical" about going to jail for five years for embezzling thousands of dollars from one's employer? Nothing! What's "logical" about not being allowed to go to a friend's house because you didn't pick up your toys? Nothing! Nonetheless, going to jail will serve as a powerful deterrent against further embezzling, and not being able to play with a friend will serve as a powerful deterrent against future disobedience (Rome, if you'll recall, wasn't built in a day).

In short, when it comes to consequences, parents should simply do what works, whether what works is "logical" or not. Isn't that simple?

Q: *My six-year-old daughter has started to test me at every possible opportunity. Every time I tell her to do something, she tells me she doesn't want to or she's too tired or something equally infuriating. If I tell her she's going to time-out if she doesn't, she says she doesn't care. If I tell her I'm taking away a privilege—like watching television for the rest of the day—she says she doesn't care. No matter what the threat, she doesn't care. Even if I follow through with it, she doesn't seem to care. I'm at my wits' end. What can I do?*

A: You can begin by stopping all these threats of time-out or annulment of one privilege or another. Every time you do so, you issue your daughter a challenge, thus creating an instant power struggle which she "wins" by saying she doesn't care what you do. Furthermore, it's as clear to your daughter as it is to me that you aren't consistent when it comes to the follow-through. You said, "Even *if* I follow through," which simply means your threats are often, if not usually, empty.

Second, you can stop telling your daughter what you're going to do when she disobeys. I know, mental health professionals have made it seem as if advance notice is mandatory, and this certainly seems like the "fair" thing to do, but in my experience, both personal and professional, *not* telling children what the consequences are for misbehaving works a lot better than the "fair" approach. Given a choice between what's fair and what works, I'll usually choose the latter.

The fact is, eight out of ten times (my estimate), there is no effective consequence parents can deliver at the moment a child misbehaves. As you've already discovered, the mistaken idea that a child's misbehavior must be dealt with immediately gives rise to a lot of empty threats—threats parents either don't or *can't* follow through with—and sets up lots of power struggles.

Here's an approach that will work a lot better than what you're currently doing. The next time your daughter tells you she doesn't want to, say, pick up her toys, just shrug your shoulders and say, "Oh, that's all right. I'll pick them up for you!" And pick them up, without a word of complaint.

At seven that evening announce, "It's time for you to start getting ready for bed."

When your daughter points out that her bedtime is eight-thirty, say, "Not tonight. Tonight, your bedtime is seven-thirty because you didn't pick up your toys when I told you to."

If it's more convenient (or if you'd prefer), wait a day or so until your daughter asks for a privilege, such as going to a friend's house. Say, "You know, I'd love to let you go to Jenny's house, but I won't because you didn't pick up your toys yesterday when I told you to."

This is called "waiting for a strategic opportunity." Remember, young children are the most intelligent organisms in the known universe. They make the connection, believe me. "Waiting for a strategic opportunity" helps parents keep their cool, avoid power struggles, and—perhaps most important—be just a bit unpredictable. I can't say it often enough: Parents! You need to keep your children slightly off balance! Better them than you.

Q: *Almost every time we take our four-year-old into a store, he begins misbehaving. How do you discipline a child when the eyes of the world are upon you?*

A: The sticky problem of controlling a youngster in public places is one parents can unstick by using a simple method I call "tickets."

Without knowing the specifics of your particular problem, let's just say your four-year-old has difficulty containing his excitement in stores. He darts away from you without warning and wants to handle everything he sees—typical four-year-old stuff, actually. In advance of your next perilous trek to a store or shopping center, cut three ticket-sized rectangles out of posterboard and draw a smiley face on each. Just before entering the store, review the rules with your child. Tell him to (1) walk with you and stay with you at all times and (2) ask permission before touching something. (For a child this age, keep it to no more than three rules!) Hand over the tickets and say, "These three tickets are going to help you remember the rules. Every time you break one of the rules, I'm going to take a ticket away from you. When we get home, you must have at least one ticket left in order to go outside. If you lose all three tickets in the store, then you will be in the house with no television for the rest of the day."

Having a discipline plan enables you to keep your balance, and your cool, when a problem occurs. In the past, when Curious George darted away from you in a store or put his fingers on expensive porcelain, you became instantly flustered. Now, however, you simply remind him of the rule and take a ticket. The keys to the success of such an approach are consistency (no warnings, threats, or second chances) and a suitable incentive.

The incentive, or carrot, can be anything the child is looking forward to doing later in the day, but again it should be a privilege. Do not offer the child a reward for proper public behavior! Contrary to what most people think, rewards are not effective motivators.

The best way to use rewards is to surprise rather than bribe. For example, if your child is extra good in the store and loses no tickets, you can (but are not obligated to) honor the achievement with a surprise ice-cream cone. But beware! Don't do this so often that the child comes to expect a reward, or you just might undo what you have accomplished. (See also chapter 22, Discipline in Public Places.)

"Tickets" is a versatile system that can be used to address a fairly broad range of misbehaviors. Take sassiness, for example. Your six-year-old daughter has a bad habit of talking back to you and calling you various creative names when you don't do as she commands. Using a magnetic clip, secure three to five (the actual number isn't that important) tickets to the refrigerator at the start of every day. Tell Her Impudence that every time she sasses you, she will lose a ticket. If and when she loses all her tickets on any given day, she will have to spend the rest of the day in her room and go to bed early. When you are finished with your explanation, she will undoubtedly sass you, giving you an excellent opportunity to demonstrate how the system actually works. Disobedience, teasing the family dog, whining, you name it, "Tickets" can handle it. The number of tickets allotted per day or situation is a judgment call, but the child should be able to beat the system fairly easily at first. Then, you can begin raising the bar by gradually lowering the number of tickets (misbehaviors) allowed per trip to the store, per day, or per whatever, until the problem is eliminated altogether.

Q: *Overall I feel you place too much emphasis on strict discipline and not enough on the need to be a relaxed, affectionate parent. Don't you agree that being relaxed is essential to good discipline?*

A: In a sense, yes, I agree. Actually, however, the most essential element of successful discipline is good communication, not—as most people seem to think—correct selection of consequences for misbehavior. As any public speaker will attest, the more relaxed someone is (to a point), the better communicator he or she will be. Good disciplinary communication saves on words. It's straightforward, to the point, and commanding (as opposed to demanding). I call it

"Alpha speech," meaning that it is communication befitting a confident leader; in this case, a leader of children.

If, for example, a parent wants her son to pick up his toys, the parent should simply say, "It's time for you to pick up these toys." Then, in keeping with the wise old observation that a watched pot never boils, the parent should walk away.

Alpha speech prevents discipline problems. Not completely, mind you, but significantly. As dog trainers will confirm, the discipline of a dog is primarily a matter of how the dog's master gives commands. Again, the key is not punishment but communication. In a perfect world, disciplining dogs and children would be completely a matter of how dog trainers and parents speak to their charges. But, alas, the world is not perfect. Good communication will prevent up to 90 percent of behavior problems, but the remaining 10 percent require that the dog, or the child, experience consequences. That's where the need to be *strict* comes in.

Strict discipline is powerful but not harsh. Strict discipline is consistent but not necessarily predictable or repetitious. For these reasons, strict discipline puts a quick end to a problem, nips it in the bud. As such, it is in the best interests of both parent and child.

Continuing my example, let's say the boy ignores his mother's command to pick up his toys. I'd advise the parent to pick up the toys herself and then inform the child that, because of his neglect, he will go to bed immediately after the evening meal. The child protests, cries, pleads. The parent holds fast. Two weeks later, the child ignores another command. He is informed that he will not be allowed to play in that day's soccer game. He protests, cries, pleads. The parent holds fast. It's another three months before this child ignores a parental instruction. By being strict, the parent has made a disciplinary molehill out of a potential disciplinary mountain.

It's axiomatic that the fewer discipline problems a parent experiences with a child, the more relaxed the parent will be. So, in answer to your question, I agree that relaxed parents are the best disciplinarians. But one way to ensure that you will be a relaxed parent is to discipline well. In other words, effective discipline must come first. The relaxation is the payoff.

Q: *I'm a single mother with custody of my fourteen-year-old son. His father, whom he sees infrequently, has mental problems stemming from battle experiences in Vietnam. My son is obviously harboring a lot of anger toward and concerning his father, but I can't for the life of me get him to talk about it. It comes out in the form of a lot of disrespect and hostility directed toward me. What should I do about this?*

A: I assume that by "this" you mean your son's supposed anger toward and concerning his father. If I'm right, you're focusing on the wrong issue. The problem is the disrespect and hostility your son directs toward you.

In the first place, when you attribute your son's brutish behavior to his feelings about his father, you're playing amateur psychologist. You're speculating (which is, by the way, all that psychologists are doing when they claim to know what causes a person to behave in a certain manner). You may be right. Then again, you may be wrong. If you're wrong, you're giving your son carte blanche to behave as abusively toward you as he pleases, whenever he pleases. If you're right, if your son is angry at his father, the question becomes "So what?"

Since when did less than perfect family situations entitle children to misbehave? My parents divorced when I was three. I had no relationship to speak of with my father until I was nine, after which I only saw him once a year for two weeks. In the interim, I missed my dad, was fairly frustrated by not seeing him, and didn't really understand why visits weren't more frequent. Nonetheless, I behaved respectfully toward my mother because she would not have tolerated anything less.

You're doing what today's parents have been "trained" to do by the media and mental health professionals: You're trying to *understand* your son's misbehavior. In so doing, you are not *acting* when he misbehaves. Because you do nothing, your son keeps on disrespecting you. Your intentions can't be faulted, but you have become your own worst enemy.

If I had disrespected my mother, she would not have tried to understand me. She would have punished me. And if I'd said, "Mom,

I claim immunity due to grieving and anger stemming from unresolved divorce and visitation issues," I'd have earned double punishment for refusing to accept responsibility for my actions. That was discipline before the Age of Psychobabble, and I daresay it was better for children, families, and our culture.

When you stop tolerating your son's disrespect, when you stop regarding him as a victim who is entitled to dump his feelings on you, when you begin acting worthy of respect, your son will begin treating you with respect. Toward that goal, I'd suggest that the next time your son blows up at you or treats you like a doormat, you say something along the following lines: "Well, isn't that interesting! Equally interesting to you, I'm sure, is the fact that you will not go anywhere except school and church for the next two weeks, during which you will receive neither friend nor phone call at this house. And every single time you act disrespectfully toward me during the next two weeks will add yet another week to your— what shall we call it?—I know! How about *therapy*?"

Your son is in desperate need of learning that women are not dumping grounds for male anger. This is a lesson only a woman can teach him. Are you woman enough for the job?

Q: *What do you think the role of grandparents should be in the raising of children? Should grandparents be expected to always support the parents' rules and methods of enforcement?*

A: I agree with the late anthropologist Margaret Mead, who once wrote, "Grandparents need grandchildren to keep the changing world alive for them, and grandchildren need grandparents to help them know who they are and to give them a sense of human experience in a [past] world they cannot know."

Grandparents can and should be one of a child's most valuable resources. At their best, grandparents are gentle teachers of the way life was, and perhaps the way it always should be. Grandparents can also be among parents' most valuable resources, demonstrating patience and tempering the often brittle seriousness of parenting with the flexibility and humor that only an appreciation for the full panorama of human life can bring.

Problems can arise when grandparents continue to perceive and treat their offspring as children long after their maturity and emancipation. In those cases, the grandchildren often become trapped in the middle of a power struggle between grandparents and parents. No one can win contests such as these, but the biggest losers are always the children.

When Eric was born, Willie and I, like many young parents, tended to be almost neurotically territorial, especially around our own parents. We were excessively sensitive to their "interference," and any suggestion from them, no matter how constructive, was regarded as a criticism.

It galled me, for instance, that my wife's parents would stuff Eric's mouth with sweets, his arms with toys, and his pockets with money. The more it galled me, of course, the more they did it. It took us years to realize that grandparents do no harm by "spoiling."

In fact, I'm now firmly convinced that it is as proper for grandparents to spoil their grandchildren as it is *improper* for parents to spoil those same children. One of the greatest pleasures of the oldest generation is making children happy, and no one has a right to interfere in that pursuit.

When Willie and I became grandparents, Eric and Nancy lived two doors away. Shortly after their first, Jack, was born, we sat down with them and said, "This close arrangement will only work if we have two understandings: First, it's our job to always spoil your kids, your job to *never* spoil 'em. If you don't do our job, we won't have to turn around and do yours. Second, when in Rome, which is our house, do as the Romans do, and when the Romans come to your house, do as the Romans do."

It's worked out just fine!

Q: *My parents live relatively close, and we see them fairly often. Spending the night with Grandma and Grandpa is a big thing for our four-year-old, who also happens to be their only grandchild. The problem is that during visits, whether we're there or not, the folks ignore our rules and let*

Michael do and have just about anything he wants. As a result, Michael is very hard to handle when we get him home, and it sometimes takes several days to get things back on an even keel. How would you suggest we deal with this problem?

A: I'm going to take the grandparents' side in this one. When our children were younger, we had the same problem with Willie's parents, whom we saw fairly often. After much frustration, we finally realized that no matter what we said or did, the folks weren't going to change. We also remembered that our grandparents had treated us pretty much the same way, and we were none the worse because of it. Finally, we admitted to ourselves that when the time came, we were probably going to spoil our grandchildren as well!

This change of attitude enabled us to realize that the control problems we were having with our children after visits with the folks weren't their fault. Blaming the children's behavior on them was buck-passing of the first magnitude. If we were willing to let the grandparents spoil the kids, we had to take full responsibility for discipline.

Taking the bull by the horns, we sat down with the kids and told them that visits with Grandma and Grandpa were vacations from a lot of our rules, but when the visits were over, so was the vacation. Immediately after every visit, we held a transitional conversation with the kids, reminding them of our expectations. If they still had difficulty with self-control, we sent them to their rooms with instructions to remain there until they felt settled.

It wasn't long before we were truly enjoying our visits with the folks, and the kids were making the transition without difficulty.

Q: *We realize we've been much too indecisive and inconsistent with our six-year-old son. As a result, he's developed some behavior problems. How is he likely to react if we suddenly transform ourselves from parent wimps to benevolent dictators?*

A: Your child may not welcome the transformation. After all, it's going to require that he give up a significant measure of control within the family. For a time, his behavior problems are likely to escalate as he struggles to return things to the way they were. As they say, "Things get worse before they get better." If you stick to your guns, however, his behavior will improve, as will the overall relationship.

Unresolved disciplinary issues impede communication and expressions of affection between parent and child. Resolving the issues removes those impediments. It's impossible for parent and child to have truly good communication with each other until the child completely trusts and feels he can rely upon the parent's authority. As they say, the horse is your authority, and the cart is an open, loving parent–child relationship.

This same is true of a teacher–student relationship. Good classroom teachers recognize that they can teach only as effectively as they govern. So, on the first day of school, before doing anything else, they put the horse in front of the cart by going over the rules. Realizing that some children will be testing, good teachers also explain exactly what's going to happen when a child breaks a rule. When rules are broken, good teachers follow through as promised. In so doing, they demonstrate their reliability to the students. The students, in turn, don't resent this. Quite the contrary, they trust their teachers *because* of it.

In the long run, the happiest children are obedient children and the happiest parents are benevolent dictators. Obviously, one can't exist without the other. So, for everyone's sake, go for it!

3

POINT THREE

The Roots of Responsibility

As I TRAVEL AROUND the country, doing talks and workshops for various parent and professional groups, I ask my audiences to participate in a small survey. I begin by asking for a show of hands on this question: "How many of you can honestly say that you expect your children to perform a regular routine of chores around the home for which they are not paid, with an allowance or otherwise?" In an audience of, say, five hundred, no more than fifty hands will go up.

Then: "How many of your parents would have raised their hands to the same question?" Hands go up everywhere, and people begin to laugh.

But this is really no laughing matter. It means that in the short span of one generation, we have managed to misplace a very important tenet of child-rearing. Simply stated, it is that children should be *contributing* members of their families. In other words, children should have chores. There are five reasons why.

- The first is a practical one. As I explained in chapter 1, the ultimate purpose of raising children is to help them out of our lives and into successful lives of their own. We have, therefore, an obligation to endow them with the skills they will need to lead successful adult lives, and domestic skills are no less important than any others. By the age of eighteen, all children, male and female, should be familiar with and practiced at every single aspect of running a home. They should be able to wash and iron their own clothes, prepare basic meals, use a vacuum cleaner, disinfect bathrooms, replace furnace filters, mow grass, and weed garden areas. They should also be responsible for earning a portion of their spending money and budgeting it sensibly. This training not only helps prepare children for adulthood, it also helps develop in them an appreciation for the effort their parents put into maintaining a household, an effort the children might otherwise take for granted.

- The second reason involves a child's sense of security. Chores *actualize* the child's participation in the family, thus strengthening feelings of acceptance and security. A child who isn't doing chores isn't participating to the fullest extent possible. The child's role in the family is, therefore, a diminished one, much like that of a baseball player who, although a member of the team, rarely gets to play. Participation generates stronger feelings of membership for both the baseball player and the child.

- The third reason has to do with self-esteem. Chores enable feelings of accomplishment. Knowing that his or her contribution of time and energy to the family is regarded as important enhances a child's sense of membership in the family, enlarges upon feelings of worth, and adds immensely to self-esteem.

- The fourth reason has to do with good citizenship. In his inaugural address, President John F. Kennedy said, "Ask not what your country can do for you, ask what you can do for your country." In other words, a responsible citizen is one who looks more for opportunities to contribute to the system than for opportunities to take from it. No one would argue that good citizenship begins at home. Our child-rearing practices should reflect this same principle. We should teach children that the reward of family membership comes more from what they put into the family than from what they take out of it. When this principle is turned upside-down, when children are allowed to take from the family in greater measure than their contribution justifies, their relationship to the family becomes parasitic. Inherent to this condition is a lack of motivation, perpetual self-centeredness, and the entirely false idea that something can be had for nothing.

- The fifth and most important reason is that chores bond a child to the values of the parents. They are a child's only means of making a tangible contribution to the family, and any act of contribution is, by its very nature, values-oriented. Think about it. When you make a contribution of time, money, or other personal resources to a political, religious, educational, or charitable organization, you acknowledge two things: that you share values with that organization, and that you want to do something tangible to help support and maintain those values. The same applies to a child's contribution of time and energy to the family. Children who are enabled to contribute to their families on a regular basis come to a clearer understanding of their parents' values. Furthermore, they are much more likely to use those same values in their own adult lives to create success and happiness for themselves and *their* children.

The proof of what I'm saying can be found in the pudding of our country's history. In what general areas or regions of this country have family values and traditions been handed down most reliably from generation to generation to generation? In rural America or, more specifically, in farm country. And what single aspect most distinguishes the life of a child raised on a farm from that of a child raised in a city or suburban environment? Chores.

That's right? As soon as they are capable, farm children are expected to perform work within their families. If they are too young to do anything but carry a milk pail, they carry a milk pail. If they are old enough to drive a tractor, they drive a tractor. And their parents don't beg, bribe, or bargain for these chores. No money changes hands (although the child may share in the profit of a certain project). There are no daily arguments over why certain work has to be done or why a certain someone has to do it. There are no temper tantrums—no screams of "It's not fair!"—and parents don't waste time and energy on repetitious attempts at justification and explanation. Doing these chores is simply *expected* of these children, and so they get done. For a child raised on a farm, the family and its values take on importance not simply because of parental modeling and enforcement but because the child performs a valuable function. Put another way, the child is given the opportunity to *invest* in the family. When someone invests in something, that something becomes worthy of protecting, of preserving. And so, when farm-raised children become adults, they cash in on that investment and use it to create success, stability, and happiness in their own lives. Eventually, they pass the same lessons on to their children, realizing there is no greater gift they can possibly give.

Willie and I didn't really begin involving Eric and Amy in housework until they were ten and seven, respectively. Until then, we had required only that they keep their rooms clean and orderly. Their growing reluctance to do anything else around the house finally made us realize the need to increase their day-to-day participation in housework.

We began by making a list of all the chores included in the housekeeping schedule, cicling those we felt certain the children could handle. Lo and behold! There was, we discovered, nothing they couldn't do, and only three things—washing, ironing, and cooking—we preferred they *not* do. We listed the materials and steps involved in each chore on separate index cards and divided them into two files, one for each child. The idea here was to leave as little as possible to the children's imaginations. Finally, we organized the schedule on two seven-day calendars, which we posted on the refrigerator. Each child's chores took up about forty-five minutes on weekdays and two hours on Saturday.

Having put all our ducks in a row, we presented the plan to the children, who—believe it or not—accepted it without complaint. Well, almost. After we had explained the system, Eric looked at me and said, "What are you and Mom going to do, watch us work?" Children are so cute.

Admittedly, during the first few weeks, we had to prompt, remind, and even at times apply a little pressure. Our quality control standards were fairly strict. If one of the children failed to do a chore correctly or completely, he or she had to redo it. A "forgotten" chore resulted in the loss of a privilege, such as going outside to play, for a day or two. It didn't take long for the children to discover that conscientious cooperation not only took relatively little time but also cost less than the alternative. Eventually, it became obvious they were taking considerable pride in the contribution they were making to the family. Besides all that, they learned firsthand the ins and outs of running a household, a necessary step toward helping them out of our lives.

Any Questions So Far?

Q: *At what age should parents begin assigning chores to children?*

A: Three is probably the most advantageous age at which to begin assigning chores to a child. A child this age has a strong need to identify with parents and expresses that need, in part, by following them around the house, wanting to get involved in the things they're doing and imitating them if direct involvement is impossible. If Dad's repairing a leaky faucet, the child wants to help. When Mom cooks, the child gets out a few pots and pans and plays on the kitchen floor.

This interest can and should be capitalized upon by starting three-year-olds on a few minor chores. In order to establish a routine, they should take place at the same time every day. Children can, for instance, help make their beds in the morning, help set the table at dinner, and pick up toys every evening before a bedtime story.

The feeling of accomplishment, along with the praise their parents give them for being good helpers, serves to enhance the children's sense of belonging and thus adds significantly to their security and self-esteem.

Because threes are so eager to please, parents should have little difficulty obtaining cooperation from them. Doing a few chores at this age sets the stage for increasing responsibilities as each child grows older. Parents are more apt to encounter resistance if they attempt to assign specific chores before age three. Likewise, children's "chore readiness" begins to wane if parents wait much later than four to begin acquainting them with this important part of family life.

Q: *What can parents do with children younger than three to help prepare them for a responsible role in the family?*

A: Parents plant seeds of responsibility by helping younger children learn to do such things as feed themselves, dress themselves, and use the toilet. Each of these accomplishments constitutes a step toward self-sufficiency and not only enhances self-esteem but also the child's receptivity to additional responsibilities.

As children take these first steps toward independence, it's important that parents be more *supportive* than *directive*. In the first place, too much direction communicates the message, You're not learning this well enough (or fast enough) to suit us. The child's reaction may well be to stop trying altogether. Parental overinvolvement also stifles the child's sense of accomplishment. In order for these learnings to be truly meaningful, the child must have full "ownership" of them.

When a child is ready to learn to use the toilet, for example, parents should provide a potty the child can comfortably use, supply training pants instead of diapers, and give encouragement. Once the props are in place, parents should stand on the sideline and let the process unfold, in the child's own way and at the child's own speed. The more parents hover, the more anxious they are about mistakes, the more frustrated the child will become and the longer the learning will take. This policy of supportive noninterference applies equally well to children who are learning to feed themselves, dress themselves, tie their own shoes, make their beds, and even read.

Q: *How much housework can parents reasonably expect of a child?*

A: At the very least, four- or five-year-old children should be responsible for keeping their bedroom and bathroom orderly. Six-year-olds can be taught to vacuum, starting with their own room. By age seven or eight, children should be responsible for daily upkeep of their bedroom and bath as well as several chores around the home. Once a week, children this age should be required to do a major cleaning of bedroom and bath. This should include vacuuming, dusting, changing bath and bed linens, and cleaning the tub, lavatory, and commode.

A nine- to ten-year-old should contribute about forty-five minutes of chore time to the family on a daily basis and about two hours on Saturday. It helps to organize the daily routine into three fifteen-minute blocks. The first of these should take place first thing in the morning (straighten room and bath and feed the dog); the second, right after school (unload the dishwasher and put everything away); the third, after supper (clear the table, rinse dishes, scrub pots and pans, load the dishwasher, and take out the garbage).

By the way, in this scheme of things, there's no such thing as boy work and girl work. It's all people work. If you are "people," then you work.

Q: *Should parents pay children for chores?*

A: In general, no. To begin with, payment tends to create the illusion that the child who doesn't want the money isn't obligated to perform the chore. Payment also dilutes the learning experience. A chore that's paid for is no longer a contribution for the sake of the family, but a contribution for the sake of money. Paying for chores puts money in the child's pocket but no true sense of value in the child's head. It may teach a child something about business but nothing about the responsibility that accompanies family membership.

On the other hand, it's all right for parents to pay children for work above and beyond the standard routine. For instance, when Eric was in high school, I didn't pay him for mowing the lawn once a week during the summer, but I did pay him for an occasional day's work of helping me cut down trees and chop them into fireplace logs. By that time, Eric knew that payment didn't mean the tasks were optional.

Q: *I must take exception to your recommendation that children not be paid for chores. It seems to me that this is a contradiction. You say children should be reared so they learn "how the real world works," but in the real world people are paid for doing jobs. According to your own standard, therefore, shouldn't children be paid for chores?*

A: As I see it, the problem with paying children for household chores is that chores should not be regarded as jobs. Rather, they constitute a *service* rendered to the family, a means—however minimal—of making a contribution to the family's welfare.

When I say that a child's upbringing should teach how the real world works, I am referring primarily to principles, not actual privileges enjoyed or responsibilities borne by adults. For example, adults can and should exercise their right to vote. The family, however, is not a democracy. Children don't elect their parents, much less state and national representatives.

Nonetheless, it is of vital importance to all concerned that children become more than simply acquainted with democracy's foundational principles. The viability of our democracy, as de Tocqueville noted in *Democracy in America* (1874), depends on the ready willingness of the citizenry to lay down self-interests and render public service. This willingness to serve does not arise spontaneously, upon demand. It is learned. If preparing children for citizenship is important, and Grandma was right that good citizenship begins at home, it follows that children should learn the service ethic within their families. I submit that the only way a child can serve his or her family is by doing chores. I also contend that doing a chore is not a service if the child is compensated in any way, shape, or form. A child should perform chores as a member of the family, period. Similarly, an adult should perform community service as a member of the community, period.

The idea that children should be compensated for doing chores is inconsistent with a more insular reality as well: Parents are not compensated for cooking meals or vacuuming floors or tending to the yard. Under the circumstances, paying children for doing chores implies that children have a privileged status within the family, free of obligation.

Unfortunately, all too many of today's parents fail to assign their children to a regular routine of chores. They act as if the only person with an obligation in the parent–child relationship is the parent. Through omission, they inadvertently teach their children that something can be had for nothing.

Most employers and managers to whom I speak bemoan the seeming absence of what I term obligatory reciprocity on the part of today's young adults, many of whom seem to think they are owed more than they owe. One manager recently reported to me that many young college graduates expect the same privileges they see accorded employees with twenty-plus years of dedicated tenure. Confusing employment with entitlement, it seems to me, is the likely outcome of a childhood devoid of tangible responsibility to the family.

Q: *Are you against giving a child an allowance?*

A: Not as long as the allowance has nothing whatsoever to do with the child's chores. Chores teach responsibility, self-discipline, time management, and a host of other essential values and skills. An allowance helps a child learn to manage money. The two lessons should not be confused. An allowance should not be used to persuade a child to do chores, nor should it be suddenly withdrawn to punish inappropriate behavior. Parents who use money to leverage cooperation from a child are unwittingly teaching that child how to use money as a tool with which to manipulate people.

Q: *When there are two children involved, wouldn't it be more fair for parents to let the children alternate chores on a weekly or daily basis?*

A: As fair as it may sound, an arrangement or this sort never works out. I find, in fact, that parental efforts to be fair almost always backfire.

Alternating chores inevitably results in several problems. The children end up arguing over whose turn it is to do what. Because none of the chores belong exclusively to either child, they take less pride in their work and do just enough to get by. When parents complain that a certain job wasn't done properly, the children point their fingers at one another. Because the chores are alternated, it takes the children longer to learn the routine. As a result, parents must constantly remind and hassle the children to get the chores done. In short, this attempt at fairness leads inevitably to frustration and conflict.

A family is an organization. As such, everyone in the family should have the equivalent of a job description. Each person's job description helps define his or her role in the family. It follows that the clearer the job description, the clearer the role. In an organization in which roles are not clear, people become frustrated and angry and the organization doesn't run smoothly. I've never heard of a business in which people exchanged jobs on a daily or weekly basis. I wouldn't recommend it for a family either.

Q: *Our fourteen-year-old son is forever asking us for money. He wants the latest clothes, shoes, and CDs. He wants money for movies, video arcades, fast food, and amusement parks. He wants money just to have money. We're slowly going broke! We give him a $10 per week allowance.*

Where it goes is anyone's guess. He says it's not enough, but when we give him the chance to earn more money by doing extra chores, he declines. Do you have a solution?

A: I can offer you a plan that worked for all concerned when our children were in their teen years, but let me begin by saying I agree with your son. You aren't giving him enough money. But by the same token, you're not expecting enough responsibility of him either. You're making the biggest, and most common, mistake made by parents of teens: You're attempting to micromanage.

As I point out in my book *Teen-Proofing*, parenting a teen is a brand new ball game, requiring new plays. Unaware of this, or perhaps unwilling to admit it, most parents fail to shift parenting gears when their children enter their early teen years. Instead, they keep right on trying to control. (In fact, because of the heightened anxiety that attends this parenting stage, most parents of teens actually try to control even more than they did when their children were younger.) Parental control works with an eight-year-old, in moderation, but it won't work with a teenager. From age thirteen on, the more parents try to control, the less able they are to mentor their children toward successful emancipation, and *mentoring* is the secret to winning.

Where money is concerned, your job is to help your son learn to establish good priorities, to budget. This is something he will learn only by trial and error, and by giving money with no strings attached, you're making it impossible for him to make errors and learn from them. You can remedy this by giving him more money. Yes, you read me correctly: more money. Here's the plan:

1. For the next month or two, add up all the money you give your son each month for discretionary (as opposed to necessary) expenses: clothes, CDs, fast food, movies, video arcades, and everything else you listed.

2. When you've collected enough data, set up a checking account with all three of your names on it. On the first of every

month, deposit into the account 75 percent of the monthly sum arrived at.

3. Give your son the checkbook and tell him that, from now on, he's to use his monthly allowance to purchase the afore-mentioned items and activities for himself. Say, "At your age, it must be demeaning to come to us for money. So you won't have to anymore!"

4. Tell him that, whereas you'll no longer be controlling how or when he spends this allowance, under no circumstances will you ever give him a loan against the next month's money. In other words, if he runs out, he's effectively grounded himself for the rest of the month.

5. Make clear that if he bounces a check, you'll pay both the merchant's and the bank's penalties out of his next month's allowance and deposit only what remains.

Now he'll be able to make mistakes and learn from them. As a consequence, he'll become more responsible. And independent! Perhaps best of all, you'll stop going broke.

Responsible Behavior

Not only have today's children, by and large, not been assigned adequate responsibility within their families, they've also not been assigned adequate responsibility *for their behavior*—in particular, their *misbehavior*.

All too often, when a child misbehaves, parents shoulder the consequences of the problem. They take on the emotional conse-quences by feeling angry, frustrated, worried, embarrassed, and guilty. They take on the tangible consequences by absorbing the inconveniences caused by the misbehavior. For example, they may be repeating instructions to the child more than once because the child rarely, if ever, listens the first time. They may be losing time at work because of the need to have frequent conferences with the child's teacher or principal. Perhaps they're repeatedly late to work because the child is never dressed and ready for school on time. They may rarely enjoy any privacy in the evening because the child fights bedtime for several hours every night.

Responsibility for a problem is measured in terms of its consequences. When parents absorb the lion's share of the emotional and tangible consequences of a child's misbehavior, they unwittingly accept responsibility for that misbehavior. In effect, the problem now belongs to them, so they will try to solve it. But the harder they try, the more frustrated they will become, because the *only* person who can solve it is its rightful owner: the child.

Situations of this sort call for an enactment of the Agony Principle. It proposes: Parents should never agonize over anything a child does or fails to do if the child is perfectly capable of agonizing over it instead. In other words, when a child misbehaves, the child should be assigned both the emotional and tangible consequences of that misbehavior. Not until and unless the agony of the problem rests squarely on the child's shoulders will the child be motivated to solve it.

In order to effect this transfer of responsibility from their shoulders to a child's, parents must draw upon the Godfather Principle. First articulated by a Sicilian philosopher known as Don Corleone, the Godfather Principle simply states that in order to make a child accept responsibility for misbehavior of any sort, the child's parents must make him an offer he can't refuse.

A Trip to the Beach

The following true story is an illustration of the Agony and Godfather principles at work.

In 1976, shortly after moving to Gastonia, North Carolina, the Rosemond family began taking summer vacations at Myrtle Beach, South Carolina. For the children, the trip was the event of the year, but Willie and I dreaded it. Five hours in a car with two young'uns in the throes of "We can't wait!" might be a useful way of extracting information from P.O.W.s, but it's no way to start a vacation.

Two minutes out of the driveway, the children would begin bickering and wouldn't stop until we reached our destination. A typical exchange:

"Make Eric stop looking at me!"

"She has her feet on my side of the seat!"

"I do not! Stop pushing me! Aaaahhh!"

"Oh, shut up, Amy! I'm not hurting you. You're such a big baby!"

"Stop calling me names! Aaaahhh!"

And, so it went, from driveway to motel. And nothing would stop it. Not begging, not bribing, not threatening to turn around and go home. Nothing.

After suffering through several of these experiences, and while anticipating yet another, Willie and I devised a way of ending the horror forever. Our salvation came in the form of ten rectangles of colored cardboard, which we called tickets.

When the appointed day arrived, we packed the car and then sat down with the children, colored cardboards in hand.

"Kids," we said, "these are tickets. Each of you gets five of them. Hang on to them, because they're important. They have to do with the rules of riding in the car. Rule One is Do not bicker. Rule Two is Do not make loud noises. Rule Three is Do not interrupt when mom and dad are talking to each other.

"Every time you break a rule, you lose a ticket. If you bicker, you both lose a ticket, no matter who started it. Now, the first thing you want to do when you get to the beach is go in the water, right? That's where the tickets come in, because if you don't have at least one ticket when we get to the motel, you won't be allowed in the water for two hours. During that time, you'll sit on the beach under an umbrella and watch the rest of us frolic in the surf."

We then gave out the tickets, piled in the car, and started down the road. Before we were out of the neighborhood, the kids lost their first tickets for bickering. Soon thereafter, Eric lost one for making a loud noise. Then Amy lost one for interrupting. By the time we were an hour down the road, they'd each lost four of their five tickets.

The next four hours were the quietest we'd ever spent with Eric and Amy, in or out of a car. They said not a word to each other or to us. They clutched those last tickets to their chests and stared out the windows. It was the start of the best family vacation we'd ever had!

Several weeks after recounting this incident at a speaking engagement, I had a phone call from a woman who had been in the audience. She had tried the technique, she said, but with no success.

"The trip there was absolutely horrendous," she said, "so we decided to give your ticket method a try on the way home. We gave each of the children five tickets, just like you said, and promised we would take them out for ice cream if they didn't lose all their tickets by the time we got home."

"Take them out for ice cream?" I asked.

"That's right. They're always asking us to take them out for ice cream. It's one of their favorite things. Well, anyway," she continued, "they were all right for a while, but then the misbehavior started and they proceeded to lose all their tickets in less than fifteen minutes. Then, realizing we had no control over them, they were worse than ever!"

No wonder! These parents had unwittingly violated the Godfather Principle by making their children an offer they *could* refuse! The trouble with promising a child ice cream for good behavior, and then threatening to take it away for bad behavior, is that ice cream—or the lack of it—is of no real consequence. Had the children stood to lose something important, such as being able to play with their friends once they got home, the likelihood of success would have increased twentyfold.

The Problems with Rewards

The problem with the approach these parents took is the problem with rewards in general. They rarely work. Not for long, at least.

In the first place, because they are basically extras, rewards are usually of minimal value to a child. Privileges such as socializing with friends or the use of a bicycle have considerable more pulling power because these are the things that define a child's standard of living. And just as an adult is strongly motivated to maintain his or her standard of living, so is a child.

In the second place, rewards are inflationary. Occasionally, a particular reward might motivate a child for a short period of time, but as soon as the child is saturated with whatever reward is being used, it immediately loses its value. At this point, in order to continue motivating the child, you must increase the value of the reward.

I often tell parents that if they promise a child an ice-cream cone for keeping a clean room for a week, the child will probably work to earn the reward for one or two weeks. By then, however, the novelty will have worn off and the child probably won't continue to keep the room clean for anything less than a hot fudge sundae. Within a relatively short time, hot fudge sundaes will lose their appeal, and the child's parents will again have to increase the offer. Eventually, in this family version of *Let's Make a Deal,* I can envision these parents saying, "Tommy, if you keep your room clean this week, we're going to send you and five of your friends to Disney World for an all-expense paid weekend, including all the ice cream you can eat!"

Absurd? Perhaps. On the other hand, I've actually heard of parents offering children one hundred dollars for each A on their report cards or two new bicycles for siblings who can manage to be "nice" to each other for a week. Sure enough, the children shape up and earn the rewards! But then it's back to business as usual—poor grades or constant bickering.

Rewards also prevent children from accepting responsibility for their behavior. Instead of helping a child learn that inappropriate behavior has undesirable consequences, rewards can result in the child developing a manipulative "What's in it for me?" attitude toward appropriate behavior. In other words, instead of learning that good behavior is rewarding in and of itself, the child learns to use the promise of good behavior as a bargaining tool to get new toys, privileges, and other goodies.

Not long ago, I explained the risks of using rewards to a gathering of parents in Miami. Afterward, a mother approached me and thanked me for my remarks. She said, "I've used rewards a lot because I was under the impression that they helped promote good self-esteem. Now I understand why every time I take my son anywhere, he asks, 'If I'm good, will you buy me a new toy?'"

An occasional spontaneous reward, used as an acknowledgment of achievement or progress in a certain area, is fine. Rewards that haven't been contracted for are more sincere and therefore more effective at promoting both good behavior and good self-esteem. Children should, of course, be praised for their accomplishments, but even praise is most effective when it's low-key and occasional.

In the question-and-answer portion of this chapter, we'll look at several other specific examples of how the Agony and Godfather principles can be used to assign responsibility for a problem to a child.

Running After the Bus

A number of years ago, while I was in Kansas City speaking at a convention of city managers, I found myself on the same bill with Tom Peters and Robert Waterman, the authors of *In Search of Excellence*, the best-selling book about corporate management. Because they were scheduled immediately before me, I had the pleasure of hearing most of their presentation.

At one point during their talk, they flashed the letters MBWA on the screen. This was not a new graduate degree they'd invented but stood for a concept they called Management by Wandering Around. That set off peals of laughter. Peters and Waterman then surprised the audience by announcing that MBWA was perhaps the most efficient and motivating of all management styles. Managers who practice MBWA are skilled at delegating responsibility, and equally skilled at staying out of the way of the people to whom they delegate. They are authority figures who make their knowledge and expertise available to the people they supervise, but they do not hover over the people who work for them, watching their every move.

They trust that their staff can and will do their jobs properly and communicate that trust by not becoming overly involved in their work. They motivate people by giving them responsibility, along with the opportunity to discover the intrinsic rewards of independent achievement. By wandering instead of bustling anxiously around, they create a relaxed work environment, one in which people are free to be as creative and productive as they are capable. In effect, instead of being bosses in the traditional sense of the term, managers who wander around are *consultants* to the people they supervise. Their general policy is one of noninterference, and they break this rule only if absolutely necessary. They are role models, teachers, guidance counselors, gurus.

Listening to and absorbing what Peters and Waterman were saying about the new manager, it occurred to me that MBWA applied to raising children as well. The most effective parents, I realized, are those who are not constantly busy in their children's lives but are relaxed and therefore create a relaxed environment in which their children can discover their potential. Instead of hovering anxiously, they act as consultants on their children's growth and development.

Parents of this sort are authority figures, but they guide and model more than they order. Their goal is not to make their children subservient or dependent but to make them independent and responsible. Toward this end, they provide a variety of opportunities for growth but allow their children a great deal of freedom when it comes to choosing or rejecting those opportunities.

Instead of taking credit when their children behave well and feeling guilty when their children behave poorly, they assign their children the responsibility, both positive and negative, for their own behavior. Above all else, they let their children make mistakes, realizing that some of the most valuable lessons in life can only be learned through trial and error. In all these ways, they send messages of trust and personal worth to their children, who are free to discover their capacities for love and creativity. In effect, these parents practice the all but lost art of Parenting by Wandering Around.

It is unfortunate that there are not more of these wonderful parents. I am thinking in particular of well-intentioned men and women who insist upon becoming too involved in their children's lives.

Because they live through their children, they take their children's successes and failures very seriously and very personally. They over-direct, overprotect, and overindulge. They take on responsibility that rightfully belongs to their children, thus robbing them of opportunities for growth.

Several years ago, I came across an article in the *Hartford Courant* written by Nancy Davis, a teacher of journalism at Miss Porter's School in Farmington, Connecticut. She wrote:

> *The advice that children need to try and fail, with supportive parents behind them, is hard for parents to take. We want to spare them the failures, big and small, which we experienced or which we see looming on their horizons. We've been told a hundred times that people learn from their mistakes, but we want our children to never make mistakes because they may be hurt in the process.*

Davis's advice to parents was simply, "Don't run after the bus." Those five words capture the essence of good parenting better than any five I've heard in a long time.

Thank you, Tom Peters and Robert Waterman, and thank you, Nancy Davis.

The Sound of Face Striking Pavement

A mother asked what she could do to get her six-year-old son to keep his shoeslaces tied.

"I know this must sound silly," she said, "but every time I look at him, his laces are flopping all over the place. It's driving me nuts!"

"Why do you want him to keep his shoelaces tied?" I asked.

"Well," she answered, "besides looking bad, he's going to trip over them someday."

"And what's the worst thing that could happen if he tripped?"

She thought for a moment. "He might fall and hurt himself."

"Badly?" I asked.

"Probably not," she answered.

"But perhaps badly enough to think twice the next time he leaves his shoelaces untied?" I offered.

After a thoughtful pause, she answered, "Maybe."

"Then I suggest you do nothing at all. Let his shoelaces flop. Let him learn the hard way."

The hard way—my dad used that phrase a lot. "There are certain things I can't teach you," he would say. "You're going to have to learn them the way everyone else does, the hard way."

In retrospect, I realize Dad was, once again, right on the mark. Some of the most valuable lessons in my life have been learned courtesy of falling flat on my face.

By and large, today's parent seems to think that letting children fall flat on their faces when the fall could have been intercepted, or even prevented altogether, is not only irresponsible but downright cruel. The prevailing attitude is it that if you, the parent, see the fall coming and do nothing to prevent it, *you* are responsible for the results, not the child.

Cedric won't do his homework, so every evening his parents sit down with him and see that it gets done. Whenever Angel has a conflict with another child in the neighborhood, her mother runs interference, calling the other child's parents, making sure things are set right. To prevent him from falling in with the wrong crowd, Roger's parents censor his choice of friends. Englebert's parents take him to a different after-school activity every day of the week and Saturday morning to make sure he stays "active."

I call this sort of obsessive hovering parenting by helicopter, and because of it many of today's children never learn to accept responsibility for their behavior because their parents are doing a fine job of accepting that responsibility for them. But responsibility isn't the only thing at stake.

Almost all learning is accomplished through trial and error. If you prevent the error, you prevent the learning. By making mistakes, one learns what works and what doesn't. Eventually, after a period of failure, the person fine-tunes his or her skills and masters the task at hand.

Standing back and letting failure occur, in a supportive but noninterfering way, gives a child room to develop initiative, resourcefulness, and numerous problem-solving skills. It also lets the child come to grips with the frustration inherent in learning any skill:

social, academic, emotional, and so on. That's how children learn to persevere, and perseverance—as we all know from experience—is the main ingredient in every success story.

It all boils down to this: If we want our children to stand on their own two feet, we must also be willing to let them fail. So let's stop tying their shoelaces.

Making Amends

Having to accept responsibility for one's own behavior develops self-control. Since the purpose of discipline is to teach self-control, any method of discipline, if it is to be effective, must assign responsibility for the child's behavior to the child. Simply put, when a child does something bad, he or she should feel bad about it and be required to take whatever steps are necessary to correct it. This is how conscience develops.

Unfortunately, many of today's children don't enjoy the advantages of this process. All too often, when a child does something wrong, the parents wind up feeling bad about it and making the compensation. Thus protected from the consequences of bad behavior, the child grows not in responsibility and self-control but in irresponsibility and self-centeredness.

There is a general tendency among adults to feel that when a child misbehaves the child should be punished. That's sometimes true, but equally true is the fact that punishment sometimes misses the point. When a child's misbehavior is hurtful to someone else, for example, it's more important that the child make amends.

A number of years ago, an upset neighbor called to tell us that Amy, then eight, had been disrespectful toward her. The implication in her outrage was that we must be bad parents for having such a bad child.

When she'd finished venting her anger, I said, "Let me assure you of several things. First, I believe what you're telling me. Second, I agree that what Amy did was completely inappropriate and there is no excuse for it. Third, I'm grateful to you for letting me know and for being so honest about your feelings. Fourth, Amy will correct the problem she's created. Last, but not least, I want you to feel free to call any time you see one of our children doing something wrong."

There was a long period of silence on the other end of the line. Finally, in an almost apologetic tone, the neighbor said, "Well, now, you know Amy is usually a very good little girl. This is the only time she's ever given me trouble."

"I'm glad to hear that," I said, "but that doesn't excuse or erase what she's done."

When the conversation ended, I found Amy and confronted her with the neighbor's report. "I'm very unhappy about this," I said. "You do not have permission to be disrespectful to *any* adult, under *any* circumstances."

She started to cry. A good sign, I thought to myself. But just feeling bad about what she'd done wasn't going to correct the mistake.

"I've decided that you're going to apologize to our neighbor for your disrespect."

Amy immediately became very agitated. "Oh, please, Daddy, don't make me do that. Make me stay inside and don't let me play with my friends, or take my toys away, but don't make me go over there and apologize, please, Daddy, please!"

"Sorry, kid, but this isn't open for discussion."

"Can I call her on the phone?"

"No, you'll do it face-to-face."

"Will you go with me?"

"No, Amy, I won't. I didn't help you create the problem, and I won't help you solve it. And that, little girl, is my final word on the subject."

When she realized I wasn't going to budge, she composed herself, walked across the street, rang the doorbell, and apologized. As I watched from the living room window, I saw the neighbor smile, take Amy's hand in hers, and nod as if to say that everything was all right.

Amy came back across the street with tears streaming down her face. There were no more punishments, no more lectures. In fact, we never mentioned the situation again.

Sometimes, when I tell this story or another like it, a listener will remark that it sounds as if I'm in favor of "laying guilt trips" on children. To a certain extent, I am. When children do something wrong, they should feel the wrong of what they've done. The only way to communicate that feeling is through the child's emotional system. In other words, just telling a child he or she did wrong isn't usually enough. The words you use must come across with enough impact to make the child feel guilty or embarrassed or sorry or all those things.

The term *guilt trip* carries a lot of negative connotations, and guilt can certainly be used in sadistic, hostile ways. At its extremes, guilt is maladaptive. People who are incapable of feeling guilt are called sociopaths. They do what they please without regard for anyone else or remorse for whatever hurt they might cause. On the other hand, people who carry around excessive feelings of guilt are neurotic. They are constantly haunted by the idea that they're doing something wrong. But guilt can also be a very adaptive emotion. Without it, civilization as we know it wouldn't exist. People won't accept responsibility for their own bad behavior unless they feel bad about it. Guilt is a message from inside that says we misbehaved and shouldn't behave that way again. The idea that guilt, all guilt, is bad, came out of the do-your-own-thing philosophy of the sixties and seventies. Well, it's high time we got our heads out of the clouds and planted our parenting attitudes in the soil of common sense.

Our job as parents is to socialize our children. You can't teach a child how to act without also teaching that child how to think and how to feel. Children won't know to feel guilty unless we first teach them that guilt is appropriate to certain situations. That's how a child's conscience develops. Once you've taught children the basics, you can trust them to come to feelings of guilt on their own, when those feelings are appropriate. Even so, there may be times, as was the case with Amy and the neighbor, when parents will need to drive the point home.

Empathy vs. Sympathy

I frequently encourage parents to stop sympathizing with their children's problems and begin empathizing with them instead. They often tell me they didn't know there was a difference, but there is, and it's a big one. Empathy involves understanding and sends the message, "What are you going to do about it?" Sympathy, on the other hand, involves pampering and sends the message, "Oh, you poor thing! You haven't done anything to deserve this!" Sympathy is like custard. The longer you stir it, the thicker and stickier it gets. Eventually, it does more to hinder change than help it.

When a child is having personal problems, a little sympathy can sometimes help open lines of communication. But, sympathy has a quickly reached point of diminishing returns. Stir too much into a situation, and you're likely to create more problems than you solve.

Why? Because, like morphine, sympathy in small amounts eases pain but in large amounts it's addictive. And once addicted, the child stops trying to solve problems and starts trying to get more and more sympathy. Since a problem has to exist in order for the child to get sympathy, problems begin to accumulate as the child settles ever more passively and comfortably into the role of victim.

When Eric entered junior high, he began having problems getting along with his peers. At first, he complained of being picked on, then that other kids were trying to get him in trouble, then that he had no friends. Initially, we regarded his complaints with a grain of salt, thinking they were nothing more than temporary problems of adjustment. As time went on, however, things went from bad to worse. We noticed that he rarely received phone calls, that he spent weekend nights at home, and that he was looking and acting increasingly depressed. On occasion, we'd hear him crying in his room. Alarmed, we started asking questions. Out came the most horrendous tale of woe we'd ever heard.

There was a group of kids at school, he said, who were not only making fun of him but were spreading rumors that he was—well, let's just say "different." He was being ostracized by the other boys and ignored by the girls. One particular group of boys had even written an obscene note to a girl and signed Eric's name. For that, he was grilled by the principal, who ended up satisfied that Eric had nothing to do with it. Nonetheless, the incident left its mark on the little guy's self-confidence.

We knew junior high kids were capable of sadistic cruelty, but this seemed beyond belief. So we sympathized. We talked, we counseled, we comforted, we even cried with him. We tried building him up by telling him what a really wonderful person he was and said his tormentors wouldn't turn out half as well. We did everything we could think of to let him know how unfair we thought the whole mess was. But things just kept getting worse. He moped constantly, he never went out, and the tales of woe became more and more woeful. Finally, we realized Eric was suffering as much from an overdose of sympathy as he was from anything else. Our good intentions had whipped a relatively small flame into a forest fire.

Finally, we sat down with him and said, "Look, kid, we feel for you, but we've noticed that you aren't doing anything to solve these problems. It's almost as if you're beginning to enjoy this little soap opera. So we've decided there are going to be no more conversations about your social problems. We've said all there is to say. Now it's time for you to get yourself in gear and do something for yourself. We're giving you three weeks in which to find a friend and start doing things with him. If you haven't done anything by then, we'll take matters in hand and begin calling some parents ourselves to see if we can arrange some activities. In other words, either you do it or we will."

The threat of embarrassment was a gentle but adequate boot in the rear. In two weeks, he had a friend. Within a year, he had more friends than he could keep up with.

That's the difference.

It's Never Too Late

In order for children to become successful at the three Rs of reading, 'riting, and 'rithmetic, their parents must first teach them the three Rs of respect, responsibility, and resourcefulness.

After I explained this concept to a group of professional educators in Phoenix, a teacher approached me to ask, "Can something still be done for a fourteen-year-old whose parents, until now, have failed to teach your three Rs?"

It may not be too late," I replied, "but in order to reverse a situation with that much history and momentum behind it, the youngster's parents are going to have to do the very thing they've been afraid to do for fourteen years."

"Which is?" she asked.

"Make their child unhappy," I said.

It's never too late. The personality of a child is not, contrary to myth, carved in stone by age six—or by age sixteen, for that matter. It remains flexible, and therefore malleable, well through adolescence.

Even an adult will find that significant events and relationships continue to mold the personality for as long as the individual is receptive to change. In the final analysis, the ability to change is a matter of choice, not chronology. The problem is that teenagers in need of "attitude adjustment" aren't likely to recognize the need. Since they aren't going to make the decision, someone needs to make it for them.

Once the decision has been made, the first step is that of getting the teenager's attention. The only way to do this is to confront the teen with full responsibility for his or her behavior. Since responsibility is measured in terms of consequences, this means the parents must stop whatever they're doing to protect the youngster from consequences.

I'm talking about a crash course in reality. This kind of emergency action demands commitment, consistency, and a complete lack of sympathy for the child's sudden plight. In addition, the parents need to let go of guilt—whether real or imagined—for past mistakes. Actually, sympathy and guilt go hand in hand. Guilt—the idea that "if I'd been a better parent, my child would be a better person"—drives sympathetic responses, which, in turn, generate compensatory behavior.

For the confrontation to succeed, parents must stop blaming themselves (dwelling in the past) and charge strategically ahead toward their objectives (focus on the future). Now, it stands to reason that, when you confront the irresponsible youth with reality, unhappiness will be the inevitable result.

The problem is that most parents don't like to make their children unhappy. They seem to think that the evidence of good parenting is a happy child. It follows, therefore, that if the child is unhappy, the parents must be doing something wrong.

Absurd? You bet! But powerful, nonetheless.

For example, the parents of an unmotivated tenth-grade boy might insist that every Friday he bring home a progress report signed in ink by every one of his teachers. To have freedom, all teachers must indicate better-than-passing work. If not, or if the report is incomplete or doesn't find its way home, the youngster has no freedom until the following Friday, when another chance to pass inspection is granted.

The heretofore irresponsible teen will greet these requirements with rage, refusal, plea bargaining, or all of the above. In other words, unhappiness.

The story is likely to last, with brief periods of deceptive calm, for three months or more. But if the parents will batten down the hatches and hang in there dispassionately, it will eventually subside and a new day of understanding will dawn in that child's life.

You see, sometimes unhappiness is not only the best form of therapy, it's the only form possible.

Questions?

Q: *Every morning, our seven-year-old drags his feet about getting out of bed and getting dressed. Both my husband and I work, and this requires that Stevie leave the house no later than seven forty-five A.M. We wake him up at six-thirty, which gives him more than enough time to get ready for school. Every morning, it's the same story. We have to call him five or six times to get him up and moving; then we have to stay behind him until he's out the door. Help!*

A: First, the only person who can solve this problem is Stevie. Second, he's not going to solve it until you make him responsible for it. Third, he has no reason to accept responsibility for the problem as long as you are willing to continue accepting it for him. Stevie will solve the problem when, and only when, his failure to get up and get moving in the morning upsets and inconveniences *him* more than it upsets and inconveniences you.

The actual mechanics of the solution are as easy as A-B-C.

A, plan your strategy. In chapter 2, I called this "striking while the iron is cold." Make a detailed list of the things you want Stevie to do in the morning.

B, communicate the plan. Say, "Stevie, we've decided we're no longer going to yell and scream and get red in the face in the mornings. From now on, after waking you up at six-thirty, we're going down to the kitchen and set the stove timer for seven-fifteen. That gives you forty-five minutes to do the things you see on this list, which we're going to post on the back of your bedroom door. When the timer rings, we're going to have inspection. If everything on the list has been done, and done properly, you may do whatever you like until it's time to leave the house. If, on the other hand, you either fail to beat the bell or haven't properly done one or more things on the list, you won't be allowed to go outside after school that day. In addition, your bedtime that night will be one hour earlier than usual. Any questions?"

C, enforce the plan. When Stevie dawdles, as he will, say and do nothing. Between six-thirty and seven-fifteen every morning, your job is to tend to your business and ignore whether or not your son is attending to his. I guarantee he will fail to beat the bell at least two or three mornings the first week. He may even still be in bed when the bell rings. If that happens, get him ready without fuss or frenzy (note the thirty-minute cushion built into the plan). That afternoon, if he starts outside, gently remind him of his self-imposed restriction and express your regrets. When he pleads for "one more chance," say, "Sorry, Stevie, but you knew the rule." When Stevie realizes that the problem is his to do with as he pleases, he will solve it. He may be stubborn, but he's not stupid.

Q: *I have a problem that is slowly driving me crazy. My two boys, ages ten and eight, bicker constantly. To make matters worse, after nearly every fracas, it's a game of who can get to Mom first with the most dramatic rendition of "Poor, pitiful me!" I know I shouldn't referee, but if I ignore them, the fighting only gets louder. If you don't have any good ideas, then at least do me the favor of referring me to a contractor who specializes in custom-designed rubber rooms. I'm going to need one.*

A: Actually, you're not refereeing as much as you are emceeing a game of "Victim, Victim, Who's the Victim?" Unfortunately, even though your intentions are good and your motives certainly understandable, by making the distinction between "villain" and "victim," you seal the inevitability of further conflict. The children aren't coming to you because they fight. They fight because you let them come to you.

When you get involved in their squabbles, you assign to one boy the role of victim and to the other the role of villain. In this upside-down set of circumstances, the victim "wins" because Mom is on his side. So, the children begin competing to be the victim. In effect, by getting involved in their bickering, you are teaching them that there is something desirable about being downtrodden. If one of the children wins by losing often enough, perhaps he will earn the coveted Victim for Life award, a dubious distinction indeed! To get them to stop playing this dangerous game, you must transfer responsibility for the problem from your shoulders to theirs.

You can use the Countdown to Confinement method. Call a conference with the children and say something along these lines: "Guess what, kids? Mom's figured out a way for the two of you to fight all you want without driving me crazy! I call it Problem, Problem, You Have the Problem! From now on, every time you guys bicker, fight, tattle, or are rude to each other, I'm going to con-fine you to your respective rooms for thirty minutes. It won't mat-ter who started the problem or who was being unfair. Regardless of who supposedly started it, you will each spend thirty minutes in your room. I'm no longer going to play "Who Done It?" with the two of you. Now listen carefully, because the third time I have to send you to your rooms on any given day it won't be for thirty min-utes. It will be for the rest of the day. You will be allowed out only to use the bathroom and to eat meals with the family.

"Oh, yes, there's one more thing. You're used to hearing me threaten, but you're not used to having me follow through on a threat. This time, I'm not threatening. I'm promising. But you'll soon find that out for yourselves."

Now, instead of fighting with one another for the purpose of getting you involved, the children must learn how to cooperate in order to *keep* you from getting involved. Aren't you clever?

Q: *I'm having a problem getting my four-year-old to go to bed and stay there. I put her to bed, she gets up a few minutes later to ask for a glass of water. I give her a glass of water and put her back to bed; she gets up three minutes later to ask me something like "When's Christmas?" I answer her question and put her back to bed, and she gets up a few min-utes later and wants to know what I'm doing. This sometimes goes on for an hour or more. Eventually, I blow my top, she starts to cry, and I feel bad. At that point, the game starts all over again. What can I do?*

A: First, make a doorknob thing out of cardboard. You know, one of those DO NOT DISTURB signs that hang in hotel room. On one side, draw a circle and color it green. Draw another circle on the other side and color it red.

Put your daughter to bed at the same time every night. As you leave her room, hang the sign on the inside doorknob with the "green light" circle showing. The green light means she can get out of bed one time. When she does, answer her question or request and put her back in bed. This time, as you leave her room, turn the sign over so that the red circle is now showing.

Say, "A red light means *stop!* This red light means you may not come out of your room again this evening. If you do, you'll stay indoors tomorrow and go to bed one hour early."

When she runs the red light, take her immediately back to her room and put her back in bed. Don't answer any questions and don't respond to any further requests. She will undoubtedly continue to get out of bed. Just keep putting her back in. Remember that it takes a child time to develop a habit and, likewise, time to catch the cure. The next day, as promised, keep her inside and put her to bed an hour early and go through the same procedure.

She'll probably run the red light several nights in a row. Then she'll catch on and you'll have a couple of successful bedtimes. Remember, if she obeys the red light, she gets to go outside the next day and her usual bedtime is restored. Over the next few weeks, expect to go two steps forward and then a step back. She should start cooperating consistently within two to four weeks. Regardless, keep using the doorknob sign every night for at least three months. It will take at least that much time for the new habit to develop fully.

Q: *Our fourteen-year-old daughter's room is an absolute disaster! The floor is littered with CDs, clothes, magazines, and other personal belongings. Her bed is never made (unless I make it) and all her bureau drawers are usually open. She maintains that, because it's her room, she should be allowed to keep it any way she likes. She has also started closing herself up in there for hours at a time to talk to friends on her phone. If we ask her to spend time with the family, she looks at us as if we're crazy and asks, "Why?" To tell you the truth, we haven't come up with a good answer. What should we do?*

A: If your daughter is anything like our Amy was at that age, you won't be able to get her out of her room with a crowbar. Today's kids go into their rooms when they hit thirteen and stay there until they get driver's licenses. I'm convinced it's a preparatory ritual of some sort. In any case, believe me, it's best. If they grace the family with more than five minutes of their presence, you want them back in their rooms anyhow.

The room itself is another matter. This stuff about "It's my room and I should be able to keep it any way I like" is hogwash. Her room is in *your* house, and the standard of cleanliness you set should be the standard she follows. She won't appreciate the value of an orderly, clean environment until you've "convinced" her to live in one for a while. Talking to her about this will only make you blue in the face.

Make a rule: Every morning, before she leaves for school, she must make her bed, straighten her room, and close the drawers. After she's gone, you inspect. If her room's neat and relatively clean, she gets to keep her phone. If it's not, you impound it, in which case the phone stays with you until room check the next morning.

Saturday becomes major room-cleaning day, which means she must vacuum, dust, and change her sheets in addition to putting everything in its place and straightening her bureau drawers. Put her weekend on hold—no phone, no social life—until this has been done, and done properly. When she says she's finished, check her work. If you open a drawer and it's crammed with junk, just say, "You have some more work to do," and walk out. Slowly but surely, she'll learn to appreciate having a clean room.

Just another example of the Godfather Principle in action. Thank you, Don Corleone!

Q: *Our twelve-year-old son has always been well-behaved, responsible, and honest. This year he started junior high school and began hanging around with several kids who are troublemakers. As soon as we found out, we forbade the association. He says we're trying to choose his friends and seems determined to disobey. It's the first really major conflict we've ever had, and quite frankly it's a bit scary. What should we do?*

A: Nothing. This is actually a great opportunity for both you and your son to learn some very important lessons. You can learn to let go, to stop being so protective. In turn, he can learn to be more responsible for the choices he makes. None of you are going to learn anything, however, unless you allow him the freedom to make certain mistakes.

Learning generally takes place by trial and error. This means that many attempts and many mistakes must be made before a particular skill is truly mastered. If the learner is prevented from making mistakes, the learning won't ever take place. This applies to learning to hit a baseball or drive a car as well as learning to make good decisions.

We can all recall making a decision that brought us face-to-face with the pavement. Instead of wallowing in self-pity, we picked ourselves up, dusted ourselves off, and carried on, slightly scarred perhaps, but a whole lot wiser. Looking back, we realize that even if someone had warned us we were headed for a fall, we'd probably have fallen anyway. These painfully learned lessons are necessary to growing up and learning to accept the consequences—good or bad—of the choices we make.

You should not only let your son associate with these boys, you should actually hope and pray he *does* get into trouble with them. Let's face it; the worst that could happen at this age isn't likely to ruin anyone's life. Let your son make his mistakes with these boys and, as a result, learn to pick his friends more carefully.

Tell him this: "You were right. We *have* been trying to choose your friends. We'd really rather you didn't hang around with those boys, but we're no longer going to try to prevent it. Whether you influence them in right directions or they influence you in wrong directions is up to you. But hear this! If you get into any trouble with them, not only will you never again be allowed to associate with them, but there will also be a significant period of time in your life when you won't be allowed to associate with anyone. You have the freedom you want, but you'd better take care of it, because along with that freedom comes a lot of responsibility."

Make it clear that if he should happen to get into trouble, you're going to hold him completely responsible for his own behavior. You will not give *any* consideration to such excuses as "It wasn't my idea" or "I didn't do anything but stand and watch" or "They told me if I didn't help they'd beat me up."

If he wants to bring these boys home with him, welcome them. Who knows? Maybe your example will open their eyes to a better set of values.

Q: *Our son started sixth grade this year. He's always had a problem tak-ing responsibility for his homework. As a result, his father and I have had to make sure he kept up with his assignments. When I went to talk with his teacher about the problem, she politely told me to stay out of it. She would take care of it, she said. With more than a little trepidation, I agreed. Unfortunately, Andrew is abusing his freedom. Most of the work I've seen has been hurriedly done. When I pointed this out to the teacher, she calmly told me she and Andrew were "working things out" and for me not to worry. Hah! I'm not supposed to worry while I see my son's grades go down the tube?*

A: You've discovered the truth in the adage, "Things get worse before they get better." In fact, I'm convinced that not only *do* things get worse, they virtually *must.*

When parents assume responsibility for a problem that right-fully belongs to a child, they end up compensating for the problem without truly correcting it. These compensations have the unin-tended effect of allowing the child to stay irresponsible. In your case, you've taken it upon yourselves to do for Andrew what he should have been doing for himself. You've made sure he brought his books home; you've stood over him, figuratively or otherwise, while he did his homework; you've checked to make sure the work was up to par.

You've been doing what many golfers do when they develop a slice. Instead of correcting the defect in their swing that causes the ball to curve maddeningly to the right, they compensate by aiming to the left of their target. In so doing, the problem doesn't get solved, but the consequences become less noticeable. In fact, the compen-sation makes the problem *worse,* because it gives the slice time to become habit. The longer the golfer compensates for it, the harder it is to solve.

Like the golfer, you've been "aiming farther left." As a result, An-drew has learned to rely on you to take up the slack in his academic life. And, like our golfer friend, your compensations have succeeded in making Andrew's problem less noticeable. He's still irresponsible, but his grades don't show it.

If the golfer stops aiming left, his next ten shots will go in the woods. In other words, as soon as he stops compensating for it, the problem will seem to get worse. But by making the problem more noticeable, it finally becomes possible to correct it.

Likewise, Andrew's teacher realizes that in order for him to begin taking responsibility for himself, you're going to have to stop taking responsibility for him. Having done what she told you to do, you're in a panic because the problem is now more noticeable and all your past accomplishments seem to be going down the tube. But that's just the point. The accomplishments were yours, not his. It's time Andrew learned to walk on his own two feet. As he does, he's bound to stumble and perhaps even fall flat on his face. That's all right. He seems blessed with a teacher who sees the problem and knows how to solve it. Trust her. She sounds like an answer to prayer.

Q: *My thirteen-year-old son waits until the last possible moment to begin doing his homework. He no longer has a set bedtime, but he must be in his room after nine in the evening. It doesn't matter how much homework he has or even whether he has a test the next day, he doesn't crack a book until he's in his room. I've talked myself blue in the face about the importance of making good grades. I tell him he simply can't be doing his best if he does homework when he's tired, but he says his grades are good enough (mostly Bs with an occasional A) and I should let him make this decision. This is driving me nuts! What can I do to get him to do his homework at a decent hour?*

A: Nothing, apparently. I can't solve this problem for you. No, make that I *won't* solve this problem for you. I agree with your son. It's his decision. Why not do yourself a favor and abandon this issue forever? You're obviously causing yourself a lot of unnecessary aggravation and being a nag in the process.

As I point out in my book *Teen-Proofing,* the biggest and most frequent mistake made by responsible well-intentioned parents of teens (note the operative qualifiers) is the attempt to micromanage. You have to micromanage infants and toddlers, and you might be able to micromanage a preschool or school-age child (nonetheless, I don't recommend it), but you cannot micromanage a teen without creating more problems than you solve. In fact, I'll go a step further and say that the attempt to micromanage a teen will solve absolutely no problems and is likely to create a slew of new ones.

Your obsessive concern about when your son does his homework falls into this perilous category. Do you really think he's going to get better grades if he does his homework when you want him to? I think it's more likely, if you manage to force him to do his homework under your eagle-eyed supervision in the afternoon or early evening, that he will rush through it, in which case his grades will drop. Why? Because you will have given him a good reason to prove you wrong.

Instead of trying to make your son do his homework when you think he should do it, give him permission to learn—the hard way, if necessary—how to manage his own time. Your job here is not to manage his time for him, but to demonstrate that choices result in consequences. Good choices result in good consequences (better grades, more freedom), and bad choices result in consequences that are undesirable (bad grades, restrictions on his freedom). For the time being, his grades are not a problem, but when he enters high school and academic demands increase, that may change, giving you the opportunity to be the agent of reality. In the meantime, take a load off your shoulders and find a more constructive outlet for all that well-intentioned energy.

Q: *Our daughter is in the eighth grade at a magnet school for gifted and talented students. Over the three years she's been there, her grades have gone from As to Cs and Ds, with more than a few Fs. She is always on restriction but seems motivated by nothing. When we talk to her about the problem, she has no answers. Should we continue restricting her? Move her back to our neighborhood school? Have her tested? We are desperate for help!*

A: In my book *Teen-Proofing*, I point out something all parents need to understand: You can respond properly to a problem you're having with a child—a problem the child can obviously control—and the child's behavior may still not change. That's just another way of saying, "Your daughter has a mind of her own." She has a problem she can control. You've done all the right things; she still has the problem. In fact, it's getting worse. Therefore, you probably need to accept that in this case you are powerless.

If your daughter had a learning problem, it's unlikely she would have ever been identified as gifted and talented. Therefore, I think having her tested will probably be a waste of money, but if it makes you feel more comfortable, by all means have it done.

Yes, I'd move her back to the neighborhood school. She's taking up space in the magnet school that another child could benefit from. And yes, I'd continue her restriction. In a situation of this sort, I don't look upon restriction as punishment. Rather, I see it as a lesson in how the real world works: If you don't accept your responsibilities, you are going to be, in effect, restricted. I'd tell your daughter that you don't like restricting her, but it would be unfair to do otherwise. Stop trying to "counsel" her out of the problem. If she wants to talk to you about it, fine. Otherwise, don't waste your breath. Something I've noticed over the years is that, quite often, when parents stop agonizing over a problem, when they accept their powerlessness, the problem begins to improve. It doesn't happen that way every time, mind you, but often enough for you to give it a good college try.

Q: *Our seven-year-old daughter is absolutely terrified of thunder and lightning. When a storm comes up, she becomes hysterical. We've talked, explained, and comforted, but nothing seems to work. Suggestions?*

A: First, I'd suggest you read, or reread, my answer to the previous question. Like those parents, you've done all the right things, and nothing has changed. Now it's time to hand the problem over to your daughter.

When my daughter, Amy, was your daughter's age, she also was terrified of thunder and lightning. She also became hysterical when storms came up. What ultimately "solved" the problem was telling her we understood her fright but could no longer allow her to be the center of attention during a storm. We told her that when she felt terrified by a storm, she had to go into a closet or under her bed and stay there until the storm passed. A child younger than, say, five needs to be held and comforted, but certainly by age six, it's time to give the child some authoritative guidance and let her solve the problem on her own.

4

POINT FOUR

The Fruits of Frustration

FRUSTRATION, ACCORDING TO nearly an entire generation of child-rearing experts (circa 1960 to the present), is bad for children. It causes stress, insecurity, and poor self-esteem, not to mention warts on the vocal chords from too much screaming. Believing this fairy tale, parents worked hard to protect their children from this supposedly terrible scourge. In the process, they gave their children too much too soon and generally required too little too late. As a result, children became increasingly spoiled, demanding, and ungrateful, while parents became increasingly frustrated. Just goes to show, what goes around comes around.

I have good news! Those child-rearing experts were wrong! Frustration isn't necessarily bad for children. In fact, a certain amount is absolutely essential to healthy character formation and emotional growth. You want proof? Here 'tis.

As I pointed out in chapter 1, the purpose of raising children is to help them out of our lives and into successful lives of their own. Parents are therefore obligated to raise children in a manner consistent with the reality they will eventually face as adults. Are you with me so far?

As we all know, adult reality involves significant amounts of frustration. We experience frustration in response not only to our own limitations but also to the limitations other people and circumstances impose upon us.

Through experience with frustration we eventually develop a tolerance for it. We accept its inevitability and determine not to let it get us down. This tolerance enables the growth of resourcefulness and other creative coping mechanisms. People who learn to tolerate frustration are able to turn adversity into challenge and persevere.

Perseverance, that all-important "If at first you don't succeed, try, try again" attitude toward life, is the primary quality in every success story. Whether the field of endeavor be occupational, recreational, social, personal, marital, or parental, the person who perseveres is the person most likely to succeed.

All the aforementioned growth takes place *because of*—not in spite of—that supposedly dreadful f-word, frustration.

Conclusion: If you want your children to become successful adults—successful in their work, their play, their interpersonal relationships, and their feelings toward themselves—you are obligated to frustrate them.

If you aren't doing so already, you can begin tending to this obligation by giving your children regular, daily doses of vitamin N. This vital nutrient consists simply of the most character-building two-letter word in the English language: *no*. Vitamin N is as important to a child's healthy growth and development as vitamins A, B, and C. Unfortunately, many if not most of today's children suffer from vitamin N deficiency. They've been overindulged by well-meaning parents who've given them far too much of what they want and far too little of what they truly need.

A Self-Test

Have you given your children enough vitamin N? Let's find out. List on a sheet of paper everything you've ever dreamed of having. Let your imagination and your greed run unabashedly wild! Don't concern yourself with whether these things are practical or presently affordable, whether your spouse shares your dreams, or whether your minister would approve of them. If you've ever coveted a particular something, write it down! What about that German sports car you've always wanted? How about a new house? Don't hold back. You want new furniture? Write it down! A new wardrobe? A boat? Jewelry? A trip to Europe? A membership at the country club? A hot tub? Write 'em all down!

When your fantasy frenzy is over, let reality intrude. Go back over your wish list and circle the things you feel reasonably certain you'll actually be able to acquire within the next five years. When I put a workshop audience through the same exercise, the answers generally fall between 10 and 20 percent. If you circle more than 25 percent of the items on your list, you're either incredibly wealthy or you don't want much. In other words, most of us must learn to contend with the fact that from 10 to 20 percent of what we want today is about as much as we can hope to acquire within five years. Remember, too, that we get what we want by putting forth sustained effort, by making sacrifices, by doing our best. And through it all, we endure all manner of . . . what? That's right. Frustration. You're catching on!

Now, on a second sheet of paper, list everything your children are going to ask for over the next twelve months. Not things they truly need, mind you, but things they simply want: the extras. Depending on their ages, they're going to want toys of every description, various items of electronic equipment, various means of fancy transportation, the latest in a never-ending cycle of clothing fads, and the cost of admission to movies, sports events, amusement parks, and rock 'n' roll concerts.

When you're through, go back over the second list, circling the things your children are pretty surely going to get within the next twelve months. Don't forget to circle things that will probably be forthcoming from grandparents, other well-meaning relatives, and friends of the family. Eye-opening, isn't it? If you're a typical American parent, you circled 75 percent or more of the items on your children's wish list.

What this means is that most of us accustom our children to a material standard that is completely out of kilter with what they can ever hope to achieve as adults. Consider also that many if not most of them attain this level of affluence not by working, sacrificing, or doing their best but by whining, demanding, and manipulating. So in the process of overinflating their materialistic expectations, we also teach our children that something can be had for next to nothing. Not only is that a falsehood, it's one of the most dangerous, destructive attitudes a person can ever acquire.

Children who grow up believing in the something-for-nothing fairy tale may never realize that the really important things in life come from within, rather than without. As adults, they are likely to be emotionally stunted, immature people, fixated at a grasping, self-centered stage of development. At the very least, they will tend to confuse the giving and getting of *things* with a deeper and more meaningful level of sharing and trust in relationships. When they themselves become parents, they're likely to confuse their children's value systems in a like manner, by overdosing them with things. In this sense, materialism is an inherited disease, an addiction passed from one generation to the next. But materialism is not so much an addiction to *things* as it is an addiction to *acquiring* things. This explains why materialists are never content. No sooner than they've acquired one thing, they want another. This also explains why children who get too much of what they want rarely take care of anything they have. Why should they? After all, history tells them that more is on the way.

Our children deserve better than this. They deserve, first, to have us attend conscientiously to their needs for protection, affection, and direction. Beyond that, they deserve to hear us say *no* far more often than *yes* when it comes to their whimsical yearnings. They deserve to learn that getting requires giving in at least equal measure. They need to learn not just the words but the deeper meaning behind them that "It is better to give than to receive." They deserve to learn the value of constructive, creative effort as opposed to the value of effort expended whining, lying on the floor kicking and screaming, or playing one parent against the other. They deserve to learn that work is the only truly fulfilling way of getting anything in life.

In effect, in the process of trying to protect our children from frustration, we've turned reality upside-down and inside-out. A child raised in this topsy-turvy manner may not, when the time comes, have the skills needed to stand on his or her own two feet.

In Pursuit of Happiness

Four years after graduating from high school, 42 percent of the class of 1980 were still "nesting" under their parents' roofs, compared with just 25 percent of the class of 1972. A 68 percent increase in eight years! Today, the figure is over 50 percent!

You'd think one reason all these young people stay unmarried and continue to live at home is so they can accumulate a nest egg, but that's not the case. The same study found that they save less and spend more than any previous generation. The fact is, most of these young people were raised by parents who gave them lots of material things but required little in return. Having grown up in a blissful state of premature affluence, these kids can't handle the relative hardship of being out on their own. So they stay at home, which frees up lots of income for discretionary things like new cars, expensive stereo equipment, and ski trips. In other words, their childhood experience of how the world works has failed to prepare them for self-sufficiency. They aren't willing to start small, to struggle, to sacrifice, to hang in there.

By and large, today's children have been overdosed not only materially but emotionally as well. They've been given too much attention, too much praise, and too many rewards. In short, we've made their lives too easy, and in so doing we've created a fantasy of how the world works. Another family therapist once summed up the situation for me quite well. He said, "This generation of parents has done a wonderful job of sharing their standard of living with their children, but a miserable job of endowing those children with the skills they'll need to achieve that standard on their own."

Looked at from a slightly different perspective, the problem is that today's parents have worked too hard to keep their children happy. As a result, children grow up believing it's someone else's responsibility to take care of their needs and wants. Never having learned to accept responsibility for their own well-being, they go through life expecting other people to make them happy and blaming anything and everything that goes wrong on someone or something else. Unfortunately, as we all know, a person who fails to take full responsibility for his or her own happiness will never be fully happy. The paradox is this: The more parents take on responsibility for their children's happiness, the more they guarantee their children's eventual unhappiness.

In the first paragraph of the Declaration of Independence, it says "that all men are created equal, that they are endowed by their Creator with certain unalienable Rights, that among these are Life, Liberty, and the pursuit of Happiness." Read it carefully. The Founding Fathers didn't say we have a right to happiness. They asserted our right to *pursue* happiness, and here's the root of the problem. When parents busy themselves in pursuit of happiness for their children, their children never learn to pursue it on their own. Yes, the pursuit is full of pitfalls and setbacks, but as bodybuilders say, "No pain, no gain." We should support children as they come to grips with the reality of frustration, but we must not protect them from it. For a child, the gain of learning to pursue happiness is measured in terms of self-esteem, so the more we pursue happiness *for* our children, the less chance they have of developing good self-esteem. There is no better reason than that for making sure your parenting cabinet is stocked with ample supplies of vitamin N.

Tantrums

If common sense tells us that vitamin N is essential to our children's well-being, why do we work so hard to provide them not only with more in the way of material things than they need but more than they're ever going to be able to attain for themselves as adults? Part of the problem, undoubtedly, has its roots in the "my children are going to have it better than I did" thinking that became increasingly prevalent following the hardships of the great Depression and World War II. But it also has to do with the fact that many parents want to avoid the consequences of not giving in to their children's demands. I'm talking about tantrums of various sorts, from the two-year-old's rolling on the floor while screaming and frothing at the mouth to the sixteen-year-old sort of stomping and slamming doors while spewing forth a steady stream of verbal abuse. Quite a few parents are intimidated, even frightened, by tantrums. So they give in. Some give in before the tantrum even starts. When they are asked, "Why do you give in?" they often answer, "Because it's easier to give in than to deal with the hassle."

That's true, but only in the short run. Giving in solves the immediate problem. It turns off the screaming, stomping, or whatever. In that sense, giving in is certainly easier. Unfortunately, the more often parents give in to tantrums, the worse the tantrums become. Every time parents give in to a tantrum, they virtually guarantee the occurrence of at least fifty more.

If you give a child a choice between getting something the hard way and getting that same thing in what looks like the easy way, the child will always choose the easy way. To a child, working and waiting for something, not to mention doing without, always looks like the hard way. Wearing down a parent's resistance and resolve by screaming and stomping and arguing and cursing seems much easier. What the child doesn't know, and what many parents don't seem to realize, is that giving in to tantrums blocks the development of initiative, motivation, and resourcefulness. Without those survival tools, the child is destined to be a less successful and therefore less happy adult.

Guilt is another reason parents give in to tantrums. To parents who mistakenly believe that the measure of good parenting is a happy child, a tantrum says, "You aren't doing a good job." They seem to reason thusly: Good parents raise happy children; tantrums are a sign of unhappiness; therefore, if our child throws a tantrum, we must have done something wrong. Thinking of this sort makes no sense, but it's very real and very common nonetheless. Take the five-year-old boy who asks for a brownie thirty minutes before dinner. When his mother says no, he begins whining and stomping around and saying absurd things like, "You never let me eat when I'm hungry!" Mom thinks the tantrum is evidence of a bad decision, one that may result in her son's feeling insecure or unloved or—heaven forbid—resentful. So she hands over the brownie, knowing full well that, as a result, the boy won't eat his supper. When, sure enough, he doesn't, she points out the connection between the brownie and his lack of appetite, as if this information is going to render him more reasonable in the future under similar circumstances. Mom's got a lot to learn.

All children can be counted on to throw tantrums of one sort or another. For one thing, children come into the world unequipped with any tolerance for frustration. For another, their original point of view is a self-centered (egocentric) one. Whatever they want, they believe they deserve. Part of our job as parents is slowly but surely to help our children dismantle that self-centeredness and replace it with a sense of social responsibility—a willingness to put personal concerns aside for the sake of family, friendship, and society. It could, in fact, be said that this is a parent's most important function. It is the essence of the socialization process, and that process involves a certain amount of discomfort. A child's natural reaction to discomfort and disillusionment is a tantrum. Looked at from this perspective, a tantrum is a child's way of divesting self-centeredness to grow up into a more mature understanding of how the world works. It's essential, therefore, that parents learn how to say *no* to their children and say it with conviction.

I chuckle inside whenever I hear a parent complain that a certain child "can't take no for an answer." I'm amused because the comment always says more about the parent than it does the child. A child who can't take no for an answer always has parents who can't really say it. It's not that the child can't take no, it's that he or she has no reason to believe it.

The fact that today's parents are not giving their children enough vitamin N is not just weakening their children's character, it also has the potential of eroding the very foundation of our democratic society. After all, it was individual resourcefulness, perseverance, and a tolerance for frustration that made this country the greatest nation on earth.

For all these reasons, the next time you give a dose of vitamin N and your child falls on the floor screaming, consider it a job well done!

Here's the Prescription!

You can start administering vitamin N to your children in the following ways:

1. Turn their world right side up by giving them all of what they truly need, but no more than 25 percent of what they simply want. I call this the Principle of Benign Deprivation.

2. Don't do for your children what they are capable of doing for themselves. "You can do that on your own" pushes the growth of perseverance and self-sufficiency. When the child says "I can't," don't argue. Just say, "Well, *I won't.*" You'll be amazed at how creative and resourceful children can be under the right circumstances.

3. Don't always rescue them from failure or disappointment. Remember that falling on one's face can be an invaluable learning experience (see chapter 3).

4. Remember that just because a child doesn't like something doesn't mean it shouldn't happen or exist. For example, the mere fact that a child doesn't want to be left with a baby-sitter

doesn't mean you shouldn't do so. For children to grow up requires that parents resist the temptation to constantly protect them from the discomfort of having to divest dependency.

5. Don't worry about treating children fairly. Remember that, to a child, "fair" means "me first," with the biggest and best of everything.

6. Remember that simply because you enjoy a good standard of living doesn't mean you're obligated to share it in full with your children. Vitamin N gives children something to strive for, along with the skills with which to strive.

7. Don't overdose your children emotionally by giving them too much attention or too much praise (see chapters 1 and 2). If you pay too much attention to your children, they have no reason to pay attention to you.

Questions?

Q: Our three-year-old daughter throws a tantrum whenever she doesn't get her way. How should we handle this?

A: I'll answer your question by telling you a story about my daughter, Amy: When she was two, and throughout the third year of her life, Amy was remarkably easy to get along with. Looking back, compared to most two-year-olds, she was relatively maintenance-free. If we told her to straighten her room, she straightened her room. Sometimes she straightened her room without even being asked. If she wanted something and we said no, she shrugged it off without a whimper. She demanded very little attention from us and was quite adept at occupying herself for long periods of time.

Then, just about the time Willie and I were preparing to heave a sigh of relief and give thanks for this unexpected reprieve, the tantrums began. And did they ever! As though determined to make up for lost time, three-year-old Amy searched high and low for excuses to do the terrible-tantrum thing. She screamed whenever we stopped her from doing what she wanted to do. She screamed whenever we refused to meet her demands, which became legion. She screamed whenever we assigned her a task, no matter how small. Sometimes she screamed for no apparent reason.

But screaming wasn't all she did. Amy began a tantrum by becoming rigid and then bouncing up and down on the balls of her feet while making a rapid "uh-uh-uh" sound that got progressively louder and longer until it became a full-blown wail. By then, Amy was usually flapping her arms and running around in circles like a whirling dervish. At some point, she would collapse on the floor in a heap and begin thrashing about.

Having become desensitized to tantrums by Eric—whose tantrums, believe it or not, were worse than Amy's—Willie and I usually sat reading the paper or some such thing until the storm blew over. After several months, however, we noticed that despite our careless attitude toward Amy's tantrums, they were getting worse. We decided to take another approach.

One fairly peaceful afternoon, I took Amy aside for a talk. "Amy," I said, "you've been screaming a lot lately. So much, in fact, that Mommy and Daddy are going to give you a special place of your very own to scream in. We have lots of special places in the house. We have special places to sleep, special places to eat, and special places to go to the toilet and take baths. Now you're going to have a special place to scream. Come with me, and I'll show you where it is."

I led her to the downstairs lavatory, opened the door, and ushered her inside. "This is it, Amy, your very own screaming place. And a fine screaming place it is, too. Why, just look! The walls are nice and close to make the screams louder, and there's soft carpet on the floor for you to roll around on. And if you scream so loud that you have to go to the bathroom, the toilet is right over here. And if you scream your throat dry, here's a sink and a cup for you to drink from.

"From now on, whenever you want to scream, just come in here and scream all you want. If you start to scream but forget to come here, Mommy and Daddy will help you remember."

During my monologue, Amy just stood there with a "You must be crazy!" look on her face. Never one to pass up a challenge, it wasn't fifteen minutes before she was screaming and thrashing around over something. I said quickly, "That's a very fine scream, Amy, but you must scream in your special place," and dragged her into the bathroom.

The first few times this happened, she would stop screaming, come back out, and begin screaming again. One of us would just as promptly put her back in the bathroom. Once she realized this was going to be standard operating procedure, the screams stopped almost as soon as the door closed. Nevertheless, she would remain in the bathroom pouting and scheming (or so I surmised) for several minutes. Then she'd emerge and, without as much as a glance in our direction, go to her room.

Within a couple of months, she had her tantrums under control. One morning, I passed her room and heard what sounded like crying coming from inside. I opened the door.

"Are you all right?" I asked.

"Yes," she said, dry-eyed.

"Were you crying?"

"No. Bumpo was." Bumpo was her teddy bear.

"Oh. Where is Bumpo? I don't see him."

Amy walked over to her corner cabinet and opened the door. There sat Bumpo, looking rather forlorn.

"In his screaming place," she announced.

Q: *The tantrum place idea sounds great for tantrums that occur at home. But what if our daughter has a tantrum in a store or some other public place?*

A: First, don't try to talk her out of it. Second, don't try to ignore it, because you can't. Third, get her out of the public eye. As quickly as possible, take her either to a remote part of the store or outside and wait there until the tantrum runs its course. If she seems determined to keep it up, go home and use the "tantrum place." In the long run, it's worth the inconvenience.

Q: *What should we say to our children when they point out, and correctly, that all their friends have a certain thing? If they don't have what their friends have, won't this hurt their self-esteem?*

A: No. Self-esteem is not a function of how many things we have, although we sometimes try to delude ourselves otherwise. It's a function of getting in touch with one's inner resources, the gifts that lie within. The more outward, material distractions there are in a child's life, the more likely the child is to search in the wrong places for self-esteem.

When they were younger, one of our children's favorite litanies was "But all my friends have one!" I never argued. Instead, I said, "I know. And I know how it feels to not have something your friends have. But your friends will share their good fortune with you, just as you will share what you have with them. That's what friends are for. In any case, you'll live." And you know what? They did!

Q: *If I say no to my son and later realize I should have said yes, should I change my mind and let him do or have what he wanted, or should I stick to my original decision?*

A: It depends. If your son handled the no fairly well, and you said it only because of stresses that had nothing to do with him, feel free to change your mind. On the other hand, if he threw a tantrum or needs more vitamin N in his life anyway, stick to your guns. Rest assured, it won't kill him or do him any psychological damage to live with parents who occasionally make irrational decisions. Isn't life a bit irrational at times?

Q: *Our thirteen-year-old has reached the age where standard-brand clothing will no longer do. Like her friends, she wants clothes with designer labels. How can we get her to understand that cost and quality don't necessarily go together?*

A: You can't, and trying will only make you blue in the face.

When Eric and Amy were into their teens, we solved this problem by opening personal checking accounts into which we deposited their monthly clothing and recreation allowances. When they ran out of money, their shopping and recreation for the month came to a halt. Through trial and error, they learned to budget, stretch their money, shop for bargains, and generally do more with less. Once they began earning their own money, our contribution went down and theirs went up. It was just another way of helping them out of our lives.

Q: *I recently read an article on "the family bed." The author maintained that children, even older children, who sleep with their parents are more self-reliant, happy, and secure than children who do not. Should we bring our children, ages seven and four, into our bed?*

A: Not unless you want two children who are *less* self-reliant and secure, and happy only if they are sleeping with you. The claims of "family bed" advocates are completely bankrupt. There is not a shred of evidence to support them, but there is plenty with which to refute them.

The point of assigning a specific bedtime for children and having them sleep in their own beds, in their own rooms, is twofold. First, it gives parents much-needed time for themselves and each other. Second, bedtime is an exercise in separation and, therefore, independence. It is, in fact, the first of many such exercises to come, and how parents handle it sets an important and enduring precedent.

Separation involves a certain amount of anxiety for parents and children, especially young children. But the issue of separation, because it demands that children become less dependent and more self-sufficient, is inseparable from the task of growing up.

In his best-selling book *The Road Less Traveled*, psychiatrist M. Scott Peck says that many people never learn to accept the inherent pain of living. When confronted with a problem, they either attempt an impatient knee-jerk solution or try to ignore it altogether. Parents who spank children for crying at bedtime fall into the first category. Parents who let their children sleep with them fall into the second. Both are failing to deal with the issue.

In thirty-odd years of working with families, I've talked with many parents who slept with their children. But not once have I talked with a parent who was comfortable with the arrangement. Why, then, weren't these children sleeping alone? The usual answer: "Because our son screams when we try to put him in his own bed." What these parents don't realize is that the longer they avoid dealing with the issue of separation, the more anxiety it will arouse in their son, and the more screams it will therefore provoke.

In Peck's terms, family sleeping is a way of avoiding a problem in the hopes that somehow, someday, the problem will miraculously resolve itself. Unfortunately, life will probably deal a different hand to family sleepers.

The child whose parents avoid confronting the pain of separation never receives complete implicit permission to separate from them. As the years go by, the parents' continued failure to resolve this fundamental issue becomes an obstacle to healthy growth and development. In my experience and, I daresay, the experience of most other clinicians, these children are generally excessively dependent, fearful, socially immature, and undisciplined.

At some point, nearly all young children cry at bedtime, and their cries make us want to draw them protectively closer. But protection of this nature is not always in a child's best interest. Children must learn to deal with separation, parents must show the way, and bedtime is a logical first place to begin the lessons. It's not as hard as it may sound. Establish a predictable bedtime and a routine to precede it. If children cry, do not—as some pediatricians and child psychologists advise—let them cry it out. Return to the bedroom at regular intervals to provide reassurance that you are still here, watching over them. If, along with your reassurances, the child hears a steadfast insistence to stay in bed, it won't be long before bedtime is accepted as routine.

Q: *My eight-year-old daughter is afraid to try new things. She also becomes easily discouraged when her first attempt at something doesn't succeed. For example, if I try to encourage her to swim three laps of the pool instead of two, she'll say, "I can't." No matter how much I encourage or* *try to pump up her self-confidence, she won't make the attempt. If her piano teacher assigns her a difficult piece, she'll hardly try it before giving up. I can't understand why this otherwise capable child has such low self-esteem. How can I help her?*

A: Your daughter's problem has less to do with self-esteem and more to do with the way you're responding to her frustrations. You're letting yourself get too emotionally involved in your daughter's performance, whether it be in swimming or piano or whatever.

Learning any new skill involves a certain amount of frustration. When your daughter encounters it, you go to her rescue. Although your intentions are good, you're actually preventing her from working through the frustration on her own, in her own way and in her own time. Her stubborn refusal to heed your words of encouragement is a way of saying *Back off, Mom.* You see, when you get involved in these situations, your daughter has to deal not only with her frustrations but with yours as well. To her, your encouragement feels like pressure. So the more you encourage, the more she resists.

Let your daughter work these things out on her own. If she wants to talk to you about problems she's having learning a piano piece or swimming the length of the pool, listen to her but let her do most of the talking. When it's time for you to talk, say, "Learning new things takes a lot of effort and patience. Losing patience means it's time to set the thing aside for a while and come back to it later." In other words, give her permission to be frustrated and even to give up, at least temporarily.

If she still insists that she "can't," shrug your shoulders and say, "Well, then don't. If you think you've done your best and you're convinced you can't do it, maybe you *should* give up. After all, if you've tried your best, giving up makes sense." Short and sweet. Then walk away.

By not getting emotionally involved in her frustrations, you let her be completely responsible for her own feelings. My dad used to call it "stewing in your own juice." When you stay out of it, you also give her freedom to try again, because now she can make the attempt on *her* terms rather than yours. Chances are, she will.

Q: *Our daughter started kindergarten this year. Every evening, after supper, I sit with her at the kitchen table while she does her homework, which never amounts to much. Missy's problem is she doesn't make numbers and letters well enough to suit herself and thinks her coloring is ugly. Consequently, she ends up doing everything over three or four times, when her first attempt was perfectly fine. The more I reassure her, the madder she gets. At times, she's made statements such as "I'm dumb!" and "I can't do anything!" Her teacher sees none of this at school. How can I help her?*

A: Let's keep things in their proper perspective: Missy is going through some major changes. She's in school for the first time; she's learning new skills; she's trying to please you; she's trying to please the teacher; she's trying to please herself; and, on top of all this, she has homework to do. Little wonder that she's feeling some pressure.

The way you manage this homework problem will be precedent-setting. In the final analysis, you want her to accept responsibility for her homework, set realistic goals for herself, and take pride in what she accomplishes. You don't want her to become a neurotic perfectionist at age five.

Two things are clear: First, you know she can do the work and do it well. Second, she doesn't get bent out of shape about her work in front of the teacher. Why? Because the teacher can't (and probably won't) give her as much attention as you can. Ah-ha! So now we know that the less attention Missy gets, the better her attitude toward herself and her work becomes. So stop overseeing her homework. Make three rules:

1. Missy does her homework in her room. No more kitchen table.

2. If she wants help, she must ask for it. If you know she's capable of doing it on her own, tell her so in a supportive, encouraging way: "Oh, you can do that by yourself. You don't really need my help."

3. She can only work on homework for thirty minutes. Set a timer. When it goes off, make her stop, whether she's finished or not. This will limit her obsessing and prevent homework from becoming a marathon.

If she complains of not being able to do this or that, just say, "I won't listen to things I know aren't true. I love you and trust you to do your best." Don't labor over this issue. The more you try to persuade her that she's capable, the more she'll complain.

Without intending to do so, Missy has manufactured this problem. There is, after all, no evidence whatsoever that it exists outside her imagination (or even outside of the kitchen). In effect, it's a soap opera, and she's the producer. When you stop being the audience, it will quickly go off the air.

Q: *Of the forty mothers with children in my four-year-old son's pre-K program, I am one of only three who work outside the home. I do so not for economic reasons, but simply because I enjoy it. My son knows his after-school situation (the school runs a small after-school program) is unique, and he makes it clear, almost daily, that he wants me to stop working so he can come directly home at the end of the regular school day. I've explained over and over again why I work, and I give him more than enough of my time in the evenings and on weekends, but nothing short of my quitting my job will satisfy him. Is there something else I can do, something I'm missing, that will help him adjust positively to his situation?*

A: Yes, you can stop talking about it with him. Letting children express their feelings freely has its place, but letting a child express the same feeling over and over again, especially when nothing is going to change, is not in the child's best interest. For one thing, allowing a child to beat a dead horse in this manner creates a scenario in which the child begins to perceive himself as a victim.

Your son is not a victim. There is nothing wrong with the decision you have made in that it does not compromise your son's development in any way, shape, or form. The more you explain yourself, the more it appears that you are pleading with him to understand and forgive. The fact is, you do not need forgiveness, and he will not understand the whys and wherefores of your decision until he is much older.

So save your breath. It's time you stopped being mealy-mouthed and started acting like an authority figure who has confidence in her own decisions.

At the next opportunity, sit down with him and say, "We have talked about my job enough. You've obviously said all you have to say, and I've said all I have to say. I know how you feel, and you know how I feel. So I've decided we're not going to talk about it anymore. From now on, when you want to talk to me about my work, I'm simply going to tell you to find something to do. If I see that you need some help to stop thinking about it, I'm going to have you do some work for me like clean your room or police the yard. Got it?"

Then, the next time he brings up the subject of your job, simply look at him and say, "I'm not going to talk about it. Have you got something to do, or do I need to find something?" Say this with a stern "I mean business!" tone in your voice. And if he needs some disengaging, provide it. Prove to him, in no uncertain terms, that you will no longer tolerate attempts on his part to beat this expired equine.

The next step in your rehabilitation will be to stop giving so much of yourself to him during the evenings and on weekends. Like a typical well-intentioned working parent, you're putting your son at the center of your attention entirely too much. He needs to see that outside of your job you are not a one-dimensional cardboard cutout with a sign reading WHAT CAN I DO FOR YOU? hung about your neck but, rather, an interesting person with a variety of interests and responsibilities, of which he is one. An important one, yes, but not the only one.

Q: *We have two boys, ages ten and seven. We've always done the same for both, thinking this was the way to prevent jealousy. It hasn't worked. They're constantly on the lookout for things one has or gets that the other doesn't. The situation is getting completely out of hand. What should we do?*

A: If it's any consolation, the same plan has backfired for thousands of parents before you and will continue to backfire for thousands yet to come.

The solution? Stop treating them fairly. In the first place, your well-intentioned "fairness" is actually unfair, because no one will ever make any effort to treat them so fairly again. The more accustomed they get to the idea that "fair" is the normal way of the world, the ruder their awakening will eventually be. In the process of being fair, you've become a slave to their demands. They find your omissions, and you dutifully correct them. So, I ask you, who's running the show?

Q: *How do I go about undoing five years of "fairness"?*

A: Just tell them the game's over. Sit them down and read them your proclamation of independence: "Hear ye! Hear ye! Let it be henceforth known and proclaimed throughout the household that your parents are no longer going to be fair. Since it has become increasingly obvious to us that you are two different people, we are going to treat you—you guessed it—differently! If, for instance, we buy *you*"—point dramatically at one of them—"something, we may not buy *you*—point, with a flourish, at the other—"anything at all. If we do something with or for *you*—point accusingly, we may not do anything with or for you"—point menacingly—"and if that's not fair, so be it. If you don't like it, and you won't, that's life! Get the point?"

Now, the important stuff. You're in the habit of being fair and your boys are in the habit of expecting it. There's only one way to break a habit, and that's cold turkey. From now on, you and your husband should conspire to plan instances of unfairness. For example, take one son to the store and buy him a new pair of shoes. Several days later, take the other to the store and buy him a new sweatshirt. Plan things for them individually, rather than collectively. It's the only way they're ever going to find out that unfair isn't terminal.

They won't like it. They will scream, rant, rave, act pitiful, and blaspheme you, and that's just for starters. When they do, you will have the urge to sit them down and explain why you're doing what you're doing and how it's in their best interests *blah-blah-blah*. Don't! They won't agree with you, much less even listen. The harder you try to get them to "understand," the more they'll rant. Pretty soon you'll begin to feel that maybe you're doing the wrong thing, and you'll try to be fair to make up for your awfulness, and—*zap!*—you'll be right back where you started. Instead of entertaining their misery, just request that they take it to their rooms and vent it against their pillows and mattresses.

Q: *Are there ever times when we should be fair?*

A: If by that you mean, "Are there ever times when we should do the same thing for both of them?"—the answer is "sure." I'm not suggesting that you never do the same thing for both of them or include them in the same activity. You wouldn't be a family any-more if you did that.

Q: *How long will it take before they adjust to our unfairness?*

A: I'd say it will take three to six months for the screaming to stop, another three to six years for them to get completely used to the idea, and adulthood before they understand why you did it and forgive you.

Q: *At least ten times a day, every day, my four-year-old daughter asks me if I love her. I always tell her I love her very much and always will. Several months ago, when this first started, I thought it was a phase that would pass quickly. Instead of tapering off, however, it's gotten steadily worse. I can't figure out what might have caused her to become so inse-cure. What would you advise?*

A: I'd advise that you help your daughter stop asking the question so much. Asking "Do you love me?" ten times a day doesn't mean your daughter is insecure. She's probably just trying to figure out what "love" means and how long it lasts. Repetition is one way children answer questions of this sort for themselves.

Illustration: If you move a brightly colored object through a six-month-old's field of vision, and then hide it behind your back, the infant won't come in search of it; out of sight, out of mind. Several months later, the same child will respond to this tease by crawling behind you to find it. Around eight months of age, an infant realizes that objects don't cease to exist when they're out of sight.

I once watched a ten-month-old amuse himself by placing a block inside a kitchen pot, putting the lid on the pot, and then immediately taking it off to rediscover the "lost" toy. Like a scientist, he repeated this simple experiment over and over again until he had proved to himself that the block was forever.

In a like manner, your daughter is trying to establish the identity and permanence of an intangible concept—an invisible idea—by taking the lid off the question "Do you love me?" time and time again.

The problem isn't the question. It's that adults are generally insecure about their ability to raise children and tend, therefore, to look for any possible indication that something is terribly wrong. We overanalyze and misinterpret events; we blow the significance of things completely out of proportion; we misplace common sense and replace it with nonsense.

At some point, your daughter probably began to sense that the question made you feel somewhat uncomfortable. Needing to understand why Mommy got so flustered, she began asking the question more and more often. The more she asked, the more flustered you became, the more she asked . . . and so on.

The two of you are riding the same merry-go-round. You don't know how to stop getting flustered, and she doesn't know how to stop asking the question. She can't help you. So, as I said to begin with, you've got to help her.

Find a peaceful, relaxed time for the two of you to sit down and talk. Tell her that "I love you" is like a piece of candy people surprise one another with, and that you would like to begin surprising her with it, too. Help her understand that you can't surprise her as long as she asks the question.

Then, the next time she asks, say something like, "Oh-oh, now it's not a surprise."

Meanwhile, make it a point to call her over to you several times a day to play "Guess What?"

"Guess what?"

"What?"

"I love you."

Personally, I can't think of a nicer surprise.

Q: *Is it okay to let an adult child live at home? If so, what understandings should exist between the parents and the child?*

A: Valid reasons for letting a grown child come home to nest include such things as divorce, job loss, and prolonged illness. Stressful circumstances such as these might temporarily interfere with the young person's ability to be self-supporting, in which case equally temporary parental help might be necessary.

"Nesting" is also perfectly acceptable during major, but not necessarily stressful, transitions in the child's life. These would include the time between college graduation or the end of military service and a job. If living at home for a few months before getting married would help the young person build a nest egg, that's fine too.

Whatever the circumstances, the arrangement should not be open-ended. Parents and child should establish goals, a specific plan of action, and time frames for reaching those goals. For example, the agreement might stipulate that the young person will be out of the house in six months. The first month will be spent finding a job, the second and third paying off debts, the fourth and fifth building a financial cushion, and the sixth finding an affordable place to live.

During this period of dependency, the young person should be required to make some form of contribution to the household. If unable to contribute financially, he or she should perform services around the home that function as payment. Once the young person has income, a sliding scale of financial reimbursement can be worked out. Grown children should, in other words, "earn their keep."

Q: *How much control should parents exercise over an adult child who lives at home?*

A: No more than they would exercise over any other temporary boarder. This arrangement involves three adults, not two adults and one child. The young person should be treated as an adult and be expected to act as such. Likewise, the parents should act as adults, not parents. This means, for example, that the parents should set no specific restrictions on the young person's comings and goings. It also means that the young person should come and go with due respect for the parents' lifestyle and values.

Q: *What if the young person violates the agreement or behaves in a manner that's annoying or offensive to the parents?*

A: The parents shouldn't lecture or punish the young person for behavior they don't like but should express their concerns in a straightforward manner. Violations of the agreement should be openly discussed, the goal being to reach understanding as to why the violation occurred and thus prevent a repeat performance. Perhaps the violation was the result of a misunderstanding, or perhaps the agreement was unrealistic to begin with and needs to be modified. If conflict continues between parents and grown child, family counseling is the next step.

Q: *What if the agreed-upon time for leaving comes and the young person isn't financially able to move away?*

A: Inventory what went wrong and why. Set new goals based on the mistakes and miscalculations that were made and try again. If the young person fails a second time to emancipate on schedule, there may be more going on than meets the eye. At that point, it may be appropriate to explore the issues and problems with a family counselor.

5

POINT FIVE

Toys and Play: The Right Stuff

I REMEMBER BEING FIVE YEARS OLD. My life was chockful of stone walls and trees to climb, lizards to catch, nooks and crannies to explore, and parks and empty lots in which to play. I had no television during those early years—didn't even know it existed—and very few store-bought toys. But my imagination had wings and fly I did, to whatever place and as whatever pretend person I pleased.

We lived for a time in a southern coastal city, and I spent many an afternoon in a park down by the waterfront, watching the big ships and dreaming of faraway places like London, where the Queen lived, and Africa, where Tarzan swung through the trees with the apes.

Every night, either my mother or my grandmother would read to me from children's classics like Kipling's *Just So Stories*, Grahame's *The Wind in the Willows*, and Thurber's *Thirteen Clocks*. Because my mother worked part-time in addition to attending college, I went to a preschool where we played games and painted pictures with our fingers and made castles out of empty oatmeal boxes and soldiers out of clothespins (the kind with no springs). Mom used to tell me we were "dirt poor," but looking back, the standard of *my* living was high. It was a special time but not out of the ordinary, because that's what childhood was all about.

But time has taken its toll on childhood—so much so that, at times, I fear we may be poised on the brink of childhood's end. Not the final apocalyptic end of children, mind you, but the loss of what being a child once was and still should (and can) be all about.

Today, instead of sending children outdoors to play, we let them sit in front of TV sets for thousands of hours during their formative years, staring at a constantly blinking, tasteless, odor-free, hands-off counterfeit of the real world. Meanwhile, their imaginations atrophy from disuse, along with their initiative, their curiosity, their resourcefulness, and their creativity.

Today, instead of providing children with ample opportunity and the raw materials with which to find and create handmade playthings, we overdose them with mass-produced toys that stimulate relatively little imaginative thought—toys that are nothing more than what the labels on their boxes say they are.

Today, instead of reading to children and letting time and teachers do the rest, we push letters and numbers at preschoolers, completely disregarding the fact that early childhood has nothing to do with letters and numbers and everything to do with play. We have, in fact, little respect for the enormous contribution play makes to healthy growth and development. "He's just playing," we're apt to say, when "just playing" is the very essence of childhood.

Before going any further, I'm going to take you on a guided tour of a typical child's life, circa 2001. Let's begin in his or her room, otherwise known as Toytown. There are toys strewn all over the floor, wedged under the bed, stuffed in the cabinets, packed onto the shelves, crammed in the closet, and even dangling from the ceiling. But wait! There's more to come! Downstairs, there are toys decorating the floor in the living room and the den. There are more lining the wall of the garage, and still more outside, rusting in the yard. If this child is not yet of school age, he or she probably attends a preschool program where most of the day is spent playing with an assortment of brightly colored plastic toys, coloring mimeographed pictures, and learning to recite and write the ABCs. How exciting! If this child is of school age, it's likely that several afternoons through the week are taken up with such seemingly essential things as soccer practice, piano lessons, and classes in social etiquette.

And yet, in the midst of all these things and all these activities, we are probably going to find a child who makes one complaint more than any other—"I'm bored!" In fact, if I were to give a name to the present generation of children, it would be the "I've got nothin' to do" generation. That is, after all, their favorite litany.

When I was five, I had five toys. They were a set of Lincoln Logs, a set of Tinker Toys, an electric train that ran on twelve feet of circular track, a set of lead cavalry and foot soldiers, and a Hop-along Cassidy pearl-handled cap pistol in a black leather holster. With the exception of this toy gun, which I was allowed to wear as often as I wanted, my mother kept those toys in a box on the upper shelf of her closet. She called them "rainy-day things." In good weather, she expected me to be outside. That box came down only if the weather was inclement or night had fallen early. But I was never bored. I was *never* at a loss for something to do. And if I had complained of being bored, I'm certain my mother would have found something to occupy my time, but it probably wouldn't have been amusing.

How can it be that today's children, for whom parents provide so much in the ways of things and activities, are so constantly bored? Actually, the question answers itself. Today's children are bored precisely *because* parents provide them with so many things and activities.

Too many toys overwhelm a child's ability to make creative decisions. A five-year-old boy today can't decide what to do next because the clutter presents too many options. So he retreats from the chaos, saying, "I've got nothin' to do." At first, his parents are annoyed by his expressions of helplessness. Eventually, however, they become fed up with his whining and complaining and buy him a new toy. It works! He stops complaining—for a while, that is.

As quickly as his interest in the new toy wanes, the child begins again to whine about being bored. What his parents are slow to realize is that, instead of solving the child's boredom, the new toy only makes it worse. In the long run, it only adds to the clutter and strengthens his growing addiction to acquired things.

This child's boredom also has a lot to do with the *kinds* of toys his parents buy. In most cases, today's toys are one-dimensional— a truck, a boat, a this, a that. The singular nature of most mass-produced playthings limits a child's ability to express imagination and creativity, making boredom that much more likely.

What it boils down to is this: With the best of intentions, we've successfully prevented today's children from getting in touch with the magical make-do of childhood. When I was a child, play was largely a matter of making do. For instance, if pirates was the game of the day, I'd borrow one of my mother's brightly colored scarves for a sash and her black galoshes for ten-league boots. A stick became my broadsword. Mom helped me make a hat by folding a sheet of newspaper. A few pieces of her costume jewelry completed the disguise. Looking at myself in the mirror, I was Captain Blood! Together, my mates and I sailed the seven backyards in search of milk and cookies. Oh, what fun!

For the most part, today's children don't know how to make do. Why? Because they've never had to. Too much has been done for them, too much given to them. Their teachers (who should know) tell me that instead of inventing games, today's children tend to mimic characters and situations from popular television programs. (That eliminates pirates from the running.) Props aren't improvised, they're purchased at a toy store. How sad. How boring!

Through the magic of making do, children exercise imagination, initiative, creativity, intelligence, resourcefulness, and self-reliance. In the process, they practice discovery and invention, which are the basics of science. Making do is not only the essence of truly creative play—which is, in turn, the essence of childhood—it's also the story of the advancement of the human race. Throughout the parade of history, the art of making do has been significant to nearly every important invention and nearly every famous discovery. The child who discovers the magic of making do is on the road to success and self-esteem. Who knows, that same child might be our next Marie Curie, Louis Pasteur, Jonas Salk, Ferdinand Magellan, Thomas Edison, or Alexander Graham Bell . . . who knows?

Charlie's Magic Make-Do Marker

Somewhere, in a present place and a present time, there lives a five-year-old boy named Charlie. One day, Charlie's parents hear strange noises coming from his room: *"Sssssssszzzzzooooommmmmmmmmmm! Pow! Pow! Pow! Pow! Nnnnneeeeeyyyooow!"*

Charlie's parents tiptoe quietly down the hall to check things out. As they get closer, the sounds get louder. Quietly, they open Charlie's door just enough to see without being seen. Charlie is running excitedly around his room, tracing sweeping arcs in the air with an empty felt tip marker turned rocketship he managed to rescue from the trash. Suddenly, Charlie stops. The sound becomes a high-pitched whine as the "spaceship" begins its vertical descent to the surface of Planet Chest-of-drawers. It lands, and for a moment nothing moves. Then *"Click, click, click,"* says Charlie, and his parents can almost see the hatch of the spaceship open and its alien commander emerge.

Instantly, the Magic Marker becomes the alien and begins to lumber ominously across the surface of the planet, looking for something to eat. The alien doesn't get very far when suddenly, from behind a wad of rolled-up underwear, there jumps a plastic Indian, with bow drawn. *"Whoooooooosssshh!"* the Indian lets fly an arrow at the alien. As the alien intruder moves to defend itself, the Magic Marker becomes a ray gun, which the alien begins firing at the Indian, making a rapid *shoom-shoom!* sound. For the next three or four minutes, the battle rages. Finally, sensing the advantage, the Indian emerges from behind the shelter of his underwear rocks, shouts a ferocious war cry, and charges at the startled alien. Realizing that death rays are no match for a crazed Indian with bow and arrow, the alien beasts a hasty retreat and blasts off in search of a more hospitable planet.

Closing Charlie's door, his parents tiptoe back to the living room. "Well," says Charlie's father. "Now we know what to get Charlie for Christmas."

"We certainly do," says Charlie's mother, and together they chorus, "A rocket ship!"

And so, on Christmas morning, Charlie wakes up to find a huge box under the tree labeled TO CHARLIE FROM SANTA Inside, he finds a replica of the space shuttle, complete with cargo hatch, command module with seating for seven astronauts, and retractable landing gear. Inside the box, Charlie finds a plastic dropcloth printed to look like the surface of the moon. The box itself, when folded in a certain manner, makes a ridge of moon mountains. Charlie is absolutely consumed with joy. But the spaceship isn't all Charlie gets on Christmas morning. There's also a battery-operated car he can steer by remote control. There's a slot-car racing set. There's a man on a motorcycle that winds up and leaps from ramp to ramp. Finally, there's a suitcase that opens to reveal a miniature city and comes complete with tiny cars to drive around the city's streets. Oh, joy! Charlie really rakes it in on Christmas morning.

Three weeks later, Charlie's mother is in the kitchen fixing dinner when Charlie drags in, looking dejected. His mother asks, "Charlie? What's the matter with you?" Charlie scuffs the floor with his toe and whines, "I've got nothin' to do."

Charlie's mother goes into cerebral meltdown. She turns on him and shrieks, "What do you mean, you've got nothing to do? You've got a new space shuttle, a remote-controlled car, a man on a motorcycle, and a city in a suitcase, not to mention all the other toys you have back in your room from birthdays and Christmases past! *How dare you tell me you've got nothing to do?*"

What Charlie's mother fails to realize is that Charlie is telling the truth. He really doesn't have anything to do. He's done everything that can be done with a space shuttle, a remote-controlled car, a man on a motorcycle, and a city in a suitcase. What Charlie really needed on Christmas morning were toys he could *do* things with, rather than toys that are nice to look at, cost a lot of money, and perform at the flip of a switch. You see, the difference between

Charlie's marvelous Magic Marker and a seventy-five-dollar plastic replica of the space shuttle is that the Magic Marker was anything Charlie wanted it to be. In the span of a mere few minutes, it was a spaceship, an alien, and a ray gun. And all Charlie did to effect these transformations was zap it with the alchemy of his imagination. But no matter how much Charlie imagines his space shuttle to be something else, it remains a space shuttle, forever and ever. Within three weeks, Charlie has exhausted all the creative potential not only of the space shuttle, but also of the remote-controlled car, the man on the motorcycle, and the city in the suitcase. And so, three weeks after Christmas, Charlie truly has nothing to do.

Transformations

Like Charlie's empty felt-tip marker, all truly creative toys have one characteristic in common: They encourage and enable children to perform what are called *transformations*. A child performs a transformation by using something—anything—to represent something else. For instance, when a child takes a pine cone and sets it upright on the ground and calls it a tree, that's a transformation. Transformations are the essence of fantasy, which is, in turn, the essence of play. An empty box becomes a boat, a car, a table, or anything else the child *wills* it to be. A child can also become someone else at will: Tarzan, Jane, or the neighborhood grocer. If a toy aids a child in making transformations, it is well worth the money spent on it, not to mention the time the child spends playing with it.

Toys that encourage transformation include creative materials such as clay, fingerpaints, and crayons. Inside, there's the everyday household stuff of empty oatmeal cartons, Popsicle sticks, spoons, shoe boxes, empty spools of thread, straws, paper bags, buttons, pots and pans, and empty toilet paper rolls. And don't forget how much fun children have turning large appliance cartons into houses! Outside, there are leaves, sticks, pine cones, rocks, and mud, glorious mud! The list goes on and on, limited only by the child's virtually limitless imagination.

As a child, one of my favorite toys was a Quaker Oatmeal box. I could make it into just about anything I wanted. I'd turn it upside down, thread a neck band of string through two holes punched in the side, and it became a drum that I played with wooden spoons. Or I'd cut rectangular notches in the top and a drawbridge in the side and it became a castle. Or I'd tape a brim to it and it became a top hat. How much did these toys cost? The price of oatmeal. How much did I gain from them? An incredible amount. After all, I'd made them with my own hands.

While your children are young, show them how to use things like pots and pans, empty boxes, pipe cleaners, and other odds and ends to make their own toys. Once you show what can be done with a box, some tape, a few sheets of construction paper, and a pair of scissors, there'll be no stopping them! Children who make their own playthings are not only learning how to entertain themselves, but are also exercising independence, self-sufficiency, initiative, resourcefulness, eye–hand coordination, intelligence, imagination, achievement, motivation, creativity—and, therefore, self-esteem. What more could a parent want? There are few investments of a parent's time and energy that will pay off better than this one.

Buying Worthwhile Toys

Realizing that the average American child is a toy addict, many toy companies make toys with purposefully (and profitably) short life spans. After all, why make toys that last when the average child is more concerned with *getting* than with the quality of what's gotten?

When buying toys for children, consider first the fact that children are inquisitive. The first question that pops into their minds when they're given something is "How does it work?" In most cases, you find out how something works by taking it apart. Unfortunately, most toys are not made to be taken apart. If you try, they will break.

Consider also that most toys are designed to attract a child's attention and curiosity but not to hold his or her interest. This obviously profitable marketing philosophy is to blame for the fact that children lose interest in most toys within a few weeks, if not days.

Not all toy companies are into making schlock, but many are. How are parents to know whether the toys they are buying their children are good investments? In addition to being safe, a toy embodies four qualities by which to measure its play value:

1. The toy presents a wide range of creative possibilities. It is capable of being many things, as defined by the child's imagination, rather than one thing, as defined by the manufacturer. In other words, it enables transformations.

2. The toy encourages manipulation. It can be taken apart and put together in various ways. Toys of this kind hold a child's interest because they stimulate creative behavior.

3. The toy is age-appropriate. You don't give a rubber duck to a ten-year-old any more than you give an electric train to a two-year-old. Most manufacturers publish the age range of a toy on its box. While not always entirely accurate, these give a fairly good idea of whether the toy and the child will "match."

4. The toy is durable. It will withstand lots of abuse.

A toy that rates high in all four areas possesses excellent play value.

When parents ask me for examples of manufactured toys high in play value, the first that come to mind are the construction sets manufactured by Lego. In my estimation, these are the only toy systems that score a perfect ten in all four categories. Coming in a close second are building sets like Lincoln Logs, Tinker Toys, and Erector sets. Art materials—clay, finger paints, construction paper, crayons, scissors—should be staples in every child's life.

By way of dolls, the cuddly so-called "adoption dolls" enable children to explore parental feelings and act out parental behavior. They're far more imaginative and creative than dolls that walk, talk, drink from a bottle, and wet their pants.

While we're on the subject of dolls, I should mention how important it is that parents not limit children to toys traditionally considered suitable for only one gender. Dolls and stuffed animals are just as appropriate for boys as they are for girls. If a boy wants to play with dolls, buy him dolls! If a girl wants to play baseball, buy her a bat and a ball! The freer children are to explore the possibilities of life, the better the choices they will make later on.

Surprisingly, most high-priced "educational" toys rate low on the play-value scale. They are typically one-dimensional and challenge a child's imagination and intellect for a relatively short period of time. Educational toys appeal primarily to parents, who mistakenly think that toys of this type will speed their children's development or get them ready for school more rapidly. For the most part, however, their educational value is shallow, contrived, and either irrelevant to a child's development or a poor substitute for cheaper but more interesting materials and activities.

Notice that the toys mentioned as being high in play value have been on the market for forty years or more. In addition to those already mentioned, toys that fit this criterion include blocks, electric trains (the child can use Legos and Lincoln Logs to make the train station and other buildings, Tinker Toys to make bridges and tunnels), Matchbox cars, small plastic figures (a bag of plastic army men or cowboys and Indians), dolls, dollhouses (the child can be taught to make furniture out of construction paper), and marbles. For the older child, buy toys that can form the nucleus of a hobby, such as chemistry sets, telescopes and microscopes, rock-collecting sets, and models. A child will get a lot more mileage from a handful of old-fashioned toys than from all the new-fangled junk in the world.

Less Is More, Part One

If I had to choose, I'd rather talk to grandparents than parents. I'm sure the fact that I'm a grandfather myself, albeit a relatively young one, has a lot to do with it. Regardless, today's grandparents—mostly the older ones—represent the last generation to rear children according to tradition as opposed to New Age psychobabble. They tell me stories, these venerable elders, of the way it used to be and still can be. If we'd heed their stories, that is.

One of the more consistent things grandparents tell me is that whereas a certain level of rivalry between siblings is nothing new, the almost constant bickering, name-calling, tattling, and even downright fighting typical of today's siblings is new indeed. This makes grandparents sad, because the siblings in question are their grandchildren.

"What's going on?" they ask. "How could things have changed so much in so short a period of time?"

I have a theory. Ironically, it's one most grandparents aren't going to like because—if I'm right—today's grandparents are part of the problem. My theory: The force driving most sibling rivalry is greed. Today's parents, with more than a little assistance from many grandparents, turn their children into greedy little materialists by buying them toy after toy after gadget after game after vehicle after gizmo, beginning before they're born and lasting forever and ever, amen.

Because today's parents feed the narcissistic spark that resides in the heart of every newborn, it grows into a flame, a fire, and a raging inferno. By age four or five, today's all-too-typical child is infected with King Midas syndrome, which is to say, he or she is a greedy little hoarder who can't share unless forced to do so, which is to say, the child can't really share at all.

As I said earlier, when I was five I had five toys I could call my own. Most people my age report between none and ten, inclusive. According to our parents, we didn't fight much over toys. That's pretty much a cause-and-effect thing. To paraphrase a line from Kris Kristofferson's country-rock classic, "Me & Bobby McGee," when you ain't got much, you ain't got much to lose. In which case, sharing is not a problem. But when you got a lot, you got a lot to lose, which means you're probably going to have difficulty when it comes to sharing.

The more material things you acquire, the more likely you are to resent it when someone else acquires something you don't have, especially if the something is presently out of the question for you;

the more likely you are to feel the other person's good fortune isn't "fair"; the more likely you are to be jealous, envious, and covetous. I need tell no one with eyes that see and ears that hear that those are the themes around which today's high levels of sibling conflict spin.

Take note, parents! Stop buying your children so many things! Stop throwing fuel on the fires of narcissism and materialism. At a certain (relatively low) level, "things" become a drug that anesthetizes the spirit. Make strong your children's spirits by keeping them "poor."

Need I repeat myself for the benefit of the grandparents in the audience?

Less Is More, Part Two

Several years ago, a couple consulted me concerning their almost three-year-old daughter. Most of the problems they described were typical of children of this age, but one was especially intriguing.

"Molly won't let us out of her sight," they said. "In addition to following us wherever we go in the house, she's constantly asking us to play with her and whining if we can't. Neither of us minds playing with her some, but we feel that with all the toys she has, she ought to have no trouble entertaining herself."

My ears perked up. "How many toys does she have?" I asked. "And what kind are they?"

"She's got so many toys you can hardly walk into her room without stepping on one," said her father. "As to the kinds of toys she has, I guess they're mostly the ones you see advertised on television."

That was all I needed to hear to know what the problem was.

First, I helped Molly's parents rate the play value of Molly's toys on a scale of one to ten. Those with ratings of less than seven were boxed and given to charity. Not surprisingly, that reduced the pile by nine-tenths. Those that remained included soft gimmick-free dolls, some stuffed animals, a set of blocks, and a dollhouse.

Next, Molly's parents went toy shopping. Instead of the junk that constitutes most of the toys advertised on television, they bought a few toys that measured up to the four criteria set forth earlier in this chapter.

To create a household environment that encouraged exploration, Molly's parents child-proofed their home. They put up anything that was potentially dangerous as well as anything that couldn't be easily replaced if broken. This ensured that Molly would be able to roam through most of the house without needing much supervision. Child-proofing also minimized the number of times Molly had to hear the word *no,* making obedience more likely.

Molly's parents also put safety latches on all the kitchen cabinets but one, which became Molly's cabinet. Her parents stocked this special place with empty oatmeal boxes, empty spools, old pots and pans, boxes of all sorts and sizes, and other safe household items that might otherwise have been discarded. Here was a place where Molly could come and rummage to her heart's content.

Last, but not least, Molly's parents went to an appliance store and obtained a large sturdy box into which they cut windows and a door. A small chair went inside, along with a few dolls and other housekeeping items—just the place for hours of imaginative play.

I saw Molly's parents several weeks later. Sure enough, Molly was entertaining herself much better than before and demanding far less of her parents' attention. "She seems bright and happy again," said her mother.

Molly's story isn't unique. In the last ten years, I've made the same basic set of recommendations to at least twenty parents. Of those, perhaps ten have had the gumption to follow through. The experiment has yet to fail. Every parent has reported the same basic results: The fewer the toys and the more space the child has in which to explore and create, the more successful the child is at occupying his or her time. And the more success the child experiences at what comes more naturally than anything else—play—the happier the child. These success stories simply go to show that sometimes less is more.

Play-Fullness

The story of Molly underscores how important play is to healthy development.

First, play exercises the skills a child needs in order to become a fully competent individual. Play is a multidimensional experience, involving nearly all of a child's perceptual, motor, sensory, and cognitive equipment. It is a total learning experience, unlike any other. Play is the catalyst of growth, as well as the medium, during early and middle childhood.

Second, as a number of studies have demonstrated, sufficient, unstructured playtime during early childhood is vitally important to the development of a well-rounded personality and healthy social skills. Children who are deprived of imaginative playtime are more likely to become either overly aggressive or depressed.

Third, play provides a nonthreatening context within which a child can explore and begin to understand the adult world. It is through fantasy play that children come to understand and work through things that might otherwise remain confusing, things like divorce, parental anger, and death.

Fourth, play helps children relieve stress and develop a sense of humor. Along these same lines, play helps children grow up to become adults who are capable of having fun.

Play is also a vehicle for significant learning, especially learning how to learn. Through play, children ask questions, explore their environments, learn essential problem-solving skills, practice social roles, and, in general, strengthen all the faculties that will enable them to realize their potential.

Unfortunately, over the last forty or more years, we have managed to place a number of obstacles in the path of the young child's innate desire to express imagination and growth through play. We have inundated young children with toys that smother their powers of creativity. We have let them sit in front of TV sets for hours upon hours while their imaginations atrophy from disuse. Instead of reading to children and letting time and the schools do the rest, we push flash cards and letters and numbers at preschool children, having lost sight of the fact that those activities are completely irrelevant to healthy growth and development.

The trend in recent years has been toward structuring the young child's time with such activities as organized sports, music lessons, classes in etiquette, and early academic instruction. We mistakenly believe that these things are more "meaningful" than play, when exactly the opposite is true. Furthermore, because so much has been planned and done for them, many of today's children have forgotten how to plan and do for themselves.

Give the Kids Their Games Back

One of the most disturbing aspects of the after-school activities craze is the trend toward enrolling children, at younger and younger ages, in organized sports programs. In my hometown, for example, children as young as five are participating in T-ball, soccer, and competitive swimming. These programs are absolutely irrelevant to the developmental needs—social, physical, and otherwise—of young children. Moreover, they can actually be detrimental, especially during middle childhood, ages six to ten.

The psychology of the young school-age child can be summarized in two words: acceptance and achievement. Self-esteem hinges on how successful these children are at creating a secure place for themselves among their peers and at establishing and attaining specific goals of excellence.

Organized sports would seem to be an ideal complement to the needs of children this age, the perfect medium in which to nurture both the inner and outer self. Not so. The primary problem is adult involvement. Adults organize these programs, raise the money to fund them, and draw up the playing schedule. Adults pick the teams, coach them, referee them, decide who plays and who doesn't, give out awards, and make up the biggest share of the audience.

But it doesn't stop there. Not only do adults play too prominent a role in planning and organizing these events, they also take it upon themselves to mediate such things as which children acquire what status within the peer group, how conflict between children is resolved, and so on.

Adults have absolutely no business being so involved in the play of children. Their presence is a complicating factor that prevents children from learning to negotiate social issues on their own. All too often, instead of being activities for children, these events become theaters where youngsters are manipulated for the gratification of adults.

The fact that these sports are competitive is not, in and of itself, disturbing. A child this age needs, and if left alone will seek out, appropriate competitive experiences. What *is* disturbing is that the children, because adults are so entangled in the proceedings, no longer play for fun but to obtain adult approval. They are not really playing at all. They are *working*, performing for an adult audience.

The difference between competitive play and competitive work can be measured in terms of emotional outcome. When children band together to play a sandlot game, one team wins and one team loses, but everyone usually manages to leave the field feeling okay. When adults direct children in an organized sports event, the children on the losing team often end up feeling angry, dejected, frustrated, ashamed, or depressed. This isn't play. This is serious business, and the stakes are high. Too high.

In this context, the child athlete's sense of achievement and self-esteem becomes defined in terms of winning and losing. Process and participation take a backseat to outcome, which isn't what childhood is all about. Everyone suffers, but the biggest losers are the children who don't get to play because they aren't "good" enough.

The basic problem—one that isn't limited to this issue—is the adult tendency to act as though children will botch the job of growing up unless we engineer the process for them. The exact opposite is true. When we place ourselves *between* the child and the task of growing up, we are no longer in a helpful position. We are interfering, and the child is ultimately less capable of dealing with life in the raw.

When he was about ten years old, Eric became interested in soccer and joined one of the teams in the neighborhood league. A proud father, I started attending the games. The stands were always packed with parents, many of them howling at the children to hustle more, be more aggressive, and so on. If they weren't howling at the players, they were howling at the referee. The coach paced the sidelines, looking very busy and very serious.

At the end of these games, while mingling with the players and their parents, I frequently overheard comments like "If you're not going to hustle, you shouldn't play" and "If you had been paying attention, that shot wouldn't have gotten by you." I was relieved when Eric told me he wanted to quit.

Several months later, Willie and I were at a local jogging track where a peewee football team was holding practice. When our run was over, we rested on the hill overlooking the field. By this time, practice had ended, and all the little players in their pads and helmets were standing in a line at the end zone, none of them older than nine. We watched in growing amazement as the head coach strutted up and down in front of the boys, bellowing at them.

"You're all a bunch of wimps!" he yelled. "You hit like a bunch of girls! Are you girls? You, Waldorf, are you a girl? Answer me, Waldorf! Are you a girl? No? Well, then, what's the matter with you out there? Are you afraid you might get hurt? Don't start crying, Waldorf, 'cause I've got no sympathy for sissy stuff."

On and on he went as my blood pressure rose, along with my sense of outrage. Willie prevented me from confronting him only by pointing out that he was twice my size and obviously mean enough not to be impressed by my opinion of his harangue. In fact, he'd have probably welcomed the opportunity to demonstrate to the team how a "real" man handled conflict.

When I was a kid, sports was one of the most important things in my life. Along with the other boys in my suburban Chicago neighborhood, I played football in the fall, basketball in the winter, and baseball through the glory days of spring and summer. Our games were all pickup games played on fields at the local school or park. We got there on our bicycles. There were hardly ever enough players to make up two bona fide teams, so we modified the rules to suit the situation.

There were never any adults at our games. We were the players, the coaches, and the referees. We yelled at one another to hustle, we praised and criticized one another's play, we razzed one another. Despite all this, hard feelings were rare. It was all part of the game, and since the game was exclusively ours, we could do with it as we pleased. In the process, we learned how to subordinate our own desires to the best interests of the group, how to be good winners and good losers, how to resolve conflict, and how to begin running our own lives.

Little League baseball was the only organized sport available outside of school sports, which didn't start until the seventh grade. Through our early teenage years, my buddies and I watched as the organized sports programs grew and began taking over the hallowed ground of our playing fields. The turning point for us came the day we were politely but firmly told to vacate a field we were playing on because a Little League team needed it for practice.

I'm aware that children rarely play pickup games anymore. Somewhere along the line, someone got the brilliant idea that sports would be more of a meaningful learning experience for children if the games were managed by adults. The adults could see to it that rules were followed, that play was fair, that the children's skills improved through proper coaching, and that conflicts were resolved properly.

The end result of all this well-intentioned meddling is that children don't have the opportunity to discover and work these issues out on their own. In addition, there's a tense and unhealthy air of professionalism that pervades organized children's sports programs. It's all too obvious that the children are on the field not to have fun but to perform for adults who are all too eager to have their egos stroked.

And so I voice my objections. And people respond by saying things like, "I know, I know, but John, sports are so competitive these days that if you don't start the kids out young, they won't be able to make the teams when they get to high school."

Hogwash! The same lame argument is used to justify teaching reading skills to preschool children. Studies show that the earlier you push reading at children, the less joy they bring to the task and the less successful they ultimately are. I suspect the same may be true of organized children's sports. And let's face it. Joy, not parental pressure, is the essence of success, whether that success is in the classroom or on the athletic field.

I say, let the kids have their games back.

Questions?

Q: *My best friend refuses to buy her children what she calls "war toys": toy guns, army paraphernalia, superhero action figures, and the like. She says they reinforce the notion that force is an acceptable way of resolving conflict. I'm undecided. What do you think?*

A: I can certainly appreciate your friend's point of view, but I don't think war toys have quite the impact on children she says they do. Unquestionably, if there were no such thing as war, there would be no war toys, but I doubt the reverse is true. Children have been playing with war toys and at war games for as long as wars have been waged. Nevertheless, there is no reason to believe that playing at war encourages actual aggressive behavior.

Children play at all manner of adult vocations and recreations. In fact, once children find out that adults do thus-and-such, they seek to understand that aspect of the grown-up world by playing at it. But a child's play does not determine a child's values. Children who play "married" and end up getting a pretend divorce are only trying to understand, through enactment, why grown-ups get divorced. Those same children aren't more likely, as adults, to think that divorce is the way to solve marital problems.

The quality and quantity of toys parents buy children certainly do have a significant effect on their development. As I've already said, too many toys of the wrong type can actually have a deprivational effect on the development of imagination, creativity, initiative, resourcefulness, and so on. But a child's concept of right and wrong, or value structure, is determined primarily through interaction with parents, *not* through interaction with toys.

The same is true of war toys and war games. They are tools, not of menace but understanding. In and of themselves, they are harmless. A child who plays at games like War and Cops and Robbers may even come to better grips with the reality of violence than a child who does not. A child who grows up in a climate of violence, however, is altogether a different story.

For the most part, I don't like war toys for the same reason I don't like the majority of toys in today's marketplace: They're too literal and therefore require little imagination. A toy gun made out of Legos or a stick is far superior to a plastic gun bought in a store.

I should hasten to mention that real guns, including BB guns and air rifles, are *not* toys. They are weapons, plain and simple. As such, they don't belong in the hands of a child, and putting one of them there does nothing but court disaster. If you want to teach a child to aim and shoot, buy a camera.

Q: *If a child asks to participate in an organized sport or take piano lessons and later wants to quit, should parents make the child stick it out?*

A: No and maybe. Children should be free to approach such things as soccer and piano with a spirit of playfulness. In a young child, the initial desire to become involved in a sport or activity is nothing more than an expression of curiosity. For this reason, a child should not feel obligated to participate, or continue participating, in a sport or activity because of parental pressure and should, generally speaking, be as free to quit as to join. "I want to" should be considered an adequate excuse for quitting.

Parents who refuse to allow a child to withdraw from something he or she has found unfulfilling unknowingly inhibit the experimental nature of these activities. A child who is not free to quit becomes increasingly reluctant to join for fear of becoming locked into something that might seem attractive at first but ultimately is not.

Children who are free to leave an activity they entered on their own initiative are in no danger of developing a "quitter's attitude" toward life. Quite the contrary. The stuff of success—initiative, achievement, motivation, and persistence—grows only when it is allowed to take root and flower within the child. Parents who appropriate those attributes and then attempt to impose them on a child are unintentionally doing more harm than good.

That being the rule, here is the exception. There is occasional value to be had from contracting with a child for specified periods of commitment regarding certain activities, especially those that involve significant monetary investment. For example, parents might require that a child agree to two years of lessons before buying a musical instrument the child has expressed interest in learning to play. In these cases, the child learns something about obligation and responsibility.

Q: *Our first child is seven months old. When should we begin reading to her?*

A: Last month. Seriously, folks, a child is never too young for reading. Parents should begin reading to a child by no later than six months of age, but six weeks is even better.

"But," you say, "she might not be able to see the pictures." That's okay. Pictures are not necessary to reading anyway.

My mother or grandmother read to me every night before bed until I was at least six years old. The books had few pictures. Some had none. I didn't know any better, so I never complained. But I did pay attention, and I did use my imagination. In fact, I probably exercised my imagination lots more than I would have, had there been more pictures. I'm not saying that pictures are in any way detrimental, only that they aren't essential.

When I read to Eric and Amy, I generally preferred books with lots of pictures because that forced us to cuddle. The pictures also became the occasion for games of "Show me . . ." and "What's this?"

Early reading stimulates language, perceptual, and cognitive development. Studies have also shown that as a child's communication skills improve, so does motor coordination. This makes sense, not only because an enriching environment stimulates a child's abilities in all areas but also because language development and motor behavior are interwoven during early childhood.

The nurturing that takes place when a parent reads to a child helps strengthen the child's sense of security. This, in turn, contributes greatly to the growth of independence. Security, independence, and intellectual competence—these form the basis of self-esteem. So you see, early and ongoing reading is one of the best investments you can make toward your child's well-being.

Don't, however, confuse the purpose of early reading with teaching a child to read. When you sit down to read to your daughter, do so because it's something you both enjoy. If you start reading to your daughter now and read to her often, you will teach her that reading feels good, and that is quite enough.

It isn't at all unusual, at age three or four, for a well-read-to child suddenly to begin reading. With enough exposure, some children figure out how to read on their own. If they don't and learn to read in the first grade, that's okay too.

Begin with books that rhyme, like those by Dr. Seuss. (My favorite rhyming book is Arnold Lobel's *The Man Who Took the Indoors Out*.) The natural rhythm of the words will hold an infant's attention better than prose. Poetry also lends itself to improvisational song, which—assuming you are able to make up and carry a tune—never fails to fascinate and delight the child in us all. Diversify into prose around the same time the child begins talking. Regardless of what you select, follow these guidelines:

- Read to your child at least thirty minutes each day.

- Choose books *you* enjoy reading. The more you like 'em, the more your child will too.

- Read slightly above your child's current vocabulary level.

- Read with feeling, with gusto. Give each character a different accent. Sing certain passages.

- Hold your child close.

- Have a wonderful time!

For more information and helpful hints on reading aloud to children of all ages, I highly recommend *The Read-Aloud Handbook* by Jim Trelease.

Q: *The preschool program our four-year-old attends has always empha-sized social and creative skills rather than academics. However, the board of directors recently hired a new teacher for the four-year-olds who wants to teach reading and math. According to her, a child this age is ready to begin academic instruction. The parents are divided on this issue, some eager for their children to have a head start, others resisting the change. What's your opinion?*

A: The fundamental question is: "What, if anything, do children gain by learning how to read and perform arithmetic problems at age four?" The answer: "Nothing."

Take two four-year-olds of approximately equal ability, teach one to read and do basic math, but wait to begin formal instruction with the other until he or she enters first grade. The result? Although the first child might outshine the second through most of first grade, by the time they both reach third grade no one will be able to determine which had the initial advantage.

The concept of readiness is at the crux of the problem. If readi-ness is defined in terms of whether four-year-olds *can* learn to read and do basic math, then most four-year-olds are ready. If, on the other hand, readiness is defined in terms of the most appropriate time to begin teaching reading and math, then four-year-olds are *not* ready.

The observations and research of Swiss developmental psychol-ogist Jean Piaget (1896–1980) suggest that abstract symbol systems such as those involved in reading and math need not and should not be introduced to children until age six or seven. Piaget maintained that intelligence develops within every human being according to a predictable evolutionary sequence. Each stage of intellectual (cognitive) growth, as characterized by the emergence of new and more sophisticated ways of understanding the world, is built upon previously existing modes of understanding.

Piaget said that any attempt to impose understanding of a certain concept "before its time" was not only fruitless but potentially harmful. He maintained that if a certain concept was introduced to a child before the appropriate developmental window was open, the child might never be able to utilize that concept effectively. Later researchers have argued that teaching four-year-olds to read is accomplished at the expense of doing permanent damage to the very nature of intelligence.

So if children are not the beneficiaries of the current vogue for preschool literacy, why the push? Because it meets the needs of some parents and some teachers, that's why.

Somehow, through a combination of misinformation and misunderstanding, many American parents have decided that since there are few skills more important to success than reading, the earlier a child reads the better. But early readers serve their parents better than they serve themselves. Early readers calm their parents' anxieties over such things as whether they're smart and whether they'll be good students. Their literacy also stands as a testimonial to the skill and good judgment used in raising them. So the payoff for parents is twofold: They're less worried and their egos are fatter. A powerful payoff indeed.

Given that parents want their preschoolers to read, a teacher who offers to teach them suddenly becomes a hot item. Everyone scrambles to get their kids into that teacher's class. What few seem to realize is that teaching four-year-olds to read is far easier and demands considerably less preparation time, imagination, and energy from a teacher than planning and carrying out a stimulating program of more creative and more developmentally appropriate activities. So the teacher's payoff is also twofold: Less work and a fatter ego.

We seem to be forgetting that education is for the sake of children, not for the sake of adults.

Q: *I am an educator who disagrees with your stand on early reading instruction. Recent studies have demonstrated that preschool children have a far greater capacity for learning than was previously suspected. By exposing preschoolers to educational opportunities such as early reading instruction, we acknowledge and nurture this potential.*

A: Your argument is the same one that's always been used to justify these programs: If preschoolers *can* learn to read, they *should* learn to read. This position is based on a limited understanding of literacy, as well as limited definitions of learning and achievement.

It's true that reasonably intelligent children as young as three can be taught basic word-recognition skills. But saying that justifies teaching preschool children to read is like saying the fact that thirteen-year-olds can be taught to drive justifies giving them the opportunity to obtain driver's licenses.

Indeed, preschool children do have a great capacity for learning. And indeed, parents and educators share responsibility for responding appropriately to that potential. The question then becomes, "What kinds of learning experiences are appropriate for preschoolers?"

We know that a preschool child's understanding of the world is earthbound. In other words, it is fairly limited to the universe of concrete, tangible things. Reading involves the intervention of an abstract symbol system—the printed word—to describe tangible and intangible aspects of the universe. Piaget's research tends to indicate that, for most children, the critical period for introducing symbol systems of this sort is around age six. In European schools, where this rule of thumb is generally practiced, there are few reading problems, compared to the spate that plagues our educational system. In the Soviet Union, formal education doesn't begin until children are seven, yet Russian children seem none the worse for it.

Just exactly what does it mean to be able to read? Literacy is traditionally defined in terms of an individual's ability to correctly recognize and comprehend words and word passages. If one adheres to this limited definition, then indeed it is possible to induce literacy in preschool children. But any definition of literacy is incomplete unless it also includes the ability to *enjoy* reading. After all, it matters not that children can read if they fail to do so for lack of enjoyment. When this third standard is applied to the issue of teaching reading to preschoolers, the complete bankruptcy of the idea is revealed.

In *The Hurried Child*, psychologist David Elkind cited studies showing that the earlier children are taught to read, the less they enjoy reading and the less they read. Every public school first-grade teacher I've ever discussed this issue with has told me that it is not at all necessary that children come to first grade with more than a basic knowledge of the alphabet. Their only hope is that their young students come to them with a desire to read that's been instilled and reinforced at home.

The trick in helping a child become literate in the complete sense of the term is no trick at all. Starting as young as six months, read to the child on a regular basis at least thirty minutes a day. There's no better way than this to prepare a child for later reading instruction.

Q: *I've put our eight-month-old son in a playpen for short periods during the day ever since he was three months old. Until recently, he's occupied himself quietly until I was able to return. Lately, as soon as I put him in the playpen, he begins screaming bloody murder and doesn't stop until I pick him up. I can't possibly be with him every minute of the day, nor can I let him be free to roam about the house. The playpen seems like the most sensible and convenient way of solving these problems. On the other hand, he hates it. What can I do?*

A: Before we go any further, understand that playpens aren't for play, not in the real sense of the term. Boredom is about all that's possible in a fenced-in area no larger than sixteen square feet. The more stuff a parent heaps in there to occupy the child, the more cluttered the pen becomes, further restricting the child's ability to interact creatively with his environment (play).

Before they begin crawling, most children will endure the relative isolation of a playpen for brief periods during the day. Crawling, however, stimulates an infant's desire to explore the world. Once your son discovers what excitement there is to be had by moving from one place to another and then another, getting his hands in the stuff of what's happenin', he's not likely to sit quietly in a playpen. Add to his curiosity the fact that a young toddler, between eight and twelve months, isn't quite sure how much closeness he wants with his mother. This business of getting around on his own is a barrel of monkeys, but it also takes him farther away from the one he depends upon the most.

So your child is caught in his *own* dilemma. He wants to be with you and he wants to be away from you, doing his own thing. He feels a bit better if he's in control of how much distance there is between you and when separation happens. If *you* walk away, he yells, but if *he* crawls off, it's goodbye. Just to make sure you haven't vaporized while he wasn't looking, he checks on you every few minutes. When you put him in a playpen, his anxiety level goes up. Not only isn't he controlling the separation, he can't get to you when he needs to.

I'd like to digress a moment and say a few things about ducks. Several days after they hatch, a brood of ducklings will line up behind their mother and follow her wherever she goes. This is called *imprinting*. After a few weeks of parading about in this fashion, they break away and begin fending more or less for themselves.

Dutch ethologist Nikolaas Tinbergen wanted to see what would happen if the imprinting process was tampered with. He placed small barriers around a circular track where mother ducks walked. As their babies followed, they had to scramble over the barriers to keep up. The result? These frustrated ducklings persisted in following their mothers long after the time that ducklings usually move off on their own.

The child who begins making motions of independence must know, beyond the shadow of a doubt, that Mother will be easily accessible in time of need. Playpens frustrate the newly mobile child the same way Tinbergen's barriers frustrated the ducklings. And as was the case with the ducklings, frustration makes your child more determined to keep his mother close.

So, by using a playpen to contain (for whatever reason) a child who has started moving about under his own steam, you increase the likelihood that he will cling to you long after most children have become more self-sufficient.

One of the nicest gifts you can give your son, once he begins crawling, is a child-proofed living area where he can crawl and putter and get into safe, unbreakable things to his heart's content while you relax, knowing he's all right. He'll experience the same insecurities as other crawlers, but instead of getting stuck he'll go right through them.

Q: *Our sixteen-month-old daughter has recently started climbing and getting into lots of things that are off limits. We have tried popping her hand whenever she picks up something we don't want her to handle, but that doesn't seem to faze her and often makes her even more determined. How would you suggest we go about keeping her out of mischief?*

A: The most effective way of keeping your daughter out of mischief is to remove the potential for mischief by child-proofing. Child-proofing a home protects the child from danger and valuables from breakage while at the same time providing the child with an open, stimulating environment in which to explore to his or her heart's content.

Take inventory, room by room, of things dangerous or valuable that are within your daughter's reach. Put childproof latches on lower cabinets, childproof covers on electrical outlets, and place gates across staircases. Bring down to your daughter's level things she can touch. Give her a low cabinet of her own in the kitchen and stock it with things like wooden spoons, pots, empty thread spools, boxes, flexible straws, and anything else that might fascinate her and help stimulate creative behavior. If you do a good job, you should be able to let your daughter roam around the house with much less supervision than you've previously provided.

When she's about thirty months of age, you can begin slowly restoring your home to its previous state. Introduce one valuable at a time, first letting your daughter see and feel the item, then putting it where it belongs and letting her know it's not a play-thing. The discrimination between "can touch" and "can't touch" is easily made at this age, as long as parents don't introduce too many interesting things at any one time.

Here's a tip for parents of toddlers when the youngster picks up something fragile, like a piece of valuable crystal: The child is almost certain to drop and break the item if an adult puts on a horrified expression, says "Give me that!" and moves rapidly toward the child with arms outstretched and hands open like claws. Panic breeds panic. Instead, control your fears, stay in one spot, squat down so you're at eye level with the child, put a smile on your face, extend your hand palm up, and say, "Ooooh, how pretty! Will you put it in my hand so I can see too?"

If you've done a good acting job, the child will smile in return and place the item gently in your palm. Let the child know this wasn't a trick by putting her on your lap and examining the object together for a minute or so before getting up and saying, "I'm going to put this up here so we can both look at it. Isn't it pretty?" This procedure satisfies the child's curiosity, saves money, and helps build a cooperative parent–child relationship, rather than an antagonistic one.

Q: *Our three-year-old daughter has recently invented, and is spending lots of time with, an imaginary playmate she calls Cindy. Her obsession with Cindy is beginning to go a bit far. She wants me to set a place for her at the dinner table and invite her along whenever we leave the house. When I suggest that Cindy doesn't really exist, my daughter becomes extremely angry and upset. Do I have reason to be concerned, or is this just a passing phase?*

A: Your daughter's fascination with her imaginary friend is just a passing phase, but an important one. Rather than being worried, you should be glad.

Fantasy thinking emerges around age three. Like any other mental attribute, imagination must be exercised in order to strengthen and grow. Cindy is your daughter's way of doing just that. She's taking a very important step toward the eventual mastery of abstract thinking. Also, since an active imagination is essential to reading comprehension, Cindy is actually helping your daughter eventually to become a successful reader.

Trying to debate the issue of Cindy's existence with your daughter is a lost cause. To a three-year-old, if something can be imagined, that something truly exists. In your daughter's eyes and mind, Cindy is as real as you are. Three-year-olds invest a considerable amount of security in their imaginary playmates. They *need* them. No wonder your daughter became upset when you tried to reason away Cindy's existence. Just as your adult mind cannot comprehend your daughter's obsession with Cindy, her child's mind can't understand your failure to accept Cindy's existence. Call it a draw and stop worrying.

At this stage of her life, your daughter is starting to form relationships with other children. Cindy enables her to practice social skills in a safe nonthreatening context and thus strengthens her ability to interact successfully with other children. When your daughter and another child play together with Cindy, they're practicing small-group social skills.

The more your daughter plays with Cindy, the fewer demands she makes of your time and energy. Instead of relying on you for occupation, she's relying on Cindy, which effectively means she is relying on herself. The more self-reliant and resourceful your daughter becomes, the better sense of self-esteem she will have.

Any way you look at it, Cindy is probably one of the best things that's ever happened to your daughter. Her invisible friend is contributing to almost every aspect of her growth and development. Instead of worrying about Cindy, relax and count your blessings.

Q: *Much to our chagrin, our six-year-old son, Robbie, has always preferred to play with dolls and other "girl" things. He also prefers playing with girls because boys, he says, play too rough. We saw a therapist who wanted Robbie to be present at the first appointment. I felt this was unnecessary, even humiliating, so we went by ourselves. The therapist accused us not only of being "resistant" but also of "enabling" Robbie by, among other things, letting him play with dolls. At that point, my husband and I walked out, but now I'm worried that perhaps the therapist was right. How serious is this sort of problem, and do you think we're enabling?*

A: Let me answer the first half of your question by asking, "If Robbie were a little girl named Roberta who preferred playing with boys and doing "boy" things, would you be worried?" I'll bet your answer is, "Of course not!" You'd just shrug your shoulders and say, with a smile, that Roberta was a tomboy. My point is, your anxiety over Robbie's play preference reflects a knee-jerk cultural bias. Unfortunately for boys, it's generally regarded as okay—even admirable—for females to do traditionally masculine things, even wear masculine clothes, but a male who prefers stereotypical feminine things is generally looked upon with suspicion, to say the least.

You neatly avoided any mention of your real worry, which is that Robbie's preference for girl things presages adult homosexuality. The fact is, masculine play preferences for boys do not guarantee heterosexuality any more than feminine play preferences foreshadow homosexuality, and that's equally but oppositely true for girls. I can't guarantee that Robbie won't, as a young adult, announce that he's gay, but I can assure you that whether he plays with dolls or toy guns at this age will have nothing to do with his later choice of sexual partners.

Are you enabling Robbie's preference for girl things? My dictionary defines *enable* as "to make possible," so in the strictest sense of the term the answer is yes, you are definitely enabling, but so what? If Robbie were my son and he wanted to play with dolls, I too would make it possible for him to do it. If, however, the therapist was using *enable* in the pejorative psychological sense, to mean you are aiding and abetting improper behavior, then my answer is *hogwash*. In the first place, Robbie's play preferences are not improper, much less pathological. In the second, it would be highly improper of you to force Robbie to play with things he doesn't enjoy.

In answer to "How serious is Robbie's problem?" I don't see that he has any problem at all, outside of the fact that his parents think he might have one. If he hasn't already, Robbie will eventually pick up on your anxiety, which will cause him to feel self-conscious about something that is really quite innocent. (In this regard, I approve of your decision to leave Robbie out of the appointment with the therapist.) Stop worrying and enjoy being a parent. You'll only get one shot at it, you know.

When all is said and done, this is a matter of Robbie's *personality*. You didn't *cause* Robbie's personality, and you can't change it. You can, however, make him feel as if there's something wrong with who he is, in which case Robbie may never become the person God intended for him to become. And I suspect God doesn't like us messing with His creations.

6

POINT SIX

Television, Computers, and Video Games: More Than Meets the Eye

IN JANUARY 1979, Willie and I sat down for what was probably our sixth conference with Eric's third-grade teacher, Mrs. Stewart, who informed us that Eric stood absolutely no chance of being promoted to the fourth grade. She had decided to give us plenty of time to digest this news, she said, rather than surprise us with it at the end of the school year. Eric was reading more than a year behind grade level and was the worst-behaved child in class: easily distracted, inattentive, disruptive, explosive on the playground when games did not go his way, and often belligerent when confronted concerning misbehavior. In addition, he rarely finished an assignment in class and therefore came with double the homework carried home by a typical classmate, none of which Eric would have done had it not been for constant pushing and prodding by Willie and me. The situation looked bleak indeed.

The most memorable aspect of the meeting, however, occurred when I suggested to Mrs. Stewart that she employ certain "behavioral" strategies with Eric. I reminded her that I was a psychologist and had some experience in these matters. I was so proud of myself!

She looked at me for several moments, an incredulous expression on her face. Then she asked, rhetorically, "You don't get it, do you, Mr. Rosemond?"

My anger rising, I responded, "Excuse me? Get what, Mrs. Stewart?"

"You obviously think I'm supposed to do something to correct Eric's problems," she replied. "Mr. and Mrs. Rosemond, that is not my job. Eric's problems did not develop in my classroom. They developed in your home; therefore, it is your job to correct them, and when you do your job I will be able to do mine."

Needless to say, I left that conference fuming. How dare she talk to me that way?

When we got home, Willie sat me down and told me Mrs. Stewart was right. Eric's problems had developed at home. It was time, she said, to stop what we were doing and do something different.

"What?" I asked.

"Well," she said, "we didn't turn out so bad, did we? Our parents did a fairly good job with us. Let's start by being the kind of parents our parents were."

Three months later, Mrs. Stewart began our next meeting by saying, "Had someone told me back in January that I would now be telling you what I have to tell you, I'd have thought he was crazy. To come straight to the point, assuming that Eric continues to make the progress he has made over the past three months, I will promote him to the fourth grade. Quite frankly, this has been remarkable. Mr. and Mrs. Rosemond, I don't know exactly what you are doing, but *keep on doing it!*"

Eric did, in fact, pass the third grade. By the end of grade four, he was an A student. In grade seven, he was inducted into the National Beta Club honor society, and apart from some occasional minor lapses, typical of any highly gregarious, risk-taking youngster, Eric did very well throughout the rest of his academic career, including college. Now in his thirties, he is a successful commercial pilot, a successful husband, and a successful father to three young boys.

What did Willie and I do between January and April? First, this is what we did *not* do: We did not provide Eric with a tutor and we all but completely stopped helping him with his homework or even prodding him to do it. We did not put him on medication, although by today's standards he qualified for a diagnosis of attention deficit disorder (ADD), not to mention oppositional defiant disorder (ODD) and a learning disability (LD)—all the big Ds. We asked Mrs. Stewart for no special consideration, such as lowering her academic standards where Eric was concerned. What we did was simply realize that psychological self-esteem–based child-rearing had not worked, although we had certainly tried it. If we were going to get our family on track, we needed to begin raising our children pretty much the way our parents had raised us—the old-fashioned, prepsychological way.

Willie and I became our parents. The term I used in *Marriage and the Family* was *autocratic*, a bad word in our generation, the generation of apostasy. We began *telling* Eric and Amy what we wanted them to do instead of asking. We tolerated no disobedience. If one of them disobeyed, we punished instead of talked. The kids came home from school one day and were told that from that day forth they were going to do most of the housework: vacuum, dust, clean bathrooms, mop floors—the whole nine yards. We turned the parenting clock in the Rosemond family back some twenty years.

Coincidentally, around this same time, someone had given me a book by journalist Marie Winn entitled *The Plug-In Drug*. As the name implies, it was about the evils of letting children watch television. Reading Winn's description of the problems she attributed largely to TV watching—not a statistically excessive amount, mind you, but a "normal" amount—I realized Winn was describing Eric to a T and convinced Willie to try an experiment: cut the kids off cold turkey from their obvious addiction to watching television.

The next day, Eric and Amy came home from school to discover that we no longer owned a TV set. It was gone, given away to a charity. Naturally, the children were devastated. How could we do such a thing? they asked incredulously. *Everyone* had television!

"No," I pointed out, "not everyone. We don't."

For the next week or so, the children whined constantly about our decision. Mind you, other changes were taking place in our family as well. The children were now expected to do housework, lots of it, every single day. Willie and I began practicing powerful parenting. We stopped badgering the children to listen and obey. If one of them didn't immediately comply with an instruction, a punishment ensued. In a matter of two weeks, their world turned completely upside-down—or, rather, right side out.

The results were nothing short of remarkable. The children began playing more creatively, paying better attention to us, and acting generally more calm, and the level of sibling conflict—much of which had centered around disputes over what TV shows to watch—diminished considerably. Undoubtedly, some of the improvement was due to the changes we were beginning to make in our parenting, but I have no doubt but that the single most critical variable in Eric's rehabilitation was the sudden complete absence of television in his life.

Later that year, I wrote a feature-length article for the *Charlotte Observer,* which they subsequently shared with more than 200 newspapers around the country, in which I laid out what I'd discovered, through both personal experience and research, concerning the effects of watching television on young children. I had come to the conclusion that the constantly flickering image on a television screen actually disables the young brain's ability to develop a long attention span. Since a long attention span is essential to impulse control, I further concluded that TV watching prevented the development of good self-control, thus "producing" behavior problems that would not, in all likelihood, have otherwise existed. Other psychologists were infuriated! I was accused of misinforming the public and promoting hysteria, and a group of psychologists in my home state of North Carolina, I later learned, even met to discuss the possibility of convincing our licensing authority to strip me of my credentials. By this time in my life, I had learned the hard way that a point of view capable of causing general outrage and uproar is either completely misguided or absolutely on target. Having witnessed firsthand the results of breaking Eric's television addiction, I was convinced I was absolutely and unequivocally on target. Subsequent experience and research into brain development has strengthened my conviction that many of the behavioral and learning problems besetting today's children are a direct result of the fact that before he or she enters first grade, the typical American child has watched close to 5,000 hours of television! Are the problems in question due *entirely* to watching television? No, that would be a simplistic and indefensible position. Nonetheless, I am convinced that watching television contributes to a certain family culture or atmosphere that breeds disobedience, disrespect, irresponsibility, whining (and a host of other dependent, helpless behaviors), depression, sibling conflict, laziness, low impulse control, boredom, and—last but certainly not least—communication problems between family members. Speaking personally, I have not watched television on any sort of regular basis since 1979. I've never seen an episode of *Seinfeld* or *Home Improvement.* I do not watch television for news or commentary or current events; rather, I read newspapers, magazines, and books, as does Willie. We do own a nineteen-inch TV set. It occupies a unassuming space in our bookshelves. It's connected to a DVD player for the purpose of watching movies, which we indulge in several times a week. We care for our grandchildren fairly often, sometimes for several days straight, during which time we never watch television, even movies, when they are awake, and they do not ask for it. When they are in our home, they play quietly and contentedly with the few toys we've stocked for them, and we never experience a moment's problem.

Since our experience with Eric (and Amy, although her "rehabilitation" was not nearly as remarkable, mostly because she's three and a half years younger than her brother), I've taken my no-TV spiel to every corner of the United States through public presentations (over 200 in a typical year), a syndicated newspaper column, and books. Hundreds of people have since shared what I now call no-TV testimonies with me, people who have become persuaded to remove television from their children's lives, if not from the home altogether. *Not one person has said anything other than it was the very best decision they ever made for their children and family.* The very best! Given our experience with Eric and Amy, this does not surprise me at all. In all likelihood, getting rid of the TV set (or at the very least unplugging the cable or antennae and hooking your set into a VCR or DVD and using it strictly as a movie machine) is the very best thing for all concerned, so that's what I'm going to try and persuade you to do. If you don't even want to consider being so persuaded, skip the rest of this chapter.

How *Not* to Raise a Gifted Child

Between birthdays two and six, the average American preschool child watches some twenty-five hours of television a week. This isn't a number I pulled out of thin air, but one that's been confirmed by one Nielsen survey after another since the early 1970s. In fact, until recently, the number was closer to thirty hours a week! The higher the educational level of any individual child's parents, however, the more likely it is that the child is watching less than the national average. Since the average reader of parenting books is fairly well educated, I'm going to adjust the above figure downward to twenty-one hours a week, or an average of three hours a day.

Multiply twenty-one hours a day times fifty-two weeks, and the preschool child of the typical adult reader of parenting books is probably watching 1,092 hours of television a year, for a grand total of 4,368 hours between birthdays two and six. Based on a twelve-hour day, this means that preschool children spend roughly one-fourth of their daily discretionary time sitting in front of a TV set.

You're probably saying, "That's not my child! My child watches no more than ten hours of television a week!" That's a perfectly understandable reaction, but I'm going to burst your bubble. Studies have also shown that most parents tend to underestimate their children's television viewing time by approximately 50 percent. They also tend not to count time their children spend watching videos. So if you think your child is watching ten hours a week, the actual number is probably much higher, perhaps even as high as my original figure of twenty-one. On the other hand, if you insist, let's say your preschooler watches an average of "only" ten hours a week. That means he or she will have watched 2,080 hours by age six. Does that make you feel more comfortable?

In order to appreciate fully what these numbers mean, you must understand that your child's preschool years are among the most important of all. Developmental psychologists and educators refer to them as the *formative* years. They are called formative because they comprise that period during which the young child is discovering, developing, and strengthening the skills he or she will need to become a creative and competent adult.

Nearly every human being is born already programmed for giftedness of nearly every conceivable form: intellectual, artistic, musical, athletic, interpersonal, spiritual. During the formative years, these programs are activated by exposing the young child to environments and experiences that push the right genetic buttons, so to speak.

In other words, releasing the richness of each child's developmental birthright requires that the child have sufficient opportunities for exploration, discovery, and imaginative play. Environments and experiences that stimulate and exercise the young child's emerging skills are, therefore, compatible with his or her developmental needs. On the other hand, environments that fail to offer these important opportunities are incompatible. Time is of the essence. Developmental research has consistently demonstrated that a child has approximately six years in which to get in touch with the many basic skills that comprise competency and creativity. The formative years are the window of opportunity for giftedness. A child of six who, for lack of opportunity, is deficient with respect to one or more aspects of giftedness will probably always have problems in those areas.

When a child sits and becomes absorbed in watching television, that television becomes his or her audiovisual environment. Since the average American child spends more time watching television than doing any other single thing during the formative years, we must conclude that television has become a primary environment for our children and will therefore influence their development in significant, far-reaching ways.

The question, then, becomes: "Does television create or constitute a healthy or unhealthy environment for children?"

For the past forty years or more, social scientists have been attempting to answer that very question. Their research has focused almost exclusively on the effects of television's content—whether, for instance, a program is violent or nonviolent, sexy or not—on the social behavior of children. This has had unfortunate consequences, because the average American parent has been led to believe that television's only danger to children is a matter of theme. If a child is watching *Sesame Street* or a family sitcom, we tend to think there's no harm. On the other hand, if the child is watching a program that contains themes of sex or violence or both, we're probably going to turn the television off, change the channel, or send the child from the room. Because of this tendency to judge the book of television by its cover, American parents are largely unaware of the more insidious and far more damaging influence of TV-watching as a *process* independent of the content of the programs.

In order to see firsthand what I'm talking about, the next time your child is watching television, look at the child instead of the program. As they say, a picture is worth more than a thousand words. Check out the illustration. Not a pretty sight, is it? Now ask yourself, "What is that child doing?" The answer, of course, is "Nothing." Not one competency skill, not one gift, is being exercised.

Regardless of the program, therefore, watching television inhibits the development of initiative, curiosity, resourcefulness, creativity, motivation, imagination, reasoning and problem-solving abilities, communication skills, social skills, fine and gross motor skills, and eye–hand coordination. Shall I go on? Because television causes the child to stare at, rather than scan, the environment, it's safe to add that visual tracking skills are not being strengthened either.

Furthermore, watching television interferes significantly with development of the attention span. Many people mistakenly believe that if children can sit mesmerized in front of a television set for two or three hours at a stretch, they must have—or at least be developing—a long attention span. That's an optical illusion. The picture on a TV screen changes, on the average, every three to four seconds. Because of this constant perceptual shift, or flicker, the TV-watching child isn't attending to any one thing for longer than a few seconds. As a result, watching television is a strangely paradoxical situation for the young child. The more time spent watching television, the shorter the attention span becomes.

Last, but by no means least, because the action on a TV set shifts constantly and capriciously backward, forward, and laterally in time (not to mention from subject matter to subject matter), television fails to promote the logical sequential thinking that is essential to an understanding of cause-and-effect relationships. This causes difficulties both in following directions and in anticipating consequences.

Once again, these failings are the same regardless of whether the child is watching *Sesame Street,* an adult movie on late-night cable, or a video rental. In each case, the child is watching in the same passive manner. This means that for the preschool child, program content is a largely irrelevant issue as far as that child's development is concerned.

As I said earlier, the preschool child's competency skills emerge and begin developing through exercise. During the formative years, play is the natural form this exercise takes. But children watching television are not playing. In fact, they aren't doing anything competent at all. Every hour, therefore, that a preschool child spends watching television is an hour of that child's potential being wasted.

One is forced to conclude that, examined from a developmental perspective, watching television is a deprivational experience for young children. It deprives them of the opportunity to discover and take delight in developing their natural potential for giftedness. And the sad fact is, that once that window of opportunity closes, it can never again be fully opened.

But don't just take my word for it. As with everything else, the proof is in the pudding. I'm saying that the child who spends a significant amount of time during the formative years parked in front of a television set is likely to be much less competent than he or she would otherwise have been. If watching television diminishes a child's potential for competency, there ought to be evidence that our TV-generation children are less competent than children of previous generations. Does such evidence exist? Indeed it does.

Television Disabilities

Since 1955, when American children began watching significant amounts of television, scholastic achievement test scores have steadily declined. As a nation, our literacy level has declined as well. Today, nearly one of every five seventeen-year-olds in this country is functionally illiterate, meaning he or she cannot read with comprehension at a fifth-grade level. The functionally illiterate individual cannot read a newspaper, a recipe, or a manual for operating a power tool. Both trends become even more alarming when one considers that academic standards are lower today than they were in 1955. Today's fifth-grade reader, for instance, is comparable to a third-grade reader from 1955.

To top it off, since 1955, learning disabilities have become nearly epidemic in our schools, both public and private. Learning-disabled children are children who can't seem to get it all together when it comes to acquiring the basic academic skills of reading and writing. Some researchers estimate that as many as three out of ten children in our schools today are learning-disabled to one degree or another. Interestingly enough, the symptoms that characterize a population of learning-disabled children and the list of developmental deficiencies inherent to the TV-watching experience are one and the same.

Learning-disabled children often have visual scanning problems. Their eyes fail to scan a line of print smoothly from left to right. They tend to exhibit problems with eye–hand coordination as with well as fine and gross motor skills. They are often not proficient at tasks requiring active problem-solving (reading, for example). They are frequently deficient with respect to active listening and communication skills. They often display social adjustment difficulties.

Their teachers typically report that these children have difficulty following a sequence of directions or the steps involved in solving a problem and frequently describe them as passive and easily frustrated by challenges. They tend to be unimaginative, and imagination is essential to reading comprehension. Last but not least, almost all learning-disabled children have short attention spans.

Thus, an almost perfect parallel exists between the list of competency skills that television fails to exercise and the symptoms characteristic of a population of learning-disabled children. But learning disabilities are just the tip of the iceberg. Again and again, veteran teachers—those who are in the best position to have seen the steady decline in competency skills since 1955—tell me that today's children are, as a rule, less resourceful, less imaginative, and not nearly as motivated as the children they once knew and taught. They also tell me that the average child's attention span seems to have shortened significantly.

I know a woman who taught second grade in public schools for forty-four years, from 1934 to 1978. In her early years, she would bring her students back from lunch and read them stories from books that had few, if any, pictures. Up through the 1940s and early 1950s, her story time lasted one hour. In the late 1950s, however, she began noticing that most of her children were no longer able to sit still and pay attention for that length of time. So she cut her story "hour" to thirty minutes. By the mid-1960s, even though she was now reading from books that had pictures on every page, she again cut story time in half, to fifteen minutes. In 1972, because her students were unable to sit and pay attention for longer than three to five minutes, she eliminated story time altogether.

I've heard stories like this one from nearly every veteran teacher with whom I've ever talked, and I'm not at all surprised. You take a child whose formative years have been dominated by television—a child whose competency skills are weak because television has pacified nearly every aspect of the inborn potential for competency—and you put that child in a classroom where learning demands resourcefulness, initiative, curiosity, motivation, imagination, eye–hand coordination, active listening, adequate communication skills,

functional reasoning and problem-solving skills, and a long attention span, and the distinct possibility exists that that child is going
to have problems of learning and performance in school.

It would be a gross oversimplification to imply that television
alone is responsible for the plague of learning and motivation problems in our schools. Likewise, it would be naive to ignore the obvious connection between the deficiencies inherent to the *process* of
watching television and the deficiencies in competency skills that
characterize not only the learning-disabled child but also seemingly this entire generation of television-overdosed children. Keep
in mind also that no other single influence has so dramatically
altered the nature of childhood in the last fifty years than the TV set.

The Plug-In Drug

Equally frightening is the addictive quality of television. The more
children watch it, the more they want to watch. If they are prevented
from watching, they often go through a period of emotional withdrawal that's stressful not only to them but to their parents. They
become sullen, moody, and irritable. They become obsessed with
television and make repeated attempts to connect with it. They
become aggressive, unruly, and anxious. Frustration and anxiety
build, choking off their ability to engage in constructive behavior.

When addicted children aren't plugged into the TV set, they
will probably plug themselves into one or both of their parents,
hassling, whining, and bored.

After reaching the limits of tolerance, parents are likely to put
them back in front of the TV set, hoping to buy a moment's peace.
They don't realize that their children's inability to occupy themselves is partly a result of the time they spend glued to the tube.
Television drains children of initiative, motivation, and autonomy
and weakens their tolerance for stress.

But why is television addictive while radio, for instance, is not?
It's a matter of different technologies. Typically, live or filmed television productions are shot using several cameras, each watching
the action from a different angle.

The networks have found that viewers will watch the screen longer when the scene shifts from one camera to the next. So shift it does, usually at three-second intervals.

This is why small children will sit for long periods, transfixed by programs they cannot possibly comprehend. The incessant shifting of reference point overrides the need for understanding. It does not interest children—it mesmerizes them.

Paradoxically, a child who sits staring at a television screen for several hours is adapting to an attention span of a few seconds and thus learning how *not* to pay attention.

After six thousand hours of this insidious training, the child arrives in a public school classroom, where the teacher discovers that the child cannot concentrate.

Since television has never required anything of its watchers, these children don't finish anything they start. They don't know why they can't sit still, can't pay attention, and can't finish their work—they just know they *can't*. And so "I can't" becomes more and more a part of their self-image.

Veteran teachers have remarked to me that, as a group, children today are far less imaginative and resourceful than children were a generation ago, when childhood TV viewing was less than half what it is today. This observation is hardly surprising. The explicit nature of the television experience leaves little to a child's imagination. In fact, it subtly discourages children from exercising their creative resources.

Over the past thirty years, we have allowed television networks to create their own myths; among them are the terms *children's program, family program,* and *educational program.*

Presumably, programs like *Sesame Street* are children's programs. But watching television is not an appropriate pastime for any children, preschoolers in particular. Television is a handicap to childhood, not a help. There really are no children's programs. The so-called children's program exists and thrives because of *parents,* not children. These shows keep children occupied, but, contrary to what their producers would have parents believe, they offer nothing of value. There are no programs for families either. The terms *family* and *program* are incompatible, because the moment a group of people calling themselves a family sits down to watch television, the family process stops.

The terms *watch* and *together* are also incompatible. You don't watch television together. You watch alone. Regardless of how many people are in the same room watching the same television, each has retired into a solitary audiovisual tunnel.

Television may not actually be spawning communication problems, but it certainly becomes an excuse for maintaining them. The more that members of a family drift apart, the more watching television becomes a convenient means of dutifully enduring one another's presence while simultaneously avoiding acknowledgment of it—all under the pretense that watching television is a family affair.

"All television is educational," said Nicholas Johnson, former member of the Federal Communications Commission. "The question is, What's being learned?"

On the surface, a child watching a Saturday morning cartoon and a child watching *Wild Kingdom* are viewing entirely different kinds of programs; one is pure entertainment, the other supposedly educational. But no one program earns the right to the term *educational* more than any other. A child watching a cartoon and a child watching *Wild Kingdom* are both exposed to the same educational message: You can get something for nothing.

Children are impressionable little people. They have no way to evaluate television's insidious message and thereby resist it.

The March 3, 1990, issue of *TV Guide* carried an article on video games that quoted Patricia Marks Greenfield, professor of psychology at UCLA and author of *Mind and Media: The Effects of Television, Video Games, and Computers*, as saying, "Video games develop a whole bunch of intellectual abilities, like problem-solving and visual/spatial skills." Greenfield also pooh-poohed the notion that children can become addicted to video games. Commenting on the observation that some children seem to become obsessed with them, she said, "Of course, kids are going to want to play till they've mastered a game, but I would call that mastery motivation rather than addiction."

Professor Greenfield needs to come down from her ivory tower and talk to people like Ken and Kathy Kelly of Charlotte, North Carolina. After determining that they would never purchase a video game unit for their five-year-old son, Kenny, they finally relented and bought him a Nintendo system. Here's what the Kellys had to say about their decision.

"We had two rules: Kenny was to share with his sister, and they could play for forty minutes a day. After just a few days, we began seeing changes in Kenny's behavior. He became irritable and bossy. He would get very upset—crying, stomping his feet—when he couldn't get to the next level in Super Mario. He constantly tried to sneak additional time, and there were several nights when we awakened at three o'clock in the morning to find him playing Nintendo.

"Kenny also began to balk at going to school. When we dropped him off, he would start crying and screaming. On several occasions, his teachers had to help peel him out of the car. He also started fighting with his classmates and sassing his teachers. He was belligerent with us and our baby-sitter.

"We couldn't figure out what was the matter. We were almost at the end of our rope when I read about a situation in your book that was very similar to our own, so we removed the Nintendo from the house and told Kenny it was broken. "Within a few days, Kenny was back. No more tantrums, no more belligerent, sassy behavior, and he started happily going to school. Needless to say, the unit will never be 'fixed,' and we'll happily go back to being the only house in the neighborhood without one."

The Kellys' experience could be dismissed if it were an isolated one, but it isn't. Over the past few years, several hundred parents (no exaggeration) have written me concerning similar video-game–related horror stories. These tales don't sound like description of "mastery motivation" to me. I've been around enough addicts and enough highly motivated people to know the difference.

Video games are not really games at all. They provoke high levels of stress and are, indeed, addictive in the sense that many children become obsessed with constantly increasing their scores (or "skill levels," as they are deceptively termed). Compared to the harm they are obviously capable of causing, the contention that video games improve certain problem-solving and visual/perceptual skills rates a big "so what?"

Unfortunately, it's what many parents want to hear.

Questions?

Q: *What guidelines do you recommend to help parents decide how much television to let children watch?*

A: First of all, I don't believe there's any justification for letting a preschool child watch any television at all. In fact, I think it makes sense to keep a child completely away from television until he or she has learned to read, reads fairly well, and enjoys reading. For most children, that point will be reached between the third and fifth grades. Once literacy has been fairly well established, I see no problem with letting a child watch programs that represent life in a realistic manner and broaden the child's understanding of the world, his or her relationship to it, and how it works. Nature specials, documentaries, historically based movies, sports, and cultural events all fit these criteria. Such programs open up the child's view of the world and stimulate visits to the library to find out more about the subject, be it whales, baseball, or the Civil War. Regardless of the quality of the programs being chosen, however, I strongly recommend that parents not allow children to watch any more than five hours of television a week.

Q: *What about programs like* Sesame Street?

A: All television programs, regardless of content, are watched in the same passive manner. From this perspective, *Sesame Street* is as much a one-way street as any other.

Programs like *Sesame Street* appeal to parents because of their supposed educational value. But the notion that preschool children can learn the alphabet, numerals, and even a basic reading vocabulary from *Sesame Street* is nothing more than hype, brought to you by the same folks who tell us that a certain toothpaste will make us more appealing to persons of the opposite sex. My reaction to the sales pitch for *Sesame Street* is simply, "So what?"

Studies have consistently failed to demonstrate that *Sesame Street* imparts any lasting academic advantage to its young consumers. In fact, as long ago as 1975, a study conducted by the Russell Sage Foundation concluded that heavy viewers of *Sesame Street* demonstrated fewer gains in cognitive skills than light viewers.

First, there's no trick to teaching children these skills. Second, children don't need to know them before they go to school. Third, a classroom provides a much more appropriate and effective environment for learning basic skills.

Q: *Television may not be doing anything wonderful for my two small children, but it certainly helps me get some time to myself during the day. Besides, I still fail to see how a few hours a day spent watching programs like* Sesame Street *can harm a child's mind. Have you ever tried to keep small children entertained all day every day?*

A: You are sadly mistaken if you think television is doing you or your children any favors. The more a young child watches television, the more that child will eventually come to depend on it as a primary source of occupation and entertainment. Every dependency encumbers the growth of self-reliance. Young children who become dependent on television will, when the set is off, seek to satisfy that dependency in other ways. Predictably, they transfer it to the next most available and receptive object or person, and Mom is usually right up there at the top of the list.

A vicious circle quickly develops. The more children watch television, the more television pacifies their initiative, resourcefulness, imagination, and creativity. When the set is off, instead of finding something else to do, they look for Mom to take over where the television left off. They complain of being bored, they whine for Mom to find something to entertain them, they demand that she become a playmate. Partly out of fear that her child will interpret any denial as rejection, Mom is at first likely to cooperate with these complaints and demands. But when it becomes obvious that the child can't get enough of her, Mom begins looking for an excuse to turn on the TV set again. Any excuse will do, but *Sesame Street* is one of the best.

There you have it. The child becomes increasingly addicted to watching television, and the mother becomes increasingly addicted to permitting it. Little does she realize that this strategy is slowly eroding the only thing that will ever give her and her child the independence they need from each other, and that is her child's ability to be self-sufficient.

What, pray tell, did children do before television? They entertained themselves, that's what! Weather permitting, they went outside to play. They made mud pies and built forts out of tree branches and skipped stones across ponds and played It and Mother May I? and pretended to be all sorts of heroes and heroines and damsels in distress, and they rarely, if ever, complained of having nothing to do. Remember? This is the television-generation child's complaint. When are we going to wake up and realize it isn't a coincidence?

Q: *Our five-month-old loves to look at television. While I watch my programs in the evening, she lies on her quilt and stares at the screen. I think she likes the play of movement, brightness, and color on the screen, but I'm beginning to worry that her fascination with the television could become a habit. I know it is detrimental for children to watch too much television, that it can hurt their powers of imagination and creativity, not to mention their reading ability. Can her early interest in the television become a habit? Should I cut back my own watching on her behalf? When, if ever, is it all right to let her start watching?*

A: In answer to your first question: Television is definitely habit-forming. The earlier a habit is formed, the more it influences the individual's attitudes and behavior. I would think, therefore, that by letting your infant daughter stare at the television screen for significant periods of time you are increasing the possibility that she will someday become a television junkie.

Movement, brightness, and color may play a part in your daughter's fascination with watching television, but the key element in her growing attachment—and possible eventual addiction—is the constant shifting of perspective and picture. If you pay attention, you will notice that the picture on the screen changes, or flickers, every few seconds.

The flicker is there to maintain the interest of the viewer. It hooks and holds the viewer's attention in its seductively hypnotic embrace. The constant flickering of the screen is stimulating in a pleasant sort of way, and positive stimulation amounts to reward. In effect, each flicker is an electronic M&M, positively reinforcing the viewer's increasing passivity. When we say a person is "glued to the tube," we aren't far wrong.

In the language of psychology, television puts the viewer on a "variable interval schedule" of reinforcement. Variable because the interval between flickers isn't constant, reinforcement because each flicker is pleasantly stimulating. Now, listen to this sentence from a contemporary psychology text: "Research indicates that learning under variable reward conditions lasts longer than learning under any other reward schedule." In other words, variable rewards result in the formation of persistent and possibly lifelong habits.

So is your daughter in danger of becoming a television addict? Most definitely. Should you curtail your own watching on her behalf? I'd recommend it, but how about on your own behalf as well? You might use the time to read. Not only would reading enrich your own life, but studies also show that young children who often see their parents reading become better readers than children whose parents rarely read.

When is it all right to let a child start watching television? Not until he or she can read well. After that time, there's no real harm in letting children watch up to five hours of television a week, preferably programs that expand their understanding of the real world.

Q: *My husband and I are seeing a psychologist because of discipline problems with our six-year-old son. Chuck has also had problems in school this year, in concentrating and in finishing work. The psychologist recently told us that part of Chuck's problem is attention deficit disorder. He said Chuck's short attention span is causing most of the problems at school and is contributing to many of the problems we are having with him at home. We agree that Chuck is impulsive and very difficult to control but are somewhat confused about the attention-span thing. If, as the psychologist said, Chuck can't control his attention-span, then why is he able to sit quietly and watch television for two or three hours at a stretch? In fact, television is just about the only thing that* will *keep him quiet. The psychologist had no explanation for that. Do you?*

A: The fact that your son can watch television for two to three hours doesn't contradict a diagnosis of attention deficit disorder. Television holds Chuck's interest in a way the everyday world doesn't because the picture on a TV screen changes every few seconds.

Not only is television's flicker highly stimulating, it also has a mesmerizing, or hypnotic, effect upon the viewer. This hook is created through the use of anywhere from three to five cameras in the production studio. Some people seem better able to resist the bait than others, but children are especially susceptible. Furthermore, television's constantly shifting perspective is perfectly suited to a child with attention deficit disorder.

Although you find that television keeps Chuck quiet, it's actually making his attention-span problems worse rather than better. He can watch television for three hours and not have to watch any one thing for longer than about ten seconds, four seconds being the norm. In other words, television is actually reinforcing Chuck's short attention span. The longer he watches, the more his short attention span becomes habit.

Where else in the real world does the scene in front of you flicker every few seconds? Nowhere. So the perceptual habits Chuck develops while watching television will be worthless, even harmful, in other environments, particularly school.

In my experience, the most effective treatment plan for children with moderate to severe cases of attention deficit disorder involves a combination of behavioral interventions along with a medication such as Ritalin to assist in impulse control and the development of a longer attention span. In addition, I always recommend that these kids be allowed to watch no more than three hours of television a week—preferably shows like nature documentaries, where content rather than production technique is the hook.

Q: *Our eight-year-old son has a learning disability that handicaps his ability to pay attention, follow directions, and correctly decipher the printed word. He's already more than a year behind in reading skills. We recently watched a talk show featuring a specialist in learning disabilities who said most, if not all, learning disabilities are inherited. Is there a way of finding out for sure whether Greg's disability is inherited?*

A: The fact is, learning disabilities come in many varieties, and no one knows for certain what causes any given one. Some may be inherited, or at least related in some way to genetic factors. Even if there were a way of making this determination, I don't think "bad genes" would be found to account for more than a small minority.

Since the early 1960s, learning disabilities have become epidemic among school-age children in America. Many say the sharp increase is due to better identification procedures. That argument doesn't make a lot of sense. Better identification procedures don't cause epidemics; they come about as a result of them. I think we've had to put more effort into research and identification *because* of the increase.

It's interesting to note that learning disabilities are not nearly as much a problem in European school-age populations as they are in the United States. Since we share much of the same gene pool, this would seem to minimize a genetic explanation and suggest that the reason for this country's epidemic may be largely environmental.

The question then becomes: "What are the most typical differences in upbringing between European and American children?"

There are many, but one of the most striking has to do with television. By and large, European children watch less than five hours of television a week, and American children watch between twenty-five and thirty. Can large amounts of television cause learning disabilities? Developmental theory strongly suggests it can.

A vast array of skills and talents is contained within the human genetic code. In order to activate this program, the preschool child must be exposed to environments and experiences that promote the exercise of those talents. In other words, the more creatively active the child is during his or her preschool—formative—years, the more talented he or she will eventually be.

Watching television is a "passivity," not an activity. It does not properly engage human potential, whether it be motor, intellectual, creative, social, sensory, verbal, or emotional. Therefore, by its very nature and regardless of the program, television is a deprivational experience for the preschool child.

Reading is not one skill but a collection of skills. In order to learn to read well, a child must come to the task with the complete collection. If pieces of the puzzle are missing or damaged, learning to read will be that much more frustrating.

Remember that the average American child has watched four-thousand-plus hours of television before entering first grade. Think of it. Can we truly expect a puzzle to endure that amount of developmental deprivation and survive intact? And let us not forget that learning-disabled children are only the tip of the "Why-Can't-Johnny-Read" iceberg. Since the early 1950s, scholastic achievement measures have slipped steadily downhill, and illiteracy among seventeen-year-olds has risen to 25 percent.

Could our love affair with television be lurking behind our national reading crisis? We may never know for sure. The question is: Is it worth the risk?

Q: *Is there any truth to the idea that watching violence on television can make children more violent?*

A: In the mid-sixties, a growing number of people became concerned about television's preoccupation with murder and mayhem. In particular, the question was asked, "What possible adverse effects could a daily dose of video violence have on the impressionable minds of America's children?"

The Report to the Surgeon General on Television and Social Behavior, published in 1972, verified that children can and often do act on the suggestion, inherent in the themes of many TV programs, that violence is an acceptable way of handling conflict and other problem situations. The idea that violence on television can stimulate violence on the playground has since become generally accepted, but the so-called smoking gun, the tie that could forever bind TV violence to aggressive behavior in children, has yet to be found.

No matter. After all, the public has a scapegoat on which to hang the growing threat of juvenile aggression; consumer advocacy groups, like Action for Children's Television, have a drum to beat; and the networks can demonstrate their sensitivity to social issues by reducing violence on television. In the final analysis, all this brouhaha costs the networks nothing.

There's definitely reason to suspect a link between television and aggressive behavior among children. Since the mid-1950s, when television first moved into our homes, the number of violent crimes attributed to juveniles has increased more than tenfold. Over the same period, big-city public schools have become a battleground, where students fight not only among themselves but also with their teachers. Even without a final answer from the scientific establishment, the anecdotal evidence strongly suggests that the television generation is also a more violent generation.

Efforts to prove (or disprove) this theory, however, might be exercises in barking up the wrong tree. The relationship between television and aggressive behavior in children may have more to do with process than content, more to do with the watching than with what's being watched.

Animal behaviorist Harry Harlow of the University of Wisconsin isolated juvenile chimpanzees in environments that offered no opportunities for play. He observed unusually violent behavior in these chimps when he reunited them with normally reared peers.

Psychologist Jerome Singer of Yale University found evidence that children who engage in frequent fantasy play are less likely to be aggressive and hostile and better able to tolerate frustration than children who, for whatever reasons, do not engage in make-believe games.

Joseph Chilton Pearce, author of *Magical Child*, writes that play is the most important of all childhood activities. It is through active, imaginative play, Pearce says, that children develop "creative competence," or mastery of their environment.

In his book *The Bond of Power*, Pearce adds that children who are not allowed extensive playtime or whose play is restricted to forms prescribed by adults (store-bought toys, adult-supervised activities) develop feelings of isolation and come to perceive the world as a threat instead of a challenge. Anxiety causes them either to withdraw or to attempt to control the world by force. In this regard, it's interesting to note that the incidence of depression, long regarded by psychiatrists and psychologists as violence turned within, is also on the rise among our nation's children.

The average American child, while sitting and staring at thirty hours of television a week, is not playing in *any* sense of the term. Watching is hardly doing anything at all. If play, especially fantasy play, is as essential to the formation of a healthy personality as Harlow, Singer, and Pearce indicate, television is fundamentally unhealthy for children regardless of the program being watched.

It is distinctly and disturbingly possible that television can so isolate a child from the world (while seeming to bring the world closer) that rage or retreat are, ultimately, the child's only options.

Q: *Do you feel about computers the way you feel about television?*

A: A growing number of experts are recommending that young children not be allowed on computers for any reason at all. These people are not technophobes; rather, they are psychologists and educators who have taken a cold hard look at the issue of kids and computers and found potential problems in the mix.

Psychologist and author Jane Healy spent several years researching the issue. She began with a favorable attitude toward educational computing but came reluctantly to the conclusion that computers stifle learning and creativity and may cause damage to both vision and posture. She even speculated that early introduction to computer "learning" may also interfere with proper brain development. Her research led to a book, *Failure to Connect: How Computers Affect Our Children's Minds and What We Can Do About It*. "We have no evidence that stands up under scrutiny," Healy says, "that computer education is helpful for learning in children under the fourth grade."

Douglas Sloan, professor of history and education at Columbia University's Teachers College, feels likewise. He charges that companies like Intel that provide free computers to schools have no appreciation for child development or a proper educational process. The motive behind their philanthropy, Sloan says, is money.

Healy would not introduce computers until the seventh grade. Theodore Roszak, a history professor and author of *The Cult of Information*, would wait until high school. Computers download information, he says. They do not teach children to think. "The Internet," Roszak told *The Dallas Morning News*, "offers electronic graffiti. The idea that [children] should be swimming in a sea of information is idiotic. The essence of thinking is mastering ideas."

Said another way, computer education may be imparting technical skills, but it is not imparting knowledge. Clifford Stoll, author of *High-Tech Heretic: Why Computers Don't Belong in the Classroom*, says the instant gratification involved in downloading information off the Internet—to which 94 percent of America's public schools are now connected—"discourages study, reflection, and observation."

But teachers and administrators, education's front line, are seemingly in thrall to the new technology. This is unfortunate because, as has been the case with every other fad embraced by public education over the last forty years, research into computer education and its effect on child development or the learning process is incomplete. Worse, much of the existing research raises lots of red flags.

Unfortunately, America's parents are also sold on the benefits of computers. If booming sales of academic programs for preschoolers are any indication, parents seem to think the sooner children get their hands on a mouse, the better. As a result, it's become difficult for schools, preschools included, to market themselves if they don't have computers in every classroom.

But some schools are bucking the trend. The Calvert School in Baltimore is one such low-tech bastion. Calvert's students are required to write daily compositions. During a visit in the fall of 1999, I was impressed by the level of literacy reflected in compositions by children as young as first grade. Headmaster Merrill Hall told me computers are not introduced until the fifth grade, and parents of children in grades K–4 are discouraged in letting their children use computers at home.

If what I saw at Calvert is any indication, Healy, Roszak, and Stoll are right. Computers and the Internet are certainly more impressive than libraries, pens, and paper, but education is not about impressive technology. It's about acquiring knowledge and learning to think, in which case libraries, pens, and paper are the clear winner.

Q: *Our board of education has just approved the installation of computers in the schools. Several questions remain, one of which is whether to make computer-assisted education available to children at all levels of instruction. As you might expect, there is no consensus on this issue. The progressives are in favor of computers at every grade level; the purists argue for a traditional education during the elementary years (K–6). We would like to know where you stand on this issue.*

A: I stand slightly left of purist and considerably right of progressive. Computer-assisted education at the early elementary level (K–3) isn't sensible, necessary, or practical.

Like any other set of abilities, intellectual skills unfold according to an immutable maturation sequence. Each stage of growth develops on previous stages and forms the framework for succeeding ones. Furthermore, each stage is compatible with and nurtured by certain forms of learning. Harm can be done either by failure to provide appropriate forms or by imposing inappropriate ones.

Computers present an inappropriate instructional format for early elementary children because, for the most part, a child's cognitive abilities are not mature enough before fourth grade for either the level of learning technology represented by a computer or the level of abstraction inherent to the computer-learning process.

It may not make developmental sense to put computers in early elementary classrooms, but I'm not surprised at the general eagerness to do so. It is typically American to try to pull the maturational horse behind a cart full of technological hardware.

I notice that several computer companies are pushing software for children as young as two or three, along with the insinuation that the child who isn't "computer literate" by the time he or she enters school will be forever a cultural cripple. This is the latest farce from Madison Avenue, the same bunch who bring you soaps that keep your hands looking younger longer and more equally delirious nonsense. Need I tell you that people who write advertising copy aren't interested in your child?

At a seminar sponsored by several big corporations, the question was raised, "How important is it that elementary children become familiar with computers?" The consensus: Not important. The technology is changing so rapidly that whatever children learn now will have to be unlearned when they enter the marketplace. The fact is, our public schools simply don't have the resources to keep up with the innovations. Furthermore, programming and design are the only two really marketable computer skills. Depending on the software package involved, virtually anyone can be taught to operate a computer in anywhere from three hours to three days. Definitely, computers are here to stay and schools have a responsibility to familiarize children with them, but not to act as if their lives and livelihood depend on it.

Since, in the history of our species, written and print communication evolved before computers, it seems logical to require that a youngster attain a certain level of proficiency in reading, writing, and arithmetic before graduating to computer learning. For instance, if we set fourth-grade achievement as the standard, some children would be ready in second grade, others not until much later.

In his landmark book *The Disappearance of Childhood*, Neil Postman makes the point that mastery of traditional literacy skills (reading and writing) is essential to maintaining an important—nay, vital—distinction between adulthood and childhood. Television and other electric media, Postman says, erase this distinction and render it meaningless.

No doubt computers represent a quantum leap in human toolmaking, with benefits limited only by our vision. But unless that vision incorporates and is tempered by an appreciation for what childhood is all about, we risk doing more harm than good to our children—and therefore ourselves—with this new technology. With this in mind, a few words from early-twentieth-century education philosopher John Dewey seems apropos: "If we identify ourselves with the real instincts and needs of childhood, and [require] only [their] fullest assertion and growth . . . discipline and culture of adult life shall all come in their due season."

Q: *We recently bought a popular and expensive video game unit for our eight-year-old son. Actually, he earned it by making good grades in school. We're beginning to think we made a mistake, however, because all he wants to do is use it. We've also seen some disturbing personality changes—a lower tolerance for frustration, temper tantrums, more conflict with his younger brother, talking back to us—and wonder if they could be related to his obsession with the video games. Unfortunately, we don't see how we can take it away or even put limits on it without seeming to break our promise. Any suggestions?*

A: You're not alone. I've heard the same story of regret from lots of parents. I said it in 1982, when the first wave of the video game craze hit, and I'll say it again: At the very least, these devices are worthless. At most, they are dangerous. The younger the child, the greater the potential for danger. (Before I go any further, I need to distinguish between the type of video games that are included in educational software and video games that are noneducational. My remarks pertain exclusively to the latter.)

In the first place, video games are *not* toys. By definition, a toy is something that provides opportunity for creative, imaginative play as well as constructive learning. Not only are video games noncreative and nonconstructive, they're also stressful. I've watched lots of children, including my own, "play" video games. They don't look like they've having fun. Typically, the body is tense, the facial expression strained. Then there's the howl of protest, if not temper tantrum, when the GAME OVER! sign flashes. If this is fun, things have certainly changed since I was a kid. I'd call this Type A behavior.

In the second place, video games lead to addiction. In this case, the "high" is a high score. The problem is, no score is ever high enough. As in a drug addiction, where the addict must constantly increase the dose in order to feel satisfied, the video-game–addicted child becomes obsessed with constantly increasing the score.

A situation of this sort can lead to exactly the kinds of behavior and personality changes you describe. Put a child—or any human being for that matter—in a stress-producing environment for long periods of time, and you're going to see negative behavior changes. Prolonged stress lowers an individual's tolerance for frustration and increases the likelihood of conflict in relationships as well as other acting-out behaviors. Eventually, the individual's coping skills break down completely. Keep in mind also that children are far more vulnerable than adults to the effects of stress.

In conclusion, I don't think you should have bought your son a video game unit in the first place. But you've raised a good point: Since you promised you would, what can you do now?

You can limit his game time to, for instance, thirty minutes a day on nonschool days only. Or, better yet, you can tell him, "We made a mistake," and take it away completely. Perhaps he'd agree to let you sell it and replace it with something of equal dollar value (but greater play value), like a new bike. Believe me, the additional expense would be worth it.

Q: *What changes did you see in your children during the four years that you didn't have a TV set?*

A: When we removed the television set, Eric was making mediocre grades in school, he didn't like to read, had no particular interests, and often complained of being bored. Amy's grades were better than her brother's, but she only read what she had to for school and had become a world-class couch potato.

After reading Marie Winn's excellent and eye-opening book *The Plug-In Drug,* Willie and I moved the television out of their lives and eventually out of ours, as well. After about three months of hearing what mean parents we were, we began to notice a definite change for the better in both children's behavior and attitude. To begin with, they stopped complaining of having nothing to do. They became more outgoing, communicative, and affectionate. They became more active socially, and we saw marked improvement in their social skills. There was less bickering between them. We saw a definite improvement in their senses of humor. They began reading more and even asked to go to the library. When we went to the mall, they'd ask for the bookstore instead of the toy store. Their grades improved, Eric's in particular.

But by far the very best result of removing television from their lives was that both children began acting like children again. Their play became more creative and imaginative. Amy would, for instance, spend entire afternoons acting out the parts to various story records. Eric built forts and log cabins in the woods behind our house.

Within a year, both kids had developed hobbies they are very much involved with to this day. Eric became quite skilled at building models and was particularly interested in World War II military equipment. He would purchase a model kit and then go to the library and research how and where the machine was used, how it was painted, and so on. When he'd done his homework, he'd build the model, airbrush it to achieve an authentic look, and then build a diorama within which to display it. Each model became not only an exercise in creativity but a history lesson. Eventually, Eric became interested in airplanes. For his high school graduation gift, he asked for flying lessons. Today, he's a pilot.

Amy became interested in music and drama. She asked for piano lessons and became involved in our local community theater, where she's since starred in *Oliver!* and played minor roles in several other productions.

What more can I say? It was wonderful!

Q: *Didn't they feel out of it when their friends talked about television programs?*

A: If they did, they never told us. I suspect it was somewhat frustrating for a while, but I'm sure they got lots of sympathy from their friends. In the final analysis, losing the TV set gave them more time to socialize, and they developed not only more friends but much better social skills. I'm sure the TV industry would like us all to believe that children who don't watch television can't relate to their peers, but it simply isn't so. Over the years, I've talked to many other parents who've had the courage to remove television from their children's lives. They all say basically the same thing: The children become more imaginative, resourceful, self-sufficient, conversational, interesting, and outgoing. Never have I heard anything negative.

Q: *When you reintroduced television into Eric and Amy's lives, how did you control it?*

A: Four years after taking it away, we bought the smallest color portable then available and set it on a bookshelf in the den. Every Sunday, the children went through the television listing and selected five hours' worth of programs, at least two of which had to be educational. Using the following form, the children listed the programs they wanted to watch, along with days and times, and turned that list in to us. If we approved, those became the shows— the only shows—they could watch. Substitutions were allowed but had to be cleared in advance. In other words, if they missed one of the programs they had selected, they were not allowed to make up the time later in the week. This method works because it hands responsibility for enforcement over to the child or children. Because children would rather police themselves than be policed, they cooperated.

Q: *If you had it do over, what if anything would you and Willie do differently?*

A: We would not let the television-watching habit get started in the first place. An ounce of prevention is always better than a pound of cure.

PART 2

It's Only a Stage

THIS "AGES AND STAGES" SECTION traces child development from birth through the teen years. My intention is, first, to help parents understand the developmental—and therefore parenting—goals intrinsic to each stage and, second, to suggest effective approaches to the problems parents are likely to encounter as they help their children, and themselves, move toward independence.

7

Birth to Eight Months: Infancy

"THE FIRST EIGHT MONTHS of a baby's life . . . are probably the easiest of all times for parents," Burton White says in *The First Three Years of Life*. "If they provide the baby with a normal amount of love, attention, and physical care," he adds, "nature will pretty much take care of the rest. . . . Nature, almost as if it had anticipated the uncertainties that beset new parents, has done its best to make the first six to eight months as problem-free as possible."

Dr. White certainly makes it sound easy, doesn't he? Still, some infants are easier than others. Researchers who study newborns have found vast differences in temperament, activity levels, how much and how loudly they cry, their reactions to different forms of stimulation, how much and how soundly they sleep, and how sensitive they are to the environment.

While more generalizations can be made about infants than about children at any other age, their differences far outweigh their similarities and are, in the long run, more significant.

All infants apply themselves, in different ways and at different times, to the many facets of growth and development. One baby may develop a true social smile sooner than another. But the baby who was slower to smile may be quicker to crawl. The crawler may still be on hands and knees when the early smiler gets up and walks. In fact, a baby of six months often seems to have chosen one or two particular areas of development to concentrate on. Put three six-month-old children in a room together, and you are apt to see one working diligently on learning how to creep, another spending most of the time experimenting with sounds, while the third is working intently to develop finger dexterity and eye–hand coordination. While each baby's timetable may vary considerably, however, the *sequence* of development is fairly predictable.

Personality traits emerge sooner than many parents expect. For instance, by the middle of the second month, babies express definite likes and dislikes, particularly in terms of what they enjoy looking at, how they want to be held, and how much stimulation they need and can tolerate.

In short, all human infants are fascinating in their own right. They begin to define who they are and what they want from you during the first few weeks of life. The following topics are of special interest and concern to parents of infants in the first eight months.

Pacifiers

There are two schools of thought regarding the use of pacifiers. On the one hand (usually the right) is the pro-thumb school (thumbers), a group of purists who promote the thumb as a natural built-in tranquilizer. The thumb, they say, is more convenient than a pacifier, and babies who suck this digit practice independence and self-control. Thumbers maintain that pacifiers are artificial and warn that children can become dependent on them.

Proponents of the pacifier (Pacifists) point out that a pacifier can be taken from a child after a certain age. Furthermore, pacifiers do not push against the roof of the mouth and upper gum as thumbs often do.

Both points of view seem reasonable, and each has its merits. There are two reasons for giving a pacifier serious consideration:

It can supplement an infant's sucking needs, and it can quiet a fussy baby.

During the first months of life, the need to suck dominates the infant's limited behavioral repertoire. Beginning as a survival-oriented reflex, the need to suck comes increasingly under voluntary control after the first eight weeks of life and gradually diminishes in strength over the next ten to sixteen months. In most cases, it disappears completely by eighteen months.

The sucking instinct is definitely stronger in some infants than in others. Most infants quickly discover the hand-to-mouth connection and by their second month spend a significant portion of their waking time mouthing various parts of their hands. By this time, they also attempt to put anything they grasp into their mouths.

Except when a child's safety is involved, there is no reason to interfere. An infant's need to suck should never be denied or obstructed, unless, of course, the object to be sucked constitutes a threat to the infant's safety. For an infant whose sucking need is especially powerful, a pacifier can be a worthwhile supplement to the hand, the mother's breast, or the bottle.

Until they are six to eight weeks old, babies may have some difficulty keeping the pacifier in their mouths. And some infants, regardless of how fussy they are or however strong their need to suck, refuse to accept pacifiers altogether.

With all this in mind, I offer the following recommendations:

- If your baby discovers a thumb (or fingers), don't interfere and don't attempt to substitute a pacifier. In the first place, it will probably be rejected. Keep in mind that when infants suck on part of the hand, two parts of the body—mouth *and* hand—are pleasurably stimulated. When babies suck on a pacifier, only *one* part of the body—the mouth—is pleasured. An infant who has experienced the added benefit of hand-sucking is not likely to settle for less.

- Periodic bouts of fussing may signal a need for additional sucking time. If your baby doesn't make the hand-to-mouth connection, try introducing a pacifier.

- Use pacifiers sparingly, perhaps only during baby's fussiest part of the day (this usually occurs in the late afternoon or early evening). The conservative approach will diminish the odds that a prolonged dependence will develop.

- Don't use a pacifier to "hold off" your baby's next feeding. A hungry baby should be fed.

- If your baby isn't particularly fussy, doesn't find a thumb, and seems content with the amount of sucking provided during feedings, there's no reason to offer a pacifier. Lucky you.

- By no means should a pacifier be used *every time* a baby cries between feedings. A baby who is obviously uncomfortable or bored should be picked up and comforted. Pacifiers are not a substitute for cuddling.

- Wean your baby from the pacifier by age six months. Past that age, pacifiers prevent a baby from learning to self-comfort (see below for additional comment).

My Peeve with "Passies"

Please bear with me while I rant and rave: What is this business of allowing children older than six months to walk/ride/be carried around with pacifiers protruding from their mouths? I see 'em everywhere! Some of the kids in question are four or five years old, for cryin' out loud! Not only does it look downright stupid (and the older the child the stupider it looks) but it also serves no good purpose other than to feed an addiction—on that need never have developed in the first place! And don't tell me, you parent for whom this shoe fits, that your child can't do without it, because he or she certainly can! Throw it away today and your child will live! So will you! And let's face it: This is your addiction, too!

That's right. We're not just talking about a child addicted to a "passy," but also a parent (or parents) who obviously cannot tolerate a crying (or chattering?) child and is, therefore, addicted to the child being addicted to having a pacifier in this mouth. Once upon a time, I thought this was benign, inconsequential. I saw no problem with parents allowing children as old as three to suck on those vile devices. For that reason, I accept my fair share of responsibility for having assisted in unleashing a monster. I hereby repent and commit myself to correcting this error.

No way should a child older than eighteen months be allowed to suck on a pacifier. A growing number of pediatricians and speech therapists are convinced that the use of a pacifier beyond that age can adversely affect speech development and contribute to serious articulation problems. Think about it: Pacifiers immobilize the tongue, possibly preventing the child from learning to properly pronounce words. The more the tongue is immobilized past the time when clear speech should be emerging, the more risk of speech problems. Not only that, but children who use pacifiers are much more prone to ear infections than children who are passy-free.

"Hold on, John!" someone is shouting. "In your ranting, you implied children shouldn't have pacifiers beyond six months. Now it's eighteen. What gives?"

Caught that, eh? Good for you! Beyond six months, a pacifier is unnecessary, even counterproductive. Beyond eighteen, it becomes a risk factor. I have no problem with parents using a pacifier during the first few months of life to establish a routine feeding schedule or calm an especially irritable ("colicky") baby. There is not even a problem with letting a toddler have a pacifier only at bedtime (albeit this isn't necessary, either). But again, evidence is mounting that when a pacifier is used throughout the day beyond six months, it actually prevents the infant from learning to calm himself. And to anticipate the next question, thumbs and pacifiers are horses of two entirely different colors. Children who suck thumbs are self-pacifying. Furthermore, unlike the case with a pacifier, a child must take his thumb out of his mouth to use his hand. To my knowledge, thumb sucking is not associated with speech problems (orthodontic problems, yes). Besides, the pacifier problem can be solved in a day, in an hour, in the next minute even! Just "lose" it, toss it, whatever.

Where "losing" the passy is concerned, a parent I know told me that when it came time for one of her kids to stop sucking on a pacifier, she simply snipped the tip off at an angle, rendering it most uncomfortable to insert in the mouth. That took care of that. No screaming, no crying, just perplexed looks.

I have to believe that the ubiquity of two-plus–year-old children strolling/riding through public places with pacifiers stuck in their maws is just one more example of how American parents are slowly but surely extending infancy indefinitely. Other symptoms of "perpetual infancy syndrome" include children who sleep in their parents' beds, suck on bottles beyond eighteen months, ride in strollers at age three and beyond, and still wear diapers during the day beyond thirty months. Why are so many of today's parents having such difficulty letting their children grow up? Maybe it's because then they'd have to grow up, too. It's a thought.

Crying

Some babies cry a lot. Some cry very little. But all babies cry. Sometimes fussiness is caused by a readily identifiable source of discomfort: The baby is hungry, has stomach cramps, or is in an uncomfortable position and needs rearranging. Other crying is unrelated to physical discomfort and seems to be an attempt at self-stimulation, a way of asking for attention. Some crying can't be explained in terms of discomfort or deficiency. Sometimes babies cry just for the sake of crying. Perhaps this is their way of announcing their existence—talking to themselves, so to speak.

By the end of the third month, most mothers have become quite sensitive to their babies' crying language and can identify the differences in tone and volume that mean *I'm hungry,* as opposed to, for example, *I'm bored.*

Most babies have regular periods of fussy crying, often in the late afternoon or evening. This daily upsurge in crying usually wanes by the fifth or sixth month.

Here are some suggestions for calming a fussy baby:

- Holding and gently rocking a crying baby will calm all babies some of the time and some babies all of the time. Every baby has definite likes and dislikes, and you may have to experiment with different positions, rhythms, and rocking techniques until you find the right combination for your little one. Music often has a calming effect. If you don't have any recorded music handy, or if you happen to feel creative, sing to your baby while you rock; singing, because it enhances language development, is actually preferable. Most infants like to be held upright so they can look over your shoulder. Sometimes it's easier for them to fall asleep in that position, too.

- If you don't have a rocking chair, or if a gentle back-and-forth motion doesn't seem to do the trick, sit on the edge of a bed and bounce gently up and down. Both of our children preferred this to the motion of a rocking chair.

- Swaddling, or wrapping snugly in a blanket, may help a baby relax. Some infants don't like being physically restricted; others are soothed by swaddling as long as they are held and rocked at the same time.

- Pacifiers can be helpful with some babies (see preceding section).

- Try burping. If no gas is released, try again in three to five minutes. A howling baby tends to swallow air, adding to the discomfort.

By the way, the fear that too much cuddling and physical closeness encourages overdependence is groundless. The opposite is true: The more secure your child feels as an infant, the more readily he or she will move away from you when the time comes.

Meet Baby's Needs as Well as Your Own

Throughout the book I will use a question-and-answer format such as what follows to elaborate on typical problems parents may encounter.

Q: *The host of a local television show recently interviewed a pediatrician who has just written a book on fussy babies. His description of what he called a "high-need baby" fit my six-month-old to a T. He is very active and alert and requires a great deal of stimulation and attention. I must hold and entertain him almost constantly to prevent him from becoming upset. If I put him down and leave the room, he begins screaming, so I carry him around with me all the time. I feel I no longer have a life of my own and find myself beginning to resent the demands of motherhood. This doctor's solution to the problems that come with a high-need baby like ours was to "wear the baby like a sweater." When the interviewer pointed out that this leaves no room for other responsibilities, he replied that meeting the baby's needs was more important than doing housework or anything else. He made it sound like our son would achieve independence sooner if we put his needs first; nevertheless, his advice left me with a rather hopeless feeling. Do you agree with him? If not, what other advice would you have for me?*

A: I agree with the doctor's description of "high-need infants." It's also true that if you repeatedly frustrate an infant's need for closeness and attention, you're going to delay the baby's independence and create other potentially serious problems.

I don't agree, however, with the doctor's statement that parents of high-need babies should "wear them like a sweater." That's similar to, "You can't spoil an infant," which, while essentially true, is usually taken to mean that parents should always pick up a crying baby. That advice is not only impractical, especially with a fussy baby, but also unnecessary.

Meeting your baby's needs involves meeting your own as well. Stated differently, you can't take care of someone else unless you also take care of yourself.

Parents who feel they must devote themselves exclusively to their babies and forget about themselves begin to develop feelings of frustration and resentment. If there's one thing a baby doesn't need, it's parents who feel that parenthood is a burden.

Somewhere between the doctor's injunction that you should wear your baby like a sweater and a state of selfish neglect, there's a point of balance where it's possible for you to meet both your needs *and* your child's.

There is no getting around the fact that fussy, high-need infants require more attention and physical closeness than the norm. And, for the most part, it's good practice to respond to an infant's cries shortly after they begin.

However, there's no harm in putting your baby down for a few minutes to take care of something you can't do with him in your arms, even if he cries during that time.

In other words, if it's practical to "wear your son like a sweater," do so. But if it's not practical, put him down and do what you must. If you leave the room, call to him every ten seconds or so. The sound of your voice isn't going to stop him from crying, but at least he'll know he's not been abandoned.

A couple of things are going to happen within the next few months that are going to make life with your baby a whole lot easier.

First, he's going to become increasingly mobile. At the moment, his intense need to explore is frustrated by the fact that he can't get around on his own. So, you do his exploring for him. You bring things to him, thus feeding his curiosity.

You have to do a lot of "entertaining," because a high-need baby doesn't stay interested in any one thing for very long. The more mobile he gets, however, the less he's going to depend on you for stimulation, and the more time you'll have for yourself.

Second, around age eight months, he's going to develop what is called "object permanence." Right now, in his mind, if something vanishes from sight, it no longer exists. That includes you. In a few months, however, he'll realize that you're here to stay, and he'll be able to tolerate your being out of sight for longer and longer periods of time.

Until then, feel free to put your baby down and go to the bath-room, brush your teeth, wash your face, fix yourself something to eat, or just sit and pull your wits together for a few minutes with-out fear of causing permanent psychological scars. I hardly think your child's long-term emotional health rests on such simplistic circumstances.

Fathers

With the exception of breast-feeding, there is nothing mothers do that fathers cannot do just as well. The obsolete notion that mothers can better fulfill their babies' needs has encouraged mothers to feel more responsible for their children than they actually are, while it has caused fathers to feel insignificant and excluded. With-out a doubt, there are differences in the ways mothers and fathers interact with their children. Each parent brings a unique set of per-sonality factors into the child-rearing situation, and each con-tributes invaluably, though differently, to the child's growth and development.

Several studies have shown, for instance, that, with the excep-tion of breast-fed babies, infants show no innate preference for one parent over the other. Other research shows that babies whose fathers are actively involved in their upbringing tend to be more outgoing, less fearful of strangers and new situations, more willing to accept challenges, and generally more assertive. I suspect these findings have less to do with fathers per se than with the fact that it's more stimulating and enriching to have two actively involved parents than just one.

Since males have not generally been brought up to think of themselves in the primary parent role, many fathers feel awkward and inept around their children at first. But a father who *chooses* to be relatively uninvolved, or whose wife discounts his significance, usually ends up feeling as though he is on the outside looking in at the mother–child relationship. Almost inevitably, this father devel-ops jealousy and resentment toward the child. Often his reaction is to put even more distance between himself and his family by becoming increasingly involved in his occupation.

The other side of this coin is the mother who feels overly protective of her role as primary parent. It is usually easier to get a somewhat reluctant father involved with his child than to get a possessive mother to loosen her grip. The overprotective mother generally ends up feeling as though she is raising her child in a goldfish bowl—she feels trapped, helpless, isolated, overly responsible, and usually ineffective. Obviously, both an uninvolved father and an overly involved mother interfere with a child's overall growth and development.

Postpartum Blues

It's not uncommon for new mothers to experience a sense of letdown and depression soon after the birth of a child. The blues may come and go in the form of infrequent mild bouts of uneasiness and anxiety, or they may be frequent and intense enough to require professional help.

Postpartum blues are probably a combination of several factors, among them:

- *Disappointment* at discovering that motherhood isn't the earth-shaking consciousness-raising event it's cracked up to be. Maybe Mom is a little shocked at her infant's wrinkled, rather flabby appearance, having expected her baby to look for all the world like the ones in the baby-powder commercials.

- *Fatigue* at being wakened one or more times night after night and being constantly on call for another human being who is not only helpless but seems to have a talent for making messes.

- *Readjustment* to a new lifestyle, new routines, and new priorities, including the fact that her own interests seem to be moving farther and farther to the back of the bus.

- *Relationship changes* with her husband, as perceptions and expectations of each other are modified. Mom may experience a sense of loss and feel that "things will never be the same."

- *Doubts* about whether she is really cut out to be a mother or whether parenthood is what she wants for herself. Almost every new mother goes through a stage in which she feels somewhat resentful toward her baby.

Any or all of these, combined with the realization that "there ain't no turning back," can be temporarily unsettling to a woman's self-esteem.

In addition to getting as much rest as you can and saving time for yourself and your marriage, new mothers should talk to other mothers. Express your feelings. You'll be surprised at how comforting and reassuring it is to find that other women experience similar emotional upheavals.

And here's some advice for the new father: Get involved! Pitch in! Offer to help with changing, bathing, feeding, and everything else that goes into taking care of the baby. If your wife seems reluctant to accept your help, it's probably because she feels she should be all things at all times to her child. If that's the case, gently point out to her that the two of you are in this thing together. If you must, insist that she let you help and even at times take over. Her reluctance may also be a way of testing your continued commitment to her. When the baby wakes up in the middle of the night, get up too and talk softly with her while she feeds the baby. If the baby is bottle-fed, take a regular turn on the night shift.

The more involved you are with the baby and the more supportive you are of your wife, the less isolated she will feel and the more resistant she will be to the postpartum blues. Therefore, the more involved she will be with you. How about that?

Can You Spoil an Infant?

Not a chance. There is no such thing as too much closeness, except in cases where a mother's anxious overinvolvement with the baby dominates her life to the exclusion of husband, interests, and friends. Most experts agree that you can't spoil an infant, but I'm afraid that many parents, and mothers in particular, have taken this to mean that babies must be picked up and comforted every time they cry. This just isn't so. There are definitely times when baby will cry (see preceding section, Crying), not because of discomfort or lack of attention but simply for the sake of crying. When this seems to be the case, it is perfectly all right to let the baby fuss for a while.

It won't take much time for you to know, from the sound of your baby's cry, what, if anything, you need to do. If the cry is an attempt at communication, don't leave an infant to cry it out. Make every reasonable effort to provide comfort. This responsiveness helps your baby develop a trusting attitude toward the world in general and toward you in particular. A sense of trust and protectedness gives children of all ages the freedom to be curious, explore the world, and become assertively independent.

Most babies cry themselves to sleep, at least for a time. Crying at bedtime helps them dispose of tensions that might disrupt the transition from waking to sleeping. There is no reason to interfere with this type of crying either. For your own peace of mind, though, you may want to look in on a crying baby every five minutes or so, until he or she is asleep. If the crying becomes more insistent, pick your baby up immediately.

On occasions when you're not sure whether the cries are for you or not, always give your baby the benefit of the doubt. Studies have shown that babies whose parents respond quickly to their cries for attention feel more secure and, consequently, cry less and less with the passage of time. They also tend to be less demanding and more self-sufficient as they get older.

Feeding

Most newborns require a feeding every three to five hours. Initially, baby's tummy won't discriminate between daytime and nighttime, but somewhere toward the middle or end of the second month, an infant may suddenly give up the three A.M. feeding and sleep from around eleven P.M. till nearly six the next morning. Don't count on it, though. Your baby may not sleep through the night for many months to come.

Feed your baby when he or she is hungry. Although some pediatricians continue to favor a strict four-hour feeding schedule, most child development experts agree the so-called demand schedule makes more sense. Actually, the term *demand* hardly fits. Infants don't make demands. When they are hungry, they cry, simply because that's their way of expressing physical tension. Being made to wait until someone else decides it's time for them to be hungry only makes them feel frustrated and insecure.

Your baby's internal feeding schedule will be fairly well established by the end of the second month. There will still be off days, however, and you will need to stay flexible.

Between baby's fourth and sixth months, your pediatrician will probably advise you to introduce solid foods into the diet. Some babies take quickly to solid food at this age and seem to enjoy experimenting with new tastes and textures. Other babies, particularly breast-feeders, reject solid food at this age and possibly for several weeks and even months to come.

Don't ever force-feed an infant! Even at this early age, the attitude you have about food will be communicated to your baby. If mealtime becomes associated with tension, and if questions of how much or what is eaten become issues, your baby will acquire a negative attitude toward meals. If this happens, I can virtually guarantee that the family dinner hour will become ever more and more of a battleground.

Introduce new foods one at a time. A new taste is less likely to be resisted if you offer it near the beginning of a meal, when the baby is hungriest. Small portions help babies get used to a new taste more gradually.

By the age of six months, your baby will take great pleasure in finger foods during part of the meal. At this age food is a sensory adventure, and babies will experiment on almost everything you give them to eat—mashing, smearing, crumbling, and hurling it to the floor.

Bottle-fed babies are usually able to hold their bottles by the time they are six or seven months old and may be allowed to do so most of the time). But it isn't a good idea to let your baby take a bottle to bed at night or for naps. Mealtime is for eating, and bedtime is for learning how to go to sleep. Babies who take bottles to bed quickly develop a dependence on them that can persist well into the second and even third year of life. In addition, the milk from a bedtime bottle can more easily adhere to the baby's teeth, resulting in a form of tooth decay known as nursing bottle syndrome. Finally, closeness between parent and child at mealtime is important throughout the first year of life.

Breast or Bottle?

Before your baby is born you will decide whether to breast- or bottle-feed. In making this decision, don't be taken in by the myth that breast-fed babies are more secure and happy than bottle-fed babies. The quality of the mother–infant relationship is enhanced when breast-feeding is successful, but nursing is *not* essential to this interaction. No evidence supports claims by advocates of breast-feeding that nursing provides a more secure foundation for healthy psychological development. If a woman would rather not breast-feed but feels she *must* in order to be a good mother, she won't do herself or her baby any favors. Furthermore, this unreasonable pressure reduces her chance of breast-feeding successfully.

In my estimation the advantages of breast-feeding are purely practical. It is more convenient. It requires no preparation or paraphernalia. Breast-feeding is a lot less time-consuming. Breast milk is preheated to an ideal temperature; you never have to worry about storage, and breasts don't require sterilization. Breast milk is free and replenishes itself. Breast milk is nonallergenic; some physicians believe that breast milk may prevent later allergic reactions to cow's-milk products.

Here are answers to some frequently asked questions about breast-feeding:

Q: *Is breast milk healthier than commercial formulas?*

A: Commercial formulas attempt to duplicate the composition of human milk, and overall the similarities outweigh the differences. The differences, though subtle, do favor mother's milk.

Q: *Are breast-fed babies more resistant to disease?*

A: Yes! Until infants build up their own defenses against infection, they rely heavily on antibodies from their mothers for protection. Many of these antibodies are present in colostrum—the yellowish protein-rich substance secreted from the breasts for the first few days after birth—as well as in breast milk itself. These protective factors temporarily immunize the baby against a broad range of infectious agents.

Breast-fed babies suffer milder and less frequent episodes of diarrhea and have fewer respiratory and gastrointestinal illnesses than bottle-fed babies. These effects are more pronounced in babies who have been nursed for more than five months.

Q: *Do bottle-fed babies gain more weight than breast-fed babies?*

A: On the average, bottle-fed babies are larger and heavier at one year than breast-fed babies. This is sometimes seen as a sign of good health; actually, bottle-fed babies gain weight more quickly than they grow in length. In breast-fed babies, the two measures tend to be in better proportion. In brief, bottle-fed babies are more likely to be overweight.

Breast-fed babies have more control over the feeding process. When they stop sucking, the mother stops nursing. On the other hand, bottle-fed babies may be encouraged to continue drinking even after their hunger has been satisfied. Bottle-fed babies are usually started on solid foods much earlier than breast-fed babies. Introducing solids prematurely can also contribute to excessive weight gain.

Bottles should *never* be used as pacifiers. Babies should be fed only when they are hungry and not necessarily every time they cry. Having a fat baby is neither cute nor desirable. Excess weight can slow a baby's developmental progress. An overweight baby is more likely to become an overweight child and, later, an overweight adult. Being overweight is not healthy for humans at any age.

Q: *Are there any other dangers in bottle-feeding?*

A: Bottle-feeding can be extremely dangerous when the water supply is unclear, refrigeration is inadequate, or preparation of the formula is not carried out under sanitary conditions. If the formula becomes contaminated, the baby is exposed to serious infection. Diluting the formula to save money can result in malnutrition. Mothers who bottle-feed need to be cautious about overfeeding and refrain from adding solids to the diet prematurely. There is nothing inherently dangerous about bottle-feeding. In fact, modern formulas are quite close in composition to human milk and promote healthy development.

Q: *Are there women who should not breast-feed?*

A: Women with active tuberculosis or a chronic infectious disease should not nurse. A nursing mother should consult her physician before taking any kind of medication. Women who commonly use alcohol, marijuana, cigarettes, or coffee should ask their doctors whether these substances might have adverse effects on a nursing infant.

Some mothers (*very* few) have an inadequate milk supply, making nursing difficult or impossible. The most common causes of milk shortage, however, are depression, anxiety, and fear of failure. All can inhibit the flow of milk. As I said before, a woman who pressures herself into nursing, but who would rather not, is stacking the deck against success. Don't let your ego get involved in this decision. Do what you feel most comfortable doing.

Q: *I have breast-fed our first child for six months. Sara takes a feeding around seven P.M. and then wakes for a slightly smaller one at ten, after which she sleeps all night. Since she won't take a bottle yet, my husband and I haven't been out in the evening without her since she was born. Naturally, we would like to have some time to ourselves, but I hesitate to introduce the bottle this early, since the breast-feeding arrangement is so convenient and satisfying for both of us. Any suggestions?*

A: It's not too early to begin supplementing Sara with either a bottle or solids, and if your approach is conservative, neither should disrupt the breast-feeding arrangement. At her seven P.M. feeding, try giving Sara one or two teaspoons of cereal, mixed thinly with formula or extracted breast milk and perhaps a small amount of baby fruit (check first with your pediatrician). The added substance may help push her late-evening wake-up time to around midnight, which would give you and your husband five continuous hours of freedom.

Now, about bottles and breast-fed babies: A breast-fed baby expects only the very best from Mom, so *you* may have more difficulty getting Sara to accept a bottle than will your husband or your sitter. The fact that she rejects a bottle from you does not mean she'll reject it from someone else, as long as that someone is patient and has experience caring for babies. If you decide to let someone else try offering Sara a bottle, it might be best if you leave the room or even the house. She might not accept a bottle from anyone if she knows you're nearby.

Your concern that success with a supplementary bottle will put an end to breast-feeding is unwarranted. Should Sara warm to an occasional bottle, she will continue to prefer your breast at least until she can hold a bottle herself. My wife and I introduced an evening bottle to our daughter at five months for exactly the same reasons. Amy accepted bottles from both me and the baby-sitter long before she would take one from my wife, and she continued to be a breast-fed baby for another eight months.

Whether or not you decide to begin the cereal supplement, and whether or not it extends the evening nap, hire an experienced baby-sitter and instruct her to offer your daughter a bottle or formula or extracted breast milk when and if she wakes at ten P.M.

Take a chance! If things don't work the first time, try again.

For additional information about nursing, contact your local La Leche League. There are quite a few good books on breast-feeding, including *Nursing Your Baby* by Karen Pryor and *The Womanly Art of Breast Feeding* published by the La Leche League. Beware La Leche's child-rearing advice, however. It's the antithesis of what you will read in this book.

Sleeping

Sometime toward the middle or end of the second month, your baby will probably begin sleeping through the night, much to your delight. In most cases, you will still need to give an eleven P.M. feeding, after which the baby may sleep until five or six the next morning. The first time this happens, you will probably wake up in the middle of the night wondering why you haven't heard anything. Check the crib, if it will make you feel better, but don't under any circumstances wake the baby up.

There is no need to whisper or tiptoe while baby sleeps. Your baby will sleep quite soundly and restfully while life goes on at a normal volume in your household. In fact, it's more important to turn down the level of stimulation while baby is *awake*. Excess noise and visual activity can provoke distress in infants and even overwhelm their defenses, making them irritable and disrupting their schedule. A baby who is constantly or frequently exposed to a high level of stimulation may fail to settle into a routine.

By the end of the third month, your baby may have eliminated the eleven P.M. feeding and be sleeping about ten hours a night. *Now is the time to begin using a consistent bedtime.* A routine will not only help your baby anticipate when bedtime is coming but will also provide the opportunity to wind down from the activity of the day and be more likely to accept bedtime when it arrives.

With or without a routine, your baby may cry when put in the crib. It's not unusual for babies to cry themselves to sleep, and many seem to sleep more soundly if they are allowed to cry for ten or fifteen minutes after being put to bed. You need not interfere with this unless the crying is obviously distressed.

Many babies continue, even after the third month, to waken for short periods during the night and fuss or make noises. These semi-waking periods are part of a normal sleep cycle. Babies require no attention during these times and, left to their own devices, will find their way back to sleep in short order. On the other hand, you can condition babies to wake up completely and repeatedly in the middle of the night by handling or feeding them every time they awaken.

If your baby hasn't started sleeping through the night by this time, don't try and force the issue by delaying the evening bedtime as long as you can. The best way to encourage a long sound period of sleep at night is to put the baby down at the first sign of fatigue. When babies are kept up past the time when they should have been put to bed, they will have more difficulty falling asleep, their sleep will be fitful, and they will be more irritable when they wake up.

At four months your baby will still take two or three naps during the day. By the fifth month, however, there may be days when there is only one. Even so, it is best to try for a second rest period, even if the baby doesn't actually fall asleep. An additional quiet time won't hurt either of you.

By the eighth month most babies sleep twelve hours a night and take just one nap during the day. (Some babies, however, take two naps until they are nearly one and a half.) Around the eighth month, many babies, regardless of how cooperative they have been in the past, begin protesting at bedtime. By this time, they can crawl, sit well without support, and pull themselves to a standing position. This mobility stimulates their interest in exploring the environment. This is an exciting time, and they may be unwilling to cease all activity when you call an end to their day. In addition, eight-month-olds are more likely than either six- or twelve-month-olds to become upset when separated from their mothers, so you may have some problems at bedtime.

This is a time for gentle firmness. Adhere to the bedtime routine you have established and, regardless of protests, let baby know that bedtime is an irreversible fact of daily life. Your decisiveness, your firm resolve, and the control you demonstrate in this situation will be an ultimate source of comfort and security for your baby.

Q: *We just spent a week of "vacation" with my parents, during which my mother and I got into it over the way I put our three-month-old son to sleep. Josh is our first child.*

I insist that the house be quiet fifteen minutes before I put him down and that it stay that way for at least one hour, until he is completely under. At that point, I only ask that people not make any sudden loud noises.

My mother called me a worrywart because of what she termed my "neurotic attitude" about putting Josh to sleep. She says that when putting a baby to sleep, the noise level in the house should stay right where it is during any other time of the day. I say noise disturbs Josh's sleep. She says Josh will get used to it.

She also says I'm already too concerned about Josh, and that if I don't get over my constant worrying about him, he'll be in control of the family by the time he's two years old. Who's right, me or my mother?

A: Your mother's right. She's tactless, but she's right.

Like yourself, most new parents believe that a house must be deathly quiet while a baby is going off to sleep. Not so. Life in the family should go on at its normal volume. The baby will quickly accommodate to whatever noise level is normal for the household and will be disturbed only if there's a sudden and significant increase from this baseline.

I don't think any studies have been done to verify what I'm about to say, but I would speculate that babies who get used to going to sleep in quiet homes sleep much less deeply than babies who go to sleep in homes that are relatively noisy. It's just a guess, mind you, but it makes sense that if the noise baseline is initially low, it will take less noise to disturb the baby than if the baseline is established at a normal level.

It seemed to work that way for our children. When they were babies, there was loud rock 'n' roll on the stereo almost constantly, sometimes until well into the wee hours of the morning. They slept right through it, I think because it was a normal part of their noise environment from day one. They are both, to this day, sound sleepers, for which my wife and I were always thankful.

They also have great senses of rhythm.

Contrast this with my two-year-old nephew, whose mother insists that everyone tiptoe around and whisper after he's put to bed. Not only does it take him upwards of an hour to fall asleep but he wakes up at the slightest noise. Come to think of it, he also controls his family. Everything revolves around him, from the time he gets up in the morning until well past his bedtime.

Concerning your mother's warning to the same effect, I don't have a crystal ball, so I don't know what will be going on in your family twenty-one months from now. I *do* know, however, that you are already setting certain precedents with Josh that, once set, will be hard but not impossible to undo.

A family should revolve around the parents, and its lifestyle should be defined by their tastes. It goes without saying that raising children requires that one make certain changes and compromises, but a family should never revolve around the presence of a child.

For all these reasons, I think you would be better to heed your mother's tactlessly given advice and get Josh used to the fact that life goes on normally around him and normally without him.

Q: *Our first child, a girl, was born six weeks ago. As yet, we haven't been able to get her on a good bedtime routine and were wondering if you might have any advice for us. Initially, we were putting her to bed at eight o'clock, immediately after her last nursing. This went well for about a week, then she started crying as soon as we put her in her crib. One of us would rock her back to sleep, but when we put her back in her crib she'd wake and start crying again. Thinking that perhaps she wasn't ready for sleep at eight, we tried keeping her up later, but the later we kept her up, the crankier she got and the longer it took to get her down. As it stands, we are playing it by ear, trying to catch her when she's most ready, but this doesn't seem to be working well either. We've heard that you can't spoil an infant, but this is ridiculous!*

A: When our son and firstborn, Eric, made his triumphant entrance into the world, he was greeted by two young anxious parents who picked him up every time he cried, day or night.

Bedtime quickly become a circus, with Eric holding out and his parents holding on. No one had ever told us most babies cry for a short period before falling off to sleep. Left to our own ignorance, we decided that crying was his way of telling us that we hadn't done something right—rocked him long enough, given him enough milk—so we would pick him up and try again.

On a good night, Eric fell asleep around ten, only to be up again two or three hours later. This kept up, off and on, all night long. Looking back on this, I guess we were trying to create a perfect pain-free world for Eric. The more we tried to protect him from discomfort, however, the lower his tolerance for discomfort became, so that by the time he was eighteen months old he could not handle any frustration whatsoever. When he was two and a half, he slept through the night for the first time.

Amy, born three and a half years after Eric, had no such luck. Several weeks before the blessed event, Willie looked me in the eye and said, with complete conviction, "*This* one's going to have a bedtime." And she did. At eight P.M., Amy was nursed, burped, and put in her crib. She usually cried for about five or ten minutes, then fell asleep.

If her crying suddenly became intense or lasted much longer than ten minutes, one of us would check. More often than not, finding nothing amiss, we rubbed her back for a minute or so, to let her know we were there, and left. Amy slept through the night when she was two weeks old.

Most contemporary authorities, including Burton White, author of *The First Three Years of Life,* maintain it's impossible to spoil an infant. This may be, but it is definitely possible to respond to an infant's crying in a way that assures you of having a thoroughly spoiled toddler on your hands.

While I agree with White that letting infants cry it out is an undesirable practice, I disagree with his recommendation that parents respond promptly to an infant's every call for attention. As I said earlier, most babies cry some at bedtime. This is not necessarily an indication of discomfort but may be a natural way of discharging tension and thus making the transition between waking and sleeping.

Rushing in every time an infant cries is just as extreme as making the baby cry it out alone. A moderate approach, such as we took with Amy, is the most sensible alternative.

Q: *My son did not sleep through the night until he was almost five months old. Shortly after that, we moved to a new house. He seemed slightly upset by the move and began waking periodically through the night again. On the advice of our pediatrician, we gave him a chance to get used to the new house and then stopped picking him up. Instead of crying himself back to sleep, he cried every night for one to three hours for nearly a month. We finally gave up and started picking him up again. Now, at nine months, he wakes up every hour on the hour throughout the night. As soon as we pick him up, he falls back to sleep for another hour. During the day, his naps never last longer than thirty minutes. What should we do?*

A: To begin with, your pediatrician's advice was inappropriate for a six-month-old infant. He should not have advised you to let your baby cry it out at bedtime or when he woke up during the night. Separation anxieties are common enough at this age without compounding them with insecurities associated with sleeping.

If your son needs reassurance, give it to him. The more available you are during the first year of life, the more secure he will feel and the better able he will be to move toward increasing degrees of independence.

Your baby is becoming overly fatigued during the day because his insecurities are overriding his need for sleep. This is another factor preventing him from settling down for a restful night.

First, establish a morning and afternoon quiet period for his nap. If he wakes up prematurely (less than one hour), try encouraging him to fall back to sleep. If he doesn't cooperate, discontinue this effort and let him out of bed.

Then begin putting him to bed at seven-thirty P.M., preceded by a winding down ritual beginning at seven. This could include a bath, a short story, a tucking-in ceremony, and whatever else you want to throw in.

When he wakes up in the night, respond *immediately* to him and do whatever is necessary to get him back to sleep as quickly as possible. You might want to move his crib back into your room until he's sleeping more restfully.

In short, let him know that your presence is not a questionable thing. Within a couple of months, he should be back on track.

Day Care

Q: *I took a leave of absence from my job to have my first baby and be totally available to her for the first three months of her life. Now people— including both sets of grandparents—are telling me I shouldn't go back to work until Kristin is at least three years old. That will mean starting over in my career, which is very important to me.*

I feel torn between my responsibilities to my baby, who means everything to me, and all the things I've worked for over the past ten years. Will putting Kristin in day care cause problems with her development or our relationship?

A: That depends upon the day care and how much you are otherwise available to her. Despite the warnings of experts such as psychologist Burton White, who advises against any day care before age three, most research indicates problems can be minimized, if not eliminated, if the day care responds to the infant's needs.

For infants, I recommend a family home in which the caregiver is looking after no more than two or three children. A small-scale home setting all but guarantees that each child will receive enough individual attention.

Because there is no staff rotation or turnover in a home setting, an infant can form a more secure attachment to the caregiver. Fewer children also means the caregiver can accommodate varied sleep, feeding, and activity schedules.

A family day-care home also gives the parents greater communication with the caregiver, who can more easily respond to parents' requests concerning how the baby should be held or fed or put to sleep than is generally possible in a larger group.

Since most states inspect and license or register day-care homes, the first question to ask a prospective home caregiver is, "Are you licensed?" Although a license doesn't necessarily mean better care, it at least guarantees the home meets minimum standards.

After starting day care, an infant will go through a period of adjustment to the environment and the new caregiver. During this transition, the baby may feel stress and express it by increased crying, general irritability, and disturbed sleep.

An initial stress reaction that doesn't begin to abate after a couple of weeks can indicate problems. It may be the child and provider are a poor match, in which case another setting might work out better.

It may be, however, that the child isn't ready for any day care at all. In either case, if a baby needs to be removed from care, parents should wait a few weeks before attempting another placement.

If the care you find for Kristin is of adequate quality and you are otherwise sufficiently involved with and responsive to her, there's little, if any, reason for concern.

In fact, day care can help the mother-child relationship by giving the mother a chance to feel adequate outside the home. The self-fulfillment a mother such as you derives from a satisfying career will, in all likelihood, have a positive effect on the baby.

A final word of advice: Don't wait until the last minute to find day care for your baby. Take time to look and compare, so that you find the best setting available. Don't choose strictly on the basis of cost or convenience. The extra time and extra money you may have to spend for truly good care will pay off handsomely.

In her book *Tips for Working Parents: Creative Solutions to Everyday Problems,* Kathleen McBride gives excellent advice on choosing a family day-care provider. Contact the child-care referral agency in your community for a list of day-care homes.

Q: *Being the mother of a three-month-old girl, I read your recent article on infant day care with interest. My leave of absence from my job is almost over, and I've been trying to find suitable care for my daughter for the past few weeks. The family day-care homes in our area are currently full, so I have no choice but to put her in group care, at least until something opens up. What should I look for in group care?*

A: Parents who are locked into group care or prefer it, for whatever reasons, should consider the following factors:

- Staff-to-child ratio: How many infants are there per full-time staff person? The lower the ratio, the more likely it is that each infant will receive sufficient individual attention. For infants, the ratio should be no higher than one caregiver per five babies.

- *Rotation and turnover:* Consistency of care allows the infant to form a secure attachment to the caregiver. Are the same staff persons in the infant room throughout the entire day, or do they change shifts in the afternoon? If so, at what point is the change made? How long has the present infant-care staff been at the center? Lots of turnover in staff probably means the center isn't a very good place to work. If it isn't a good place to work, it's probably not a good place to leave a baby.

- *Experience and training:* How and how often are staff persons trained, which certificates do they hold, and how much experience does each have working exclusively with infants?

- *Environment:* The infant room should be bright and airy, with no door. An open-floor play area for crawlers that's fenced or divided from the remainder of the room and either carpeted or covered in mats is preferable to three or four individual playpens. The crawling area should contain a few chewable playthings that encourage exploration and stimulate motor development as well as one or two relatively large soft cushions or tunnels the babies can crawl over and through.

- *Cribs:* Although so-called stacking cribs are less visually appealing, they do offer more floor space. Are the infants allowed ample time on the floor, or are they confined for most of the day to their cribs or individual playpens? If the center uses traditional cribs, there should be plenty of space between them. Each crib should contain no more than one or two crib toys to occupy babies who are waking up or needing a little quiet time.

- *Equipment:* Look for such things as one or two baby swings, adequate changing-table facilities, and tables with built-in chairs for the babies who are eating solid food. Make sure that babies are always held and talked or sung to when drinking from bottles, as opposed to have bottles propped in their mouths.

- *Staff:* How and how quickly do the caregivers respond to crying? How actively involved are they with the babies? Do they pay attention only when a baby is crying or are they calmly busy almost all the time? Is their tone soothing? Do they handle the babies gently or somewhat abruptly? Most important, do they enjoy their jobs?

Finally, do the director and staff seem interested in you, the parent, and are they sensitive to the anxieties you feel about putting your baby in day care? Are they warm, patient, and reassuring? Do you feel you'll be able to communicate effectively with them? You may not know it yet, but their relationship with you is every bit as important as their relationship with your baby.

8

Eight to Eighteen Months: The Toddler

FOR CHILDREN BETWEEN eight and eighteen months old, the world is changing rapidly. By the eighth month, a typical infant sits upright alone, crawls, pulls up to a standing position, and may even sidestep around (cruise) the perimeter of things. Improvements in eye–hand coordination and finger dexterity also take place. For instance, it is now possible for the baby to pick up small objects (buttons, crumbs, and so on) between thumb and index finger (a pincer grasp). This stimulates interest in the world of tiny things and correspondingly increases the risk of injury.

During the next ten months the child makes tremendous gains in motor, communication, and intellectual skills. It is a period of "tooling," when the infant is outfitted with the skills and information needed to begin mastering the environment.

These maturational events are truly groundbreaking. They are the seedlings of self-sufficiency. For the first time, the child can do a significant number of things independently. Driven by an insatiable appetite for discovery, he or she moves from place to place, putting the pieces of the puzzle together into a coherent picture of the world. The child has become an explorer, a collector of information, an active participant in the overall scheme of things with one all-consuming purpose: to *know,* to penetrate the mysteries of the universe. Why? Because it's there!

Shrinking Violets

This new freedom, as always, has its price. At the same time that the child is experiencing this acceleration in motor, perceptual, and intellectual skills, the mother is probably calling the pediatrician to ask why her baby is so reluctant to separate from her in the presence of other people. And why, the parents ask, does baby constantly check on them, as if afraid they will vanish at any moment?

There are several reasons (or one reason in several parts) why children this age seem so eager to try their wings one moment and so fearful of venturing away from their parents the next.

For starters, the ability to explore the world on their own rearranges their priorities. The quality of *things*—their texture, taste, and movement patterns—are of prime importance now. In the short span of several weeks, the world becomes a radically different place, and the prospect of venturing out by themselves into this alien landscape is both exciting and frightening. It's exciting because of the exhilarating sense of accomplishment that goes with opening a new door; it's frightening because taking those first steps into unknown territory is risky. A child of this age wants to take those steps, but not without making certain that the primary security figures are still there. That's you, Mom and Dad. You are your child's insurance policy!

Up until now, most of what babies have seen, heard, or touched has been courtesy of the primary caretaker (usually their mother) who carried them, fed them, moved objects within their grasp, played with them, and so on.

Mother has been synonymous with gratification of the infant's needs for food, comfort, and stimulation. And, from the child's egocentric point of view, their identities have been blended. The baby has not distinguished "ma-ma" from "me."

As the infant discovers the ability to do things independently, a sense of separateness from Mother begins to develop. This is the first stirring of a sense of identity, the beginning of self-consciousness.

For the first time, the infant has a *choice*. With the ability to control, to a certain degree, the distance between self and Mother comes the need to decide how close to be. He or she must balance the need for security with the urge to become ever more independent.

The child is now pulled in two directions simultaneously. One voice says, "Hey, kid, you can do it yourself!" But the child who answers that call gives up some of the security that goes with having Mom right there to do everything. So the other voice pleads, "No! Not yet! It's too much to deal with all by yourself! Get Mom over here before she slips away forever!"

How well the child resolves this conflict depends on the answer to one critical question: How responsive and supportive is the environment to the child's explorations and inquiries? Is the primary experience exhilarating or frustrating? Are discoveries joyous or painful? Do caretakers assist or obstruct this playful work? Is the environment stimulating or boring? The future is in this child's hands. How often are they slapped?

For a time, the child seeks intuitively to restore equilibrium by gravitating closer to Mother. The link with Mother is vital; her presence is essential to the child's continued security.

Not surprisingly, other people become one of the most threatening elements of the expanding universe. They tend to move in before the child has a chance to size them up, and they often want to snatch him or her up, out of Mother's arms and into their own. The only protection is to cling and scream.

Unfortunately, because few adults understand the reason behind these rebuffs, grandparents often feel hurt, fathers often feel angry, and mothers frequently feel responsible for everyone else's hurt feelings.

The following questions and answers illustrate the clinging-toddler phase.

Q: *I am the mother of a delightful but very mother-oriented one-year-old. He gets upset sometimes if I just leave the room. He won't let anyone else hold him if I am in sight, sometimes not even his daddy. Needless to say, this gets very frustrating for me at times. I nursed him until he gradually weaned himself at eleven months, and I wonder if this contributed to his being so clingy. I thought letting him nurse for as long as he wanted would promote independence.*

A: When you leave the room, panic sets in because *he* is not controlling the separation. It's one thing for him to crawl away from you; another entirely for you to walk away from him.

And yes, breast-feeding can promote the growth of an independent spirit, but so can bottle-feeding and being held and comforted. But before your son can take those first tentative steps toward independence, there must be no question, no lingering doubt whatsoever in his mind as to whether you will remain close at hand. He must reassure himself that you will stay there until he doesn't need you to be there any longer.

If he wants to cling, let him cling; if he wants only you to hold him, *you* hold him. The more receptive you are to his expressions of need, the shorter this phase will last.

The evidence clearly shows that the harder the child has to work to keep Mommy close, the more clinging he will ultimately become. This does not mean that putting a child in day care or leaving him with a sitter must be traumatic. At those times it is best for Mommy to hand him over quickly. The longer Mom hangs on and hangs around, the worse things become.

If, instead of closing in on him with outstretched arms, people will just sit and wait, he will eventually get around to approaching them. If they make no sudden movements, he might hang around long enough to make friends. At this somewhat fragile time in his life, he will feel most comfortable when closeness happens on *his* terms.

Q: *I have my ten-month-old son in a mothers'-morning-out program one morning a week. He cries almost the entire four hours unless one of the teachers is holding him.*

In the program, there are ten children, ranging from six to eighteen months, and three teachers. Ricky has attended since he was three months old, but the problem didn't begin until a couple of months ago. He's also doing the same thing at our church nursery.

He's an otherwise secure child. At home, Ricky will play by himself for more than an hour at a time. He enjoys his familiar baby-sitters and going to other people's homes when only one or two other children are present.

He is an only child, and I do have a lot of time to spend with him. I sometimes feel guilty about taking him to mothers' morning out, but I also feel I need a few hours a week to myself. Am I wrong to continue taking him? Will he outgrow this stage?

A: The problem is twofold. First, Ricky is right in the middle of the first of two separation crises that occur during early childhood. This one started on schedule around his eighth month and will probably last until his first birthday or thereabouts. The next has its onset around eighteen months and lasts for several months thereafter. Second, Ricky is made even more anxious by the fact that in both mothers' morning out and church nursery, there is a noisy gaggle of children, some of whom are much older, much more active, much more aggressive, and therefore much more threatening. Comparing Ricky's reaction to mothers' morning out with his reaction to being with one other child his own age is like comparing apples to watermelons.

Console yourself with the fact that things could be much worse. At least Ricky is content to play alone for long periods of time when he knows you're there. He also can tolerate being left with a sitter. Many children this age cling tenaciously to their mothers, refusing to let even fathers or grandparents hold them.

Infants can't tell us why they feel and act the way they do, so developmental psychologists have to make educated guesses when it comes to explaining much infant behavior. Ricky's anxiety over separation probably has a lot to do with his rapidly expanding ability to move around in and explore the environment. Previously, his moving about was done courtesy of you and your husband, mostly you.

Like most other human beings, Ricky wants to have his cake and eat it too. He wants to move around on his own, but he also wants to make darn sure you're not going to slip away while he's not looking. Somewhat paradoxically, he doesn't *need* you quite as much but seems to *want* you that much more.

The evidence clearly shows that the more upsetting a separation is to a child of this age, the longer this phase will last. In other words, it will probably pay in the long run for you to avoid, at least temporarily, situations that cause Ricky great separation distress.

Instead of leaving him in mothers' morning out, hire a sitter to come into your home one morning a week. In a lot of cities, there are Rent-a-Granny services that provide child care of this sort. If you can't arrange for a sitter on Sunday morning, it might pay for you and your husband to alternate staying home from church until Ricky is older and feels more secure in a group of small children. Wait a couple of months after he starts walking and try again.

Q: *What is the appropriate amount of praise for a fifteen-month-old? I praise my toddler for specific accomplishments, but I don't make a huge deal out of it. I want him to know that I'm proud of him, but I don't want him to need my praise for everything he does. I have a friend who is teaching her child of the same age to clap for himself whenever he does anything nice. The mother also praises him every time the child says anything, even words he has known for months. Am I wrong in fearing that this amount of praise is too much and will lead to future problems?*

A: Your intuitions are right on target. It is not only unnecessary to praise a child, regardless of age, for every single accomplishment, it is also counterproductive in the long run. Too much praise creates a dependency on being praised that inhibits, rather than promotes, accomplishment and independence. Having a toddler clap for himself is well-intentioned silliness. Furthermore, once a child is fairly proficient at something, the message from his parents should be, in effect, What you're doing isn't special, it's simply the right thing to do.

In another twenty-one months, your friend is going to wonder why her three-year-old won't leave her alone.

Discipline

Q: *What is the best approach to handling unwanted behavior from my thirteen-month-old? One thing she likes to do is shake the dining room chairs. She pulled one over on her once, but that didn't stop her. Now, when she shakes the chairs, I tell her "No!" and put her in her playpen for about one minute. This behavior has since decreased. Is this type of punishment okay for a thirteen-month-old, or should I just take the chairs out of the dining room until she's older?*

A: A stern reprimand followed by a brief time-out is certainly appropriate punishment for a young toddler. If you want to strengthen the message a bit, you might leave her in the playpen for two or three minutes, but longer than three is probably overkill. Don't expect quick results, however. As I point out in *Making the "Terrible" Twos Terrific!* this age child doesn't really pay much attention to consequences. Be as consistent as possible and be patient. If your daughter is slowly tearing the dining room chairs apart, it's probably advisable to put them out of reach, but if the only problems are the racket and the chance she'll pull one over on herself again, I'd leave them where they are. Actually, having a chair topple over on her—which, unless the chairs in question are especially heavy, is threatening to neither life or limb—will probably cure this faster than a combination of *no!* and time-out in the playpen.

Magical Mischievous Tour

Sometime between eight and fifteen months, a child discovers that the world is full of magic and that he or she is one of its foremost magicians. When a child becomes a magician, the old saying "The hand is quicker than the eye" is never more true.

Around this time, parents may find cryptic messages scrawled on the walls in lipstick, pages torn out of the family Bible, the contents of the toilet in the tub, all the books out of the bookshelf, all the clothes out of the dresser, and the kitten in the refrigerator. The magician's quick hand is, of course, the child's. The slow eye belongs to the parent.

Parents don't seem to mind at first. They laugh and praise the young magician for these tricks. "Isn't that cute?" they say.

Then they become jealous because the child's magic is better than their own. Their faces go red, their eyes grow cold, and they begin applying the old quick hand to the slow rear, just to prove they haven't lost their touch. "Isn't that awful!" they say.

The young magician tries in vain to make the old ones understand by inventing more tricks, pulling more pranks, performing more and better feats of legerdemain, only to be reminded on the slow rear. The young magician learns fear, and this is the Waterloo. Fear will slow the best hand down. The old tricks stop working. In years to come, when all magic is forgotten and the eyes get slow, the magician will be ready to become a parent.

Toddlers and parents live in different worlds. Toddlers live in a wonderland of enchantment, where every sight, sound, and touch is new. Everything that happens in a toddler's world happens for the first time ever and for no one else.

The small child does not have words enough to explain the amazing things that happen in this world; no words to tell why paper shreds and glass breaks. There are no reasons for anything except "just because." No wonder children believe in magic.

The Cookie Tree, a children's book by J. Williams, now out of print, should be required reading for all parents. It begins:

> *The village of Owlgate was quiet, and tidy, and nothing surprising ever happened there. Everything had a place, and everything was in its place. Everybody knew why things happened, and everything happened just as it was supposed to. Nothing surprising ever happened because nothing surprising was allowed to happen. "That way," said the people of Owlgate with satisfaction, "you always know where you are."*

We parents live in Owlgate. We have reasons and places for everything. We work hard all day long giving reasons and finding places and making sure things stay put. Words have taken the place of wonder, and if something cannot be explained it isn't there.

When an egg falls on the floor, a twelve-month-old may see a piece of the sun spill out; the parent sees a mess. Tiny fingers reach for things that come apart or fall and bounce and break or splatter and spread out in all directions. In Wonderland, it's magic. In Owlgate, it's mischief, and mischief is the reason for messes. But in mischief, there is also the thrill of discovery, and therein is the reason for Learning, with a capital *L*.

Young children do not have enough language to understand the *whys* and *why nots* of things in Owlgate. They discover the world by experiencing it directly. The splat, bounce, and break of things are defined by a child's own action, and it is through action that they discover all the different things the world is made of, how it comes apart, what's inside, what happens to what, and when, and how. They must experience *all* of this before they can ever make sense of the words we use to describe the *why*. And so, messy magical mischief is also the reason for Language, with another capital *L*.

Children who are allowed to roam about being mischievous learn that words can also be used in magical ways. They learn language quickly, and they learn to use it well. Mischief also flowers into imagination and creativity. A scientist is, after all, nothing but a grown-up magician, making the mischief of progress.

The mischievous nature of a child's curiosity is the force underlying all learning and accomplishment. At the same time, it is also the source of many childhood accidents.

During this critical developmental phase, it is essential that certain physical boundaries be established, both to ensure the youngster's safety and to provide an environment that encourages exploration, learning, and creativity.

Toddlers cannot predict what objects and situations in their surroundings might be harmful, nor are they able to appreciate the value of irreplaceable or expensive household treasures. Their nature *demands* that they touch, feel, and taste everything within reach. Powered by an insatiable appetite for discovery, they are most alert when in motion, exploring for novelty everywhere. At some point, it is inevitable that this exploratory drive will aim a toddler toward fragile ceramic figurines, antique glassware, the African violet collection, and everything else within reach.

By far the easiest, least expensive, and most sensible way to reduce the obvious risk is to put these objects well out of reach, as soon as the toddler is able to grasp them. By child-proofing your house in this way, the boundary between *can touch* and *don't touch* is established by the child's own physical limitations. Parents who fail or refuse to child-proof must constantly watch where their toddlers are and what they are doing. These parents never have a moment's rest, and their children cry a lot.

I can hear you now: "But Michelle has to learn what she can't have, and besides, it took me years to collect all these things." You have a point. Your daughter must eventually be taught the difference between what she *can* have and what is out of bounds. But the connection between reaching for a certain object and a slap on the hand or a loud *no!* is established (maybe) only at great cost to the parent's peace of mind and the child's sense of confidence and capacity for learning.

Protect your valuables and breakables by putting them up and away. Chasing a child around the house, frantically trying to cover all bases, is a losing proposition. You cannot win, because the child has more energy and determination.

Relax and enjoy your parenthood. Feed a child's curiosity, but not with African violets. Provide a variety of objects around the house of different colors, shapes, and textures, but not a lot of toys. Let children "discover" things that are unbreakable. When they find them, teach them to play Put and Take with you. Play *with* your children, not *against* them.

Before you visit friends or relatives, call and ask if they would help make the visit a more relaxed and pleasant one for all concerned by gathering up their treasures and closing off certain rooms. "Please don't think me rude, but I'd so much rather talk with you than worry about what Michelle is doing behind my back."

Child-proofing is even more essential when objects and substances that are potentially harmful to children are involved. Cleaning fluids, paint, medicine, pins, glass bottles, plastic bags, aerosol sprays, and tools must be out of a child's reach. Electric sockets can be fitted with childproof plates. A lock on the door to the basement steps is a deterrent to broken bones and concussions. Lower cabinets can be fitted with childproof latches or cleaned out and made safe and fascinating to crawl into.

Playpens

Playpens have their pros and cons. Used wisely and sparingly, a playpen can perform a service for parents and provide baby with a safe place to play. If misused, however, a playpen can be an obstacle to normal development. When left unattended in playpens for long periods, children become bored and frustrated and even depressed.

Use of a playpen after a child is old enough to walk is even more damaging. There is evidence suggesting that children who spend lots of time confined in cribs or playpens suffer delayed speech and are less coordinated. A handicap imposed on a child in this way is not easily undone.

As your child grows, use the playpen less often and for shorter periods. When he or she begins crawling, allow plenty of free time to roam and explore. The more that children are able to exercise their curiosity, the more intelligent and creative they will become. If you use the playpen while ironing, washing, or cooking, set it up near you and talk to your child while you work. This keeps him or her alert and stimulates language development.

Protect your child's health by providing a safe environment to explore without having to experience frequent frustration, boredom, or punishment. By establishing these physical boundaries in a loving, sensible way, you not only ensure safety but promote your toddler's development and provide a more relaxed atmosphere for yourself.

The rule is a simple one, as expressed in the following sonnet, reportedly written by Shakespeare's evil twin, Bobo.

After crawling, don't confine,
Child-proof for your peace of mind,
Allow your child to freely roam,
In the safety of your home.

Biting

During the first year of life, biting is almost exclusively exploratory in nature. An infant's mouth is as primary an organ of discovery as are the eyes and hands. Furthermore, the sensations that arise from using the mouth to explore things are extremely pleasurable, so nearly everything gets put in there.

Infants learn to discriminate tastes, textures, and temperatures by mouth. They find out what is food and what isn't by chewing on everything from ashtrays to zwieback. They find answers to the same questions about people: I wonder what Mommy tastes like. *Ummm.* Not bad! Hey, she does interesting things and makes new sounds when I do that. Wonder if she can do that again? As an added bonus, infants discover that biting relieves teething pain and feels plain ol' good, by gum!

Sometime close to the beginning of an infant's second year, biting becomes a way of being playful and affectionate. It's a way of saying, "Hey, I love you! Wanna play?" Biting continues to feel extremely pleasant, and your child doesn't know that you are not sharing this ecstasy.

As toddlers grow into their second year, they encounter an ever-increasing number of frustrating situations. They may well make the discovery that by biting down very hard on something, they can release the tension that builds up in these encounters. A likely target is the someone most closely associated with their frustration.

Here's the tale of a typical biter and my advice to the bitee.

Q: *I have a fourteen-month-old son who bites me several times a day. Sometimes he is clearly frustrated by me, but sometimes he bites for no reason whatsoever that I can see. This has been going on for the past three months and is getting worse. I have tried spanking, putting him in his crib, and biting him back (on the advice of my pediatrician), but nothing seems to get the message across. He only bites* me, *and I don't understand what I could be doing to cause it. What should I do?*

A: Don't take it so personally. He's not biting you because he hates you or because you deserve it, he bites you because you're *there*. You are the person most available to him. You frustrate him more than anyone else because you share more time with him than anyone else does. Throw in the fact that toddlers are easily frustrated, have no self-control, and love to sink their chops into things, and you have a typical fourteen-month-old biting his typical mother.

Your son bites you at different times for different reasons, but he continues to bite because you have never insisted that he stop. Thinking about what you might be doing to "cause" his biting has prevented you from taking action on the biting itself.

Put yourself squarely in the present tense and *do* something about it. As much as possible, prevent his toothy attacks, even playful ones. Surely you can tell when one is on the way. Every time he tries to bite you, regardless of whether he succeeds, face him and say *no!* Then pick him up, turn him around so he faces away from you, and take him to his room. Put him down on the floor (*not* in his crib) and walk away, leaving the door slightly ajar as you go. He will "hear" the message clearly.

When he emerges, he will probably come straight to you. If he wants the reassurance of being held, hold him, but do not talk about the incident. If he is still agitated and tries to bite you again, repeat the sequence.

When he learns that you are not a willing victim, he may try biting someone else. Again, whether or not you are able to prevent that from happening, say *no!* and put him in his room. If you aren't at home, improvise with an out-of-the-way chair.

By the way, biting a child back sometimes works, but more often it makes the problem worse. I don't recommend it because it confuses the child, puts parents in the position of modeling the behavior they want eliminated, and is likely to start a let's-see-who-bites-harder contest.

This method should bring noticeable improvement within two or three weeks. As usual, commitment is the key. And that, my friends, is the honest tooth.

Weaning and Eating

Q: *I'm having trouble getting my fifteen-month-old son to give up drinking from a bottle. He drinks from a cup during meals but cries for his bottle whenever he is upset or sleepy. Should I refuse to give it to him?*

A: There is much to lose and nothing to be gained by struggling with your son over a bottle. When we make issues out of things like bottles and thumbs and security blankets, children are likely to become more desperate in their attachment to them.

Allow your son to drink from a bottle whenever he expresses a need for that source of comfort. Insist, though, that he follow your lead and drink from a cup during meals. I strongly advise against filling a bottle with milk or any sugar-sweetened liquid, such as iced tea or fruit punch. The sugar in these drinks greatly increases the risk of tooth decay. As his parent, the decision regarding what goes in the bottle is yours. Fill the bottle with unsweetened (strained) fruit juices or water only, and stand firm on this decision.

Your son will probably lose interest in the bottle quickly if you begin to water down the juice and gradually (over several weeks' time) increase the proportion of water until you have eliminated the juice altogether. During this process, leave the bottle, filled with water or the water-juice mix, where he can reach it without asking for your help. He will eventually forget about the bottle, and so will you.

By no means should a child who is capable of drinking from a cup be encouraged to continue drinking from a bottle. Nor should parents offer a bottle as a pacifier. Allow a child access to the bottle, simply and naturally. As with so many things, the more of a problem you make of it, the more troublesome it will become.

Q: *How far should one go in encouraging an eighteen-month-old to eat a balanced diet? I cater to his whims for breakfast and lunch, but for dinner I put a small amount of what we're having in front of him. Unless we* *are having some sort of bean dish (which he loves), he will say "All done" and sometimes try to throw his dish on the floor. Then he will ask for his milk over and over until we give in. (We always give him a big glass of milk before bed.) Should I just give up on dinner and let him have milk?*

A: I don't see a problem with that. Neither did the pediatrician I consulted. He and I agreed it sounds like your son's nutritional needs are being met, although adding a liquid multivitamin supplement is probably a good idea. If he's hungry at dinner, he'll eat. If he wants milk, let him drink milk. If he hasn't eaten dinner in a week and you begin to worry, take care of yourself by heating him up some beans. A three-year-old should not be catered to at the dinner table, but catering to an eighteen-month-old is not likely to create a long-standing problem.

At this age, everything in the environment is fascinating; everything must be explored. Infants will touch everything they can, and anything that passes inspection by the hands goes to the mouth. After being tasted, chewed, and mashed, if the tongue says "Yes!" down the hatch it goes.

Q: *My daughter, thirteen months old, has begun playing with her BM. If I don't catch her in time, she scoops it out of her diaper and smears it all over herself. What is most upsetting, however, is that she also manages to eat some of it. The word "aakey" usually keeps her from putting certain things in her mouth but hasn't worked with this. I try to keep my cool, but I'm just about at my wits' end. What can I do?*

A: Given the opportunity, most children will play in their bowel movements, just as they will play in the dirt from your potted plants, the sugar bowl, oatmeal, or whatever. To an infant, a BM is no different, except she made it! How delightful! Another bit of magic from the world's greatest magician.

Rest assured that there is nothing abnormal about this behavior (at this age), and nothing is wrong with your child. Furthermore, aside from what we might *think*, there is nothing dirty or unhealthy in what she is doing. Granted, it's a mess, but no more than a rather exasperating example of recycling.

Nor is there anything especially significant about this behavior. The trap, however, is that we big people have an outstandingly negative reaction. We are repulsed, disgusted, and infuriated at having to swab the decks afterward. No matter how we try to keep cool, it's difficult not to let our true colors show, thereby tipping the child off to how significant the whole business is to us.

Make a big deal out of something, and it will become a big deal. Any exaggerated reaction on your part (spanking, screaming, fainting, throwing up) is probably going to set the stage for a repeat performance.

I would suggest that you maintain as much cool as you possibly can and wash her up without any special to-do. If you need a break to recover, put her back in her crib and take five (or fifteen).

Bedlam at Bedtime

Q: *We can't seem to get our fifteen-month-old daughter to go peacefully to sleep at night. We've even tried keeping her up until she's absolutely exhausted, but no matter when we put her down, the moment she hits the crib mattress she starts to wail. And wail. And wail! Don't tell us to let her cry it out, because we just can't. Besides, she's already proven she can scream nonstop for almost an hour. The only thing that seems to work is rocking her to sleep, which takes about twenty minutes, then staying in there and rubbing her back for another ten or fifteen minutes once we put her in her crib. The added problem is, if she goes down crying, she almost always wakes up screaming in the middle of the night. There must be a better way! What is it?*

A: Indeed, there is a better way to put an infant to sleep. Known as J.R.'s Guaranteed No Mo' Sleepless Nights, it involves three easy steps to permanent bliss while at the same time answering forever the question, "How do you keep 'em down on the bed, after they've seen the alternative?"

There are three steps to take.

Step One: Set a definite bedtime and stick to it. Do not—I repeat, *do not*—try to wear the infant down by keeping her up long after reasonable people have gone to bed. Contrary to popular belief, the later you keep your daughter up, the more agitated she will become and the more difficult bedtime, when it finally arrives, will be. Instead of waiting for a signal from your daughter that she's ready for sleep, make the decision for her. Somewhere between seven-thirty and nine P.M. is probably reasonable.

Thirty minutes before bedtime, start putting her through the preliminaries, which might include a bath, a snack, and a story. When the appointed hour arrives, put her down with a brief tucking-in ceremony and promptly leave the room, screams not withstanding.

Step Two: Assuming the child screams, go back into her room every five minutes and repeat the tucking-in ceremony. If you must, lay her back down, reassure her that the world as she knows it still exists, kiss her, and exit, stage left. Do not pick her up and do not stay longer than one minute. Five minutes later, if she's still at it, go back in and repeat the procedure. Sooner or later, she will begin to tire of this foolishness, and her screams will turn to whimpers. At this point, you should extend the interval to ten minutes, or whatever your common sense and intuition advise. If, however, she goes back to full throttle, return to the five-minute plan.

True, she may scream for a couple of hours at first, but after several nights of this, she will scream less and less until, after a few weeks, she will scream for only a few minutes, if at all. Look at it this way: At present, you spend approximately forty-five minutes getting her to sleep, more if you count the fact that you are keeping her up much too late to begin with. With this method, if she screams for two hours, you will have gone in twenty-four times at less than a minute each for a total of around twenty minutes.

Step Three: Should she wake up in the middle of the night, which is likely for a week or so, repeat Step Two.

Lest you have lingering doubts, I've been pushing this plan for at least twenty years, and it's yet to fail. Just call me the Sandman.

9

Eighteen to Thirty-six Months: The Terrific *Twos*

I THINK OF THE TERRIBLE TWOS and an image of children screaming, throwing things, playing in makeup, eating soap, breaking
china figurines, saying *no!* to everything—running amok while
Mommy and Daddy chase, grab, spank, yell, scream, and run amok
too. To be honest, it's not exactly an image. It's a vivid memory
starring the inimitable one-and-only Eric!

To live with Eric at twelve was to wonder if this was the same
child who didn't sleep through the night until he was two and a
half years old. Could he be the same child who was dubbed Mr.
Mad or Mr. Tough, depending on his mood, by two of our best
friends? Thirty years ago, no one could have convinced me Eric
would be sane when he grew up, much less the mellow, thoughtful, delightful person he is today.

It took me several years and another child to learn that two-
year-olds can be terrific. There's no question about it, their reputation for terribleness has to some extent been earned. But the
difference—terrible or terrific—is not primarily a matter of the
child. It's a matter of the parents.

The most dramatic and significant transition in the development of any individual occurs between eighteen and thirty-six months. It is a revolution, involving sweeping changes in every child's experience both of themselves and of the world. Naturally, your two-year-old's behavior takes some dramatic turns as well.

This can be one of the two most stressful periods in the overall life of a family, the other being around early adolescence. But it doesn't have to be. As with most endeavors, the key is understanding, which can help make the terrible twos *terrific*.

"I'm Me!"

Infancy is a time of almost total dependency; infants must rely on parents and other people to feed, bathe, dress, change, and even move them from place to place. Between eight and eighteen months, children make rapid gains in problem-solving (cognitive), motor, and communication skills. They begin to experiment with cause-and-effect relationships, discovering in the process that they can manipulate their environment. Children between eight and eighteen months old are collectors of information. They are constantly on the move, harvesting facts with their hands, eyes, and mouths. At this stage the process is random. The child has no blueprint—just an irresistible urge to know everything there is to know about every "thing."

Throughout these meanderings, toddlers absorb an incredible amount of information without, however, knowing how to *use* it. Then, sometime around the eighteenth month, children realize they can act upon the world to *make things happen*. At this point, their guidance systems switch from automatic to autonomous pilot. Before, they were explorers; now they are *experimenters,* alchemists, out to create history—their own, at the very least.

From this moment on, things will happen the way toddlers want them to happen, and people will do what they want them to. Full speed ahead and damn the torpedoes!

As the "sense" of their environment is revealed, toddlers begin interacting with it to *solve problems*.

A fourteen-month-old, seeing a jar of cookies on the kitchen counter, will reach in vain and point and yell until someone comes along to lend a hand. Several months later, this same child pushes a chair to the counter, climbs up, and gets the cookies.

As the mind expands, so does the world. In no time these youngsters are consumed with excitement, with no way to express their exhilaration except through activity. They are on the go constantly, getting into everything, climbing up on counters and bookshelves, climbing down out of crib and car seat, always one step ahead of you. They won't take no for an answer. After all, what does *no* amount to when everything else around and inside says *yes!*

One of the limitations nature has imposed on two-year-olds is a gap between physical and intellectual development, favoring the latter. Their bodies have not caught up with their minds. They may be able to see the solution to a problem but may *not* be able to make their bodies perform the movements required to carry it out. For example, a child may know that a certain shape fits into one certain space in a puzzle but be unable to make the finger movements needed to maneuver it in.

This frustrating disparity is often expressed in sudden, violent, and sometimes destructive tantrums. Trying to lend a helping hand usually leads to more rage. The child would rather do it alone and fail than watch you succeed. That's understandable. Whose growth is this anyway?

Sometime around the middle of the second year, a child realizes, in one relatively sudden, insightful moment, that "I'm *me!*" It's the blooming of individuality, of self-consciousness. It's the biggest "Aha!" of all.

The next eighteen months or so are spent in defining who *me* is and establishing clear title to that psychological territory. Much to the child's dismay, it turns out that these boundaries are not all-encompassing. He or she is not the only *me* in the world but one of many.

At this age, children must learn that independence means less than being able to do as they please. Just as the task of the child is to establish autonomy, the parents' task is to begin the process of socialization, of communicating and enforcing boundaries, limits, and rules governing the child's expressions of independence.

It gradually dawns on the child that becoming a separate, independent person means giving up a corresponding measure of attachment to other people, Mommy and Daddy in particular. These sacrifices and disappointments can be overwhelming. For all these reasons, the third year of life is a relatively uncertain time with few dull moments.

Dominated by the central question of whether it is more advantageous "to be or not to be (independent)" the child is a study in paradox: clinging and cuddly one minute, demanding and defiant the next, wanting the best of both worlds, and slowly—painfully—realizing that there is no middle ground.

This is the second time the infant has had to deal with issues of separation, the first time having occurred between eight and twelve months (see chapter 8).

"Don't Leave Me!"

It isn't unusual for eighteen- to twenty-four-month-olds to respond to the temporary uncertainty of this internal revolution by demanding more visual, physical, and verbal contact with their parents. For a short time they may need someone to hold on to, a port in the storm.

If parents are fairly tolerant of their child's determined clinging, the child will, within several weeks or months, gain all the reassurance needed to move through this metamorphosis.

Q: *My son is twenty months old. He has been a delightful baby but has recently started clinging to me somewhat more than before. He follows me around the house and wants to be held a lot. How should I handle this?*

A: Your son's need to cling expresses, paradoxically, the realization that he is a person in his own right. He has made the discrimination between "me" and "you." He now knows you are not a blend:

you and he are two people, and that fact places psychological space between you. This distance allows him to begin testing his wings— to move farther away from you and into the environment.

This metamorphosis, however, carries with it a certain degree of uncertainty at first. You no longer seem as available and accessible as before. He doesn't know how great the distance between the two of you will become. He wants to fly, but he does *not* want to give you up. He doesn't have the words to express his anxieties, so he follows you from room to room, reassuring himself that this change is not the beginning of some disappearing act. In other words, before he can take one giant step forward, he must take one baby step back. In this game of Mother May I? your answer must be "Yes, you may." If he wants to be held, hold him. If he wants to follow, let him. The fewer obstacles in his path, the less disruptive this transition will be for everyone in the family.

The Roots of Rivalry

The birth of another child into the family during this period of transition can be very disruptive. Older children often act as if the new baby were a tiny trespasser who sneaked into the picture while their back was turned. Feeling that this small someone will take their coveted place next to Mommy and not yet fully committed to giving it up, they rush back to close the gap.

Q: *We have a two-and-a-half-year-old daughter and a six-month-old son. Off and on, ever since the baby was born, our daughter has asked us to rock her at bedtime. She has also asked to have her bottle back. We have not, in spite of several tantrums, given into these requests, but now there's an additional problem. We began our daughter's toilet training about five weeks ago, with success at first. A couple of weeks ago, however, she began refusing to go if prompted and now she has more accidents than not. They seem to be almost deliberate, and this disturbs us. She now says she wants to be put back in diapers. Should we stop for a while, put her back in diapers, and try again later?*

A: One thing your daughter does *not* need, regardless of what she asks for, is permission to backslide.

The problems you describe are typical of what can happen when less than three years separates one child from the next in a family. When the second child was born, your daughter's position in the family shifted, creating anxiety and distracting her from the basic task of growing up. The reasons for this kind of developmental stall are not at all mysterious, and such problems are generally short-lived. The arrival of the baby reminded your daughter, at an inopportune time, of how wonderful it was to be carried and rocked to sleep and bottle-fed and have Mommy change her diapers.

Your task is to reassure her that her place in the family, while different and changing, is still secure and protected. And you must convince her, firmly but gently, that she has no choice in the matter.

The time for bottles, being rocked to sleep, and wearing diapers has passed. She is obviously ready for training, and it should proceed. Keep her in training pants, except at night. She probably won't stay dry at night for another year. Do not follow her around asking her if she needs to use the potty. When she gets up in the morning, take her into the bathroom, point to her potty, and say in effect, "Remember to put your wee-wee and poo-poo in here today. If you want Mommy to help you, just call me." If she asks to be put in diapers, tell her she is a big girl who wears pants during the day and diapers only at night. If she has an accident, change her without fuss. Then take her into the bathroom and remind her once again where to put her business in the future.

Continue, even in the face of resistance, to relate your expectations to her in a clear, calm voice. I've said it before, but it deserves repeating: The more effectively authoritative the parents, the more successfully autonomous the child.

Q: *We have two boys: One has just turned three and the other is sixteen months. My problem is with the older one. He wants my attention almost constantly throughout the day—"hold me, read to me, play with me, help me!" If I can't go to him immediately, he whines and cries until I do. He's* *been this way since shortly before our second child was born, but it seems to be getting worse. It is extremely frustrating for us all. What is the problem, and what can be done about it?*

A: It sounds as though his demands are beginning to dominate the family. It is in everyone's best interest, including his, for you to act before the problem gets firmly rooted in your lives.

Set aside two specific times during the day: a time with him and a time without him. Perhaps your time with him could be during the younger child's nap. In any case, set aside at least thirty minutes to spend totally with him, doing what *he* wants to do. Take the phone off the hook and don't answer the door.

For your time away from him—at least thirty minutes—stay out of his sight and relatively inaccessible to him (it may help to have another adult take over during this time). Go to your room and lock the door. Take a drive or a walk. Mom's time out is just for Mom.

The rest of the day, let common sense tell you whether to comply with his requests for attention. If you can give him your attention without interrupting something else, fine. But if giving him attention means stopping what you are doing, say *no* (assuming he's not in dire straits). If he acts as though he can't live with that, take him to his room with the suggestion that he "cry here."

I suppose it's the need we parents have to be all things to our children that works us into holes like this. "Good" mommies don't make their children cry. "Good" mommies sacrifice everything for their children. Those are the sort of whips we flog ourselves with. But there is a difference between being a good mommy and being a slave.

As you dismantle his present set of expectations and start to build new ones, he will yell. He has learned that sobbing brings you around in short order. His crying also means he senses a change in the rules and rituals that govern his relationship with you. The uncertainty of not knowing what's going on or where you are headed will stimulate a healthy amount of distress. Nonetheless, the best way to help him deal with his discomfort is to chart your course confidently and stick to it.

You might also consider finding a preschool program for him to attend several mornings a week. The break would do you both good.

James Dean

As the second birthday approaches, the child's personality clamors even more persistently for recognition. Young children have little, if any, appreciation for the virtue of moderation. They tend toward extremes in their behavior, so when the self is discovered, it emerges in exasperating ways. "I don' wanna! . . . No!"

Rebellion is nothing less than an expression of the toddler's need to be a separate person and assert a now-flowering identity to its utmost. It is important for parents to realize that this behavior, in its many manifestations, has a definite place in the overall scheme of things. However infuriating, it is an exclamation of growth and becoming.

If all this is put in its proper perspective, parents are less likely to overreact. Remember, parents run the show, regardless of the child's protests and contrariness. It is our responsibility to establish limits and enforce them in firm yet gentle ways. When we respond to these small mutinies out of fear or anger, we have, in essence, lost control of ourselves. This not only increases a child's anxiety but feeds the fantasy that he or she is more powerful than we are. The power struggle that inevitably ensues leads nowhere.

The patterns established at this early stage in the parent–child relationship will tend to endure, and as the mold sets it becomes more and more difficult to break.

Q: *My two-year-old has recently started ignoring and testing me whenever I ask her to do something. Can you tell me anything about handling this behavior?*

A: What you describe is typical of two-year-olds. In fact, rebellion is a healthy ingredient in any child's developmental process.

Encourage your daughter to recognize your authority and cooperate with the limits you set by using more than just your voice when giving directions. For instance, if she ignores you when you ask that she come away from the television set, move her away gently. At the same time, repeat your request and give her something else to do, such as, "Sit down here, and I will get you some pots and pans to play with."

This show-and-tell technique can even be used with commands such as "Pick up your toys." Your child's resistance can be overcome by gently moving her through the paces, as though you were physically teaching her what you expect.

Q: *Is it too much to expect a two-year-old to pick up his toys? Our little boy, when we tell him to do this, just stands there and looks at us. We've tried everything from spanking him to trying to make a game of it, but nothing has worked. At most, he will pick up one toy and put it where we tell him, but that's it. Any ideas?*

A: Your first question, concerning the appropriateness of expecting a toddler to pick up toys, must be considered in light of the fact that the typical child this age has already acquired more than fifty toys. Now, I think it is excellent training in responsibility for parents to teach a toddler to pick up after himself. This training should begin around eighteen months of age. But fifty toys? I don't think so!

Even expecting that only ten playthings be picked up and put away presents a task much too daunting for the average two-year-old. Keep in mind that *all* toddlers have attention deficit disorder (ADD is a developmental thing, folks!). They have great difficulty in focusing on tasks that do not engage the imagination, which includes picking up toys. Furthermore, I'm aware of no reliable method of turning this into play. Nor am I aware of any punitive method that will persuade a toddler to play "ten pickup," much less "fifty pickup." Telling a two-year-old he can do something he wants to do after he picks up his toys usually results in nothing but frustration for both parent and child.

The solution to this vexing problem lies neither in play nor in punishment, but in managing the situation so that the task is doable. That can mean only one thing: giving your toddler access only to that number of toys he can and will pick up. And how many is that? No more than one, at least to begin with.

I recommend that parents of toddlers operate a toy library, restricting the number of toys the child can check out at any given time to one. This library ought to be maintained in some relatively secure place, at least until the child understands the routine and the rule. The child selects a toy to play with. When he's done, he simply brings it to the parent in charge and exchanges it for another one. When the child has "gotten it," the number of toys checked out at any given time can increase to two. But, until the child is at least three years old, two should be the limit.

Parents who use this approach also discover that a toddler needs very few toys. Ten, in fact, is more than enough to keep a toddler occupied throughout the day.

"John," someone asks, "do you mean . . . ?"

Exactly! The "toy library" approach promotes longer periods of independent play, meaning, of course, that Mom and Dad are able to enjoy relatively long periods of uninterrupted time. It's certainly paradoxical, but a toddler can play imaginatively for a much longer period with one toy than with ten. At three, a toddler's ability to make choices begins to become overwhelmed, and he or she begins to whine and do other annoying things that are more a function of circumstance than personality.

I've never heard of this approach failing.

Aggression

Two-year-olds are extremely territorial. The space immediately in front of them, and everything in it, is "mine!" Intrusions into that territory threaten the child's self-concept and therefore provoke distress. The more passive child cries, while the more assertive child strikes out in some way. Brief but intense clashes over space and toys are commonplace in a group of toddler twos.

As if that weren't enough, they are virtually oblivious to one another, insensitive to each other's feelings, and incapable of remorse. A two-year-old can give and take on a limited basis with adults and older children but has a difficult time doing the same with another two-year-old. Put two or more children of this age together, and you have all the makings of a good fight. But this is nothing to lose sleep over. In a way, their willingness to tangle reflects healthy, expressive personalities.

Q: *We are best friends, writing to you about our children, two girls, ages twenty months and two years. Both children are fairly easygoing—until they are in the same place at the same time. When they get together, which is almost every day, they fight constantly. It looks as though they dislike each other. They pull hair, snatch toys away from each other, hit, scratch, and refuse to share. This is all the more puzzling because with other children they get along fine most of the time. What's going on, and what can we do to stop it?*

A: You have inadvertently stumbled upon the recipe for Instant Tot-bash: Take two toddlers between eighteen and thirty-six months old. Blend them together for two or more hours almost every day. Sit back. Watch them bash each other. (Warning! This mixture is highly volatile and will, in almost every instance, undergo spontaneous combustion.)

The level of aggression you describe is not only typical but heralds the blossoming of two healthy, demonstrative personalities.

The most important thing to keep in mind is your friendship; it is the catalyst to the conflict. The friendship brings the youngsters together frequently. The more children this age are together, the more likely they are to do battle. It is actually better, when pairing two-year-olds, to select ones with similar temperamental characteristics. Two passives or two actives will mix far more compatibly than an active and a passive.

Don't let the friendship be an obstacle to letting the problem solve itself, which it eventually will do. Both of you have an investment in the children's liking one another. Their relationship, had it been affectionate, would have affirmed and strengthened your own bond. But if you want their relationship to be an extension of your own, their conflict may become threatening to you.

Use your friendship as a way of coping with their rude interruptions. As much as possible, let them have enough space and time to work things out for themselves. At the same time, give each other permission to intervene whenever the warfare seems to be getting out of hand. Two-year-olds can and will hurt each other without ever "intending" to.

When a toy is snatched, gently take the toy away from the snatcher and give it back to the snatchee. Then keeping the screaming snatcher away from the snatchee. If need be, remove her to another place until she calms down. If they both go bonkers at the same time, separate them until they relax.

Above all else, keep your sense of humor about you, and be an example of harmony that the children can follow.

Q: *When my two-year-old has a friend over to play, they fight over toys almost constantly. Today he pushed a little girl down for no reason. I spanked him and sent him in the house. Did I do the wrong thing?*

A: I was intrigued by your use of the phrase "for no reason," because it illustrates how we big people often misunderstand the behavior of children.

When your son pushed the little girl down, he did so for no reason of ours but just "because." That is the way toddlers are. They fight over toys because they want everything *right now,* and there is only one way to skin a cat, and there are no rules—just things to want—and waiting is not fun at all. That is why at this age, and in this situation, neither a spanking nor any other form of punishment will make any connection. "Reasoning" won't complete any circuits either.

Take time to comfort both the pushee and the pusher. They are both upset, so reassure them that their world is still safe. Then involve yourself in their play, showing them, with your own actions, how to play side by side without a battle. Be a facilitator, a moderator. Remember, however, that the game is theirs, not yours. If things flare up, hold them both on your lap and say soft things.

Will this solve the problem? Not today. But in time they will learn moderation and reason. Meanwhile, remember that you are the only one with patience. Use it.

Q: *We have two girls, who are four years and eighteen months old. I've heard that the second born is more aggressive, but this is ridiculous! I actually have to intervene to keep the baby from hurting her big sister. If Audrey is playing with something and will not give it up when Polly wants it, Polly will kick and bite and throw things at her. I know that an eighteen-month-old has very little self-control, but what can I allow Audrey to do in her own defense?*

A: It sounds as though Audrey is very tolerant, patient, and gentle with Polly, especially in light of the abuse she takes from her. Polly is entering her "first adolescence." During this stage, children tend to be extremely demanding and rebellious and, when frustrated, will often react with a tantrum or some form of aggression. So the situation you describe is not at all unusual.

You are, in some ways, fortunate that Audrey is not younger. If that were the case, both children's self-centered territorial instincts would clash dramatically, and you would be having an even more difficult time.

From this point on, Polly needs, as much as anything else you can give her, the constant presence of a firm yet gentle hand. It is time for her to begin learning who is the proper authority in her life and what is appropriate behavior with you, older adults, peers, and Audrey.

Audrey should *not* be made responsible for protecting herself against a toddler who knows little about restraint. As much as possible, however, allow the children to work out their own arrangement concerning toys and other things. Tell Audrey that you do *not* want her to strike back when her sister attacks, but to protect herself first by getting away from Polly and, second, by asking for your help in resolving the conflict.

When a toy is involved, see that Audrey gets it back and attempt to substitute something for Polly. This will not always sit well with her. If she throws a tantrum, take her to her bed or crib (with the side down), or put her on the floor (if carpeted), and walk out of the room. By doing this you will let her know that there are definite, constant rules concerning expressions of frustration that occur when the world does not turn according to her whim.

Q: *Two days a week, my two-year-old son attends a mother's-morning-out program that includes children as young as eight months. At present, he is the oldest child in his class. In the meantime, the problem is that he's hurting some of the babies. Almost every time I pick him up, I get a report of an incident. The teachers have been very patient, but I can tell they're slowly reaching the end of their rope. The other day, he hit a baby on the forehead with a toy and drew a little blood. What should I do?*

A: You should photocopy this page and give it to the teachers.

For the following reasons, toddlers and babies should never be grouped together in any sort of day-care situation:

- Generally speaking, toddlers simply don't get it where babies are concerned. They don't understand that these little bundles of movement and sound are human beings. No amount of explanation, furthermore, will turn on the light of understanding. The typical toddler is not old enough to understand that a baby is human, with feelings, until his or her intellectual (cognitive) skills are mature enough to grasp this concept, at which point the toddler in question is no longer a toddler.

- Because they don't get it, toddlers tend to relate to babies as if they were just another plaything. In their attempts to figure out what babies are, they poke, pinch, bite, and maul (as they tend to do with dogs and cats). And lo and behold, they get a fascinating array of reactions—from both the infants and nearby adults.

- Some toddlers, when reprimanded for something, will stop doing the something in question right away. Others, for whatever reason, will continue doing the something in question no matter how many times they are reprimanded. The former category contains a disproportionate number of girls; the latter an equally disproportionate number of boys. Regardless, you can't predict what's going to happen if you mix a baby and a toddler of either gender.

- Toddlers don't know their strength and don't, furthermore, understand that the experimenting they do on babies is often hurtful. To take one example, they don't know that lying across a baby's face shuts off the baby's air supply. In short, the potential risk requires that an adult always be present, if not to prevent hurt (which isn't always possible), at least to intervene before the hurt becomes life-threatening.

The same problem often arises in a family setting when one sibling is a toddler and another is an infant. As emergency room physicians and pediatricians will attest, the annual number of infants who are seriously injured by toddler siblings is not insignificant. This is one reason why most child development specialists say three to four years is the ideal interval between siblings.

In short, this problem has arisen because of misjudgment.

The Dracula Syndrome

Biting, relatively common to toddlers and two-year-olds, strikes an especially dissonant chord among adults. It is, from our civilized perspective, irrational and barbaric.

When there's a biter in a group, we tend to lose sight of any other aggression that might be taking place. The biting becomes the focus of attention, and the child who bites becomes a scapegoat. If another child begins to bite, the blame falls on the first biter, who must have "infected" the second.

If the biting takes place in a nursery school, as is often the case, parents may develop the mistaken idea that the teacher, through neglect or ineptitude, "allows" children to bite. What we need to realize is that toddlers give no warning when they are about to attack—they just attack.

Not long ago, for example, I was asked into a day-care center to observe an eighteen-month-old biter. There were five toddlers in the group. I had been in the classroom for about forty-five minutes when this child did his thing. There were three adults in the room at the time. None of us could have anticipated his attack, and we were not able to prevent it.

Parents can't do anything about what takes place in the classroom either. In fact, the more responsible that parents feel, the more likely it is that biting will be talked about in the home and during the ride to and from the center. This attention only increases the odds of the child's biting again and again.

There is nothing "wrong" with a toddler who bites. He or she simply learned, probably through a chance combination of instinct and accident, that teeth are an effective weapon. Now the toddler must be taught to restrain this impulse—one of many lessons in self-control.

Q: *I am the director of a day-care center and would like your comments on a situation in our toddler classroom, in which there are six energetic and assertive children, ranging in age from seventeen to twenty-four months. Three months ago, one of the little boys began biting occasionally, usually when another child was trying to take a toy away from him. Despite our efforts to stop him, he still bites once or twice a day, generally when the activity level of the group is high. The biting has triggered a reaction from this group of parents that has been difficult to handle. All of them are up in arms over this and insist that we do something to stop him. He is not an unusually aggressive child in other ways and is not the only child in the room who has bitten. Both the teacher and his mother are beginning to feel defensive. Can you offer any suggestions?*

A: His parents must not talk about biting with him or around him (unless, of course it also takes place at home). It is not even necessary to keep them informed of incidents in the classroom. The less they know, the less fuel they bring to the fire.

Biting is more likely to occur during periods of general excitement, so separate the biter from the group when the activity level goes up. Provide him with a less active alternative until things settle down. When he does bite, or even tries to bite, the teacher should face him immediately with a firm *no* and sit him in a chair facing the group. She must do this as quickly as possible, *before* tending to the wounded child. The biter may be allowed out of the chair after the victim is calm and has returned to the group.

Q: *My two-year-old occasionally bites himself when he is mad because he can't have his way. What can I do to stop him? Does this mean he is insecure or that something is troubling him emotionally?*

A: To your first question, my answer is, Do nothing. Children of this age are largely uncivilized, and the ways they express their anger are, likewise, quite primitive. They scream, throw things, roll on the floor, strike out at objects or people nearby . . . and sometimes they bite. Their targets include toys, furniture, parents, other children, and themselves. It is possible to "cure" toddlers of biting other people, but virtually impossible to prevent them from biting themselves. In the first place, you can't predict when it's going to happen. It is somewhat like lightning, except this bolt will often strike more than once in the same place (usually the arms or hands).

Parents become alarmed and confused by self-biting and generally respond with one form or another of uncivilized panic. They shriek, run for help, struggle to separate teeth from arm, or faint. They are also likely to feel guilt at having "caused" the biting, in which case the child ends up being held and pampered.

All those reactions send this message from parent to child: "I lose control when you bite yourself." Biting becomes an issue of great significance, and the child capitalizes on the issue as a source of power and reinforcement.

Giving your son attention for biting himself makes it more likely to happen again. So, as I said, do nothing. Pretend to be busy with something else. If your child shows you the bite marks, tell him how sorry you are that he hurt himself and go about your business. If he breaks the skin, calmly help him wash and apply antiseptic to the area. If there is any doubt about his being adequately protected from infection, call your pediatrician. Watch the wound for festering or failure to heal. By reacting calmly, you lessen the chance that it will happen again.

The answer to your second question is no, he is probably not insecure or emotionally troubled. Many children bite themselves (more than parents are willing to admit). Two-year-olds teethe on themselves purely to play and test your reaction. There are many superstitions about the meaning of "odd" behavior, but often the behavior occurs initially because children are simply children. It continues because parents overreact.

On the other hand, if you live with an older child who has developed this practice into a habit that occurs whenever he or she is frustrated, or a child who bites more than occasionally, I recommend a talk with a therapist.

Q: *My brother and his wife have a big problem with their son, Axel, who recently turned two. For the past six months or so he has been biting people, adults and children alike, and often for no reason. We are not talking about a little nibble, but an all-out bite. He has drawn blood from his victims on numerous occasions. As a consequence, most of his older cousins don't want to be anywhere near him. The other day, I was holding his hand as we were walking down the driveway when I suddenly felt his sharp little teeth sink into my wrist. He recently drew blood from a six-month-old baby his mother was tending. Those are just two of the latest incidents. No one seems to know what to do, and discipline—his parents are trying light spankings and one-minute time-outs—does not seem to be working. Any insight you may have would be a great help to the entire family.*

A: To begin with, it's not unusual for toddlers to bite. In any playgroup of five or more toddlers, it's all but inevitable that one will be, or become, a biter. In and of itself, this is not abnormal or an indication of anything wrong, either with the child or with the family situation. Biting is a primitive response to frustration, and toddlers are primitive. As a group, toddlers reflect our original nature: self-centered, territorial, instant-gratification oriented, and aggressive, even violent. You can't begin to do much about this until a child is into the third year of life, when discipline needs to begin in earnest, and only powerful and consistent discipline will turn a savage into a relatively civil human being by the child's third birthday. Why are so many of today's three-year-olds still acting like toddlers? Because their well-intentioned parents employ discipline that is neither powerful enough nor consistent enough to turn the trick. In the case of your nephew, let me assure you that light taps on his bottom and a minute in a chair are the equivalent of blowing smoke in the teeth of a hurricane.

You cannot talk a toddler out of biting. You must respond immediately and in a way that persuades him not to bite—ever again, preferably. I actually have no problem with a spanking and time out. Applied with moderate force and followed with a relatively long period of time out (five to ten minutes for this age group), spanking might work. The problem is that most two-year-olds are still in diapers, unfortunately, and a swat to a padded rear means nothing.

Will your nephew outgrow this? Perhaps, but I hear of too many four- and five-year-olds who are still biting to want to take the risk. By that age, the problem is far more difficult to solve, believe me. To nip this in the bud, I'd recommend a combination of moderate spankings (the best research on the subject indicates moderate spankings are effective across a wide spectrum of misbehaviors at this age) and ten minutes of time out. Then, before the child is released from the chair or other confinement (a small room with a gate, for example), he must apologize to his victim and kiss the boo-boo.

Many, many women of my mom's generation have told me that they solved this problem before it became a problem by biting the child back. They describe a retaliatory bite that is just hard enough to cause pain without breaking the skin. Most of these women tell me that one such bite was enough to make a permanent impression, figuratively speaking. Let me assure the reader that fighting fire with fire in this fashion is *not* confusing to a child. But let me also make clear that I am not recommending this approach, only relating it as a matter of historical interest. On the other hand, one is moved to wonder, "Is there anything new under the sun?"

Tantrums

Children usually begin having tantrums around the age of two. Tantrums happen for a variety of reasons. First of all, they are an inevitable by-product of even the most normal healthy childhoods. Children become frustrated and angry just as we do, but they can't see that there is more than one way to skin a cat. They also have difficulty expressing their frustrations and knowing what questions to ask. If at first they don't succeed, they just might have a tantrum.

A cardinal rule is don't respond to tantrums by taking over the problem. The child who is rescued often enough by his or her parents learns that tantrums solve problems. If you child has a this-dumb-toy-won't-obey-me tantrum, take the dumb toy and tell the out-of-control child that it will be returned when he or she is calm.

A second rule of thumb is don't give in to demands because of tantrums. It's true that giving in turns off the screams, but it also guarantees their eventual return.

Spankings don't cure the tantrum habit either. In fact, they *increase* the likelihood that tantrums will occur. You can't fight fire with fire.

Parents tend to exaggerate the significance of tantrums. Suffice it to say that when adults make mountains out of a child's molehills, the child will learn to build mountains. For instance, some parents feel that tantrums occur because they have made some mistake in dealing with the child's demands (which they mistakenly interpret to be expressions of need). It stands to reason, if they *are* to blame for the child's tantrum, that they must right the wr   as quickly as possible. So, having said *no,* they say *yes.* Or, having spanked, they then give the child more than he or she originally demanded, to keep their guilt at bay. These maneuvers work. The tantrum stops, the parent is relieved, and the child, learning that tantrums are a successful means of obtaining things, throws more and better ones.

Other parents react to tantrums with anger rather than guilt. To them, the tantrum is evidence that the child does not accept their authority. They see the tantrum as a mutiny and react by demonstrating their authority on the child's rear end. The paradox is that a spanking, in this situation, is *not* an expression of authority. It is a display of fear, panic, and desperation. Parents who are truly in control and secure in their feelings of authority are aware that an occasional tantrum is normal for any young child. If spanking stopped tantrums, the tantrums would stop. But they don't; both continue, more and more often.

Between eighteen and thirty-six months, tantrums are almost a reflex response to anything that is frustrating. And two-year-olds are easily frustrated. They want more than their stomachs can hold or their arms can carry. In fact, an occasional tantrum is a healthy expression of the child's need to experiment with being a rebel.

Keep tantrums occasional by reacting to them calmly and matter-of-factly, in the manner of an authority who is in control.

Let's say your two-year-old daughter has a tantrum. Simply pick her up and carry her to her bedroom. Deposit her in her bed. If she still sleeps in a crib, leave the side down so she can get out. If she can't get out, put her on the floor. Then leave, because there is nothing to discuss. If you *must* say something, say, "You may have your tantrum in here."

As you leave, pull the door partly closed. If she comes out before her frenzy has subsided, gently put her back in. When she is quiet and comes out, do not mention the tantrum. It's not important.

This is neat and simple. Do this whenever a tantrum occurs, and they will never become a major issue. Parent is still boss. Child is still child. Molehills are molehills.

The occasional tantrum can be handled best by letting it run its course and then being there when it subsides to help the child cope with whatever is causing the upset. Frequent tantrums, however, are often an indication that parents are not enforcing rules consistently. One day, Miranda wants a cookie before supper and gets it because Mom is too tired to be firm. The next day, she is refused a cookie before supper because Mom took an afternoon nap, so she throws a tantrum. Mom may spank her, give her a cookie, put her in her room, throw a tantrum too, or all of the above. This kind of inconsistency places stress on a child. Stress provokes tension, fatigue, and tantrums.

Remember what Grandma did when you told her you were running away from home? She probably said, "That's a wonderful idea. You should have left to see the world long before now. After all, you're six years old and time's a-wastin'. So I'll help you pack and fix you a sandwich." And there you were back at Grandma's door twenty minutes later, having seen quite enough for six years old.

Grandma had some fine ideas. She could tell the big people from the little people without a program, and she never needed a scorecard. So let's lift a page from Grandma's memoirs and see if tantrums can be handled with some homemade reverse psychology.

Pick a calm time when everyone in the family is feeling relaxed. Sit down with your young one and say something like, "Miranda, we want to talk with you about tantrums. A tantrum is when you are very angry and scream and throw things.

"You have about ten tantrums every day, so we decided to give you a special place to have them in. We will call it your tantrum place. Your tantrum place is the downstairs bathroom" (or any relatively private place in the house).

"From now on, when you want to make a tantrum, go—or we will take you—to your tantrum place, close the door, and make it. You may make all the tantrums you want in there. No one will bother you."

Whichever place you choose, make it seem it's the best location in the whole house to make tantrums in. Nowhere else is quite good enough for the fine tantrums that Miranda makes.

"We decided to give you the bathroom, because it seems just right for making tantrums. It's small, so the tantrum will be louder. It has a toilet you can use if you have to. There is a light switch for you to turn off and on to make tantrums bigger. You can lie down on the comfy rug and kick and scream. When the tantrum is done, you have tissues to dry your tears and water to wash your face. We hope you like it. In fact, it would be all right if you want to go in there *right now* and make a tantrum, just to see how well it works."

Chances are that she will make a few trial runs the first day, and then, finding that the thrill is gone, will have increasingly shorter tantrums and less frequent ones. As she begins having fewer tantrums, point this out to her and thank her for helping keep the house quiet.

Should she forget about her special place and begin making tantrums in the living room, say something like, "Oh-oh, remember the tantrum place. You had better get in there quickly before your tantrum is all over." If necessary, take her there while she is screaming, firmly but without anger.

If she continues to have an occasional tantrum outside while you aren't around, or in her room by herself, let these run their course without notice.

Is it a trick? No. The parents are not one-upping the child with an elaborate practical joke. It's actually a game in which everyone learns something valuable about dealing with stressful situations.

I've seen this technique work with children between the ages of two and a half and five, the ages at which tantrums occur most frequently. Children older than five probably will not cooperate in the game so readily and may simply have to be told, "I do not like tantrums. From now on, when you have a tantrum, I am going to put you in the downstairs bathroom. When you go in there, the door will be closed. You are not to open it and come out until the tantrum is completely over. If you come out before it's over, I will put you back in again."

If Grandma's game doesn't appear to be working, then you may need to be more firm. If nothing you try appears to be having any positive effect, consider seeking professional help. Whatever you decide, if at first you don't succeed, don't throw a tantrum.

Q: *My youngest, a boy, is twenty-six months old. When we visited relatives recently, my nephew—three months older—was very aggressive with my son, often pushing him down. My son began screaming at the top of his lungs any time his cousin came near him. Since then, he has continued to scream whenever he's upset—a short earsplitting scream that is incredibly annoying! How do you reason with a two-year-old? Help! My supply of earplugs is running out!*

A: You can't reason with the unreasonable. Your son learned that screaming would move adults to make things better for him, so the screaming has generalized to any and all upsetting situations. Not a problem. Create a tantrum place in your home. It can be a carpeted alcove, an upholstered chair, or any other comfortable, well-defined area. Tell him screaming is special and deserves a special place. Equate his tantrum place to the bath place (tub) and the eating place (table), as in, "Every special thing has a special place."

When he starts screaming, take him immediately to his tantrum place, telling him he has to stay until he stops. Then walk away. If he follows you but has not stopped screaming, put him back. You may have to do this several times at first in order to get him to stay until his tantrum is over. The key to success is to act completely nonchalant, as if the screaming doesn't bother you bit, but you simply can't allow him to scream just anywhere.

The Bedtime Blues

Q: *We have an eighteen-month-old girl who has, until lately, always gone to bed (at nine o'clock) very pleasantly, fallen asleep quickly, and slept through the night. In the past several weeks, she has become a monster at bedtime. She screams, becomes rigid, and goes into a rage when we leave the room. I have always rocked her for several minutes before putting her down. Now, the moment I stop rocking, she starts yelling. This went on for three and a half hours last night, as we did everything*

*we could think of. Finally she wore herself out in my arms. She has also
been waking up briefly in the middle of the night. What have I done to
cause this, and what can be done to stop it?*

A: You haven't done anything to cause her screams. Her Jekyll to
Hyde transformation at bedtime is the first stage of a revolution
commonly called the terrible twos.

Gone are the days when she would smile and coo pleasantly as
Mommy and Daddy put her to bed. Cribs are confining and not
compatible with her new way of thinking. Gone are the days when
a few minutes of rocking was enough. What right does Mom have
to stop rocking? None! She has also figured out that life goes on in
the house after the lights go out in her bedroom. It's a trick! How
dare you?

To make bedtime go more smoothly, you must first rid yourself
of the paralyzing idea that she screams because you have done
something wrong. She screams because *you* have done something
to *her*, and she will not stand (or lie) still for it. There may be no
way, short of letting her sleep with you (*don't* do that!), to put her
to bed without screams for a while.

Next, keep it firmly in mind that her bedtime exists solely for
your sake. The importance of putting a child to bed is so daddies
and mommies can be husbands and wives again. Bedtime is an
exercise in learning how to separate the child from the marriage
(see chapter 18, Bedtime). With that in mind, I recommend that
you move bedtime back to eight o'clock. Between seven forty-five
and eight, move her through the preliminaries. Then put her in her
crib and, screams or no screams, leave the room. Remember: In hesitation, all is lost.

I realize how difficult it is to forget you are parents when there's
a child screaming in the house. So put yourselves on a schedule.
Take turns checking in with her every ten minutes. Walk with
feigned casualness into her room, say a brief something about
going to sleep, lay her back down, give her rigid body a kiss, and
walk out. As she begins to get the message, you can extend the time
between checks to fifteen or twenty minutes.

While she rages, you and your husband can talk, play back-gammon, read, or do whatever you enjoy doing together. Support and help each other make the transition from parent to spouse. Real people again. Now *that's* something to look forward to.

Q: *Our twenty-month-old son is putting us through some changes. He is becoming more active and refuses to take an afternoon nap. In addition, he has learned how to climb out of his crib. Bedtime is becoming a battle. What can we do?*

A: Before you do anything, you need to understand how important these changes are to your son's growth and development. On the surface, this behavior may appear to be symptoms of rebelliousness, so it's no surprise that you've engaged him in "battle." But there's more going on here than meets the eye. The transformation taking place is more accurately described in terms of an underlying process, the fertile soil from which this "rebellious" behavior grows.

The metamorphosis from caterpillar to butterfly has begun. Caterpillars fly and babies climb from their cribs. As your son's sense of himself expands, so does his view of the world. Everything takes on new and exciting dimensions, stimulating his wonder and his activity level. Who can blame him for not wanting to stay in a crib?

The not-so-simple act of climbing out of the crib is much more than an athletic event. It requires and expresses a feeling of trust, an irrepressible confidence in his ability to accomplish new things (scale new heights, so to speak). Most of all, it acknowledges that he has given himself permission—and he senses that you have, too—to begin uncoupling from you to become independent. He no longer has to stay put just because you put him there.

Take the path of least resistance. Instead of trying to make him stay where he is determined not to, begin a gradual changeover from crib to bed. Dismantle the crib (with his help) and put the mattress on the floor. Let him sleep there until he learns the boundaries of the mattress and no longer rolls off in his sleep. Then move him to a regular bed.

You might want to put up a childproof gate at his doorway, especially if you live in a two-story house. The gate will secure him in his room after you put him to bed but will allow him to roam within reasonable boundaries until he's ready to sleep. In this way you aren't forcing him to lie down, but you are setting limits on his activity after bedtime. If he stands at the gate and screams, return to his room at regular lengthening intervals (begin with ten minutes) to calm him down and tuck him in with a firm message about going to sleep. This will take some effort for several days but will eventually pay off.

The best solution to his increasing activity level is to childproof your home, if you haven't done so already. This not only guarantees the child's safety but your peace of mind as well.

As for nap time, trying to make him sleep is a losing proposition. You can still require that he remain in his room for one hour every afternoon, though. Continue putting him to bed for a nap as part of his daily routine. If you must, use the gate to keep him in his room. Once he gets accustomed to this regular down time, he will probably start napping again. Whether he sleeps or not, use the time for yourself. For the next few years, in fact, the more time you can make just for *you,* the better off *he* will be.

Q: *When we put her in her crib at night, our eighteen-month-old daughter gets on all fours and rocks back and forth, banging her head against the headboard. It's a gentle but persistent banging until she falls asleep, which is usually within ten minutes. Is this normal?*

A: Depends on what you mean by normal. Most toddlers don't bang their heads as they're going to sleep, so from that perspective, your daughter's head-banging isn't normal. On the other hand, if a toddler who's perfectly normal in every other respect bangs her head gently to help herself go to sleep, then her head banging *is* normal.

The research differentiates between pathological and nonpathological head-banging. Pathological head-banging in children is usually associated with serious neurological, developmental, or emotional problems. In other words, an observant parent would know something was wrong even if the child in question wasn't banging his or her head. The bottom line: Don't worry about it.

Your daughter has discovered this rhythmic and gently stimulating activity helps her go to sleep. Lucky you, considering the alternative: screaming bloody murder for thirty minutes or more. (Remember, a toddler's head is quite soft, so gentle head banging is probably not the least bit painful to her.)

The bottom line: Don't worry about it. Be grateful.

Einstein Didn't Talk Until He Was Three

Q: *We are the parents of an active and alert twenty-month-old boy who doesn't talk. He has a limited single-syllable vocabulary that includes "ma-ma," "da-da," and "bye," but whenever he wants to say something else, he acts it out with gestures. He has no trouble understanding anything we say to him, but we wonder if he has a problem. Up until now, we've put no pressure on him to talk, but it has been suggested to us that we not do things for him unless he uses words to tell us what he wants. What are your thoughts on this?*

A: A three-word vocabulary at twenty months is not cause for concern. In one sense, your son's vocabulary sounds fairly extensive.

We all have two vocabularies: one active, or expressive; the other passive, or receptive. Our active vocabulary consists of words we use when we talk (or write), while our passive vocabulary includes all the words we understand. We generally understand more words than we use, and in children the difference is marked. Your son's passive vocabulary is probably the more accurate reflection, at his age, of how well he is progressing in language development. From this point of view, he is obviously doing fine.

Well, then, why doesn't he talk more? Probably for several reasons, all having to do with his age.

He stands on the threshold of the terrible twos, a traumatic eighteen months in the lives of most children. It is the agony and ecstasy of childhood—and parenthood as well. The child who is almost two views and acts on his world as though he were the center of all experience. He also takes his first tentative steps toward independence. And tentative they are, since his need to be cuddly and close is still powerful. His need to feel independent is satisfied by being in control of situations—and people. His continued dependency needs are met through involvement with you, his parents. All these needs are, paradoxically, satisfied by not talking. He is able to control certain situations, prolong your involvement with him, and receive plenty of attention in the bargain. Isn't he clever?

So cooperate with him, casually and matter-of-factly. Don't try to force him to talk by ignoring his pantomimed requests. That would create a useless and frustrating power struggle. He is, after all, becoming adept at gestural language, an art that will enhance his overall communication skills in the long run.

Talk to him, but don't require him to talk back. When he's ready and has found other ways to satisfy his need for attention, he will no doubt discover that talking works better than charades.

When a child is twenty-four months old, a speech and hearing evaluation might be appropriate if several of the following indicators are present:

- The child uses less than a twenty-word expressive vocabulary.

- The expressive vocabulary is not increasing, or the child shows no interest in talking.

- The child is becoming increasingly dependent on gestures.

- The child is becoming visibly frustrated by attempts to communicate.

- The child does not respond when spoken to or seem to understand simple directions.

- The child does not show an understanding of what you want when you show a picture and say, "Point to the puppy," "Show me the ball," or "Where's the hat?"

Q: *Our two-year-old isn't talking yet, and we're worried to death about it. He babbles, and it's obvious to us that he's trying to say words, but he doesn't say anything intelligible except ma-ma and da-da. We've had his ears tested, and the doctor says everything's okay and not to worry. What should we do?*

A: You should listen to your doctor. Stop worrying. If your son's hearing is fine and he's attempting speech, he'll talk in his own time. Indeed, your son's a bit behind the curve—a bit, mind you—in his speech development, but that's somewhat typical of boys. The norm is established by counting in all the girls, and the average girl begins talking intelligibly about three months earlier than the average boy. If your son was not attempting speech, I'd be giving you a more cautious answer, but everything sounds fine to me.

You didn't say, but you may be worried that a delay in speech means your son isn't all there in the intelligence department. If so, you can put that neurosis to bed as well. While a significant speech delay in combination with little or no attempt at speech is likely to signal more pervasive developmental problems, a slight delay isn't a reliable predictor of anything. According to rumor, Einstein— yep, the one and only Albert—didn't talk until he was three. My first grandson, who—it goes without saying—is gifted, didn't begin talking intelligibly until almost three either.

10

Three-Year-Olds

A CHILD'S GROWTH, like that of every other living thing, proceeds through a sequence of stages. Each stage, or phase, is defined by new ways of interacting with the environment, and each successive theme is an extension and elaboration on previous ones.

Three-year-olds begin to build a sense of initiative, or purposeful self-confidence, upon the trust and autonomy acquired during the wonderful ones and the terrible twos. During the eighteen months before the third birthday, children are busy forging a clear sense of who they are. As you might expect, the young self-image is fragile, like a clay pot that hasn't yet dried.

The omnipotence felt as a two-year-old has turned inside-out. Once upon a time, the child ruled the world. Now all that is left to claim are a few toys and a vague, shifting sense of identity, and even that small territory is a struggle to maintain. Is it any wonder, then, that three-year-olds are so easily threatened by such things as the dark, loud noises, and bumps on the head?

Owies

Physical injuries, no matter how minor, strike too close to home for the three-year-old's comfort. Even the slightest pain from a tiny scratch can dislodge the tentative grasp three-year-olds have on the "me" that must be guarded so carefully, lest it slip away as mysteriously as it came. Furthermore, three-year-olds have no way of knowing that wounds heal, which inflates their fear and feeling of helplessness.

Q: *Our usually easygoing three-year-old has recently started acting more sensitive to pain than he used to be. He gets almost hysterical over a little scratch or scraped knee. I won't even attempt to describe his reaction to a cut. We have tried to get him to realize that his injuries aren't that bad, but it doesn't help. We don't know what more we can do. What suggestions do you have?*

A: Threes (and young fours) have a reputation for overreacting to mild pain in the manner you describe. It will do no good to try to persuade your son that his perception of these traumatic events is inaccurate. There are some things only time can teach. The more you do, the more you talk, the more exaggerated his reaction is likely to become. Simply tend to his wound, put your arms around him, and sit quietly until he calms down. Your being there is all he needs to restore his misplaced sense of togetherness.

Isn't it nice to know we don't always have to talk so much?

Fears

Fears are common to three-year-olds. Leading the list are fear of the dark, fear of being left alone, and fear of things that go bump in the night.

Three-year-olds often misinterpret ordinary events as threatening because of the interaction of three characteristics:

1. The need to protect their recently acquired and still fragile sense of identity. As children grow in self-sufficiency, they must come to grips with the anxiety associated with letting go

of their parents. Fears dramatize this process. They are symbolic, fantasy-laden expressions of the young child's feelings of vulnerability.

2. The flowering of imaginative thought. Threes have the ability to conjure up mental images of things real and unreal but lack the ability to control the process.

3. The inability to separate *word* from *thing*. If there is a word for something, it *must* exist. Threes can't separate fact from fiction because both are represented in the same medium—language.

Parents often misinterpret a child's fearfulness as a symptom of insecurity or upcoming emotional problems. They react as if the fear were the child's way of saying, "You guys aren't taking care of me." They feel responsible for this anxiety, so they try to protect the child from it. Unfortunately, the parents communicate *their* anxieties and actually *increase* the child's sense of helplessness.

Trying to reason the fear away usually doesn't work either. The rational explanation and the imaginative fear are on separate incompatible wavelengths. A reasoned approach only heightens the child's sense of isolation: If the parents don't see things the same way, the child really is at the mercy of whatever seems to be "out there."

The most effective approach is first to acknowledge the fear: "I know the dark can be frightening when you are three years old." Then identify with the child: "When I was three, I was afraid of the dark too." Finally, provide reassurance: "I'll be downstairs in the living room, and I will take care of you."

Stay close enough to make the child feel protected, but not so close that your presence validates the fear.

Q: *Believe it or not, my three-and-a-half-year-old son is afraid of newspapers. He says he doesn't like the way they smell and refuses to enter a room if one is there. He is also afraid of other paper products. He won't sit at the table if there is a napkin at his place, won't blow his nose on a tissue, and wants me to clean him after he goes to the toilet. He has* *become quite insistent about all this and has a tantrum if we do not cooperate. What should we do?*

A: Newspaper is a new one to me, but it isn't any more significant than garden-variety fears of the dark or of frogs.

Young children do not see the line we draw between fact and fancy. Their playful innocence makes them vulnerable, for the same process that turns bath toys into sailing ships can also bring shadows alive in the night. With a bit more exaggeration, children see themselves as victims of sinister forces beyond their understanding or control.

By acceding to your son's demands and rearranging the world in order to protect him, you inadvertently become part of the drama, thereby giving validity to his fright. "Newspaper can hurt me. I know it can, because Mom and Dad protect me from it. Other kinds of paper can hurt me too," He can also use this issue to manipulate you and gain control of certain family situations. It is no surprise, for instance, that his fears have disrupted mealtimes and hooked you back into helping him go to the bathroom. Power struggles between children and parents almost always involve conflict over bedtime, meals, or the toilet.

Your son is saying, "I will come to the table only on my terms. I will only go so far in using the bathroom by myself." However, he is not actually in control of himself or of the situation. He is convinced his fear is real. The more you cooperate, the more his original insecurities increase, and the more fearful he becomes.

You must help him distinguish between what is real and what is not. It is essential that *you* define for him the way the family functions. While I see no harm in letting him choose for himself whether to enter a room in which there is a newspaper, you must not let his panic persuade you to remove it. About meals and the bathroom, make no concessions. Tell him, "You are one person in this family, and your place at the table will look like everyone else's." Insist that he sit with the family during meals and use his napkin appropriately. Firmly refuse to assist him in the bathroom.

Give the problem back to him. After all, *he* invented it.

Intellectual Growth

Three-year-olds gradually learn to deal with delay of gratification. A two-year-old will always choose the immediate reward—even if it is less attractive—over the one he or she must wait for. Three-year-olds can hold off for a short time, provided they have something to occupy them in the interval. This ability to postpone gratification indicates a strengthened tolerance for frustration and increased self-control.

Three-year-olds demonstrate a remarkable memory for past events. When my children were three, they continually amazed me with their ability to describe, in precise detail, events that had happened months before—ones I had almost forgotten and could not recall with comparable clarity.

Threes are also able to retrieve information selectively for problem-solving. For these reasons, children of this age show more variety in their approaches to problem situations. A two-year-old, seeing no other alternative, will often fly into a rage if the first attempt to solve a problem doesn't work. Three-year-olds, having experienced the same initial failure, are more likely to try one or two other strategies before being overwhelmed by frustration.

Three-year-olds learn from their mistakes and use feedback to modify their problem-solving techniques. The emergence of trial-and-error thinking is one of the two most significant intellectual events occurring at this age. The other is the flowering of creative, imaginative thought. Threes are suddenly interested in making things. They enjoy coloring, painting, working in clay, and building things out of whatever material is available. But more than anything else, three-year-olds *pretend* and, if left to their own devices, will spend a major portion of their day engaged in self-directed imaginative activity. This timely happening is a perfect complement to their growing independence and initiative. For the first time in their lives, threes are capable of occupying and entertaining themselves for relatively long periods.

Three-year-olds use their intellectual freedom to explore and come to grips with their initiation into the social side of life. Their almost constant imaginative play is a way of practicing and preparing for greater social responsibility. Three-year-olds are literally playing at growing up. This ability mentally to represent entire social scenarios also allows three-year-olds to keep enough distance between themselves and actual events to keep their anxiety level under control and protect their still-fragile self-image.

Q: *My friend and I both have three-and-a-half-year-old boys who will enter four-year-old kindergarten this fall. I'm concerned because her son knows how to write his name and can identify lots of colors and even— get this!—all fifty states. His parents are now working with him on the names of the state capitals, which he's picking up fairly quickly. My son can't write his name yet and shows no interest all in memorizing anything. Do I have cause to worry?*

A: Worry about what? You have something to worry about if your son

- can't converse fairly well and clearly

- shows no interest in playing with other children

- regularly messes himself

- can't occupy himself independently and creatively

- sits for long periods of time staring at the wall

- throws wild tantrums during which he bangs his head on hard objects

but the fact that he doesn't write his name and perform mnemonic tricks on command is no cause whatsoever for concern.

With due respect to your well-intentioned friends, who are probably convinced their pet human is gifted, any three-year-old possessing average intelligence whose parents invest the time can be taught to write his name, correctly identify all fifty states, and so on. A young child's mind, uncluttered as it is, can absorb all sorts of irrelevant junk. It's truly too bad, even pathetic, that some parents are so eager to be seen—and see themselves—as superior to the rest of us that they waste their young children's precious time in these ways.

The fourth year of life is for learning how to play with others, for practicing proper manners, and for spending independent time inquiring, imagining, and creating. To force upon a three-year-old tedious and completely irrelevant memory drills is brain abuse, pure and simple, even if these exercises are conducted as "games." Let me assure you, when both children—yours and your friend's—are in their teens, no one will be able to tell which one knew the names of all fifty states when he was three. I might, however, venture to predict that your son will be the happier of the two.

I asked a recent audience, "How many of you entered first grade not able to identify all twenty-six letters of the alphabet?"

Lots of hands went up, and let me assure the reader that this audience had not been bused in from a local rehabilitation center for adult illiterates. It was, in fact, composed entirely of people who worked for a large high-tech corporation. Later, several managers told me the best potential employee was not necessarily one who'd made the best grades in school but rather one who was creative, resourceful, industrious, and required little direct supervision. Those attributes are learned during the third and fourth years of life. Evidence suggests, furthermore, that occupying a child's time with rote exercises—even teaching a child of this age to read—may be counterproductive. One study, for example, found that teaching children to read during their preschool years increased the chances of their not enjoying reading as a teen.

So if you've been obsessing about the possibility that your son is behind the preschool performance curve, you can stop. By showing no interest in memory drills, he's telling you he's a happy well-adjusted three-year-old who's not the least bit interested in performing at dinner parties. In this case, the child knows best.

Imaginary Playmates

One day shortly after my son's third birthday, I sat downstairs listening while he played upstairs in his room. After nearly two hours of animated conversation and much activity, Eric bounded down the stairs. Alone.

"Who were you playing with?" I asked.

"My friend," he said, a gleam in his eye.

"And what is your friend's name?"

"Jackson Jonesberry," he said, with obvious pleasure.

I have no idea where he got the name, but I like to believe it came from the same place Jackson did.

When my daughter was three, she created not one but a whole group of imaginary friends, including Soppie, Honkus, and the inimitable Shinyarinka Sinum.

The appearance of imaginary playmates is an unmistakable sign of the three-year-old's interest in peer relationships. With Jackson Jonesberry or Shinyarinka Sinum, a child can satisfy this strong need for peer affiliation while at the same time practicing social skills in a safe and controlled context.

When Eric was three and four, we lived in a rural area where there were few opportunities for play with other children. For nearly two years, he played with Jackson and several other invisible friends—invisible to Willie and me, that is, for to Eric they were very real. I am certain he could "see" them.

There is no need to worry about the amount of time children spend in this sort of play. Adults should not interrupt or intrude when a child plays in this manner. When it is necessary to interrupt for practical reasons, do so with utmost respect for the "guest." Adults should *never* question the existence of such an invention.

In light of the importance of imagination to social and intellectual growth, I cannot urge parents too strongly to keep children this age away from television. It can distract and eventually overwhelm the young child's imagination.

Children watching television learn to depend on something outside themselves for creative stimulation. They do not learn to be creative. Children watching television are not preparing for a larger role in life. They learn how to be spectators instead of doers, followers rather than leaders. A child watching television is not practicing independence or exercising initiative. That child learns only how to be complacent, dependent, resourceless, and irresponsible.

This is true regardless of the program, *Sesame Street* included (see chapter 6, Television, Computer, and Video Games).

Kid Klutz

During the fourth year of life, children may act as though they are becoming *less* instead of *more* coordinated. Typically, they trip and fall more often, their feet get tangled when they run (he's got two left feet), and they drop and spill things and generally play the role of Kid Klutz (he trips, he spills, he stutters, he walks into walls). They may also begin stuttering—repeating themselves, backing up, and holding on to certain sounds.

Paradoxically, this physical and verbal awkwardness arises because the three-year-old is trying to orchestrate thought, language, and movement. Up until this time, the child focused on each of these developmental areas in relative isolation from the other two. Now, he or she is putting them together in a coordinated system.

Whereas before children concentrate separately on learning to walk and to talk, they now try to walk and talk at the same time. This example, while oversimplified, expresses the essential character of this stage in a child's growth. It is a time of reorganization and integration, and at first the pieces don't work as well together as they did individually.

Unfortunately, parents often react as though the child has suddenly developed a problem. They become anxious, lose patience, and try to help overcome the "difficulties." This makes a problem where there was none. The parents' anxiety tells the child something is "wrong," and minor difficulties become traps. This is particularly true in the case of stuttering.

The general rule is, have patience and be supportive. If your daughter spills her milk for the thirteenth time in twelve days, instead of blasting her self-esteem ("What's the matter with you? Why can't you do something as simple as hold a cup"), say something like, "Oh-oh. Here, take this rag and help me clean up. I remember spilling my milk when I was three years old, too."

Stuttering can usually be prevented if parents take the time to listen and show interest in what the child is trying to say. If your son starts stuttering, here is what *not* to do:

- *Don't* complete his sentences for him.

- *Don't* say things like "Slow down" or "Take a deep breath and start over."

- *Don't* discuss his stuttering when he can hear you.

- *Don't* interrupt him or tell him to come back when he is calm and can talk "better."

Talk slowly to children who stutter. If they have trouble telling you something, ask questions they can answer in three words or less. If they complain about stuttering, let them know that sometimes even big people have tubble tralking.

Social Growth

By the age of three, the child's almost intolerable self-centeredness gives way to a more social view of self in relation to others. He or she learns to take turns (which precedes true sharing) and to play *with* (instead of simply around) other children.

Three-year-olds occasionally act as though they can look at a situation from someone else's point of view. Expressions of empathy are rare, though, to anyone except their primary caretakers and children with whom they are familiar. Three-year-old playmates comfort each other and are sometimes even penitent when they bruise one another's feelings.

Three-year-olds can form transient play relationships with other children their age or slightly older. Proceed with caution, however, when mixing three-year-olds for the first time. They don't understand the value of social foreplay. Instead, they rush into intimate and risky interactions with one another. This causes as many disastrous first encounters as rewarding ones. And first impressions definitely count with three-year-olds. Children who hit it off well generally continue to do so, while children whose first encounter was filled with friction are likely to have subsequent difficulty getting along.

But close encounters of the worst kind can be prevented if adults are sensitive to the risks involved in putting children of this age together, and if they give the children adequate supervision, structure, and guidance until they are playing smoothly with one another.

This is a good age for introducing the young child to group day care. Be careful when selecting a preschool, because the value of the experience depends on the quality of the program. By and large, however, research indicates that developmentally oriented group care produces an increase in constructive goal-oriented behavior, an increase in cooperative play, an increase in assertive behavior, improvement in conflict-solving skills, and improvement in the child's ability to adapt to new situations.

Three-year-olds carefully observe other children and imitate them. This "monkey see, monkey do" tendency, although exasperating at times, is important to the growth of social skills. On one level imitation is a game, an almost ritual exchange between children that forms positive cooperative social bonds. On another, it is a way of acquiring problem-solving skills. Researchers have found that once a three-year-old watches another child cope with a stressful event, he or she can employ similar strategies to deal with the same situation. On yet another level, imitation is a low-risk way of experimenting with new forms of behavior. If they are nothing else, three-year-olds are experimental little people, and therefore somewhat unpredictable.

It's a try-anything-once age. They go through this phase of their lives trying on any and every behavior imaginable, seeing if it fits or adds something interesting either to their own image of themselves or that image they see reflected in other people's reactions to them.

The first three years of a child's life are spent building a relatively enduring personality—a basic wardrobe. For the next two years or so, the youngster window-shops for accessories—bits and pieces of behavior to add variety and spice.

Three-year-olds are likely to borrow these tidbits from anyone, but playmates and older children figure heavily in what they bring home. The mimicry three-year-olds love is clearly a sign that they are beginning to identify with other children and are exerting considerable influence as role models for one another.

Episodes of regression to behavior reminiscent of infancy are also common, all the more so when there's a new sibling involved. These include increases in bowel and bladder accidents, asking for a bottle, using baby talk, and wanting to be carried and held more than usual.

Most of these harmless excursions back in time are best handled by looking the other way. However, if several repeat performances in a short period tip you off that a pattern is developing, it's necessary to intervene authoritatively before the mortar sets.

Q: *My husband and I would appreciate your suggestions on a situation that has us puzzled. Our three-and-a-half-year-old son taught himself to use the toilet when he was just two. Since then he has enjoyed playing with his diapers, training pants, and various articles of toddler clothing, which we let him do. Recently, after being at the home of a friend his age who is not toilet trained, he came home, put on several pairs of training pants, and wet them, just slightly. He has done this twice since, and we aren't sure what it means. I've also noticed that, on occasion, his penis gets hard when he is playing with putting on diapers or training pants. Should we forbid him to wear them? I might add that we are expecting a new baby in four months. Could this have anything to do with it?*

A: I don't get a sense of anything unusual from your letter. Your son sounds like a typical three-year-old. Not that lots of threes dress "down" in diapers and old clothing, mind you, but typical in the sense that a child of this age is imaginative and experimental and enjoys role play.

There is no need to forbid him to play in his old clothes. I would suggest, however, that you convey clearly your rules and expectations about them.

It is probably unwise to let him play with the diapers. He may think he has permission to wet them, especially after the new baby arrives and he notices that his younger sibling enjoys this prerogative.

As for the arousal of his penis, keep in mind that a three-year-old's sexuality is diffuse and capable of responding to any form of pleasurable stimulation. In this case, putting on his diapers and training pants must arouse warm feelings associated with the many pleasurable experiences of infancy—being held, having diapers changed, wetting his pants. Similar physical responses are fairly common in boys and girls (although in a less obvious manner) who suck their thumbs or nuzzle favorite blankets.

Lies

A three-year-old's sense of fantasy is so much a part of the child's personality that the distinction between what is truth and what is not is hazy. The meaning of "truth" is not *really* clear until a child is nearly seven.

Young children don't completely understand the concept of responsibility either. To them, things simply happen, and the extent of their involvement is not always clear in their minds. Therefore, don't expect threes (or even fours, fives, or sixes) to be completely truthful. And don't regard it as a moral weakness when they aren't.

Children of this age are easily frightened into concealing the truth. If the threat of punishment is present, the child's natural defense is to try and avoid pain by saying, "Not me." If this works, the child will feel relief at having been spared the parents' wrath.

There is also a certain rush of exhilaration at realizing that a concealment has "worked." This exhilaration can be habit forming. The greater the threat and the more risky the concealment, the greater the thrill of getting away with it. And so the child rolls the dice again the next time and keeps on rolling.

Occasionally, the concealment falls flat, and the parents score with a spanking. Some of the time, though, it works so the parents are at least confused, and the child scores. The child who tries five "hoodwinks" with only one success will probably go on playing the odds.

Q: *Our little boy, who is three years old, will misbehave and then, when we confront him, deny he did anything. We punish him anyway, but it makes us upset because he acts so hurt. We wonder if he knows why he is being punished, or if he really believes he did nothing wrong. How should we handle these situations?*

A: Remember that an ounce of prevention is worth a pound of cure. Don't give your child an opportunity to conceal something you already know he did. Instead of asking your son, "Did you tear all the leaves off my African violets?" make a firm positive statement, such as, "You tore the leaves off my African violets. I am very angry. You must clean up the mess and go to your room." Ask the child no questions, and he'll tell you no lies.

If you see your son misbehave, or if circumstantial evidence points to him as the culprit, don't open the door for argument by asking the obvious question. Extracting admissions of guilt or apology is not necessary. Save time and trouble by making statements that tell the child you know what happened. Ignore his protests and alibis. You'll be doing him a favor.

When several children are playing together and something goes wrong, it's not worth the effort to play Who-done-it? Besides, children are quick to make a scapegoat of one child in the group, usually the smallest or one who has taken lots of blame in the past. They cannot be relied on as impartial witnesses. Where siblings are involved, say, "This happened while you were playing together, and you will both be punished for it." In cases where your child is one of a group, break up the action and direct the disciplinary lesson at your own offspring.

Concealments are less likely if the threat of spanking is not an issue. Punish by taking away privileges: bicycle, outside play, having friends over, and so on. It's true that spankings take less time, but in this case they seldom have a lasting effect. On the other hand, it's too easy to let "You can't go outside for three days" slide after the first day, so make the consequence short but meaningful.

Punish the act and disregard the concealment. Don't promise your son that things will go easier if he tells the truth, or that he will be punished doubly if he lies. This sort of plea bargaining is extremely confusing and tells the child you *expect* him to lie. Unless you want the seed to grow, this idea must not be planted in a child's mind. A child who misbehaves should be punished immediately. No deals or legal mumbo-jumbo should divert attention from what happened.

"Mine?"

Until recently, from the three-year-old's egocentric (self-centered) point of view, there was but one territory and one set of possessions—the child's. Part of growing up is accepting the disappointing fact that everyone else owns a piece of the pie too. This requires that children civilize their view of the world by learning what is implied by the words we use to define *possession*.

This is a difficult task, because the lines separating *mine* from *yours* are largely invisible. There is, for instance, nothing distinguishing about the "my" in "my fire truck."

The possessive pronouns—mine, yours, his, hers, theirs, ours—are abstractions referring to ownership. Three-and-a-half-year-old children find it difficult to comprehend abstractions, which are one step removed from their world of color and sound and touch and taste and smell.

To a three-and-a-half-year-old, "This fire truck is red" makes sense because red can be seen. It can be experienced *directly*. "This fire truck is *mine*," however, makes no sense. "Where and what is *mine*?" puzzles the child.

Attempting to understand abstractions, the youngster translates them into behavior. Oftentimes this behavior runs counter to the intended message. For example, the word *don't* is also an abstraction, referring to the *absence* of some action. "Sit on the dog" makes sense to a three-and-a-half-year-old because the message is concrete, down-to-earth. On the other hand, "Don't sit on the dog" complicates matters considerably. The child is perplexed and, in an attempt to resolve the confusion, does the obvious, which is to plop down on the dog. Because we fail to see the child's behavior in its proper context, we say the child is "disobedient" and "knows better." Far from it.

Q: *During the past three months, on four separate occasions, our three-and-a-half-year-old daughter has shown me objects she had concealed and taken from a playmate's house or the day-care center. After each incident, I talked calmly and tried not to make a big deal out of it, but I'm not sure this is the right approach. Is this more serious than I'm willing to admit? Should I have punished her? How would you suggest I deal with it if it happens again?*

A: Not to worry. Nearly every child this age tries the sticky-fingers routine. This is not to be confused with stealing. The motives are anything but similar. In fact, your daughter is, in the most literal sense of the term, *innocent*.

During the preschool years, "taking" is an experimental behavior, no harm intended. She is, first of all, testing your reaction: "What will Mommy do if . . . ?" I applaud your daughter for inventing such a clever and ingenious way of defining the difference between *mine* and *yours*. By taking what she has been told is someone else's, or what rests at someone else's house, your daughter is attempting to define the concepts of possession and ownership.

What to do now? Help her out. She's asking a question. Give her the answer. React calmly and directly. "Oh. You took a toy from

David's house. This toy belongs to David. This toy is *his*. You and I are going to take the toy back to David's house and give it to him."

It is extremely important that you return the item immediately, while the question is fresh in her mind. It is equally imperative that your daughter accompany you on this mission. It is *not* important that she confess, apologize, or hand the item back herself. These requirements only serve to punish the question and muddle the answer. It is sufficient that she see you apologize and transfer the item to its owner. Keep the lesson simple and straightforward. No need to spice it with either guilt or grief.

Q: *Our five-year-old daughter and our next-door neighbor's three-year-old daughter play together a lot. The problem is that their child has not been taught to share and will pinch, bite, slap, and kick our daughter if she tries to play with one of her toys. In fact, if our daughter takes her own toys outside, and the three-year-old gets hold of one of them, it's the same story. Meanwhile, even if the child's parents see what's going on, they do nothing. They seem to think it's cute, even though my daughter sometimes ends up crying because she's so frustrated. Up to this point, I've told our daughter to let the child have her way, but it's getting out of control. Should I tell her to be just as aggressive?*

A: The first thing that comes to my mind is the old adage, "Two wrongs don't make a right." No, I would not teach your daughter to strike back at a younger child. She has every right to protect herself from this child's assaults, but hitting is not the ethical response in this situation.

The second thing that comes to mind is a question: Why do you continue to let your daughter suffer this undersocialized child's behavior? (Note that I am using the term *undersocialized child* as a euphemism for a more old-fashioned four-letter word that begins with *b* and ends with *t*.) It's rather obvious that this child's behavior is not going to change anytime soon. She is not going to outgrow her aggressiveness. It will have to be disciplined out of her. But that's a moot issue, given parents who think it's cute. Playing with this child must be more stressful than fun for your daughter. Therefore, the logical solution is to suspend the relationship indefinitely.

"But John," you might say, "that might cause a rift between ourselves and our neighbors!"

Well, there's a price to pay for everything, a downside to every solution. As such, you need to weigh whether it is better for your daughter to continue to pay the price of your inaction, or better for you to pay the price for the action you take to protect her. Besides, you can do this in a way that minimizes the possibility of a rift. Simply tell your neighbors that the "age chemistry" between the two girls doesn't seem to be working very well at the moment and you've decided to suspend the relationship for a year or so until the girls are better able to get along. You can add that perhaps a prolonged period of absence from one another will "make their hearts grow fonder." By not giving the impression that the problem is their daughter's behavior, you leave the door open for a future reconciliation.

It's not at all unusual for children who are three years old or thereabouts to have difficulty sharing. My grandson Patrick, for example, at the age of three was firm in his reluctance to share anything with anyone. Why this is typical of this age is anyone's best guess, mine being that toddlers are just beginning to grasp the concept of private property. This enables them to exercise a greater degree of control over their immediate environment, including playmates, while at the same time making a clear assertion of their identity. So, whereas not sharing needs correction, in and of itself it is not bad.

Unfortunately, some of these "nonsharers" tend to become aggressive toward other children who try to play with their toys. Needless to say, their outbursts are not consistent with Marquis of Queensberry rules. The three-year-old is undersocialized; therefore, when he or she strikes out aggressively toward another child, the assault is likely to look distinctively savage to the civilized onlooker.

The first problem, simple, garden-variety nonsharing, can be solved parents and other caregivers who are firm in their expectation that children share and who provide the disciplinary structure within which sharing can be learned. One way to do this is to use a simple kitchen timer to signal when the toys in question have to be exchanged. In most cases, once children have learned to take turns in this fashion, they begin spontaneous sharing in almost no time at all.

The answer to a three-year-old who hits, kicks, pinches, and bites is to immediately remove the child from the group, even if it's a group of two, until he or she is ready to apologize and share. If an aggressive incident occurs twice in the same play session, I'd recommend confining the child—even at the tender age of three—to his or her room for the remainder of the day, along with an early bedtime. If it occurs in a play group, I'd recommend separating the child from the other children from, say, midmorning (when the second incident hypothetically occurs), until the child is picked up by a parent at the end of the day. If one wants the aggression to stop, which should be everyone's aim, and quickly, the consequence must be memorable. It must create a strong mental imprint that will hopefully begin to inhibit aggressive outbursts. Meanwhile, adults should definitely use the opportunity to counsel children on nonviolent means of handling similar future situations.

In the final analysis, however, nipping behavior of this sort in the bud requires parents who absolutely will not tolerate it. So, yes, aggression takes place at preschool, and if the child is three or older, parents should follow through with a punishment at home. Some research indicates that when parents do not take strong disciplinary action concerning aggressive behavior when it first emerges, the problem can grow from molehill to mountain in no time.

"Play Wif Me!"

For the most part, three-year-olds have resolved the conflicts surrounding the issue of dependence versus independence. But not completely. There are still times when they are tempted to give up the ground they have gained and retreat to the old lifestyle that guaranteed comfort and security. Independence involves risks. Remember, the three-year-old has no map to show the way. Dependence, on the other hand, is secure and addictive. One way of expressing this internal tug-of-war is to pull on Mommy and say, in essence, "Be my playmate."

Q: *About how much time each day should I spend playing with my three-year-old son? I don't work, so I've got just about all the time he needs.*

A: A very tricky question, for which there are no definite answers. At this age, there should still be plenty of time when the two of you sit down together just for the fun of it, but your responsibilities do *not* include being his playmate.

In fact, although he may want you to spend your day playing with him and be rather insistent about it, that is exactly what he does *not* need from you at this stage.

He does not require that much or that kind of attention from adults. He needs adults for protection, affection, and control. He needs adults to read to him, to organize and arrange his play space, to reinforce his initiative, to encourage his independence, and to give him ideas he can use to take off in new self-sustaining directions.

Psychologist Burton White, author of *The First Three Years of Life* and an authority on preschool children, has said that one of the most accurate indicators of developmental health in three-year-olds is the ability to occupy and entertain themselves for significantly long periods of time.

That doesn't mean parents should stop playing with their children after their third birthdays. Three-year-olds need to know that their parents are still available to them. Keep in mind, however, that the more of a playmate a parent is, the more the parent's authority and the child's autonomy are undermined.

Set limits on when you will play with him and when you won't. Don't be afraid to say *no* even if he screams. Find a morning preschool program and enroll him three days a week.

And while you're taking care of *his* independence, don't forget about your own.

Q: *I have two sons, three and five, with whom I'm at home during the day. Approximately how much time should I be spending in one-on-one, sit-down-with-them, direct play? I want to do it enough that they are stimulated and given attention, and yet not so much that I hamper their creativity and ability to play independently.*

A: You are by no means obligated ever to get down on the floor and play with three- and five year-old children. If you feel like doing so, fine, but by age three, children should be able to keep themselves occupied quite nicely. I know, the "attachment parenting" hoax is causing today's parents (moms especially) to feel they're being lazy, if not downright irresponsible, if they don't do the "Mommy is your playmate!" thing for 23.8 minutes a day, every day, with each of their kids.

During the first two years or so of a child's life, as we have seen, a home should be child-proofed so that the child can roam and explore pretty much at will. If parents take the time to create a safe, interesting environment, even toddlers can keep themselves occupied for relatively long periods of time. Certainly, for parents to want to play with children of this age, to make them smile and laugh, is a good and natural thing. And most definitely, parents should read to children every day from no later than eight months to at least when the child is reading well alone. But by age three, the child should be a self-starter and self-sustainer where play is concerned. Behind any three-year-olds who can't play on their own are parents who haven't taught them how or have created an environment that does not promote it (one where the television is on all the time, or the child has too many toys), or both.

My mom, a single parent for most of the first seven years of my life, is a good example of what I'm talking about. Instead of playing with me, she taught me how to occupy myself creatively. She bought me finger paints and showed me how to use them. On a rainy day, she'd put butcher paper on the kitchen floor, and I'd finger-paint while she went about her tasks. By the time I was five, Mom had taught me how to work with papier-mâché, with which I made a tunnel for my train set, animal "sculptures," and many other works of art. She bought me Lincoln Logs and taught me how to build with them. Once she had taught me how to do something, she expected me to be on my own from that point on.

My mom was by no means unique for her generation, because other people my age report similar memories of mothers who'd demonstrate but not "play." Did we get enough attention? On average, I'm sure we did, and where one of us did not receive enough attention, that had nothing to do with a mom who didn't get down on the floor and play. By today's standards, we baby boomers were just shy of neglected; nonetheless, we had acceptably happy childhoods (again, on average), which is about as happy as a childhood ever gets anyway. Most importantly, the peers I've spoken to about this are unanimous in feeling that their childhoods would not have been one bit happier had their mothers served as their playmates 23.8 minutes a day.

And look here! You have not just one child who has reached his third birthday, but two! Not only can you reasonably expect each of your boys to play on his own, you can and should expect them to be playmates.

In a nutshell, you don't teach your child to play by playing with him. Instead, you teach him that he doesn't need you in order to play.

Naps and Bedtime

Q: *My daughter is now three and a half. Even when given an hour's opportunity for an afternoon nap around two o'clock, she doesn't go to sleep. Then, by five-thirty, she falls apart. She cries and is touchy and can hardly sit up and eat her supper. If she goes to sleep around three-thirty, I try to wake her after an hour or so, or she will be up until nine-thirty or ten. Is this just another stage?*

A: It sounds as though your daughter may no longer need an afternoon nap, but this transition from nap to no nap won't happen overnight. For a while there will be days when she will obviously need to sleep and days when she will not feel the need as strongly.

During this transition stage, she is likely to resist taking an afternoon snooze, for the simple reason that being awake is far more exciting than being asleep. Remember that children become upset when their routines are disrupted. This transition, then, because it involves shifting bedtimes back and forth, may be unsettling. You can count on her being cranky and out of sorts at times.

A routine would help her make this difficult adjustment. You must establish the routine, and you must enforce it in the face of occasional resistance. With this in mind, establish a bedtime. This decision should take into consideration such factors as work schedules, what time everyone needs to leave the house in the morning, where the child spends her days, and so on. In the end, however, parents should decide when *they* want the child in bed. Every child needs parents who spend private time together regularly. So let's say that you choose eight-thirty as the time when you want your daughter tucked away.

To make this happen, begin at eight o'clock to prepare her for bed. Turn off the television, turn down everyone's activity level to idle, give her a warm bath, send her to the potty, offer a small (preferably sugar-free) snack, read a story (in bed), talk softly with her about pleasant things that happened during the day, kiss and cuddle her, turn out the lights, and leave the room. If she resists sleeping, make it clear that she must stay in her bed with the lights on. Enforce your decision calmly, but as firmly as necessary.

If her biological clock is attuned to the norm, she will sleep until about eight o'clock the next morning. Depending on how active her day is, she may or may not want to nap. If she falls asleep of her own accord, allow her to sleep no more than one hour. In the evening, whether or not she takes a nap, begin again to wind things down at eight o'clock, aiming for that eight-thirty bedtime. The most important thing to remember is that *you* establish the routine and *you* program her to fall into it through calm, consistent enforcement. The pattern will eventually become fixed, and she will make her own adjustments concerning naps according to her needs.

"Mine!" (Emphatically)

Q: *My nearly three-year-old daughter masturbates excessively. At least, I think it's excessive. She started when she was about six months old, seemingly to help herself fall asleep. That didn't really bother me. Now, however, I'm concerned because she would rather do this than just about anything. How do I get her to stop?*

A: It's not at all uncommon for girls your daughter's age to have discovered the "magic button" and be somewhat obsessed with pushing it. Masturbation is more common in girls this age than it is in boys, which may have something to do with the fact that little boys are generally more active than little girls. In any case, it's nothing to worry about, not in and of itself. (I must mention, however, that excessive masturbation—if not an obvious outgrowth of early attempts at self-pacification, as is the case here—may be a sign of sexual abuse. Parents with suspicions or concerns along these lines should contact their child's physician.)

A child of this age is very much a pleasure seeker, with a limited sense of what adults generally consider right or wrong, which is why a toddler keeps climbing up on the counter for the cookie jar, no matter how many times you say no. My point here is that you can't punish or persuade a young child to stop masturbating. And needless to say (I hope!), shaming the child is definitely *not* the answer.

So, what to do? Tell your daughter that children are not allowed to do "that"—give it a neutral name or just call it rubbing—anywhere except in a certain bathroom (or any place in the house that isn't awful, just boring). Furthermore, if caught doing "that" anywhere except the bathroom, they have to go to the bathroom and stay for five minutes. It's the rule. Period.

Now, it's important when you apprehend your daughter in the act that you not make a big deal of it. Just say, "You know the rule. You have to go to the bathroom for five minutes."

If she promises to stop, say, "That's okay, but you still have to go to the bathroom because it's the rule. You can stop in there." It's important that you not make this seem like punishment, which it isn't. It's simply a gentle means of helping her begin exercising some control over something she's probably going to continue doing, for a while at least.

That's right. Once a little girl finds this particular button, she's going to keep pushing it, and the more attention she gets for it, the more adult hysteria it generates, the more she's going to push. You can get your daughter to limit her masturbation, but she probably won't stop completely until she finds a sufficient number of other things and activities with which to occupy her time.

Along those lines, if she's not already involved in a preschool program, enroll her in one. Don't let her watch much television, if any. Keep her as active as possible, but don't run yourself ragged. This is not a test of how good a mother you are. In the final analysis, where your daughter puts her hands has nothing whatsoever to do with you. Keep that perspective, please.

11

Fours and Fives

THE PLAY OF THREE-YEAR-OLD CHILDREN is open-ended and improvisational. They are self-starters and can occupy themselves for relatively long periods of time, but they are playing solely in the present, the here and now. They have no objectives in mind; they play simply for the sake of playing.

Four- and five-year-olds begin to establish goals and direct their activity toward accomplishing them. If you ask a three-year-old, "What are you doing?" you will usually get this answer: "Playing." A four- or five-year-old answers the same question more specifically, telling the purpose of the activity: "I'm building a boat."

This ability to conceptualize and work toward a predetermined goal is the next step in the child's drive to master the environment. It signals the emergence of *achievement motivation*—the focused desire to accomplish, to create, to do.

Fours and fives express their need to achieve in a variety of ways. They begin to form definite interests, and more often than not these interests are gender-related. Typically, boys identify with the role model their fathers present and show an interest in similar things (such as sports, automobiles, gardening, and carpentry). They express more need for Daddy's approval and companionship and engage in activities associated with their fathers. At the same time, little girls are forming close ties with their mothers and exhibiting clear preferences for behavior and activities that are—relative to the standards in the home—feminine in nature.

Gender identity also stabilizes. Four-year-olds realize that boys grow up to be men and girls grow up to be women. The emergence of precocious "sexual" behavior in children of this age is their way of exploring and thereby understanding all that is implied by the mysterious differences between males and females.

As you might expect, the strategies the children use to obtain answers to their questions are direct and unself-conscious. It's the age of "Let's play doctor" and "Show me," and it's bound to cause parents some consternation.

"You Show Me Yours"

I heard them all giggling and laughing upstairs in my daughter's room and went upstairs to see what was so funny. They all had their clothes off, every stitch! They were all hopping around the room, hitting each other with pillows. I just stood there. My mouth wouldn't work.

Timmy had been in the bathroom for a long time, so I went to see if he needed any help, and there they were. I thought I had prepared myself for anything—but two boys?

Every time I look around, Emmy has her hand inside her pants. She does it everywhere. I've tried everything I know to stop her, but it only gets worse. I'm embarrassed to take her anyplace.

It happens in the best of families. There you are, managing things smoothly, coping with the occasional expected hassles, but at least there's *one* thing you don't have to deal with for another ten years—or so you think. Then one day you happen to look in on the little ones who have been playing so well together for half an hour . . .

Sometime between their fourth and sixth birthdays, most children discover that their bodies have pleasure places where touching feels almost as good as a chocolate ice-cream cone tastes. There's nothing perverted or wrong in liking ice cream, and there's nothing unnatural about children wanting to know about their own—or someone else's—body once they discover the mysteries within.

A child's curiosity does not readily obey the green and red lights that adults set up to define what is right and what is not. It never occurs to a child who indulges in immature sex play that this is doing something wrong, and the idea that this delightful discovery is forbidden can be confusing and destructive. After all, it's the child's body, and it feels good. When adults look sickened, shout, slap the offending hand, or say it's bad, the message is that making oneself feel good is wrong.

Children hear people saying there's something wrong with their body and it mustn't be touched. Eventually, what they find delightful and good is scrubbed from their thinking, replaced by words like *disgusting* and *nasty*. Embarrassment, shame, and guilt can easily become attached to a child's body image and translated into the wrong ideas. The final conclusion: "I'm *bad* to want to feel good."

There's a further danger in punishing or showing disapproval of such self-discovery. If children's interest in their bodies is punished, if it becomes tinged with shame, the children will hide it from sight.

It is essential that our children feel free to talk with us about sex and related matters. If a young child's unashamed openness is punished, it is unlikely that later, as a teenager, this youngster will feel comfortable approaching Mommy and Daddy with questions, doubts, or problems concerning sexuality.

What to do? There are no easy prescriptions, but here are some general guidelines.

Children, like everyone else, have a need for privacy and a right to it. Don't intrude on their world, either at regular intervals or simply because they are being "too quiet." If you happen to find your child exploring his or her body in the privacy of a bedroom, let it be. No harm, physical or psychological, has been done to the child and certainly no harm to anyone else.

Children who explore themselves in public places must learn that bodies are a private, personal matter. Tell them something like

"I know that feels good, but the living room is not the place to do it. If you like, you may go to your room where no one will bother you." This will help the child develop self-control without defining the act as forbidden. In public, the straightforward approach is also best: "Please take your hands out of your pants while we are in the store. You may do that in your room when we get home." When there are two or more children together, simply divert their attention and briefly mention that what they are doing is not allowed: "You two are not allowed to play together like that. I want you to put your clothes on and come downstairs. I need your help in the kitchen."

Keep in mind that it is natural for young children to show an immature interest in sex, one way or another, and there is no difference at this age between curiosity displayed toward one's own body and curiosity displayed toward other bodies of either sex. Be honest and simple when answering the questions that may come up. Keep a straight face even if you feel bewildered or shocked. Respect the child's right to privacy, but at the same time say that there are appropriate times and places for everything.

Q: *Our five-year-old daughter has recently started masturbating by rubbing herself between her legs. We have tried to ignore it, but several times have had to tell her to stop because we were in public. Her kindergarten teacher says she is also rubbing herself in class. In all other respects, she is a happy well-adjusted child with no obvious insecurities. Can you help us understand why she started doing this and give some suggestions for handling it?*

A: In all likelihood, your daughter started masturbating because she accidentally discovered rubbing herself between her legs felt good.

In a well-adjusted child, who is active and enjoys good relationships with peers, there is no cause for concern. Plenty of young children make this same discovery. You just don't hear parents talking about it for obvious reasons.

As you have learned, masturbation cannot be ignored. Nor *should* it be, since it is imperative for the child to learn that it isn't an acceptable thing to do when other people, even parents, can see.

So you are obligated to say something about it. I recommend something along these lines: "We've noticed you seem to enjoy rubbing yourself between your legs. That's all right, but it is one of those things that shouldn't be done where other people can see you. We've decided you can rub yourself if you want to, but you must go to your room first. We also think there are better things to do with your time, like reading or playing outside. If you have trouble finding other things to do, let us know and we'll help."

Short, noncritical, and to the point. At school, her teacher should have a similar conversation with her and assign her a special place to go if she feels an overwhelming urge. Chances are, she'll never use it.

She will probably continue to masturbate occasionally at home for several months. Eventually, she'll tire of it and use her time more wisely.

If, however, you notice her spending increasing amounts of time in her room, then ask your pediatrician for a consultation.

Q: *Just the other day, I caught my five-year-old daughter and the boy next door, also five, playing at being a little more grown up than I felt was appropriate, if you know what I mean. They had been playing in her room for quite some time when I went back to check and ask if they were interested in a snack. There they were, laughing and giggling, with nothing but their underpants on. When I opened the door, their reaction told me they knew what they were doing wasn't proper. I'd rather not tell you what I said, because I don't want the whole world knowing if I blew it. But please tell me—and other parents who may someday find themselves in similar situations—how things like this ought to be handled.*

A: To begin with, what your daughter and her friend did is not unusual at all for four-, five-, and six-year-olds. Children at this age have lots of questions and very few inhibitions, which can make for some exciting moments, as you've already discovered.

Naturally curious five-year-olds are fascinated by the beginnings of life. They want to know where babies come from, what pregnancy and birth are all about, and what newborns are like.

Sooner or later, they begin asking questions that deal with the sexual aspect of this whole mystery. And we answer the questions, with an emphasis on the general and simplistic, because that's all their little minds can grasp.

Your five-year-old daughter is a concrete thinker, which is to say she needs more than words to understand transcendental things like sex and death and fly-fishing. She needs pictures and demonstrations and other audiovisual aids. But when words are all adults will provide, and vague ones at that, your young one is left to her own devices. Somehow, she must translate the words into something concrete to which she can relate. So at the first possible opportunity, she grabs some other child, who probably has similar questions, and says, "Hey! Let's act this whole sex thing out! Then maybe we'll understand it better!" They shift gears into pretend and away they go, to the chagrin of parents who catch them at these innocent sports.

Low-key is the secret of success in situations such as these. Simply say something like, "You may not play this game, or games like it, until you are much older. Please put your clothes back on. Buddy, I think it would be best if you and Laura-Ann didn't play together for the rest of the day, so I'm sending you home."

In most cases, a cooling-off period of a day or so is advisable, but it shouldn't be put to the children as a punishment. In fact, there's no reason to punish at all, unless one or both of the children have already been told that the game is forbidden. You should also let the other child's parents know what happened and how you dealt with it. Under normal circumstances, and most of these circumstances are normal, there's no need to give the children the third degree or rush off to the psychologist's office. However, if this kind of behavior begins happening with some regularity, I'd recommend a professional evaluation. Repetitive behavior of this sort may be a symptom of sexual abuse.

A single mother told me a funny story. One day she caught her six-year-old daughter and an equally young male playmate out behind the garage pretending to be "married." Obviously, the game had gotten a bit out of hand, so she brought her daughter inside for the rest of the day. In the ensuing discussion, the mother asked, "Did the two of you pull your pants down?" A look of panic froze the little girl's face, and she quickly answered, "No, Mommy, we were just thinking about it!"

Art Linkletter was right. Kids do say the darnedest things.

Q: *My five-year-old son has a fascination with pregnancy. He has often put pillows in his clothing in order to appear pregnant. Last night, I found him asleep in bed, clutching a doll, with a big orange bouncy-ball kangaroo toy under his nightshirt. Should I be concerned?*

A: This is, admittedly, a new one for me. I did a search of the literature and was unable to find any research or even theoretical writings on the subject of little boys who pretend to be pregnant. Since I think it unlikely that your son has invented a hitherto unknown psychological disorder (pregnancy envy?), I'm confident you can chalk this up to a very inventive imagination. Your description of the most recent incident, however, caused me to think that perhaps he is actually pretending to be a pregnant kangaroo. Still, this should only be considered a problem if he begins bounding around the house and wanting to box with other members of the family.

Around this age, children begin to realize that human life has a beginning and an end. Lacking the sophistication of language necessary to pose some of their questions, they often "act out" their curiosity in baffling and sometimes exasperating ways (like playing doctor). Parents can, and sometimes do, make mountains out of molehills by overreacting to this sort of creative innocence. In the final analysis, orange bouncy balls under nightshirts are no more indicative of psychological problems than games of "You show me yours and I'll show you mine."

Your concern reflects the tendency on the part of today's parents to attribute esoteric psychological causes to behaviors that do not fit some preconceived notion of what is normal. In this fashion, parents often scare themselves witless worrying about things that deserve nothing more than a chuckle. The fact is, sometimes a young child will do something for no reason at all other than it occurred to him or her to do it, in which case, the something in question means nothing at all either.

The problem, of course, is that today's parents trust "experts" more than they trust their own common sense, and we experts have duped our rapt audience into believing that parenting is a science of sorts, or at the least a perilous process fraught with psychological pitfalls. As a consequence, it is the rare person today who is truly appreciative of the innocence and simplicity of a child and in possession of a full measure of common sense and intuition where children are concerned. As regards creative, imaginative, fantasy-oriented behavior of the sort you describe, the proper question is rarely "What does it mean?" but rather "What, if anything, should I do?" And by the way, if no answer to the latter question pops to mind, it may be best to do nothing, to take an old-fashioned wait-and-see attitude. Left alone, most behavior of this sort will run its course in due time.

In the case of your son's fantasies, my suggestion is you do nothing except have a camera ready for the next time a precious, priceless example of pregnancy envy or wallaby wannabe occurs.

Moral Development

Four- and five-year-olds are forming an elementary sense of moral values. They aren't capable of abstract thought, however, so they define *good* and *bad* in terms that are closely related to their need for approval. "Good" is doing what their parents approve of, and "bad" is what they disapprove of.

They are not yet able to apply moral concepts to a wide range of situations. For example, a four-year-old boy may be able to tell you that it would be wrong for him to take something from his friend's house (the concept of possession being fairly well established by this time), but he would not be able to apply the general principle that "stealing is wrong." If asked the question, "Why shouldn't you take a toy from Barry's house?" he would probably answer, "'Cause it's Barry's toy."

Furthermore, he doesn't understand why certain behavior is acceptable in some situations and not acceptable in others. He relies almost exclusively on signals from his parents and other adults to make these subtle distinctions and adjust his behavior accordingly.

For these reasons, it is essential that parents establish rules and guidelines solely in terms of what will and won't be allowed under each specific set of circumstances. The more talking and explaining parents do, the more the essential message—the rule—gets lost in a torrent of words.

Talk, Talk, Talk

Mikey is four years old. He's a smart little fella, full of mischief and stubborn as a mule. His parents are very conscious of the way they are raising him. They don't want to make *any* mistakes.

They believe the best way to teach Mikey the difference between right and wrong is to reason with him, thereby helping him understand all the complicated *whys* and *why nots* of the world. Let's look in on Mikey's household to see if we can find an example. Ah, yes, his father is "reasoning" with him now:

"How many times do I have to tell you, Mikey, it's not nice to hit someone who is a guest in our home and then call him a poo-poo? Reverend Diggs is our minister, and he deserves to be treated with respect when he comes to visit. Hitting people and calling them names is bad manners. It's not polite. You know better, don't you?"

Mikey nods.

"I thought so. When you hit someone who is a guest in our house and call them a name, they feel bad because they think you don't like them, and Mommy and I become angry when you do things like that because we've talked with you about hitting and name-calling before and" *blah-blah-blah.*

Poor Mikey. He hasn't the vaguest notion of what his father means, but he knows enough to stand there and pretend to take it all in. He knows he's in trouble, but what's this about someone's name being called?

The truth is, Mikey isn't old enough to understand most of what his father is saying. In fact, the more his father talks, the *less* Mikey understands.

His father is well meaning enough, and he certainly has a point—Mikey must learn to express his affection in some other way. But Mikey didn't know. He got carried away in his excitement. Unfortunately, at the end of his father's monologue, Mikey won't have learned much. In fact, the monologue is so confusing to a four-year-old that by the time it's over, Mikey will probably have forgotten how it all started in the first place.

The process of learning to talk involves more than learning to make certain sounds. It's like building a house, except this "house" takes at least twelve years to build and another six or eight years to put on the finishing touches. Talking involves learning thousands of associations between patterns of sound (words) and the things (nouns) or actions (verbs) they represent. Then the child must learn how and when to use all the qualifiers (adjectives and adverbs) that assign values to the nouns and verbs. Then comes learning how to classify and organize words into larger units of meaning. Finally the child develops an appreciation for words that refer to ideas rather than objects. And through this entire process, the child is also learning a complex set of grammatical rules, without which none of this makes any sense. Complicated, isn't it?

Mikey's "house" already has a foundation. The walls for the first floor are slowly being put together. But his father is throwing roofing shingles at him.

At four years, the Mikeys of the world can understand only words referring to things and actions, stuff they can see or feel with their senses.

Words like *respect* and *polite* evaporate in Mikey's brain. The key to understanding is not practice, it's maturity. Mikey's parents could drill him for a week on the meaning of *respect,* and he still wouldn't know what it meant. He won't be able to understand *respect* next year or even the year after that. In fact, an understanding of words like *respect* won't begin to emerge until Mikey is about seven or eight years old.

Let's go back to Mikey and his dad for a moment.

"Do you understand what I'm saying, Mikey?"

Mikey nods.

"Good. Now I don't want you being disrespectful to our guest, and that includes name-calling. Do you understand?"

Mikey nods.

"Good. Now I want you to go tell Reverend Diggs you're sorry."

Mikey is a clever little munchkin. He has learned to escape the firing squad by nodding his head at just the right moment. He can tell when to nod by the changes in his father's tone of voice and facial expression.

Mikey will even apologize to the pastor, but he won't know why he's saying, "I'm sorry." He doesn't know what *sorry* means either. So the next time there is a visitor, Mikey is just as likely to get excited and hit and say "poo-poo," and then everything will start all over again. Mikey's father will talk a mile a minute, and Mikey still won't know what he is talking about.

If you *must* reason with a young child, remember that you are helping build a house. Make sure it's a solid structure. Don't try nailing on the roof before the walls are up. Observe three rules of thumb:

First, speak with the child immediately, before the memory fades away.

Second, use simple words that refer directly to what was done, who did it, and *who* it was done to. Don't use words that refer to morals or ethics (such as *deserve, respect,* and *polite*).

Third, do your reasoning in fifty words or less. Say your piece, and (if you feel it is necessary) assign some form of punishment. "Mikey, you hit Reverend Diggs and called him a poo-poo. We don't hit or call people poo-poos. Go to your room. Your timer is set for five minutes. You may come out when the bell rings."

Enough said. Mikey understands.

Ask Them No Questions

Most lies young children tell are told because adults ask questions when they already know the answers.

For instance, four-year-old Minnie McSweeney is playing alone in the living room while her mother fixes their lunch. Suddenly, Mrs. McSweeney hears a loud crash from the living room and rushes in to find a vase in pieces on the floor and Minnie looking sheepish. In a demanding tone, Mrs. McSweeney asks, "Minnie McSweeney, did you knock this vase over?"

The question presents Minnie with a choice. She can admit to knocking the base over, but Mommy sounds angry, and that could mean a spanking. Or Minnie can plead innocent and hope for the best. Either way, her odds aren't good, but Minnie decides in favor of deception. "No, Mommy," she replies, "I didn't knock it down. I was just playing and it fell. Honest."

Now Mrs. McSweeney has a dilemma on her hands. What's more important, the broken vase or the lie? If she responds only to the broken vase and ignores the lie, does she miss an opportunity to nip lying in the bud? Perhaps she should punish Minnie for lying, making it clear that, had Minnie told the truth, she wouldn't have been punished at all. That, however, may give Minnie the impression she can avoid the consequences of her misdeeds by simply 'fessing up.

Suddenly, a minor incident has become thoroughly complicated. Every possible solution generates another problem. Furthermore, the problems aren't likely to end with the broken vase and Minnie's denial.

Because Mrs. McSweeney is sensitized to the possibility that Minnie will lie when confronted with a misdeed, she is likely to set up more tests of Minnie's truthfulness. The more questions she asks, the more lies she gets, and the bigger the issue of Minnie's moral depravity becomes.

A child caught up in situations like this learns parents expect her to lie, so she does. To prevent this problem from taking root, remember the golden road to honesty and truth is by way of the old maxim, "Ask me no questions, and I'll tell you no lies." For instance, Mrs. McSweeney could have said, "Minnie McSweeney, you broke my vase and now you must help me clean it up."

I'm reminded of an incident involving my daughter, Amy, who was five, and my son, Eric, then eight. Eric had begun saving his weekly allowance in a coffee can decorated with colored paper and crayon. One day, he and Amy were in his room and I was one bedroom over, relaxing. It registered that Eric came out of his room and went downstairs. Soon after, Amy emerged from Eric's room, walked into her bedroom, and shut the door. A minute or so later, Eric returned to his room. Amy then opened her door and went downstairs. Several minutes after all this, Eric was standing next to me, looking upset.

"Dad," he said, "I need your help. While Amy was in my room, I took my money out and counted it. Then I put it away and went downstairs for a drink of water. Now my money's gone and Amy's the only person who could have taken it. But if I ask her for it, she'll say she doesn't have it and we'll get into a fight. So will you tell her to give it back to me?"

After thinking it over, I said, "Yeah, you're right. This is one situation involving the two of you that I'd best handle. You just go into your room and I'll take care of things." Walking to the top of the stairs, I called for Amy.

She peeked around the corner. "Yes, Daddy?"

"Come up here. I want to talk to you." When she reached the top step, I knelt down at eye level with her, extended my hand palm up, and said, "Go get the money you took from Eric's room and give it to me."

Immediately, her eyes grew wide, her chin dropped, and from behind this mask of utter incredulity she said, "What money?"

"Eric's money," I replied. "The money you took from his room."

Again the mask and the innocent voice. "I didn't take any money from Eric, Daddy. I don't know what you're talking about."

"Yes, you do, Amy. When Eric left his room, you took the money from his can and put it either in your room or downstairs. Now go get it and put it in my hand and we'll all forget this ever happened. I'm not waiting any longer."

Slowly, the mask dissolved, only to be replaced with a look consisting of equal parts disgust and wonderment. Her eyes narrowed. "How did you know?" she asked.

I lied. "I know everything."

"Do You Believe In . . . ?"

Q: *I have a five-year-old daughter with whom I feel I have an open and trusting relationship. The problem that I am at a loss to deal with involves my religious views. Through family members, kindergarten, and friends my daughter is exposed to a belief system that I do not share. I am not necessarily opposed to this, but I feel reluctant to share my religious views with her for fear that, if she repeats my thoughts and ideas, she will be ostracized at a time in her life when she is not able to deal with it. And yet she is beginning to ask me questions. In the past I have responded to questions with, "Yes, lots of people believe that." Now, she asks, "Do you believe it?" How do I maintain the openness we have without endangering the relationships she has with others?*

A: More important than the need to protect your daughter from having differences of opinion with other children is her need to know exactly where you stand on these issues. At this time in her life, her need to identify with you takes precedence over peer affiliations and peer approval. You are her primary role model, and she is consciously striving to pattern herself after you—your behavior, your interests, your ideas. She looks to you to set the standards and wants only to follow your example. And, yes, she *will* identify with your beliefs and claim them as her own.

You are also her primary source of security and will continue to be for the next seven years or thereabouts, as she goes about finding a comfortable place for herself within her own generation. Before she ventures into new social territory, however, she must have a blueprint for behavior, and the directions must be clear. She depends on you to show her the way, but in this instance, it sounds as though she's having some difficulty reading you.

If you make it difficult for her to pin you down (remember, she doesn't know that you are trying to protect her), she will become hung up on the question, "What does Mommy believe?" The evasive quality of your answers will frustrate her and stimulate feelings of insecurity. In an effort to reduce her anxiety, she will fixate on the religious issue until you clarify matters for her.

Furthermore, she may interpret your discomfort as a sign that you are ill at ease with your own beliefs—that perhaps you feel something is wrong with them. Otherwise, why the game of hide-and-seek?

I also think you may be overestimating the significance of religious beliefs to acceptance among her peers. A child's religious views, or the religious persuasion of her parents, is relatively insignificant to the social process at this age. Young school-age children don't ostracize one another because of differences in race, religion, politics, or what-have-you unless their parents encourage them to. The exception would be the child who wore her differences on her sleeve.

Answer her questions. I would suggest, however, that instead of telling her what you *don't* believe, you answer her primarily in terms of what you *do* believe. Keep in mind that five-year-old children cannot understand philosophical abstractions. Explain your beliefs clearly, concisely, and concretely.

For the sake of trust.

"I Hate You!"

Q: *Whenever I make my five-year-old angry, she tells me she hates me. This happens when I make her do something she doesn't want to do or refuse to give her something she wants. Nearly every time, I have to discipline. If I try to explain myself to her, she just gets more upset and more belligerent. What am I doing wrong?*

A: The only thing you're doing wrong is taking her seriously. Children your daughter's age think in absolutes. In other words, things are either black or white; there are no in-betweens. So when you frustrate her by making her do something odious like setting the table, or refuse to give in to a demand, she "hates" you. If, on the other hand, you let her do just as she pleases, she "loves" you.

You're attributing too much significance to your daughter's use of the word *hate*. When an adult says he or she hates someone or something, it indicates a deep loathing, a repulsion that often carries with it feelings of ill will. When your five-year-old says "I hate you!" it means you've done something to make her mad. Since five-year-olds are still fairly self-centered, it doesn't take much to make them mad. It's part of a parent's job to set limits on what children can and can't do. Limits are frustrating. So, if a five-year-old is going to hate anybody, it's going to be the parents.

When you react to "I hate you!" as if it's something to be taken seriously, you make matters worse. Acting as if she really understands the implications of what she's saying gives it credence. She sees it gets to you, so she starts saying it more often. The more she says it, the more seriously you take it, and the more credence you give it and . . . get the point?

At the very least, the more she says it, the more it's likely to become habit. A further danger lies in the fact that young children don't question their parents' beliefs. If the parent believes a certain way, the child "believes" it, too. It follows that if you act as if you believe your daughter truly hates you, she might begin believing it as well.

For all these reasons, you must not tolerate your daughter's saying things of this sort. On the other hand, you mustn't respond in an emotionally charged way. Letting her see that it makes you mad or upset will only make matters worse. You have to stop taking the words themselves seriously, while at the same time making it clear that talk of this sort is not allowed.

First, strike while the iron is cold by sitting down with her and telling her that, while you understand you sometimes make her mad, saying "I hate you!" isn't an appropriate way of handling her anger. Tell her you're going to send her to her room for fifteen minutes whenever she lets it slip.

This preliminary conversation puts you in position to strike while the iron is hot. The next time she loses control and says she hates you, don't threaten, warn, or admonish. Just send her to her room for fifteen minutes. If she quickly apologizes, say, "I know you're sorry, and I accept your apology, but you still have to go to your room." Use a timer to let her know when the fifteen minutes is up. That prevents having to deal with fifteen minutes of "Can I come out now?"

"I Need You!"

Q: *My four-year-old daughter Marnie is driving me up the wall. She can't seem to get enough of my attention. To begin with, she follows me from room to room all day long. If I tell her to leave me alone for a while, she looks hurt, so I find myself letting my frustration build until I can't take it anymore, at which point I explode. Then she cries and I feel guilty and things start all over again. In addition to following me, she asks me to do things for her that she is capable of doing for herself—help with her bath, dress her, zip her coat, carry her in stores, and so on and on and on. Manipulation is the term my pediatrician used. But labels won't solve the problem. Meanwhile, I feel like I'm going down for the third time. Help!*

A: Oh, all right! I'll help! Anything to get you to stop pestering me!

I'll bet that sounds familiar. Kind of stings a little bit too, doesn't it?

"But John," you might say, "I really need help, whereas she doesn't truly need me for all those things."

Maybe so, but keep in mind that she is as convinced of her needs as you are of yours. In other words, she is not, as your pediatrician says, manipulating you. She is as much a victim of the vicious circle as you. Furthermore, she is not *in* control, she is *out* of control.

As things stand, your feelings of helplessness are a direct reflection of hers. You feel helpless to stop her and she feels helpless to stop herself. Furthermore, her independence is simply an extension of yours. Her only salvation (and yours) is your ability to control her, however misplaced it might be.

The least painful, fastest-acting method of reestablishing control in a situation such as yours involves three steps.

1. Make a list of the things she asks you to do for her that she can either do for herself or that you want her to learn to do independently. Then assign a value of either 1 (things she can do quite easily), 2 (things that might frustrate her slightly, but which she is still capable of doing), or 3 (things she doesn't know how to do, but can learn) to each item on the list.

2. Draw an elongated rectangle on a sheet of paper, divide it into five boxes, and number the boxes left to right from five to one. Make thirty copies of this chart.

3. This is the crucial step. I call it the Conversation, and it must be done with *authority*.

Sit your daughter down at some relatively peaceful time and clearly spell out a new set of rules for the relationship. It could go something like this: "Marnie, I'm going to talk to you about following me around and asking me to do things for you.

"First, following me around: I've decided that you can follow me five times a day and no more. I'm going to keep track of how many times you follow me by putting this chart up every morning and marking out a number, beginning with five, each time you follow me. When all the boxes are gone, you can't follow me anymore. If you do, I will put you in your room for ten minutes. Every morning I put up a new chart and we start all over again.

"Next, asking me to do things for you that you can do for yourself: Here is a list of all the things you want me to do for you that you could be doing for yourself [go over it]. Now, here is a second list of the things I will still do for you [all the twos and threes from the master list]. If you want me to do something for you and it's not on the list, I won't do it. If it's something new, I'll decide whether you need my help or not.

"If you scream or cry because I won't do something, you'll go to your room until you get control of yourself. In weeks to come, this list is going to get shorter and shorter and shorter until there is no list and you're doing everything you don't need me for on your own [cross out the twos over several weeks' time, then start on the threes]. We're going to call it Marnie's Growing-up List because growing up means you learn to do things without Mommy's help."

The only thing left is to be firm and follow through. When she follows you, simply say, "You are following me, so I have to take a number off your chart." (Important! Don't threaten, just remove the number.) If she asks for help with something that isn't on the list, just point that out to her and go on with what you were doing. "Sorry, Marnie, but that's been taken off your list."

The first several weeks might be tough, as Marnie tests your resolve and adjusts to a radically new concept of what Mommy is for. Then again, she might welcome the structure and the control and things might go smoothly from the start. In either case, just keep one thing squarely in mind: You're doing this for her.

Q: *Our four-and-a-half-year-old daughter constantly asks for reassurance that we're not just going to take her someplace, like preschool or a baby-sitter's or church nursery, and never come back to get her. She separates from us easily enough, but never without asking, "Are you coming back for me?" and "When?" This happens regardless of how familiar the place and people where we're leaving her. Likewise, we always tell her, "Of course we're coming back and we'd never leave you," but the next time we take her someplace, we get the same questions. We don't know how she became so insecure, because we've always been reliable and she's never had a bad experience away from us. Do you have explanations or suggestions?*

A: I'll bet you do the same thing with one another your daughter is doing with you. Proof: When one of you leaves the house to drive to some relatively distant place, your mate gives you a hug and a kiss and says, "Promise me you'll drive carefully." And you say, "I promise," as automatically as you say "fine" when someone asks how you feel.

In a sense, asking someone for a promise of safe driving is the same as asking "You will come back, won't you?" Call it insecurity if you will, we all have it to one degree or another, and separation from a loved one is perhaps the likeliest trigger.

The problem with the separation issue is, it never goes away. It's with us from the day we're born till the day we die, and so is the anxiety. Most of us develop fairly effective ways of dealing with insecurity by the time we're three or four years old. One of the most common coping mechanisms is termed a "separation ritual."

A separation ritual, as the name implies, is an essentially meaningless exchange between two people about to separate. The person who initiates the ritual is usually asking for reassurance that the separation isn't permanent. The other person, usually the one leaving, is obliged to reassure. Obviously, there's a certain amount of absurdity involved in all this, because no one can ever predict for certain that any given separation *won't* be permanent.

So mothers tell their children to "be careful" when riding their bikes around the neighborhood, and wives make their husbands promise to drive safely when they're about to embark on a business trip, and your daughter asks if you're coming back when you drop her off at preschool.

Parents easily lose perspective on things like this when their own children are involved. I suppose it's because we're so afraid of warping them that we're supersensitive to any indication that we already have. But fear not! Your daughter is no more insecure about separating from you than the average four-year-old. And, relatively speaking, she's no more insecure about separating from you than you are about separating from one another.

The most truthful answer to "Are you coming back for me?" is "I don't know." But the point of ritual is that no one wants to face the truth, just like no one really wants to know how you are today, and you don't really want to tell them. The proper thing to do, therefore, is simply provide the reassurance your daughter's asking for: "Yes, we're coming back for you, because we love you."

Q: *I am a first-year teacher of four-year-olds in a private pre-K program. In my college program in child development, it was axiomatic that one always answers a child's questions, but I'm beginning to wonder. I have* *a boy in my class who asks questions constantly. He's intelligent, cute, plays very well with the other children, and has a wonderful imagination. But most of the answers to his questions are obvious. For example, I'll be cutting out an animal figure with scissors and he'll ask, "What are you doing?" If I ask him back, "What am I doing?" he'll tell me. Under the circumstances, do I have to answer these questions? How should I deal with this?*

A: The basic intent behind the idea that adults should always answer young children's questions—to promote intellectual curiosity—is a good one, but there are exceptions to every rule. Unfortunately, many child development programs treat this issue as if there should be no exceptions ever, which is why you're beginning to get frustrated concerning this little fella's constant stream of queries.

The answer to your first question is no, you are not, by any means, obligated to answer each and every one of this child's questions. You are obligated to *respond*—with kindness—but your response can certainly be a firm but gentle refusal to answer.

In the final analysis, it's in this little boy's best interest for someone to help him discover that he can answer many of his questions himself. As it stands, a question occurs to him and he impulsively blurts it out. You can help him learn to control that impulse and begin thinking through many of the word problems that occur to him.

During a planned private moment, tell him he doesn't need to ask so many questions. He's smart, and he can answer some if not most of them without your help, if he just thinks a little while. From now on, tell him, you're going to answer some of his questions but not all of them. Where the others are concerned, you're going to help him answer for himself or simply remind him that he can answer for himself and leave it at that.

I'd be sure to hold a conference with his parents beforehand, by the way, so they understand the philosophy behind what you'll be doing. It may be that they're experiencing a similar issue at home and would welcome your guidance.

For example, when your little interrogator asks what you're doing when the answer is as plain as day you simply say, "Oh, you don't need me to answer that question," or "You can answer that without my help," or "That's the kind of question we talked about," or something along those lines. You can also ask questions that help him discover the answers for himself.

A number of years ago, concerning a similar situation involving a six-year-old girl, I recommended that each day her teacher give her ten "tickets," rectangular pieces of laminated construction paper adorned with question marks. If the girl wanted an answer to a question, she had to give up a ticket. When she ran out of tickets, the teacher couldn't answer any more questions. Within a week, this little girl, who everyone had thought was insecure and seeking attention, was asking fewer than five questions a day and looking much happier for it.

Just as you can either give a man a fish or teach him how to catch them, you can give a child an answer or teach the youngster how to think.

Q: *My five-year-old daughter was so nervous on the first day of school that she threw up shortly after getting there. Since then, she's been crying every morning about having to ride the bus. She weeps on the way to the bus stop, weeps while she's waiting, and I have to almost literally push her on it when it arrives. I have to admit, I've given in and taken her several days. Every time, she promises me that if I'll take her "just one morning," she won't cry again. No such luck. When I ask her what she's afraid of, she can't tell me, and her teacher says she's fine by the time she gets to school. A counselor friend of mine says my daughter's manipulating me. What do you think?*

A: I think the ideal that children manipulate their parents has been vastly overblown. The very concept implies a mental maturity that the typical five-year-old doesn't possess. No, a young school-age child who's crying every morning about riding the bus to school isn't trying to manipulate—as in conspiring against one's parents with aforethought—she's genuinely upset.

Your daughter is *really* scared, but there are two kinds of really scared. In the first, the child is really scared of an event that has happened or might well happen. Your daughter's fear would fall into this first category if, for example, the bus had been struck by an eighteen-wheeler and turned over the first morning she rode it. In this case, her fear would be reality-based and you would need to take affirmative action of some sort. (Tangent: Do you know that the government seat belt law, especially as it pertains to children, can be legally ignored only by the government? I encourage my readers to put pressure on local schools to install seat belts, with shoulder harnesses, in school buses.)

The second kind of really scared involves either a fear of something that has never happened and has a slim-to-none chance of ever happening, or a vague undefined feeling of fear that the child can't put in words ("I'm just afraid!"). I'm reasonably certain your daughter's fear is the second kind. She's obviously not afraid of school itself, or the teacher would be seeing a problem. And the bus driver can probably tell you your daughter calms down by the next stop.

I'm sure you've said everything you can possibly say to your daughter about her fear. You've done what you can to help her solve the problem; now it's her turn. In fact, the only person who can solve it is your daughter, and believe me, an otherwise emotionally healthy five-year-old is completely capable of getting a fear of this sort under control.

Tell your daughter she has to ride the bus every morning. As usual, you'll walk her to the stop and wait with her if you have the time, but you will not drive her to school again, regardless of promises she might make. Assure her that it's all right to cry, that sometimes crying helps people get over fears of this sort. Don't promise her anything special if she doesn't cry, and don't make a big deal of it the first morning she's able successfully to "suck it up." On that auspicious day, just tell her you're proud of her and let that be it. After all, getting on the bus without tears is no big deal.

If your daughter sees firm resolve on your part concerning this matter, it too will pass within a relatively short period of time.

Toy Correctness

Q: *To make sure neither of our children—a five-year-old boy and a four-year-old girl—develop sexist attitudes, we buy them equal numbers of "boy" and "girl" toys. If, for example, we buy our son a truck, the next toy he gets is something typically thought of as a toy for girls—perhaps a dollhouse. Regardless, our daughter winds up playing with her dolls and our son plays with his trucks. We don't let them watch television or see videos that could reinforce sexual stereotypes, and my husband is as likely to wash the dishes as I am to change the oil in the car. What's the explanation for this, and what else can we do to address this problem?*

A: To the first part of your question, my answer is, I don't know. According to the latest evidence, male and female brains are different in significant ways. That suggests that males and females perceive differently, emote differently, and think differently (generally speaking, of course). If this is true, it's just a short hop to the idea that males and females tend to prefer different sorts of things and activities, and that such differences would be evident from an early age.

To the second part of your question, my answer is, Probably nothing. You can, however, stop thinking of this as a problem and let nature take its course. I agree that parents should do what they can—short of being neurotic about it—to prevent children from developing dysfunctional gender stereotypes. I stress *dysfunctional* because I think some gender stereotypes make good sense (but to avoid unnecessary controversy I won't go there). I doubt, however, that the toys one plays with as a child are a significant factor. I'll just bet that when you and your husband were children, you played with toy dishes and he played with toy cars. Today, you can change the oil and he does the dishes. I played with toy guns as a child; nonetheless, real guns scare the you-know-what out of me and I certainly don't equate them with masculinity. In short, our childhood toys didn't warp our thinking about gender matters, and your children's toy preferences aren't likely to warp theirs either. Theories to the contrary are urban myths, nothing more.

I've heard of boys who like to play with dolls and girls who prefer toy trucks to Barbie (whose physical dimensions have been the subject of much psychosocial hyperbole), but examples of that sort are most definitely the exception. Furthermore, where one of these children is concerned, the parents will almost always testify that they had absolutely no influence over the preference and that all efforts to "correct" it ended in failure.

So, it would appear destiny may be at work here. Buy the typical girl a truck and a Barbie, and she will end up choosing to distort her own body image. Buy the typical boy a dollhouse and a GI Joe, and Joe will eventually demolish the former in a fit of military pique. In neither case, however, can anyone make any accurate predictions concerning what these children's gender attitudes will be twenty years from now.

My advice: Give it up. You're spending twice as much money on toys as you need to. Stop trying to make Mother (or Father) Nature bend to your values and let your children simply be themselves. Having some experience in these matters, I can assure you they will be themselves regardless.

12

Six to Eleven: Middle Childhood

THE PSYCHOLOGY OF THE young school-age child can be summarized in two words: acceptance and achievement. Self-esteem for these youngsters hinges on success at creating a secure place for themselves in the social matrix of their peer group and at establishing and attaining specific goals of excellence.

A child must now learn to address a variety of challenging and often demanding tasks. In doing so, he or she draws on the trust, autonomy, initiative, and imaginative playfulness acquired during the preschool years.

Children whose preschool years were a success are prepared to meet the social, intellectual, and emotional challenges of middle childhood. They are able to take reasonable risks with confidence, they are increasingly self-rewarding and self-motivated, they accept increased responsibility and even seek it, and they continue to experiment with new expressions of independence and autonomy.

On the other hand, children who arrive at this crossroads with a burden of unfinished business may have difficulty in the new roles expected of them by parents, teachers, and peers.

Going to school introduces new social, emotional, and intellectual pressures. For the first time the child must adapt to a new set of intellectual and behavioral expectations. Being a student requires greater independence of thought and behavior, places greater distance between children and their parents, introduces them to new authority figures, and brings them into closer proximity with their peers.

As children broaden their social base and expand their range of interests and activities, they establish significant and relatively enduring precedents for themselves within their peer group. Their social personalities are negotiated through interaction with other children and defined in large measure by the roles they are assigned or acquire within the tribe.

Most children, by the time they are six years old, have internalized the behavioral limits taught them by their parents. From this time on, a child's attention shifts toward learning the implicit and explicit rules that mediate behavior within the peer group. This moral judgment is further elaborated through participation in rule-governed activities—such as competitive games and structured play—and the relatively formal atmosphere of the classroom.

Although capable of applying moral and ethical principles across a fairly wide range of situations, a school-age child's moral judgments tend to be dogmatic, rigid, and egocentric. Typical peer conflicts at this age involve arguments over whose point of view is "right," who behaved correctly, who broke a rule, and so on. Young school-aged children compare themselves to each other in every conceivable way. Everything is a contest, from the absurd to the trivial.

Q. *I have an eight-year-old who is supersensitive. He believes everything other children tell him. Recently, he proudly told one of his friends that he had sold twenty tickets to the school fair. The other child said that he had sold one hundred tickets (which wasn't true). My son believed him and felt terrible because he hadn't sold as many. I've explained how and why children sometimes stretch the truth, but my son continues to believe unquestioningly. What can I do to help him understand?*

A: In any competitive situation, there is a risk that someone may experience emotional pain. Learning how to compete involves learning to accept and deal with losing in such a way that it doesn't threaten self-esteem.

In this respect, the "supersensitive" child is at a disadvantage. Supersensitive, however, is a label *you* have selected and attached to him. It actually says more about you, his parents, than your son. Because you think of him as fragile, you are inclined to react protectively when the competition puts him down.

It is understandable for parents to feel protective when their children hurt, but reacting protectively is not always in a child's best interest. Supersensitive becomes a self-fulfilling prophecy when parents' reactions prevent children from confronting situations on their own and learning from them.

In other words, you may be doing too much taking care of him when what your son needs is enough space to learn how to take better care of himself. An overdose of sympathy can be addicting.

I suggest you simply reflect the content of these situations back to him in a fairly objective way, while acknowledging his feelings and helping him to explore more successful ways of handling these problems. For instance, "Mark wants to be better at selling tickets than you, and you want to be better than Mark. When Mark told you he sold one hundred tickets, how did you feel? . . . Do you think Mark really sold one hundred tickets? . . . Why did he tell you that? . . . Let's talk about what you can do next time something like this happens, so you don't end up feeling so awful. . . . Have *you* got any ideas?"

Take the emphasis off self-pity and focus his energy on solving the problem. His self-confidence rests on being able to do that for himself, and he needs to hear you say, "I know it's hard but you can do it."

You may have to settle for a sensitive child, but he can still be super!

Q: *We recently moved into a neighborhood where there are many children about the same age as our eight-year-old daughter. The other children gang up and pick on her almost constantly. I have watched them take* *things away from her, tease her until she cries, make fun of her, exclude her from their games, and call her names. She comes home crying several times a day. I have talked and talked with her about staying away from them, but as soon as we talk and she stops crying, she goes back for more. She gets along fine with each of the children individually, but as a group they are mean to her. Should I handle it by not letting her play with them for a while or letting her play with them only if I supervise? Or should I talk with the children or their parents?*

A: Don't do any of the above. The correct answer is, Stay out of it.

Something needs to be done, but the doing needs to be done by your daughter. There is more going on than meets the eye.

The treatment she is getting comes with being the new kid in town. Her arrival threatens to rearrange the fragile structure of the group as well as to break up some of the tenuous alliances the old-timers have with one another. So the group reacts protectively. You said it yourself: Individually, the children have nothing against her; collectively, she is treated as an untouchable. She is being slowly initiated into the group's pecking order.

The more serious problem is a paradox: You must act to prevent your daughter from growing into a victim role, but you must not interfere in the victimization. The role of victim is a seductive one because it evokes a potent yet destructive reinforcer—sympathy.

Furthermore, by accepting the underdog's definition of herself, along with the notion that she needs you (and only you) to help her, you can become that person's "lifeguard." You get to feel competent and needed, a strong temptation to resist. And finally, the "villain," by virtue of the victim's helplessness, gets to feel powerful. Each role complements the other two. Villains need victims who need someone else to give them sympathy and a helping hand. This triangular drama is addicting and self-perpetuating because everybody gets something out of the arrangement. It's a soap opera, every bit as enticing and repetitious as any you can find on the tube.

Back off. A victim without a lifeguard must either sink or swim. A victim who starts swimming is no longer a victim. I'll bet your daughter can swim. Obviously, she is in no real danger and wants to be with these other children, so let the problem be hers.

If you don't have a kitchen timer, get one. Every time your daughter comes home crying after an encounter with her tormentors, tell her she needs a rest and she must stay indoors for thirty minutes. Set the timer to signal when she can go back outside. During this time, you can listen and reflect her statements back to her, but don't discuss her anguish in sympathetic terms. Persistent crying should be done in her room alone.

If she is playing outside and you hear her crying, go out and bring her in, with the same instructions (these suggestions do not apply to cuts, bumps, bruises, and other injuries to the body). She may want to know why you aren't doing something about the horrible ways the kids treat her. You can say something like, "Those aren't *my* playmates. They are *your* friends, and *you* will have to learn how to get along with them. I can't do anything except to talk to you about it. Do you want to talk?"

Perhaps the most difficult thing about being a parent is having to make certain decisions that force your children to stand on their own, even when they tell you they can't.

Q: *We have a son, seven, who has a tendency to be rude and bossy to his friends when they come over. Not always, but often enough to concern us, he will refuse to share toys with them, order them around, and become angry and verbally abusive toward them when they don't do what he wants. We've spoken to him many times about his responsibilities toward his guests, but his behavior doesn't change. He tells us that these other children treat him the same way when he is in their homes. Even if this is true, it makes no difference. We have thought about sending his friends home when he is rude to them, and we have considered ignoring it altogether and just letting them work it out. Which approach do you favor?*

A: For the most part, I'd just let the kids work it out, but if the situation really gets out of hand, send the other children home and confine yours to his room for a few hours. There is another way of handling it, but first you should understand that your son's behavior is perfectly normal for a child of this age. Furthermore, his little friends no doubt treat him likewise when he is in their domain, not out of spite but simply because this kind of social behavior at this age is more the norm than the exception.

The territorial instinct is as basic to human psychology as it is in the animal kingdom, the difference being that, among us humans, efforts are made to cloak it in a mantle of politeness. When we say that a child "can't share" or "must be the boss" in a group, we are referring to the fact that that child's territorial instinct has not yet been completely socialized.

For reasons that probably have more to do with biology than upbringing, the territorial instinct is stronger in some children than others. In a group of two-year-olds, for instance, the more territorial tots will occupy and aggressively defend certain play areas, while the less territorial ones will shy away from conflict.

Our culture, for better or worse, rewards territorial people; they create high expectations for themselves, pursue goals aggressively, and, consequently, get things done. They're the go-getters of the world and probably, as a rule, more intelligent. In thirty years, our highly territorial two-year-olds will probably be executives giving directions while tots who were more passive will be taking them.

So, your son is territorial. Slowly but surely, he's learning to socialize his inner yearnings to always run the show when he plays with other children, particularly equally territorial ones, whom he is likely to choose as friends (birds of a feather, you know). As a three-year-old, he reluctantly learned to take turns. Later, he learned to give and take. At this stage, he can share, but if the sharing takes place on his turf it must also take place on his terms. When he's on a friend's turf, the roles reverse.

When my daughter was your son's age and equally territorial with her equally territorial friends, my wife and I would occasionally employ the "humiliation method." Most of the time, we just left the children to their uncivilized selves, but if Amy really started lording it over another child, one of us would step in and say something like, "Amy, I can't believe what I'm hearing from you. You're being very rude to your friend, and that is certainly not the way we treat guests in our home. I'm sure that your selfishness is hurting your friend's feelings. It's also hurting mine to hear you treating her this way. If you don't stop right now, I'll have no choice but to send your friend home and keep you in your room the rest of the day."

We never had to follow through with our promise, because Amy would straighten up after one of these talks. They took place every now and then for a couple of years until there was no longer any need for them. Eventually, if she was with a friend and wound up running the show, she did so politely. I couldn't ask for more than that.

Q: *Our nine-year-old son seems uninterested in making friends. Both at school and in the neighborhood, he seems content to play by himself, even when other kids are available. He's been like this since he was very young, and we always thought he'd grow out of it, but the older he gets, the more concerned we have become. We've tried pairing him with more assertive children, but with little success. We'd like to help him improve his self-esteem to where he'd feel socially comfortable. Do you have any suggestions?*

A: Whoa! Slow down! What makes you think this is a self-esteem problem? The fact is, some children are socially outgoing, while others, like your son, are more introverted. The child who prefers solitary pursuits over social interaction doesn't necessarily have a problem. Introversion is simply a personality characteristic, and recent studies have determined that an individual's social style is strongly influenced by genetic factors. The fact that your son has never shown great interest in other children suggests that this feature of his personality may have roots in his genetic makeup.

Don't confuse his social reticence with shyness, either. A shy person feels genuinely uncomfortable in social situations and avoids them for that reason. A person who is a loner by choice doesn't necessarily feel self-conscious or anxious when alone. The loner simply prefers it.

Trying to stimulate extroversion by matching your son up with outgoing children isn't going to work and may even backfire. Children of similar social styles tend to get along better than children of opposite social styles. In other words, two outgoing children or two relatively passive children will play together more successfully than one outgoing child and one introverted child. Matching your son with an extrovert may cause him to become intimidated and make him that much more inclined to avoid social interaction.

As I said, this isn't a self-esteem issue, but it could become one, especially if your son begins to sense that you think something's wrong with his social performance. If he begins to feel he's not living up to your expectations, he could conceivably develop feelings of self-doubt and experience a lowering of self-esteem.

I suggest you leave this issue alone. Don't worry about it. Like they say, "It takes all kinds." Let him find his own social comfort level and, for the most part, make his own social choices. When opportunities present themselves, you might match him with other children who are similarly inclined, but I wouldn't suggest that you go out of your way to manufacture these opportunities or push them in his direction.

Now, the fact that we're talking about the possibility of genetic influence doesn't mean this part of your son's personality is written in stone. This isn't like having either blue eyes or brown. Genes *influence* personality, they don't make final determinations. During his teen or early adult years, his social style may change in response to the peer group. Then again, it may not.

Either way, he'll work it out. Trust him.

Q: *Our seven-year-old is in second grade in a public school. However, all the other children her age in our neighborhood attend the local private school. We decided to buck the system and put her in public school because we believe in the concept of public education and want to support it. We also feel that public school children receive a more well-rounded educational experience and, because they go to school with children from all walks of life, make a better adjustment as adults.*

Our problem is this: Because she doesn't go to school with the children in the neighborhood, she finds herself left out of things like neighborhood birthday parties and spend-the-nights. Likewise, she doesn't have class-mates to play with after school. We've invited some of her classmates over, but importing children just isn't the same as playing with neigh-borhood kids.

Our daughter has started to complain of having no one to play with, and we're beginning to worry that perhaps our decision to put her in public school is becoming a real handicap for her. What advice do you have for us?

A: Like you, I also believe in the concept of public education, and both our children attended public schools and North Carolina universities.

However, I am also a realist who believes that there are times when practical considerations must outweigh philosophical ones. Your daughter is at an age when her social experience is of extreme importance. Increasingly, her social success will bear significantly upon her security and self-esteem.

In fact, the social and extracurricular aspects of school are as important to a child's overall growth and development as the academic aspect. A frustrating social experience is likely to result in diminished self-esteem, which in turn can impair motivation and school performance. In other words, if the "social" domino falls, it's going to topple others as well.

In my practice, I've seen children who were seriously depressed and doing poorly in school because they felt they had no friends. When the social problems were corrected, these children usually began making better grades.

If you think you've given the present situation your best shot and it doesn't seem to be improving, and you're confident that your daughter would be happier with her neighbors in private school, make the move. All things considered, it sounds like the wise thing to do.

Your concerns that private school might adversely affect your daughter's ability to make a successful adjustment to a more pluralistic adult society is shared by many, but there really is no basis for believing that private-school children have any more adjustment problems in adult life than children who grow up attending public schools.

Nor is there evidence that private-school children are more elitist or prejudiced or suffering from any of the other personality quirks that some narrow-minded critics would attribute to them.

Junior Jekyll
and Master Hyde

Q: *My son is six years old and in first grade. At home he is a real problem—disobedient, boisterous, and generally hard to handle. I went for my first conference with his teachers braced for the worst. Instead, they told me he is one of the better-behaved children and one of the best readers in the room. I had no idea. Since then, I've tried to get him to read to me at home, but he refuses (as usual). I don't get it. What am I doing wrong? Or what are they doing right?*

A: Children are far more likely to engage in conflicts with their parents than their teachers. This is number thirty-nine of the time-honored Fifty Ways to Grieve Your Mother: Be the teacher's perfect precious and bite Mommy on the leg—or on her ego (whichever is more vulnerable).

There are at least five reasons why number thirty-nine has become a tradition with children.

First reason: A teacher's role is more clearly defined than a mother's. There's vast territory for children to explore in the relationship with their mother, because the limits of that relationship are vague. So anything goes—or can at least be tried. Teachers are for teaching, which they do from eight A.M. until three P.M., Monday through Friday, nine months a year. The teacher's status as an authority figure is clear and has institutional support. But if it makes you feel better, consider that plenty of teachers who have no problem managing thirty children in a classroom can't get a handle on the one they have at home. A teacher's a teacher and a mother's a mother, and never the twain shall overlap.

Second reason: Mothers tend to take out one heck of an emotional mortgage on each of their children, with lifetime payments and no insurance. This investment makes objectivity almost impossible. A mother's self-esteem, sense of competence, and well-being are all too often tied up in her children and their behavior. There can be a problem of separating who is who. Teachers are paid to be objective. Aren't they lucky?

Third reason: Rules are more clearly defined at school than they are at home. Parents often expect good behavior without defining exactly what *good* means. Furthermore, parents are more likely to make exceptions, overlook things (hoping they will go away), and fight with each other over how to enforce rules. Parents often act confused, which is not lost on children. A teacher's rules are usually few and clear. The are enforced quickly, with few exceptions, and the spouse is not in the classroom. The teacher is clearly the boss.

Fourth reason: In school, a child can observe the behavior of other children and follow their example. This can and does work both for good and ill, but the group usually pressures its members to behave in ways that enhance its image. Classmates expect every child to contribute to the collective identity and shun children who detract from that image.

Fifth reason: At home, within the family, the entire course of a child's upbringing is charged with the issue of autonomy and independence. The basic question of how much independence is possible, and by what means it is obtained, is central to a child's participation in the family. By its very nature, this issue *demands* that children be somewhat rebellious. Some conflict between parents and children is not only inevitable but healthy. It is the parents' responsibility to the child to contain that rebellion within safe and reasonably appropriate limits.

At school, on the other hand, the central issue is achievement, which often requires cooperation. Because rebellion is incompatible with the expectations of the classroom, the likelihood of conflict between teacher and student is considerably lessened. Children who rebel in school are those for whom the challenge is too great or not great enough, those who have not been able to rebel effectively at home, and those who have difficulty fitting in the social configuration of the group.

Your little James Dean is a rebel with a cause at home, because he has developed a consuming sense of autonomy and an appreciation for his own individuality. He cooperates with the teacher because he has developed a sense of initiative and a will to achieve.

Congratulations on a job well done.

Organized Sports

Q: *What do you think about organized, competitive sports for children? Our son is eight years old, and the current craze among the neighborhood children his age is Peewee football. Actually, the adults appear at least as excited about it as the kids. The way the parents behave at the games makes me wonder whether they haven't got big money riding on the outcome. The same mania sweeps through the neighborhood in the spring, during Little League season. We are caught between wanting our son to feel he's part of the group and not wanting him to learn, at this age, that winning is the most important thing in life.*

A: Organized activities of this nature are inappropriate during middle childhood (ages six to ten). Though organized sports might seem ideal for children at this competitive age, it's not so.

To begin with, adults are overly involved in these activities, in terms of both their presence and their emotional investment. Adults organize, raise the money, draw up the playing schedule, pick the teams, coach, referee, give out awards, and make up the biggest share of the audience.

But it doesn't stop there. Not only do big people play too prominent a role in planning and organizing these events; they can also be found defining and mediating social issues, encouraging rivalries, conferring status as they see fit, and resolving conflicts.

Adults have no business being that entangled in the play of children. Their involvement is a complicating factor that prevents children from learning to resolve certain critical issues on their own. Instead of being activities for children, Peewee football and Little League baseball become theaters where youngsters are manipulated for the ego gratification of adults.

That these sports are competitive is not, in itself, disturbing. Children this age need and, left to their own devices, will seek out appropriate competitive experiences. What *is* disturbing is that the children who are caught up in these sports don't play simply for the sake of the game—for the fun of it—but to obtain adult approval. In fact, they don't really play at all. They *work,* performing for the crowd.

The difference between competitive play and competitive work can be measured in terms of emotional outcome. When children band together to play a sandlot game, one group wins and one group loses, but everyone usually leaves the field feeling okay. When adults direct an organized sports event, the children on the losing team often end up feeling angry, dejected, frustrated, ashamed, and depressed. This isn't play. This is serious business, and the stakes are high—too high. Under pressure from adults to perform, the child athlete's sense of achievement and self-esteem becomes defined in terms of winning and losing. Process and participation take a backseat to outcome, which isn't what being a child is about. Everyone suffers, including the children who don't get to play because they aren't "good" enough.

The basic problem—and one that isn't limited to this issue—is the adult tendency to act as though children will botch the job of growing up unless we engineer the process for them. The opposite is true. When we place ourselves *between* the child and the challenge of growing up, we are no longer in a helpful position. Instead, we are interfering, and to that extent the child is ultimately less capable of dealing with life.

Guidance, support, encouragement, supervision—these are things children need from us. Carry them too far, however, and they become pure meddling.

Allowances

No one has more right to complain about inflation than this country's children. Recent trends have conclusively proven what old-timers in Maine have been saying all along: "As the economy goes, so goes the allowance." Recent concern over the effects this allotment can have on the economy is reflected in the increasing number of questions I've been receiving on the subject:

Q: *At what age should a child be started on an allowance?*

A: As a rule of thumb, it makes sense to start a child on a small allowance at the same time the school begins instruction in the mathematics of money. Preschool children are generally unable to grasp that the amount of money they have places an upper limit on what and how much they can purchase. In the child's eyes, there is no correspondence between the size or desirability of an item and its cost. Until a child is old enough to understand the idea of exchange and deal with the complexities involved, I recommend that parents limit any experience with money to certain exercises in *paying* for things.

Q: *Should my son be required to earn his allowance by doing chores around the house?*

A: Absolutely not. The question of how much the child is expected to contribute to household maintenance is completely unrelated to the allowance issue.

The child's allowance should be for the sole purpose of providing opportunities to practice efficient money management. It should never be manipulated to persuade the child to carry out assigned duties, nor should it be suddenly withdrawn as punishment for inappropriate behavior.

Chores are for developing responsibility, self-discipline, and other essentials, but it takes the better part of childhood for this lesson to take hold. Given a choice between developing some responsibility and riding a bicycle, most children will choose the latter. Therefore, parents must make the choice and, once made, enforce it.

It boils down to a simple matter of obedience, for which there is but one effective incentive—parental authority. In the end, children do chores because they are *told* to do them.

Parents who exchange money in return for chores are unwittingly undermining themselves. When money is used to mediate this aspect of the parent–child relationship, people lose sight of the basic issues of authority and obedience.

Every child needs to learn the value of chores, and every child needs to learn the value of the dollar, and parents need to make sure the lessons don't get mixed up.

Q: *Is it all right for parents to give children a chance to earn extra money by doing special work beyond what's expected of them?*

A: Certainly. Chores are those jobs that are part of the household routine—taking out the garbage, feeding the pet iguana, and so on. It's perfectly acceptable for parents to contract with their children for work other than regular chores, though deals of this nature should be the exception rather than the rule. No one should forget that, within the family, work is not done for money but simply because it needs to be done.

Q: *What should children be required to spend their own money for?*

A: That's an interesting question. In the first place, an allowance is not the child's money, it is the *parents'* money, shared to teach the child how to use it.

Parents should keep tabs on how the child intends to use the money and retain the right of refusing to let it be spent it irresponsibly or in ways that are incompatible with the values of the family. Parents need to teach their children how to be intelligent consumers: how to recognize quality, how to compare, how to shop for value.

It goes without saying that a child should *not* be required to pay for essential food, clothing, books, or school supplies. The allowance is not meant to establish the child's standard of living but to supplement it.

Q: *How much should a child receive each week?*

A: Something between two little and too much. If the amount is either insufficient or excessive, the child may not learn to set responsible spending limits.

Determine the actual figure by taking into consideration age, the socioeconomic level of the family and peer group, how involved the child is with activities outside the family, where the family lives, and, last but not least, the current rate of inflation.

Real Boys Don't Eat Quiche

Q: *My nine-and-a-half-year-old son prefers to play with his five-year-old sister's dolls and toys. When I tell him he cannot, that it isn't right for a boy his age, he pleads, begs, whines, and cries until I can't stand it any longer. If begging doesn't work, he becomes angry and verbally abusive, saying things like, "I hate you! . . . You're mean! . . . You hate me! . . . I hate my toys! They're no fun!" Eventually, I always give in. I don't think he's doing this to get more attention from his father and me, because even before his sister was born, he would play with the neighbor girl's toys before he'd play with his own. He has no really close friends (male or female), which also concerns me. I've tried speaking to him logically and quietly; I've tried yelling; I've tried ignoring it. I've even tried to embarrass him, telling him that other boys and girls will think he's strange. Nothing I have done will convince him to change. Do I have a reason to be worried? What can I do?*

A: Your son's preference for dolls and "girl" toys is unusual but not necessarily abnormal. There is no law that boys must play with trucks and trains and sports equipment or that girls must play with dolls and wear pink.

Unfortunately, we tend to be far more rigid in our attitudes concerning what is and is not appropriate sex-role behavior for boys than for girls. We accept the little girl who likes to climb trees and play baseball, but criticize the little boy who wants a Barbie doll for Christmas.

The problem does not lie with your son's preference for his sister's things. The problem is that you have made his choice of toys into a major issue, at the crux of which is the question of his autonomy. As long as you fight with him over whether he has a right to like dolls, he has no choice but to fight back. In the process of defending his turf, he builds walls around it that not only keep you out ("Eventually, I always give in") but keep him in. He won't have the freedom to expand his range of interests until you put an end to the battle.

I'm not suggesting that you ignore him. I'm suggesting that you give him complete permission to play with whatever he wants to play with, whenever he wants to play with it. And not just permission but encouragement.

He needs to hear it from you, so tell him: "I've been making a big mistake. I wanted you to be like other little boys, so I tried to make you plays with things like trucks and trains instead of dolls. Now I realize that what you play with isn't important. What's important is that you're happy. So if playing with dolls makes you happy, it's all right with me. If you want some dolls of your own, we'll go out and buy some."

I can't guarantee he will ever express more interest in "boy" toys than he does now. But I can guarantee that he will never feel comfortable with them until he is absolutely certain that you accept him, regardless.

The fact that your husband received only passing mention in your letter makes me wonder whether he is sufficiently involved with his son. If Dad isn't there enough to make a difference, he needs to realize that he should be and can. Studies have shown that the quality of the father–son relationship has a direct bearing on a boy's success in social relationships. This seems to be more important when the father is in the home than when he is absent.

It sounds as if your family has needs of the kind that are best and most quickly realized with the help of a competent, experienced family therapist. Ask your pediatrician or family doctor to find one for you.

Q: *I am a teacher and this concerns one of my students, a ten-year-old fifth-grade boy with pronounced effeminate mannerisms. He prefers to play with girls and is fascinated by makeup, women's clothing, hairstyles, and other female things. He is not only an object of ridicule here at school but, according to his mother, catches a lot of flak from his father as well. Apparently, Dad is most disappointed at the way his only son is turning out. The boy talks to me a lot about the rejection he feels from both his classmates and his father, but I really don't feel qualified to counsel him. All I can do is lend a friendly ear.*

My questions: What is the likelihood of the boy developing into a homosexual? If it is strong, is there a possibility that therapy can help him "turn around," or is it too late?

A: Based on your description, I'd say that chances are considerably better than average that the boy will eventually become homosexual. Keep in mind, however, that personality and behavioral characteristics during childhood are unreliable predictors of an individual's later sexual orientation. Contrary to the prevailing stereotype, effeminate mannerisms and homosexuality don't necessarily go hand in hand. The boy's fascination with makeup and women's clothing is actually the more significant warning sign.

Under the circumstances, individual therapy probably couldn't do much more for the boy than help him cope with the ridicule and rejection with which he's faced. In other words, a therapist wouldn't be able to do significantly more than what you're doing, and since he already trusts you and feels comfortable with you, I see no reason to transfer that relationship to someone else. Don't underestimate your ability to give this youngster sound advice. As long as you don't take it upon yourself to "cure" him of his effeminate ways, you're as qualified as anyone else to talk with him. A friendly ear is exactly what he needs.

It's the parents who could truly benefit from counseling. It sounds like a predictable situation has developed in the family. The father is verbally aggressive toward the boy, partly out of disappointment, but in actuality his anger is a defense mechanism that masks deep-seated feelings of guilt and responsibility. I'd venture to guess that the father further projects his feeling of failure by blaming his wife for the boy's behavior.

The more rejecting and verbally aggressive the father is toward his son, the more the mother acts protective. This not only serves to strengthen the boy's identification with his mother but further alienates him from his father as well. The closer the boy gets to his mother, the angrier the father gets and the more he blames his wife for the problem. The end result of all this mess is that the feminine side of the boy's nature comes increasingly to dominate.

What the boy needs more than anything else is an open and accepting relationship with his father. Therein lies whatever possibility still exists of helping the boy develop better self-esteem and a more appropriate sexual orientation.

The father needs to realize that his fears are self-fulfilling. The more angry and rejecting he is, the less effective he is as a role model. The mother, too, needs to understand that her protection is as much a part of the family problem as her husband's anger. Finally, the guilt both parents feel needs to be confronted. All these issues are much too explosive to be handled outside of therapy.

If you have any influence whatsoever with these parents, encourage them to talk with a qualified professional counselor, and fast!

This Too Will Pass

Q: *We have a boy, six, and a girl, eleven months. Several years ago, our son went through a period of extreme defiance. We became firm with him, and although he remained headstrong he settled down considerably.*

Three months ago we began having the same problems with him again. Getting him to obey has become a constant battle. We generally prevail, but not before much arguing, crying, and gnashing of teeth.

Nicky recently told us that we give more attention to his sister. Although he is loving and gentle toward her, he pouts when we spend time with her.

We've tried to explain she needs more of our time and attention right now, but he's not impressed. We don't know whether this is a normal reaction to a second child or whether we're doing something wrong.

A: You're not doing anything wrong, and Nicky's behavior is, for him, a normal reaction to a second child.

Burton White has found that, generally speaking, three and a half years is the ideal interval between siblings. Contrary to what many parents think, the chance of problems with the older child increases not only as the interval between siblings shortens from White's magic figure but also as it lengthens. In other words, you are just as likely to have adjustment problems with a spacing of five and a half years as you are with a spacing of one and a half.

The problem with early spacing is that the first child has yet to resolve the conflict of dependence vs. independence that virtually defines most of the second and third years of life. By three and a half, most children have achieved a satisfactory degree of autonomy and are not threatened by the arrival of another child.

The problem with late spacing, particularly in the case of a first-born, is that the older child has settled comfortably into the role of "only." That is your son's territory, so to speak, within the family, and he is not prepared to share it with anyone else.

For the first eight months, the new baby's relative passivity and helplessness pose few problems for the older child. But as the second child begins to move about independently and make active demands on the parents, the older child's perception begins to change.

What was once cute and cuddly, a baby whose helplessness made the older child feel big and responsible is now seen as an intruder.

Responses to this perceived threat vary with the individual's temperament and history. The older child may become somewhat aggressive toward the baby or may regress in one or more ways (baby talk, wetting "accidents") to get attention.

Nicky has engaged in two predictable strategies. First, he is demanding more attention from you, even when you are obviously occupied with the baby and cannot give it. Then he puts on a display of pouting. Second, he is engaging in behaviors that once brought him a great deal of attention—defiance, tantrums, and so on.

As his role in the family changes, Nicky is struggling to keep things as they were, using tactics that worked before.

The answer? Be firm. You must not cooperate with his perception of the situation. He is getting enough attention for his age, although less than before. You can help your son make the necessary adjustments by telling him the truth.

"Yes, Nicky, you are right. You *are* getting less attention than before because now there are two children who need attention instead of one.

"Your sister is a baby, and babies need more attention than six-year-olds. You are getting plenty of attention from us as it is. When you want attention and we can't give you any right then, you must find something to do on your own. We are also going to stop arguing with you about doing what we say. If you don't obey us when we tell you to do something, we will send you to your room until you decide to do it. That's the way it's going to be. Any questions?"

Nicky's security has been temporarily disrupted. Parental authority is the cornerstone of any child's sense of security. If you want to restore Nicky's security, therefore, you must exercise your authority.

Q: *Our eight-year-old occasionally asks me to hold him on my lap and cuddle him like a much younger child. Do you feel this is inappropriate for a child his age? Could it be an indication of insecurity? Should I let him or not? There are times when I'm simply not in the mood for an eight-year-old on my lap, but I don't know how to say no without making him think I'm rejecting him. Do you have any suggestions?*

A: To your first question—is it inappropriate for an eight-year-old to sit on his parent's lap?—the answer is no, unless the child never wants to sit anywhere else.

During years six to ten, sometimes called middle childhood, children are gradually transferring dependency needs from parents to peers. They are becoming less involved with their parents and more involved with other children their age.

Up until now, everything the child did or wanted to do was measured against the parents' value system, consisting of a fairly constant set of do's and don'ts. During middle childhood, the peer group introduces a new set of expectations, which are not always compatible with the values the child learned at home. The almost inevitable discrepancy between what the child's parents have taught and what the kids on the block require in order to be part of the gang is one source of conflict for this age child.

Children seek to ease the tension generated by this conflict in a number of ways, always seeking to reconcile the often irreconcilable differences between the generations. They lie about their parents to their peers and lie about their peers to their parents. They deny that any conflict exists between the inclinations of the group and the values their parents hold dear ("I didn't think you'd mind"). They suffer mild periodic spells of selective amnesia ("I forgot"). They scapegoat somebody ("George did it! We told him not to!").

A second source of stress and conflict is the challenge of growth itself. Growing up is like conducting a guerrilla war, where the ultimate objective is to conquer some uncharted territory—in this case, adulthood. The child spends five years or so establishing a base of operations from which to develop and test strategies. Subsequent forays, tentative at first, become increasingly bold and far-reaching as the terrain becomes more familiar. But always in the back of the child's mind is the knowledge that whenever things get too rough, it is always possible to beat a hasty retreat to home base.

At this early stage of the game, the safest strategy is to take two steps forward and one step back—into Mom's lap, for instance.

Your son is simply seeking to maintain as close a relationship with you as possible during these trying times. He needs the reassurance of knowing that you will still be there whenever he needs you. There is no harm in his asking and no harm in your saying "sure."

Now, whether you say *sure* in any given situation should be solely a matter of whether you feel, at that moment, like having a relatively large child on your lap. If you don't feel like it, say *no*.

I suggest you talk with him about this. Begin by reassuring him that sitting on your lap is not only all right but something you enjoy as well . . . sometimes. Let him know there will be times when it won't be convenient for him to sit on your lap and times when you will just want to sit by yourself. Prepare him to hear you say, "Not right now." Then the next time he asks and you don't feel like having him sit on your lap, say, "Remember our talk? This is one of those not-so-good times."

When it comes right down to it, telling our children our true feelings is simpler and less painful than trying to conceal them.

Q: *Our eight-year-old son will not go up to his room alone after dark because he's certain there's "something" up there that's going to get him. We've tried leaving all the lights on upstairs after dark, we've talked ourselves blue in the face, we've even searched every upstairs nook and cranny with him to prove there's nothing for him to be afraid of.*

Once he's under the covers he's fine as long as the hall light is on and his door is open. Are fears of this sort normal for a child his age? How would you suggest we deal with them?

A: Yes, fears of the dark and carnivorous beasties lurking therein are quite typical of children your son's age. The cause is developmental, not psychological. Children of this age are highly imaginative and, studies tell us, extremely suggestible. It doesn't take much for even the most secure child in the middle years to come to believe that a one-eyed flying purple people-eater lives in the closet waiting for that single unguarded moment.

As you've already discovered, no amount of talk, however logical, will dispel the child's irrational notions. Also, I hate to tell you this, but your method of proving that no monsters live in your upstairs was as counterproductive as it was thorough.

Looked at from the perspective an eight-year-old, going from room to room on a monster hunt only confirmed your son's belief that one might be there. It's too bad that most adults can't remember how to think like children. We could save ourselves a lot of time and exasperation if we did.

The best approach involves a combination of understanding and nonchalance. You must also retain your sense of humor, even if the child's is lost. Above all else, give the child responsibility for the problem. You must be careful not to enter into the drama, which you do by taking these fears seriously. Handled properly, this situation can become a valuable lesson in the power of positive thinking.

To illustrate: When our daughter, Amy, was around your son's age, she too began expressing fears of the dark, along with a reluctance to put herself to bed.

I told her, "When I was your age I thought there was a monster under my bed. He was so real I could almost see him. He had horns like a bull, scraggly yellow hair, one red eye, and green scales all over his face like a fish. He was very, very ugly, and I knew that if I got too close to my bed after dark that he would reach out from under it, grab me, and eat me!"

Amy laughed at the thought that her daddy could be so silly.

"Even though I was afraid of the monster, I knew I was just pretending. So I pretended a way of beating the monster at his own game. Every night when it was time for bed, I would run down the hall that led to my bedroom, slap the light switch off as I came through the door, and leap into bed. That way I never got close enough to the bedside for the monster to get me. And here I am. I lived to tell the tale. I suppose he got tired of trying to catch me and left.

"Now, your mother and I know that you're smart enough to figure out a way of beating your monster and getting rid of it. The reason you have to figure it out all by yourself is because anything we think up for you won't work. Also, once you figure it out, don't tell us, because it will stop working. That's just the way these pretend monsters are."

Over the next few days, I asked her several times if she had figured out a way to beat her nighttime monster, quickly reminding her that she wasn't to give me any of the details. Less than week had passed when, in answer to my question, Amy gave me a sly smile and said simply, "Yes."

And that's all there was to it.

13

Eleven to Fourteen: The Tweenager

"Whenever I ask him to do something, he just sits there as though I don't exist. He's unpredictably temperamental, too—swings back and forth between joy and misery as if he's riding an emotional seesaw. And when he's in misery, watch out! Nothing I know of will satisfy him. But the worst thing to deal with is this idea that he can do whatever he pleases, without regard for anybody else. And stubborn? Ha! If I say go, he wants to stay. If I want to stay, he wants to go. Loving one minute, don't-touch-me! the next. To tell the truth, I've about had it. Sometimes I think it's either him or me. There are times when I feel the urge to throttle the little monster, but I always snap back to reality moments before my hands wrap around his throat.

ANOTHER TWO-YEAR-OLD, RIGHT? Wrong. The monster this parent is complaining about hasn't worn a diaper for ten years.

Introducing the large, economy-size version of the terrible two: He pouts, he stomps his size-seven feet, he bellows at the top of his lungs. Ladies and gentlemen! A big Bronx cheer for that second most terrible of all terribles, the tweenager!

And no, this is not a misprint. I use the phrase to refer to an eleven-, twelve-, or thirteen-year-old, a three-year period in a youngster's life that is completely unlike the years immediately before and after. Most eleven-, twelve-, and thirteen-year-olds are no longer children but they are not quite adolescents. They are betwixt and *between,* therefore the term *tweenager.*

The tweenage years can be a miserable time both for tweens and for anyone else who has to deal with them day in and day out, parents and teachers in particular. There are many outward similarities between the terrible twos and the equally terrible tweens, so much so that many writers refer to the second eighteen months of life as the *first* adolescence.

Like the two-year-old, the tweenager is a rebel in search of a cause. The defiance of parental (and most other) authority is blindly reflexive. However, the tremendous growth of language during the intervening decade has replaced the monosyllabic *no!* with a peculiar form of self-centered ranting that makes no sense to anyone but the speaker.

And, like the toddler, the tween is an emotional basket case, careening wildly from one passionate extreme to another—a bull in the china shop of feelings.

It's another two years of almost certain temper tantrums, which burst forth any time the tweenager's inevitably unreasonable wants are not catered to. The more unreasonable they are, the greater the force of explosion.

This volatile character was portrayed brilliantly by young Michael Landon in *I Was a Tween-age Werewolf,* Hollywood's in-depth study of preadolescence. (Regrettably, the *w* was left on the cutting-room floor by a junior editor who read it as a misspelling.)

The two-year-old is also father to the tween in his or her maddening self-centeredness. Tweenagers are willing to inconvenience anyone to get what they want. And excuse *you* for leaving your foot where our royal tween-ness might step on it. Any empathic weaknesses that might interfere with this me-first obsession are suspended for the duration.

Again like the two-year-old, the tween cannot decide whether to be dependent or independent. But whatever the role of the moment, Freddy the Freeloader or James Dean, it's darn sure going to be on the tween's terms and no one else's. Tweens will, for instance, curse their parents for having the gall to restrict their freedom, insisting on taking care of themselves, come what may, and then ask for money, a ride somewhere, or more likely both.

But there is method to this madness. Just like the two-year-old, whose behavior is the echo of a consciousness that is rapidly expanding, and propelling the toddler from explorer to experimenter and observer to doer, the tween is making a similar leap in the ability to flush out the mysteries of the universe. After ten years of grappling with the logic of concrete, measurable relationships, the tween is beginning to grasp the abstract, the hypothetical, the stuff of no-stuff-at-all. Not surprisingly, the tween is as hopelessly drunk on this process and its attendant revelations as the two-year-old was.

Add an overdose of hormones, put the mixture under ever-increasing peer pressure, and you've got a guaranteed two or three years of Katy-bar-the-door-and-jump-back-Jack.

Ah, but amid this mayhem are two reasons to rejoice: most tweens are potty trained and very few of them bite.

The tweenage years are a time of transition—a symphony or, more aptly, a *cacophony* of change involving the whole child and dramatically altering the child's definition of self and world.

Changes in the structure and chemistry of the body and corresponding emotional upheavals bring tweenagers face-to-face with their emergent sexuality.

About this time, the brain begins to process and organize information in a radically different manner, adding new dimensions to the tween's perception of the world and further complicating the self-image.

Preadolescents tend to be introspective; that is, they think a lot about themselves, sometimes to the point of obsessiveness. They reflect upon and evaluate their own behavior, their feelings, and even their thoughts. This ability to look within brings into clearer focus not just the person-that-is but also the person-that-could-be, the ideal self. Comparisons between the real (present) and ideal self generate either aspiration or anxiety, depending on such factors as how much discrepancy there is between the two and whether the preadolescent has a basically positive or negative self-regard.

Because they scrutinize themselves so carefully and speculate on the thoughts of other people as well, preadolescents often believe they are constantly watched, usually by peers. Therefore, and quite understandably, they are given to "performing" for their imagined (but not necessarily imaginary) audience. This explains why young teens are so generally self-conscious about how they look, spending hours (or so it seems to the one waiting to use the bathroom) primping before every public appearance, however routine.

During this critical period the child transfers most security needs from parents to peers. The peer group bridges childhood (when the child relied on the parents) and adulthood (when the healthy individual is primarily self-reliant); it is a social laboratory where rules and roles can be practiced, evaluated, and incorporated. Gradually, the clique becomes a thing of the past as the preadolescent turns toward forming stable friendships and participating in large-group activities.

Early adolescence is a time of great psychological vulnerability. The young person's self-concept is ambiguous and therefore fragile. From a developmental standpoint, the child's task is to establish identity—an enduring sense of who he or she is and is becoming. This is not easy for someone caught, for the moment at least, between the comfort and security of childhood and the uncertainty of adolescence.

Q: *Do you have any suggestions for parents on how to endure the early teenage years successfully?*

A: There are four keys to parental success during early adolescence.

The first key is *understanding*. Parents must realize that the needs of their child are changing radically during the early teenage years. Socially, the peer group is becoming more important, both as a source of approval and as a source of values. For better or worse, young teens begin pulling away from family and identifying more with their own generation.

Intellectually, the child's mental processes are maturing, unleashing the capacity for abstract critical thought. Tweens test this newly expanded ability—of course—on their parents, arguing and criticizing at every possible opportunity. Also, the young teen's physiology, both internal and external, is changing at an alarmingly rapid pace. In defense, he or she projects the resulting dissatisfaction onto the outside world. Complaint, thy name is tweenager.

The second key combines *tolerance and accommodation:* tolerance because early adolescence is rarely permanent, accommodation because the radical changes taking place during this critical developmental period require equally radical changes in how parents respond to their children. Often a child's accelerating need for freedom catches parents off guard, and they react by hanging vainly on to a style of child-rearing that no longer works.

True, most tweens want more freedom than they can handle. On the other side of this coin, however, are parents who fail to let the young teen experiment with a sufficient amount of freedom. The child, faced with parents who want to keep things the same, rebels. It is important that parents learn when to restrain and when not to, so that this time in the child's life is not defined primarily in terms of struggle. Parents who hope to weather the onslaught of early adolescence by digging themselves in are fighting a losing battle.

The third key is *communication.* Parents must be willing to listen to these young teens, even when they make no sense: to listen to their fears, their expressions of insecurity, their hopes, their ideas, and their opinions; to listen to their many complaints—about friends who don't do right and parents who are never right—and to reflect the majority of their moanings and groanings back to them in an accepting, nonjudgmental way.

There are still plenty of occasions, however, when young teenagers need to hear what their parents think about a certain subject or issue. Parents should not ever be reluctant to say, "We understand how *you* feel; now we want you to listen to how *we* feel." Note the subtle difference: Parents need to understand their children but require only that their children listen. During childhood, understanding is almost always a delayed reaction.

The fourth key is *involvement*. There is no better antidote to the potential pitfalls of peer pressure than parents who are interested and involved. Take the time to ask questions, to listen, to participate. It's one of the best investments you can make in your child's future.

Q: *In a talk I heard you give in Ohio, you warned of the pitfalls of trying to micromanage a teenager. This is a new concept to me. Can you help me understand just what constitutes micromanagement where a teenager is concerned?*

A: Parents who micromanage, or attempt to do so, will do just about anything to prevent their children from learning life's lessons the old-fashioned "hard" way. They don't understand what pre-modern parents—their own parents, in many cases—meant by such sayings as "You made your bed, so lie in it" and "I knew if I gave you enough rope, you'd hang yourself." Parents who micromanage obviously believe they can do with their children what their parents were unable to do with them: Impart wisdom and common sense with words. As a consequence of their misdirected good intentions, they create far more problems than they solve, if they solve any at all.

I was reminded of this during a conversation with two parents from a large city in Georgia. The father mentioned that his wife and sixteen-year-old son were having difficulty getting along. She immediately rolled her eyes and said, exasperation dripping from her voice, "I only want him to stop waiting until the last minute to do his homework and study for tests." In other words, she only wants what is clearly best for him. Therefore, she certainly qualifies as caring, responsible, and all that good stuff. But in those same nineteen words, she was revealed herself to be a compulsive, shoot-herself-in-the-foot, world-class micromanager, which is why she embroiled in perennial conflict with this lad. Instead of letting him learn that decisions (like waiting until the last minute to study for a test) have consequences (poor grades, no driving privileges), she was trying her level best to get him to make the decisions she'd make (at forty-something!) and prevent him from experiencing any consequence other than having to listen to this mom's nagging.

It's quite simple, really. She gives him grief, so he gives her grief in return, the only way he can—by driving her nuts.

In the workplace, the micromanager creates four reliable problems: communication problems, conflict, deceit, and disloyalty. A perceptual myopia causes this boss to believe that the blame for this behavior lies exclusively with the employees, thus justifying even more micromanagement. The micromanaging parent creates the same four problems, blames the child, and justifies even more micromanagement.

During our active parenting years, Willie and I developed some pet parenting mantras, one of which was, "You make your decisions, and we'll make ours." The children quickly figured out that this meant we were going to give them as much rope as they needed with which to hang themselves, make them lie in whatever beds they made, and learn their lessons the hard way. That was the crux of their education in good decision-making, and they proved themselves able students, albeit not without some reluctant experiences with ropes and beds.

For obvious reasons, one often has no choice but to micromanage to some degree during early and middle childhood. But what is often necessary and works with, say, an eight-year-old is completely counterproductive with a child just four years older. As it is written in Ecclesiastes, "To everything there is a season." Would that more parents understood how that applies to child-rearing.

I Was a Tweenage Misanthrope

When I was twelve years old, I hated everything. There was so much to hate I couldn't remember it all. To keep it straight, I wrote it down, and in keeping with this stark no-frills view of the world I titled it my Hate List.

My Hate List filled several pieces of lined notebook paper, both sides. It was in my possession at all times so I could refer or add to it at a moment's notice. Nothing and no one was immune. Naturally, my parents were at the top of the list—in CAPITAL LETTERS surrounded by exclamation points. I hated every one of my teachers, even the ones who were tolerant of my abrasiveness. I hated them if they gave me a C, and I hated them if they gave me an A. I couldn't be bought.

I hated my brother. I hated my sister. I hated my neighbors. I even hated my friends. Each one took a turn on my list. I hated books, homework, the guy who ran the neighborhood store, the barber who cut my hair too short every time, grass because it had to be mowed, leaves because they had to be raked, cars because they had to be washed, my room, girls, white socks, white Levi's, police, and all food except hamburgers, French fries, and Cokes. I hated my mother's hamburgers. She made them awful just to punish me for spending my meager allowance at the Burger Palace. I hated having an allowance. It was demeaning. I hated having no money.

I hated acne medications, my clothes, my shoes, my jacket, the stupid hat my mother bought me, and the galoshes my father made me wear when it snowed. But most of all, I hated me. I couldn't stand the sight of myself in the mirror.

"Yuk! Look at that face. No wonder Linda avoids me. I'm ugly! I hate Linda. I'm short, I'm skinny, my face breaks out, I've got freckles, my biceps are concave, my ribs show, I have dandruff, my hair is red, I can't suntan, there's no hair on my face. . . . O Lord, please don't make me put on shorts for gym anymore—my legs are too skinny and my knees are too knobby. Why do I have to wear glasses? Why do I have to wear braces? My arms are too long, my nose turns up, my ears stick out, my chin is too pointy, I can't play football, I can't fight, nothing good ever happens to me! I'm a reptile. I'm a worm. I'm a bug. I deserve to be squashed!"

What a dirty trick it is to be twelve. You ain't nothin'. You aren't a child. You aren't a teenager. You aren't an adult. You need your parents and you wish they'd leave you alone. You want friends but you don't know how to be friendly. You want to be one of the crowd; you want to be different. You're always on guard, protecting a fragile sense of who you are or wish you were.

Confusion. Resentment. The victim of a cosmic joke. Twelve is the pits. But there is one way out.

Thirteen.

Keep Both Hands on the Wheel

Preadolescence can be emotionally tumultuous and confusing for all concerned. Unfortunately, in many families it is a time when limit-setting begins to break down. It is easy for parents to let themselves be intimidated by their children's emotional upheavals and begin allowing them more responsibility than they can handle in order to avoid confrontations. Exactly the opposite is called for. This is a time for reaffirming your authority rather than allowing your children to dismantle it. Although they will surely reject the notion, it's also a time for children to know that hands other than their own are ready to take the wheel.

Q: *Six months ago, we moved from the East Coast and settled in a nice community in the Midwest. The adjustment has been difficult for all of us, but it seems to have particularly affected our twelve-year-old son. This once outgoing and popular child has formed no close relationships since the move. In fact, he seems to avoid children his own age and has taken to associating with children several years younger. We have spoken to him about making more of an effort to find a friend, but he stays put, spending most of his free time in his room, watching television. He has also become more dependent and attached to his father and me. How can we help him?*

A: I suggest you start by talking with your son about how generally upsetting the move has been to everyone in the family, how difficult it was to leave old friends and find new ones, and so on.

The disruption of a move often causes the preadolescent to regress to earlier forms of behavior. Your son may seek out younger children because they are more accepting, and because his status among them is virtually guaranteed. He is also likely to act more dependent on his parents.

Be understanding and supportive. Encourage and help him expand his activity away from home. A gentle assist from you in the form of arranging for his involvement in activities sponsored by the community, church, or YMCA may be helpful.

Finally, I can't urge you strongly enough to remove the television from his room and limit his access to the family set to a maximum of one hour in the evening. His absorption in television is a way of retreating from the challenge of carving out a niche for himself in his new surroundings. Every hour spent staring at the tube further dampens his initiative and increases his inertia.

Q: *Our thirteen-year-old has recently started threatening to run away from home. He is the second of three boys, three years younger than one brother and three years older than the other. He complains about everything: we expect too much of him, he never has anything to do, we are "easier" on his younger brother, his older brother gets to do more than he does, and so on. It seems as though he's miserable nearly all the time. He can be loving and cooperative—but has not been for at least three months. Should we be concerned about his threats? We hear them two or three times a week. What should we do?*

A: I don't think there's much possibility that he actually will leave for good—not anytime soon, that is. The ones who run with the intention of staying gone don't talk about it much beforehand. They just *go*, and the pressures pushing them to that extreme are far more serious than the typical tweenage blues you're describing. In a similar vein, people who repeatedly threaten suicide are seldom the ones who (except through miscalculation) end up in the morgue. In both instances, the threat is a dramatic way of calling attention to oneself: "Hey! You better look at me, 'cause it might be your last chance!"

There are victims and there are "victims." Included in the former are real-life runaways and real-death suicides. A "victim," on the other hand, is nothing more than a caricature of tragedy—too involved in wearing this particular mask to even consider playing a lesser role. Included in the latter group are, quite often, middle children and tweenagers. Congratulations! You've got two for the price of one.

In one sense, the middle child is a tweenager throughout childhood. Born both too late and too early, he or she rails against the injustice of having an older sibling who enjoys more freedom and a younger one who seems to get more attention ("You let him get away with murder!").

Middle children want the best of both worlds without having to pay the price. They want to be gloriously independent and securely taken care of at the same time. The lure of becoming a victim is almost impossible to resist in this irreconcilable dilemma. "I'm gonna run away!" is a frustrated, exaggerated expression of this conflict. It is both a battle cry for freedom and a plea for more attention.

As middle children move into their tweenage years, the middle-ness is compounded. Woe is them! Insult upon injury! The straw that broke . . . and all the rest.

I am less concerned about your son's threats than the feelings behind them. Understand that this is a particularly stressful transition in his life and an equally important time in the life of your family. Keep communication open, but beware of allowing the child too powerful a voice in defining crucial issues. The questions (or challenges) children of this age raise are often superficial or irrelevant, only distracting from, and preventing resolution of, more important problems facing the family.

For instance, concern over threats of running away can mask the more salient issue of "What does being a member of this family mean when you are thirteen years old?"

Q: *Several times in the past six months, we have found panty hose, usually several pairs at a time, in our twelve-year-old son's room (he will be thirteen soon). He says he took most of them from his aunt's house (he sometimes baby-sits for her children). He denies ever wearing them but can't (or won't) explain why he is so interested in them. We don't understand what his problem is, since he seems like such a typical well-rounded boy in every other way—he is active in sports, makes good grades, and has lots of friends. What do you think is going on, and how should we handle it?*

A: You're right. What you have is a typical, well-rounded twelve-year-old boy expressing his emerging sexuality in a rather unusual but by no means abnormal way.

And *he's* right, too. He probably *doesn't* know why he's attracted to panty hose; he just knows he is. Let's face it—part of the mystery and magic of sex at any age is that words are inadequate to express why it feels so darn good. It just does, and that's enough. For instance, if I try to explain why I'm sexually attracted to my wife, I end up *describing* her. Fine, but why am I attracted to that particular combination of characteristics? I dunno. Just am.

The only problem with the panty hose is that most adults are narrow-minded about expressions of sexuality by a child. We tend to have definite ideas about what is and is not appropriate. So when a twelve-year-old elopes with a pair of panty hose, we freak out because it doesn't fit our preconceived notions of what is okay. Another facet of the problem is that we think of the differences between children and adults in purely quantitative terms. A twelve-year-old possesses less "adultness" than a thirty-year-old—he is smaller, less practical, and so on.

But childhood is not just the lowest eighteen rungs of life's ladder; it is a different ladder altogether. Children play a different game, particularly when it comes to things like sex. In fact, the basic difference between children and adults is that children learn about such things by playing, while adults think of learning as a very serious undertaking.

Around the age of twelve, your son became increasingly, irresistibly, attracted to the female body. He could hardly contain his curiosity. But he had to. The average twelve-year-old has enough presence of mind to know that the female body is off limits for a few more years. But it just so happens that there are these things called panty hose that women wear over a very intriguing area of their anatomy. So . . .

He's only playing. Just learning, in a safe and harmless way. In this case, panty hose are transitional objects—items the youngster uses to help him come to grips with the changes taking place in his body, in his mind, and in his emotions. He is interested in them because the "real thing," besides being off limits, is too threatening at the moment.

If your son were not "typical"—if his behavior were extremely unusual in other respects or if he isolated himself from other children his age or seemed depressed—more concern would be appropriate. But even in that context, panty hose would be the *least* relevant detail.

Take this ideal opportunity to let him know that you understand how panty hose can be intriguing (but *don't* analyze his interest for him). Tell him that as his body matures and his feelings about women change, you are there to help answer his questions and discuss his concerns. If the door is open, he will walk through it, and when he discovers that you're willing to listen without judging or criticizing him, he will seek your counsel more often.

Q: *A communication problem has recently developed between us and our eleven-year-old son. We used to be very close and affectionate toward one another. He's always been a child who would tell us what was going on in his life and talk to us if he had a problem. That all changed shortly after he started sixth grade this year. He's more distant, seems uncomfortable when we show affection toward him, and is no longer open with us about what he's doing in school or with his friends. If we try to engage him in conversation, he gives us one-word replies to anything we say or ask him. According to his teachers, he's well liked by his classmates, but his grades are starting to slip. What would you suggest?*

A: I'd suggest that what's going on may be nothing more complicated than preadolescence, and that you would do well to stay pretty much out of the picture, at least for the time being.

Preadolescence, the tweenage years, begins around age eleven and lasts through age thirteen. Before this important transitional stage, the child's security is invested primarily in relationships with parents, self-esteem is primarily a function of parental approval, and the quality of sense of identity (self-concept) is tied predominantly to his or her role within the family.

The task of preadolescence is to find a secure niche within the peer group. This requires youngsters to put some distance between themselves and their parents. And so, around age eleven, the child begins withdrawing security from the family and investing it in peer relationships. Increasingly, self-esteem becomes a function of peer approval and self-concept a measure of how successful the youngster is at finding a relatively stable role within the peer group.

As you can imagine—and probably remember—this metamorphosis generates its share of anxiety and insecurity, which explains why children of this age often look worried and troubled.

But to whom can they talk? Not to friends, because to do so would be a tacit admission of weakness. Not to their parents either, because that would be an admission of continued dependence. The tweenager is having to make a lot of adjustments, and—aside from being understanding, patient, and supportive—there's probably little that parents can do that will significantly ease the process.

Although he may at times act as if he wants nothing to do with you, your son is actually trying to figure out how he can develop a place for himself among his peers and still keep you on his team. Without realizing it, you're doing half his job for him. Every expression of concern on your part affirms the security of his relationship with you. And so he seizes the opportunity to turn the tables on you a bit. You pursue, and he plays hard to get.

I'd suggest you back off a bit and let him begin assuming a greater share of responsibility for the relationship. You might issue an open invitation of the "if you want to talk, you know where to find us" sort. As far as his grades are concerned, a slight slip is no cause for alarm, but if they continue to deteriorate, you might consider reading a book such as my *Ending the Homework Hassle*.

Q: *Our thirteen-year-old son, an only child, is generally well behaved and does well in school. This past summer, the three of us decided that William would begin working in his father's business one day per week during the summer and one weekend day during the school year to earn money and develop a good work ethic. We've had nothing but problems since. He claims that having to work is causing him to miss out on a social life and is robbing him of a "fun" childhood. This is causing great conflict between him and his dad and a lot of family problems overall. If William were your son, would you make him live up to the agreement?*

A: Not if making him live up to the agreement is going to create uproar in the family, I wouldn't. If William, upon discovering what he agreed to, wants to back out, I'd let him. At this age, trying to force compliance will succeed at the risk of precipitating great rebellion on William's part. Besides, the fact that he doesn't want to work for his dad doesn't indicate he's going to be a lazy good-for-nothing when he grows up.

You asked what I would do if I were William's dad, so here goes: I would tell him he didn't have to work for me if he didn't want to. Under the circumstances, however, I had decided to give him a weekly allowance of, say, $20 (or a limit of $80 per month), with which he was hereafter going to be responsible for purchasing his own nonessential clothing and recreation, unless the latter included other family members. Under no circumstances would I ever advance him money toward the next week or month's allowance. If he felt he needed more money, he was either going to have to ask me for work or ask neighbors if they have jobs for him. If he asked me for work and I found myself having to stand over him, however, I'd fire him, and that would be the end of it.

A management plan of this sort—which I've spelled out in great detail in my book *Teen-Proofing*—would force him to budget his money and begin confronting economic realities, including the principle that "money doesn't grow on trees." He would have a good measure of fiscal independence, he would learn by trial and error to make sound spending decisions, and the present tension in the father–son relationship would be defused.

I would also assign William at least one after-school or after-lunch chore per day (in addition to making his bed in the morning and keeping his room neat and clean), Monday through Saturday. His allowance and his chores would be completely independent of one another, however. In other words, he would do chores for free, simply because he was a member of the household. I wouldn't

397

stand over him in this area either. If he didn't do one of his chores, I wouldn't nag. I'd simply do it for him. But! If I did one chore for him throughout the week, his weekend privileges or freedoms would be revoked.

I don't believe in micromanaging a teenager (or a child of any age), but I don't believe a capable child should be a freeloader, either. Do yourselves and William a favor and let him learn his life lessons the hard way. Stop trying to cram them down his throat.

Q: *The last couple of times we've gone out to eat as a family, our twelve-year-old daughter has refused to go with us. Is it better to let her have her way or insist that she come along? In the latter instance, of course, we're all going to be miserable.*

A: Well, you may be asking the wrong guy this question, because I am an inveterate misery-avoider. My wife, Willie, is cut from the same chicken wire. When our children became teenagers, they often wanted to stay home when we went out to eat "as a family." We quickly learned that if we insisted they come along we'd be miserable. So we stopped insisting.

If you trust your daughter to stay home alone, and you trust that she's safe, I see no point in making her be a member of the family when she'd rather have some private time. One couple I know solved this problem by simply telling their young teenage son that if he wanted to stay home he had to do housework. If he chose to go out with them, and he made them miserable, he had to do housework when they got home. Sometimes, staying home was so important to him that he'd do the work. At other times, he went along with the family and kept his misery—if there was any—to himself. In either case, the parents were happy.

Childhood's End

Q: *Our eleven-year-old daughter recently told me she has been having "scary thoughts" lately, including thoughts of dying, us being killed, and other vague feelings that something terrible is about to happen. The* *thoughts not only frighten her but also cause her to feel guilty, particularly the ones about us getting killed. We have a good relationship and she's been open with us about this. We recently read an article about a psychological disorder that involves obsessive thoughts of this sort. Could something serious be going on here? How should we handle it?*

A: The psychological disorder you read about is called obsessive-compulsive disorder (OCD). It often begins during adolescence and is characterized by obsessive thoughts or compulsions—ritual behaviors that the individual feels compelled to perform. Recent research suggests that OCD results from a chemical imbalance within the brain and is best treated using a combination of medication and psychotherapy.

I am in no position, of course, to make a diagnosis. Chances are, however, your daughter's problem isn't serious. Persistent disturbing thoughts of one sort or another are fairly common to pre-teens and teens. Often, they are a byproduct of the transition from childhood to adolescence.

Along with physical changes that are taking place during this time, profound changes are taking place in how a child organizes and processes information. Specifically, the child becomes capable of thinking in far more complex and abstract terms—in other words, like an adult. Comparing the child's brain to a computer, it's as if the child's thinking program is suddenly and significantly upgraded. This new capacity is exciting, but some aspects also may be initially confusing, even frightening.

When my daughter, Amy, was about twelve, she began having fears of dying. They usually began at bedtime, preventing her from falling asleep. When she shared her anxieties with me, I explained them in terms of mental growing pains.

"At this point in your life, Amy," I told her, "you're beginning to change from a child into an adult. You can see the changes happening in your body. What you can't see are the changes happening in your brain that affect the way you think about things. As you go through this transition from thinking like a child to thinking like an adult, it may sometimes feel that you're not in control of what's going on in your mind. Sometimes, a frightening thought may just pop into your head, or the same thought may occur over and over again. No matter how powerful these thoughts may feel, however, they don't have the power to cause things to happen that wouldn't have happened anyway.

"The important thing," I went on to say, "is that you talk about these things with either Mom or me. The worst thing you can do is bottle them up inside, because then they have nowhere to go and they just start bouncing around in there to make you feel more and more confused. The best way to get them out of your head is to talk about them, and that's one reason why we're here."

Amy and I continued to have occasional talks about this over a period of about six months. Each time, I provided the same reassurance and basically the same explanation. To my knowledge, the thoughts didn't go away that quickly, but Amy became less and less fearful of them and therefore better able to control them.

The fact that your daughter shared the problem with you indicates you have a healthy relationship in which there is good communication and lots of trust on her part. With you there to provide the foundation of support and security, there is little chance that this will develop into something major. If, however, the problem persists longer than a few months without any improvement, it would be prudent of you to seek professional help.

"Hello? Is Anyone at Home in There?"

The phone rang and thirteen-year-old Eric jumped to answer it.

"Yeah? . . . Huh? . . . No. . . . Uhhh. . . . Yeah."

He emitted a series of unintelligible sounds and hung up. The "conversation" lasted less than thirty seconds.

"Wrong number?" I asked.

"My girlfriend."

"Your girlfriend? You've got to be kidding! You actually talk that way to someone you know? It sounded as if you have a speech problem—sort of semihuman, you know?"

"That's the way we talk to each other all the time."

"No it's not."

"Whaddaya mean?"

"I mean it may be the way some of you talk to each other, but it's not the way *you* are going to talk to anyone, not on our family phone you're not."

Soon thereafter, my wife and I put both children through a crash course in making and receiving telephone calls, including "Hello?" "May I take a message?" and "Thanks for calling."

Good phone manners, we pointed out, are as important as manners in any other area, perhaps even more so, since your voice is all you have with which to make your impression on the other person.

From that point on we never cringed when one of the children picked up the phone because they projected a friendly, positive attitude.

As time went on, however, I discovered Eric was right in one respect: many of them do talk to each other that way, "them" being young people in their early teens.

I think it has something to do with their self-consciousness, which has something to do with wanting to appear aloof, which has something to do with wanting to make oneself less vulnerable. In any case, their phone manners are generally abominable.

I was brooding on this problem one afternoon shortly after Eric had drawn my attention to it, when the phone rang. I picked it up.

"Hello?"

"LemmespeakaEric."

"Chip [not his real name]? Is that you, Chip?"

Chip was one of Eric's friends. I would kid around with Chip a lot.

"Yeah."

"Listen, Chip, that was atrocious. I mean it was just awful, and I'm going to pretend you never called and hang up. You call back and let's try it again from the top, okay?" and I hung up.

Fifteen seconds later, the phone rang again.

"Hello?"

"Uhhh, I wannatalkaEric."

"Better, Chip, better but not quite right, if you know what I mean. Let's try it one more time from the top." And I hung up.

The phone rang again.

"Hello?"

"Uhhhh, ha-ha-ha, uhhh . . ."

"What do you mean, 'Uhhhh, uhhhh,' Chip? Do I have to spell it out for you? Look, try it one more time, but this time when I pick up the phone, I'll say, 'Hello?' and you say, 'Hello, Mr. Rosemond, this is Chip and I'd like to speak with Eric if he's home.' Got it? Oh, and Chip, a British accent would really snap it up." And I hung up again.

The phone rang again.

"Hello?"

"Hello, Mr. Rosemond—uhhhh—this is Chip and I'd—ha—ha—ha—like to [phony British accent] speak with Eric—ha—ha—ha."

"Gosh, Chip, I'm sorry, but Eric's not home. May I take a message?"

He hung up.

The "Talk"

Q: *Our oldest, a son, just turned twelve. He's in the sixth grade and be-ginning to show some interest in girls—talking on the telephone, mostly. When and how should we begin his sexual education? Neither of our parents ever sat down to talk with us about such things, so we don't know how to go about it.*

A: As a young teen, one of the things I dreaded, and hoped to for-ever avoid, was the "Talk." That's when your father walks casually over to you and says, with this really serious, I mean *terminal*, look on his face, "Son, I think you and I need to talk." And you act stu-pid at first, like you don't have any idea what he means, all the while calculating how you're going to handle this uncool situation. But before you can say anything, he's already started his spiel, and all you want to do is get out of there, but you can't because it's your father. So you pretend to listen.

Or you do what I did, which was to lie. "Hey, listen, Dad, before you go any further, I think I can save you some time. This guy came and talked to our health class last year, about—you know, and—

well, he was pretty good, and—well, I don't think it's really necessary for me to hear it all over again, but I appreciate your concern and I'll be sure and come to you if I have any questions, okay?"

Boy, did *he* ever look relieved.

As my son approached adolescence, I looked back on that truncated conversation with a mixture of humor and perplexity. I wasn't comfortable with the format my father chose, and neither was he. But what was the alternative? In the process of pondering this dilemma, I realized that my feelings of unease as an adolescent were due in part to the fact that sex was, at the time, a threatening subject for me, and so it is for many adolescent males. One way of keeping the anxiety it arouses at bay is for the young teen to deny that he needs to know anything about it.

But a second reason for my discomfort was that I had no choice in the matter. Dad had decided it was time for my education and that was that. In other words, *his* needs dictated the moment. I'm sure he felt obliged to "do his duty" toward me and approached the subject the only way he knew, but I felt backed into a corner and so took the quickest way out.

I came to the conclusion that what my son needed from me was not a rundown of the facts, but the freedom to ask questions. If his sexual education was going to be meaningful, he would have to feel in control of it.

So, I took the initiative to issue an open-ended invitation. I think we were going somewhere together in the car when, for whatever reason, the time felt right for me to say what I had to say.

"Son, as you get older, you're going to become more and more interested in girls and you're going to have questions and—"

He interrupted. "Uh, look, Dad, before you go any further, this guy came and talked to our health class last year and—"

"Yeah, I know, he was pretty good and answered your questions, right?"

"Right. How'd you know?"

"Same guy came to my health class when I was your age. But I'm not finished. All I want to say is that when you have questions or anything at all you want to discuss concerning women and men and sex, I'd like you to ask me. I'd rather you asked me instead of one of your friends, because their answers and opinions might not be correct. And remember: There's no such thing as a dumb question."

Boy, was *he* ever relieved. But he *did* come to me with questions on more than a few occasions, and I took those opportunities not only to answer his questions but to add a few editorial comments as well. In addition, he occasionally said or did things that allowed me to make further adjustments in his attitude.

With our daughter, the only modification my wife and I made in this basic approach was to prepare her for her first period.

Basically, we tried to get across to both of them that the secret to a successful sexual relationship with someone has less to do with techniques and biology than with attitude and values—specifically, how well you respect yourself and how well you respect the other person. You can't package that attitude in one fact-filled conversation. It's something you model for them every day in what you say and what you do. In that sense, a child's sex education begins the day he or she is born.

Q: *My wife and I recently discovered that our thirteen-year-son, on two separate occasions, had gone into our ten-year-old daughter's room and cut up one of her panties. Our third child knew about it too, but the thirteen-year-old asked them to not tell. Thinking this a bit weird, our first inclination was to call a therapist. Since then, my wife has had insomnia. When she does sleep, she has bad dreams. She tells me she feels violated herself and has expressed the feeling that our son is a "stranger" who is capable of even more outrageous things. Is my wife overreacting? Should we get our son into therapy? I suppose you need to know that he has apologized to his sister, seems genuinely remorseful, and has accepted his punishment, which amounted to being grounded for a month.*

A: I'd say your wife is overreacting, but on the other hand it's important that neither of you underreact, either. A young adolescent male's sexual curiosity is to some degree undersocialized, meaning this age male has yet to learn to say no to certain of his sexual impulses. For example, he may know that something (like cutting up his sister's underpants) is wrong, but his sexual feelings are often so urgent, so all-consuming, that they override the admonitions of his conscience. As a consequence, the young teenage boy is likely to express his sexuality in ways considered downright bizarre by adults. Indeed, if an adult male cut up a little girl's underwear, he definitely would be considered perverted, sick, and perhaps even a menace to society. Such diagnoses do not apply, however, when the perpetrator is thirteen.

If your son had physically violated his younger sister, if he had exhibited no remorse when his act was discovered, if he persisted in destroying her underwear in spite of being punished, significant concern would be warranted. None of those apply. Therefore, I'd certainly keep an eye on the situation for some time, but I don't think you have anything to worry about. Along these lines, I do not think he would profit at this time from seeing a counselor, but if you would feel more secure if he (or the two of you) spoke to a professional, then by all means make an appointment.

The act of vandalizing a sister's underpants at age thirteen or thereabouts is not predictive of bizarre sexual behavior later in life. I've talked with many a responsible well-adjusted male adult who has admitted to having had some very strange fetishes during early adolescence. (Which is not to say that some fetishistic teenage boys don't ever grow up to be sexual deviates, but this is probably more the exception than the rule.) Keep in mind that the young male teen is less mature and generally shorter than his female classmates and usually can't even get the time of day from them. These fetishes are, generally speaking, a harmless way of channeling a lot of pent-up sexual energy.

Your son did something inappropriate but relatively harmless. He has apologized and been punished. It's time for the family to move on.

14

Fourteen to Nineteen: The Teen Years

IF YOU HAVE TEENAGE CHILDREN, their going to the mall becomes an issue. So do parties and riding around and dating and curfew and concerts and going to the beach and . . . need I go on? All these things became issues in our home when our children entered their teens.

Not since the children were two were my wife and I confronted with such a push for independence. Even though we knew it was coming and did our best to prepare, adolescence still occasionally managed to sneak up behind us and yell *boo!*

Thankfully, those times were few and far between, but then were blessed with two children who took pride in doing the right thing. I think about parents who haven't been so fortunate, for whom life with a teenager or teenagers has been like dominoes falling, and I wonder how things can go so right for some and so wrong for others.

After thirty years of working with families, no one can tell me that luck—for lack of a better term—doesn't have something to do with it. I've heard enough horror stories from caring, conscientious parents to convince me that caring isn't all it's sometimes cracked up to be.

Please don't misunderstand me. If you *don't* care, then you will most certainly reap the harvest of your neglect. But caring and doing all the things caring parents are supposed to do still doesn't guarantee everything's going to be all right. And that's what's so scary, isn't it?

The question I am most often asked by parents of teenagers is "How much freedom should we give?" I must admit to not having a specific answer to that one. I only know that teens are generally guilty of wanting more freedom than they can handle. But then parents are generally guilty of giving less freedom than teens can handle. Somewhere between the urge to fly the nest and the urge to keep them from flying too far too fast there is a happy medium. Finding it is the trick.

Then comes "What should teenagers be doing in their free time?" and again I have no formula. "A variety of things" is perhaps the closest I can come to an answer. I smell trouble when a teenager seems obsessed with doing only one thing, or only a few, whether it be listening to rock music, hanging out at the mall, or doing homework. For my wife and me, things like going to the mall and riding around were not issues as long as they were just two of many things our children wanted to do. Nor were there magical ages at which we allowed Eric and Amy to go to concerts or wear makeup or date. The better our children took care of the privileges they had, the more privileges we gave them.

That last question is followed closely by "How can parents tell if their teenage children are doing things they shouldn't be doing?" The answer: If you care to know, then you will know. You'll know because they'll act as if they're keeping secrets.

If you want to minimize the possibility that your teenage children might, among other harmful things, become sexually active or experiment with drugs (including alcohol and tobacco), the best insurance policy involves open lines of communication.

I find that humor is perhaps the best medicine for opening those lines of communication and keeping them open. Likewise, nothing clogs those lines quicker than a parent who takes things too seriously.

I once heard a parent jokingly remark that the teenage years were, for parents, "the best of times, the worst of times." That may be so, but let's not forget that the teenage years are possibly the best and worst of times for our children as well. The fact that we've already walked in their moccasins means we can understand them better than they understand us. And a little understanding can go a long way.

Q: *We are worried about our fourteen-year-old daughter. She's become extremely rude and disrespectful, and the more of an audience she has, the ruder she is. She constantly calls attention to herself by acting silly and obnoxious and seems determined to provoke us one way or another. We're also concerned that she seems to have little or no interest either in school or in spending time with friends. Up until the last year or so, she was a sweet, affectionate child. What could be the matter and how should we handle it?*

A: Before adolescence, a child's self-concept is closely tied to parental approval. As adolescence approaches, the source of self-esteem shifts from parents to peers. The task facing the young teen is one of finding a viable niche in the culture of the peer group, one that draws positive attention.

This important transition involves a certain amount of insecurity. To gain approval from peers, the youngster must conform to prevailing peer-group standards. In the process, parents come down off the pedestal they previously occupied and are replaced by friends as a major source of influence.

As the parents and the child adjust to new roles and expectations of one another, some friction is inevitable. An abnormally high degree of conflict or rebellion, however, usually spells trouble. It means that either the child's friends are exerting a decidedly negative effect, or the child is having social problems and, outward appearances aside, is depressed. Depression can wear a number of masks, but self-directed anger is almost always a feature.

Your daughter's lack of involvement with her peers may mean she has yet to find her niche. Feeling rejected and self-conscious, she draws attention to herself by acting silly and obnoxious. This has the unintended effect of driving her peers farther away.

Inwardly, she blames herself for her social problems, but she deals with her anger by projecting it outward, onto you. You become her whipping post.

First, confront her in a way that opens the door for communication and support. Say, "We think your recent behavior is a way of hiding some unhappiness that you need to talk out. If you don't feel you can talk with us about what's bothering you, let's find a counselor you can talk to."

During this conversation, it's important that you not criticize her or imply that her behavior has hurt you in some way. That kind of approach will put a quick damper on communication.

Second, encourage involvement with peers. Urge her to do things like invite a friend over to spend the night or go to the movies. Depending on how much social paralysis has set in, you might even need to insist. Consider getting her involved in a church-sponsored youth program. If you don't attend a church, you can still find a program that would welcome her participation.

Third, keep your cool when she lashes out at you. Don't take it personally, because it really isn't. Let her know, however, in straightforward nonemotional terms, how her behavior appears to others. Be honest and straightforward with your feedback, as in, "That was rude. It's not necessary for you to behave that way to get our attention. What is it that you're really wanting from us right now?"

In a sense, her verbal barbs are a test of your strength. She wants to know, "Are you strong enough to see me through this uncertain time of my life?"

If things don't get better quickly, call your family doctor or area mental health association and ask for a referral to a therapist who specializes in adolescent issues.

Q: *Our fourteen-year-old daughter recently told an adult friend of ours that she didn't get along with us. This came as quite a surprise because although we have occasional conflicts over the usual things—what she can do, when she has to be in, and so on—we didn't feel we had any major problems.*

We don't want to betray the confidence she has in the friend by confronting her with what she told him, but we feel we need to do something. How would you handle this situation?

A: Unless you have reason to feel that there is something amiss in your relationship with your daughter, I wouldn't advise you to do anything. The fact that she told someone that she doesn't get along with you is more of a comment on her age than it is on the status of your relationship with her.

In the first place, it isn't cool to get along with your parents when you're fourteen. Even if you do, you're reluctant to admit it. Children of this age are seeking to establish autonomy and an identity separate and distinct from who their parents think they are or want them to be.

This struggle to become your own person, to define yourself, is, in fact, the central theme of early adolescence and is the reason for most of the tension that exists between parents and children during this stage of development.

So if someone asks a fourteen-year-old, "Do you get along with your parents?" the likelihood is great that the answer will be *no*. But *no* doesn't mean that there is more than a normal amount of tension in the relationship. *No* may simply be an expression of the young teen's need to feel autonomous.

Consider also that your daughter may have unburdened herself shortly after a conflict with you. Teens are given to dramatic exaggeration. If they've just had an argument with their parents, they'll say they never get along with them even if they generally do.

In short, I wouldn't worry about it, and I certainly wouldn't confront her with what you've heard. Bringing her feelings out in the open will give them more attention than they probably deserve. Attention can make a mountain out of a molehill.

Q: *Our fourteen-year-old daughter's room is a pigsty. Her clothes are heaped on the floor where she took them off, her closet looks like the aftermath of Armageddon. Papers, books, and CDs are strewn everywhere.*

*Gaudy rock posters are all over the walls, and her bed is never made
(except on the day I change the sheets). Millie and I have had a running
battle over the state of her room for as long as I can remember. Her position is that she lives there and so should be able to decorate and maintain it according to her standards, rather than mine. I don't see how she
can stand to live in such a mess, much less find anything she wants in
there. She says it's none of my business whether she knows where things
are or not. What do you say?*

A: I say your daughter's argument is far better than yours. She's
perfectly right—whether she can stand the mess or knows where to
locate her possessions is none of your business.

Here's your argument: Millie should keep her room orderly and
clean because she'll be happier if she does. Question: How do you
know? Answer: You don't. Millie has told you she's perfectly happy
with her room as it is. It's really quite presumptuous of you to tell
her she'll be happier if she does things your way.

I say it's time you told Millie the truth. The first part of the truth
is that the reason you want her to keep her room clean is because
you'll be happier if she does. The second part of the truth is that
you pay the mortgage, so your standards should prevail.

Now get in there and insist that your daughter keep her room
clean and orderly. Sure, her tastes are different from yours; you can
respect that, can't you? Millie can have her CD collection and her
rock posters, as long as they're put neatly away in their cases and
tacked neatly to her walls. The issue is not what constitutes good
taste, it's what constitutes *clean* and whether children should obey
their parents.

Apply the Godfather Principle and make her an offer she can't
refuse. On school days, her room must be neat and clean before she
leaves for classes or she can't socialize with her friends or talk on
the phone after school. On other days, freedom and privilege are
earned by first accomplishing the same chore. If she wants to trash
her room while she's in there, fine. But it must be untrashed before
she can do what she wants to do. Define *neat* and *clean* as clothes
picked up and put away properly, floor cleared of obstructions,

closet organized, top surfaces of furniture tidy, and bed made. (In future, have her change her own sheets.)

She's bound to want to fight you about this. Don't! Just enforce the rules, without concern for whether or not she likes them.

Q: *Do parents ever have the right to search a teen's room or read a diary? My fourteen-year-old daughter and I are having a dispute over this issue. Although I've never searched her room or looked in her diary, I maintain that, as her parent, I have the right to do so at any time, especially if I think she's up to no good. My daughter says her room is her private domain and I do not have the right even to set foot in there without permission, much less conduct a search. Who's right?*

A: That's a tough question. Both points of view have merit, but neither can claim to be the final word.

For instance, I agree with your daughter that parents should respect a teen's privacy. With that privilege come certain responsibilities, however. Your daughter's concept of "private domain" implies that she is responsible to no one but herself where her room is concerned. That is simply not so.

She earns and maintains her privacy by, first, keeping her room clean and neat, in keeping with the standard that prevails in the rest of the home. Second, she is not entitled to do as she pleases in her room. The rules of the household extend beyond her doorway, and she should be expected to abide by them. For instance, she should keep the volume on her stereo low enough that it doesn't interfere with someone else's peace of mind.

Nor does your daughter have the right to shut herself in her room for long periods of time, only coming out to eat and perform other vital functions. With the benefits of membership in the family goes the requirement of participation. For some teens, however, the only question is "What can my family do for me?" They have little appreciation for the flip side of the coin, "What can I do for my family?" (See chapter 3.)

In other words, you should expect of your daughter exactly what society expects of us all. We are entitled to privacy, but we are not allowed to do as we please with the privilege. Our homes are our castles only as long as we abide by certain rules and regulations.

In most communities, for example, there are restrictions that prevent using a private residence as a commercial business. Nor are homeowners allowed to accumulate garbage in their front yards or disturb the peace of the neighborhood with loud noises. If your daughter wants to be treated as an adult where the privacy of her room is concerned, she must be willing to act like one.

For the most part, you are wrong in saying that parents have the right to search a teen's room at any time. A search motivated by mere curiosity will do nothing but undermine trust and communication. If the teen's conduct is above suspicion, the parents have no right to violate a young person's privacy. On the other hand, if parents have significant reason to believe that the teen is, indeed, up to no good, they have more than a right to search for evidence, they have a responsibility to their child to do so.

If your daughter has been lying about her whereabouts and activities, if she has been violating curfew and other rules with regularity, if she frequently comes in looking and acting unusual, if she has been skipping classes in school, if her grades have taken a sudden turn for the worse, if she tries to keep you from finding out who her friends are—then trust has already been broken and you do have sufficient cause to conduct a search.

If, however, a search reveals that you were wrong to suspect wrongdoing, then your child deserves a confession, along with an explanation and an apology. Trust is, after all, a two-way street.

Q: *I've heard that the greater the number of organized activities—church youth groups, athletics, scouting, school organizations, and so on—that teenagers are involved in, the less likely it is they'll get messed up with drugs and sex. Do you agree and, if so, how much should parents dictate to a teenager concerning extracurricular activities?*

A: There is nothing so deadly as boredom during the teenage years, and I believe that parents should promote involvement in the types of events and activities you mentioned.

The recipe for a teen in trouble, whether the trouble be alcohol, drugs, or sex, is equal parts negative peer pressure, parental under-involvement, and boredom. Let a teenager just wander in search of something to do, and he or she will eventually wander into a crowd of kids who are themselves wandering. Sooner or later, they'll stumble onto the opportunity to experience something forbidden. Lacking anything better to do, they will accept, and keep on accepting, the invitation.

Several years ago, I did an informal study of well-adjusted teens. These were young people ages thirteen through seventeen who, according to their parents' reports, made good grades, got along well at home, enjoyed an active social life, and seemed happy with themselves. Without exception, these youngsters were active in at least one extracurricular activity through their school, church, or community. In addition, every one of them had a hobby. To their parents' knowledge, none of them was using drugs or alcohol, nor were they sexually active.

I know what some of you are saying: "C'mon John, don't be so naive! Just because their parents don't know something is going on doesn't mean it isn't."

I disagree. Parents who are interested and involved in what their children are doing with their spare time will usually know when something is wrong. They may not know the specifics, but they will *know* nonetheless. The test for trouble is simple. Ask yourself, "How often do I have a feeling of general discomfort concerning who my child is with, where my child is, and what my child doing?" If your answer is once a month or more, you had better take a closer look. Parents often ignore the signs. Then, when the beast finally rears its ugly head, they claim ignorance.

Remember also that most teens will sooner or later drink a beer or two, take a drag off a joint, and tread dangerously close to "too far" sexually. There's a difference between trying and using. The difference is made by parents who care.

Concerning how far parents should tell to a teenager what to do with spare time, I don't see anything wrong with parents mandating that a teen get involved in a certain activity as long as that mandate is the exception rather than the rule. Part of our job, after all, is to help create and maintain "well-roundedness" in our children's lives. If we see a gap, we have every right to fill it—if our children won't take the initiative to do so. Oftentimes, their reluctance to get involved in something is based on inadequate information, misperception, or the unfounded fear that they won't fit in.

There have been a few occasions when my wife and I told our teenage son what he was going to do with his time. Although he might have initially complained about our decision, he always ended up appreciating it.

Sometimes it pays to remind ourselves that we really *do* know best.

Q: *About two months ago, our fourteen-year-old son got mad at us and ran away from home. We finally found him two days later at the home of a friend whose parents didn't know we were looking for him. He left because we put him on a week's restriction for not coming home on time. He was a perfectly delightful kid until about a year ago, when he began acting like a complete jerk—talking back, giving us grief every time we asked him to do something, and becoming belligerent when he didn't get his way. We're at our wits' end with him. To make matters worse, he's using this running away thing to get what he wants from us. If things don't suit him, he starts talking about leaving. He obviously knows how upset it makes us. To hear his teachers and friends' parents talk about him, you'd think he was a saint. What should we do?*

A: For starters, you should stop living in fear of his running away. Based on what you told me in your letter, it's not a likely possibility.

I make a distinction between running away and running off. Lots of kids run off. They get mad at their parents and escape to what is usually a fairly safe haven—a friend's house, a neighbor's barn—for a few days. It's an impulsive, dramatic way of handling frustrations. Kids who run off have every intention of coming home and often make it very easy for their parents to find them.

Running away, however, is a horse of quite a different color. This is serious stuff, not soap opera; these kids don't want to be found. They're almost always from very unstable families, where conflict is the norm. Frequently, these kids have been the victims of physical or sexual abuse. To escape the dead-end street, they hit the road.

Your son didn't really run away; he merely ran off. And there's nothing in your letter to suggest he's likely to decide suddenly to leave on a cross-country hike.

Yes, living with a young adolescent can certainly be the pits at times. It's important to distinguish between normal adolescent behavior and real problem behavior. Here's my test for truly troubled teens:

1. Was he or she a behavior problem long before the onset of adolescence?

2. Do other adults (teachers, neighbors, other kids' parents) also have difficulty with him or her?

3. Is he or she using drugs or alcohol?

4. Is he or she sexually active?

If the answer to all four questions is *no,* there's every reason to believe that this too will pass. If the answer to even one of them is *yes,* I would advise that you get some professional help, and fast.

Your letter suggests a *no* to all four. Therefore, I don't think you have anything to fear save fear itself. In that regard, you mustn't allow your son to intimidate you with threats of running away. The next time he lets one slip, shrug it off by saying, "Help yourself, but when you decide to come home, remember that you're going to be grounded one week for every day or part of a day that you are gone." That will give him something to think about.

The more you soften your approach in order to prevent another incident, the worse his behavior will become and the more likely it is he'll pull this kind of stunt again. When he needs discipline, discipline him. In fact, it sounds like a major crackdown may be in order.

I won't wish you good luck, because luck has nothing to do with it. Instead, I'll wish you "good hanging in there!" Firmness is certainly in order.

Q: *Our fourteen-year-old son looks at least two years older and is more mature in many ways than most boys his age. He recently started hanging around with a group of boys who are two and three years older, all of whom have driver's licenses. These boys don't have bad reputations; in fact, they're all good kids who make decent grades and stay out of trouble. Still, we are concerned. Should we insist that he find friends his own age?*

A: If I was in your shoes, I'd leave well enough alone. I can certainly understand your concerns, but it sounds as if your son can relate better to boys who are slightly older. He probably regards the behavior of the typical boy his age as more than slightly puerile and wants to avoid guilt by association. These older boys have affirmed his image of himself as older than his years. They accept him and, given that they are good, responsible kids, I have a suspicion that they are acting as your son's mentors. Good role models can help him channel his social maturity in constructive directions. If my suspicions are correct, the relationship is probably going to help your son to take a later leadership role within his peer group. In short, instead of this situation being a prescription for trouble (as it might be under other circumstances), I think it's actually helping your son stay out of trouble.

In my book, *Teen-Proofing,* I caution parents of teens against letting their anxieties drive a tendency to micromanage. Not only do parental attempts at micromanagement prevent a teen from learning by trial and error (the emphasis being on *error*)—the hard way, as my stepfather would have put it—it's also a sure prescription for rebellion and, therefore, ever-escalating parent–teen conflict. If you want your son to continue being open and aboveboard with you, you'd do well not only to back off but also to welcome his friends into your home with open arms.

Yes, keep an eye on the situation, but that's your job regardless. If you sense trouble brewing, let your son know what your concerns are. In that event, you should make it clear that whereas you're not going to try and choose his friends, you are going to hold him 100 percent responsible for the choices he makes while he's with them. As I tell parents over and over again, it's not your job to always prevent your child from getting into trouble; rather, it's your job to make sure your child learns what he needs to learn if and when he *does* get into trouble.

In the absence of trouble, you don't have much of a job. Enjoy the vacation.

Q: *Our sixteen-year-old daughter has always been a moody, uncommunicative child, but in the last couple of years it's gone from bad to worse. She hangs out with a group of kids who all share the same gloomy, pessimistic view of the world. Her grades are bad, and she's started smoking cigarettes, drinking, and using pot. I had to take her to the ER once because she drank so much she passed out and her friends panicked. She won't talk about anything of substance with her father or me. If we try to get her to open up, she clams up even more. We've told her we can't let her drive, but she doesn't seem to care. For her latest offense, we restricted her to the house for two weeks, but all that did was precipitate a declaration of war. Is there some other disciplinary approach that might help?*

A: I don't think you're describing a discipline problem; therefore, a disciplinary approach is not called for. It sounds to me as if your daughter is depressed. I'm not in a position to make a definitive diagnosis, but when the behavior is self-destructive, the peer group (assuming there is one) consists of like-minded fatalists, and discipline hasn't done anything but make matters worse, depression is what comes immediately to mind.

Unfortunately, by the time today's children reach their teen years, overexposure to the media has programmed significant numbers of them with the fatalistic notion that life is a soap opera with no possibility of a happy ending. A generation or so ago, alienated teens were displeased with the state of the world, but most of them (yours truly included) were activists of one sort or another. We didn't like what we saw, but we were determined to bring about change. Today's alienated teens are horses of a different color. They tend to be negativists who seem intent upon elevating their brooding to a high art. Sometimes, as current events make painfully clear, this brooding turns to plotting, and the result is often something highly destructive to self and others.

In the last thirty years—one generation, mind you—the teen suicide rate has more than tripled. This strongly suggests that teen depression is rapidly becoming epidemic, if it isn't already. Other markers, including widespread binge drinking and self-mutilation, point to a similar conclusion. I'm convinced, furthermore, that when it comes to teens, depression is a communicable disease. So a basically healthy kid who begins associating with depressed peers is at serious risk for becoming depressed, in the clinical sense of the term. I'd even go so far as to speculate that associating with depressed peers can adversely affect brain chemistry in such a way that an otherwise harmless episode of self-pity can rapidly cascade into full-blown depression.

The bottom line: I think your daughter is depressed, but I can't say for sure. The markers are there, but a letter is no substitute for a clinical consultation. Therefore, I strongly recommend that you take your daughter to a child psychiatrist—preferably a woman—who specializes in adolescence. There are several new non-narcotic medications that can very possibly—in combination with counseling, of course—help your daughter begin to see that while life may not be a bowl of cherries, it's not a can of worms either.

In the meantime, given her drug and alcohol use, I wouldn't let her drive, but I'd make clear the prohibition isn't a punishment; rather, your love for her leaves you no other choice.

Q: *Our twelfth-grade son, an honor student, has recently told us he doesn't want to go to college. Instead, he wants to become a BMW mechanic. He's already picked out a training program that's out of state and relatively expensive, but that's not the issue. Needless to say, we just assumed he would go to college and get on a professional track. We've talked until we're blue in the face about wasting his talents, looking at all his options, and the like, but he's like a brick wall about this. What would you suggest we do?*

A: I'd suggest you go to the dictionary and look up the word *emancipate.* To save you some time, my highly authoritative *American Heri-*

tage Dictionary of the American Language says it means, in part, "to release [a child] from the control of parents or a guardian." That means letting the child, in this case your son, start to make his own decisions, discover for himself which ones are mistakes, and learn his own lessons.

You may be asking the wrong guy this question because I still resent my high school guidance counselor's telling me I couldn't (not *shouldn't*, mind you, but *couldn't!*) take auto shop because I was college bound. As a result of his "advice," not only did I never have the opportunity to discover for myself whether or not working on cars was my karmic destiny, but I'm also at the mercy of expensive and seemingly very happy mechanics when it comes to anything but an oil change, and even that's getting too complicated.

Your son is smart indeed. As a senior in high school, he's already figured out there's a big difference between the measurable riches of earning a lot of money as, say, a lawyer and the immeasurable riches of vocational satisfaction. I disagree that he's wasting his talents, and I double-disagree that he's not looking at all his options. I take it you mean that someone with a high IQ shouldn't work on cars. I believe that was my guidance counselor's message also. Have you looked under the hood of a car lately? I have, and I've come to the conclusion I don't want anyone with a mediocre IQ working on mine. I've also had the opportunity, in the last year, to work alongside a mechanic on some jobs I needed done, and I was in awe of his ability and his smarts. Where your son's options are concerned, it seems to me he's looking at more options that you even began to consider for him. You put him in a pigeonhole because he's an honor student. He refuses to accept the assignment. I say, "You go, boy!"

This is not about a teenager who's making bad decisions. This is about parents who are having a problem letting go, parents who are perhaps wanting nothing more than to tell all their friends their son is training to become a *(fill in the blank with some high-paying high-prestige profession)* and need to get over the notion that he's under some obligation to be a "trophy son."

Cheer up! After all, you'll soon be driving a BMW and getting most of your work done for free. Tell your son to keep me in mind when he finishes that training program.

Curfew

When Eric and Amy were in their early teens, my wife and I made an astonishing announcement to each of them. We said, in effect, "We don't want to be your parents anymore." By that we meant we no longer wanted to reprimand, scold, restrict, or exercise the power of office in any punitive manner.

We went on to say, "You are well aware of the rules, and well aware of the consequences of violating those rules. You're also intelligent and responsible. So, we're counting on you to keep us from having to be parents. Here's the deal: If you obey the rules, you'll find that not only will we stay off your back but your freedoms will steadily grow, and grow, and grow."

Having secured their undivided attention, we popped the Big Q: "How would you like to have more freedom than just about anyone you know?"

"That would be cool," they said, feigning nonchalance.

"Then all you have to do is obey the rules. We want you to have lots of freedom, but with freedom comes responsibility. You prove to us that you're responsible by respecting the limits we set on your freedom. You respect those limits and the freedoms expand. It's as simple as that."

Take Eric's curfew, for example. When he was fourteen, his curfew was ten o'clock on nonschool nights. The rules were simple. We had to know and approve of where he was and what he was doing, and he had to be home before ten.

"But some of my friends can stay out later," he complained.

"If you obey the rules for six months, your curfew will become ten-thirty. You break the rules and we start counting another six months from there. If, after earning a ten-thirty curfew, you obey the rules for six months, your curfew will become eleven, and so on. Sound good?"

"It's a deal!" he said.

Two months later, he came in fifteen minutes late. He gave us some song and dance about not knowing what time it was, and he forgot to wear his watch, and his friend's pet iguana got sick and they had to take it over to the vet, and we just smiled and shook our heads and said, "See, now we have to be your parents." His six-month waiting period started over from that night.

He figured things out quickly. Six months later, his curfew became ten-thirty. Six months after that, it became eleven o'clock. By the time he was seventeen, we trusted him enough to let him spend spring break at the beach with a couple of buddies.

The principle is a simple one. Children will take responsibility not for things that are handed to them on a silver platter but for things they must earn. The things they earn, they take care of. We all take care of the things we invest in, don't we?

I never cease to be amazed at parents who give their children nearly everything they want and then wonder why their children don't take care of what they have, take their parents' benevolence for granted, behave irresponsibly and even dangerously, or all of the above.

Willie and I did not dedicate ourselves to making Eric and Amy happy. Instead, we tried to instill in them the qualities and skills they'd need to create their own happiness. The payoff was twofold. First, the children obtained nearly all the freedom they could want. Second, so did we.

You know, it's kind fun not being a parent.

T-Shirts

This is the story of fifteen-year-old Eric and the T-shirt. It can finally be told because I bought the rights for an undisclosed sum.

The story begins at a Van Halen concert Eric attended. Before he went, he had asked our permission to buy a tour T-shirt. We granted it with the stipulation that the T-shirt not be black or sleeveless or bear any reference to drugs, alcohol, or sex.

"Why can't it be black?" he asked, in that indignant I-demand-an-explanation-for-this-injustice tone that is universally characteristic of fifteen-year-olds.

"Because we don't like black T-shirts," we replied.

After several exchanges, the issue was put to rest by our offering to rescind permission to buy any T-shirt at all if an agreement on color could not be reached. Eric agreed to our terms.

He returned from the concert with a white knit shirt emblazoned with the Van Halen logo and WORLD TOUR '84. On Monday morning of the following week he came downstairs ready for school wearing you-guessed-it.

"Sorry, Eric, but we aren't going to let you wear your T-shirt to school," I said.

"Why not?"

"Eric, would you like to donate your new T-shirt to Goodwill?"

"I won't wear it to school."

It's truly amazing how quickly he sees the light.

Eric didn't wear his T-shirt to school, but he wore it everywhere else. It seemed like weeks went by when he wore nothing but the T-shirt. I was beginning to think maybe the band had bought advertising space on his chest.

Meanwhile, Eric spurned the other clothes we had bought him—clothes he had picked out himself, clothes that were supposedly "in," clothes that were not getting any bigger while he was. Not only this, but there was a certain—let us say—attitude that Eric projected when he wore his Van Halen T-shirt. It wasn't quite defiant. It wasn't quite macho. It wasn't quite anything we could put our fingers on, but it was definitely an attitude. The final straw was when he wore it to school on the final day of his junior high school career. Upon discovering this, his mother confiscated the T-shirt.

Several weeks later, as Eric, his godfather Rob, and I were driving to the beach to play golf, the subject of the T-shirt came up. Eric began complaining that he couldn't understand why Mom had taken it away, and he didn't see anything wrong with wearing it to school anyway, and it just wasn't fair.

I agreed that it didn't seem exactly fair.

He got excited. "Will you talk to Mom about giving it back to me then?" he asked.

"No," I said, "I won't."

Again: "Why not?"

"Because I plan on living with your mother for at least another forty years and with you for another three. I think you can figure that one out."

All I heard from the backseat was a disgusted sigh.

Rob and I spent a good hour talking to him about the importance of proper dress and the impression one's clothes make on other people. At the end of this eloquence, all Eric could say was, "I want my T-shirt back."

"Eric," said Rob, "if you were smart instead of mad, I'll bet you could get it back."

"How, steal it?"

"I'm not going to tell you how, because you should figure this one out for yourself, but I'll give you a hint: It's called *diplomacy.*"

For several moments, the car fell quiet. Then Eric said, "I'm never going to get my T-shirt back, I just know it."

"Diplomacy, Eric," said Rob.

About a week later, Eric came down to the dinner table wearing the T-shirt. I asked my wife how Eric had managed to get it back. "He asked me for it politely and promised not to wear it away from the house," she answered.

Which goes to show: Adulthood happens one step at a time.

Wheels, Part One

"Dad! I've decided what kind of car I want to get when I'm sixteen. Look at this!"

"Eric," I said, brushing away the copy of *Car Trader* he'd stuck in my face, "I've told you a hundred times, I'm not buying you a car when you turn sixteen. Look here! Read my lips! I'm . . . not . . . buying . . . you . . . a car."

"Why not?"

"I've told you why not."

"Yeah, but why not?"

"Because I've told you why not."

"But can we talk about it?"

"We've talked about it before."

"But Dad, can we talk about it today?"

"No."

"Why not?"

He wouldn't give up. He had started in on me when he was fourteen and kept it up relentlessly for a year and a half. I mean every day. And every day I told him he wasn't getting a car.

"Why not?"

"Because you don't need a car of your own. We have two cars. You'll be able to use one."

"Right, the station wagon. Forget it. I won't drive a station wagon."

"Nerdmobile, eh?"

"Right!"

"Well, Eric, nerd sort of runs in the family. I was a nerd, you know. It's probably inevitable—genetic, even. You'll be a nerd too, sooner or later. If driving a station wagon doesn't do it, wearing glasses will."

"I don't wear glasses."

"Then you have to drive a station wagon. It's either one or the other. We nerds don't have a lot of options."

"Dad?"

"Yes, son."

"Will you buy me a car when I'm sixteen?"

"No."

"Why not?"

Relentless.

My reasons for why not were philosophical (giving a sixteen-year-old a car would serve only to reinforce, one more time, to a kid already firmly convinced it was so, that something can be had for nothing), ideological (parents who buy cars for their kids are indulging their children's capitalist/materialist/bourgeois obsessions), and psychological (buying a teen a car is a way of compensating for never having spent time with the kid when time really mattered).

And finally, I had practical objections, firmly rooted in reality. I didn't think I could afford it.

Sixteen came and so did the driver's license, and Eric started driving my car. (He was true to his word—he *wouldn't* drive the station wagon.) It was inconvenient, and it was irritating to get in my car after he'd driven it to find the seat pulled up under the steering wheel, the rearview mirror aimed at the floor, and the gas gauge on empty. And he couldn't get a job because he didn't have reliable transportation, which meant I had to pay for his gas and insurance. And so, tossing my self-righteous, pompous principles out the window, I broke down and bought him a car—a completely restored 1966 Mustang. It was the car I had wanted when I was a teenager.

I surprised him with it during our summer vacation at the beach. You should have seen the look on his face. It was worth every penny of it.

And, I've since concluded, it was one of the best moves I've ever made.

I put the title in his name, you see, and I said, "This is yours, lock, stock, and barrel. I bought it, but you have to pay for the insurance, the gas, and all repairs. Welcome to responsibility!"

Eric got a job soon thereafter. He was never late with an insurance payment, never late to work, and never was his car anything but clean. He grew up two years in the first nine months of ownership.

And, man, was I happy! Not to mention proud.

Wheels, Part Two

Q: *With the start of the school year upon us, and with a child about to turn sixteen, my wife and I were wondering what your feelings were about high school kids having jobs during the school year. Our daughter, who has always been a fairly good student, says she wants to get a job. We're not sure it's a good idea. Do you think we should let her, and, if so, what kinds of rules should there be?*

A: I think you should let her. Your daughter's initiative and willingness to accept obligations outside of home and school, especially one that will allow her less time with her peers, should definitely be encouraged. At the very least, she'll find out that she really isn't ready for a job. Either way, it will be a tremendously valuable learning experience, one she shouldn't be denied.

If she were not already a fairly good student I would probably advise that you tell her she can get a job when her grades come up. When she shows improvement in her grades, you allow her to work a certain number of hours per week. She shows further improvement, you let her increase her hours, and so on. In that case, her desire to work would present you with a strategic opportunity—a chance to turn her motivation for doing one thing (getting a job) into motivation for something else (better grades). In the long run, seizing upon a strategic opportunity benefits the child more than the parent, although it may take the child awhile to figure that out.

When our children turned sixteen (separately), we told them if they wanted to drive they had to pay the difference in our insurance premium. That meant they had to get jobs, the only stipulation being they could not work more than fifteen hours a week to start. We gave them a two-month grace period, during which we picked up the insurance tab. After that, no work, no drive.

So, they each went out and got a job. Eric stocked shelves in a drugstore. Amy worked behind the counter in a yogurt shop. They started at minimum wage, which meant that after they paid us their share of the insurance, they had a little more than half their paychecks left to do with as they pretty well pleased. We should be so lucky!

We also informed them they couldn't keep their jobs unless they kept their grades up. "We'll give you one grading period to adjust to this," we said each time. "If your grades go down, you'll be allowed to continue working, but you'll be on probation until the next report card comes out. If the grades haven't come back up by then, you'll have to quit your job, which means you won't be able to drive."

By linking grades, jobs, and driving privileges together, we created circumstances that began to approximate adult realities. Sixteen-year-olds need experiences of that sort, ones that prepare them for dealing with the complexities of independent living.

And that's what it's all about, remember? The purpose of being a parent is to help your children get out of your life and into successful lives of their own.

Letting Go, Part One

Raising Eric has been the most significant learning experience of my life. Through him, I discovered more about children than a hundred books could have taught. I also discovered a lot about myself, particularly during his teen years.

Not just living with a teenager but living with a teenage son opened a window on my own adolescence. More than a breath of fresh air, it was a look backward in time.

Like most teenagers, I never truly knew who I was or understood why I did the things I did. I only thought I understood myself and tried to get everyone else to go along with the deception. In order to cover my insecurities, to hide them from myself and the world, I cultivated an attitude of insensitive aloofness.

Nothing bothered me. I did not run when it rained. I did not wear a hat or earmuffs in below-zero weather. In other words, I was cool. This was the early sixties, and cool was in for the teenage boys of my generation. We were masculine only to the extent that we were cool. There was only one alternative to cool and it was definitely not an option.

In this little charade, I was also in control. I was in total control of myself and my surroundings. No one ran my show but me, not even my parents. You had to be cool to be in control, and since I was obviously in control, I was cool, right? Wrong!

I wasn't cool and I wasn't in control. I was kidding myself and the joke was on me. I was insecure and not a little frightened of suddenly losing my tenuous grip on reality-according-to-Rosemond. But I would not admit this, even to myself.

Eric has helped me see all this and put it in new perspective, to recapture those lost years of my life. As I watched him grow into and through adolescence, I saw him doing pretty much the same things, for the same reason: holding the hounds of insecurity at bay. There's been a déjà vu quality to the whole experience, as if I were watching myself, twenty years younger. Sometimes I haven't been able to keep from laughing at the teenage me I've seen in Eric.

When he was in the seventh grade, for instance, I drove him to school nearly every morning. The junior high was on my way to work, so it was convenient and gave us some time together. When eighth grade rolled around, I continued to drive him.

One morning about a month into the new school year, I stopped for a light at an intersection two blocks from the school. Without warning, Eric jumped out of the car, saying something like "I'm gettin' out here, Dad. See you later. 'Bye."

He continued to get out at the same intersection over the next two weeks. Unable to figure it out, I finally asked why, and he gave me some lame excuse about joining up with friends and walking the rest of the way. He wasn't telling me the real reason, so I decided to figure it out. Something about what he was doing seemed vaguely familiar.

Several weeks later, after having all but forgotten my mission, it came to me. Of course! I remembered being thirteen years old, and I remembered how hard I worked at that age to create and maintain the illusion within my peer group that I didn't have any parents. Come to think of it, none of my friends had parents, either. We were cool.

Thank you, Eric. Thank you for helping me be a kid again. In some ways, it was a lot more fun the second time around.

Letting Go, Part Two

He was gone. Number one son Eric, that is. Just like that. One day he was home, the next he was off to his first year of college at North Carolina State University.

We took him up on a Thursday, helped him move in, and were back home on Friday. Seemed like the fastest twenty-four hours of my life.

Try as I did, I just couldn't make it go any slower. Besides, it was obvious he was doing his best to get us back on the road as quickly as possible.

Once he was settled into his dorm, we said our goodbyes and left, stopping downstairs for a soft drink. As we sat there, talking with two other parents, Eric walked by the window, headed in the direction of the women's dorm. The kid didn't waste any time.

That's when it hit me, watching him walk away from us like that.

He looked so—well, *purposeful*. Like he knew where his life was going, and it sure as heck wasn't back in the direction of home.

Right then and there I realized his childhood was over. He'd never be the same again, and neither would I.

There were many times during his last three months at home when I caught myself trying desperately to fix some minuscule flaw I thought I had detected in his behavior. I found at least one of these must-fix-its every day.

"Eric," I'd say, "you need to listen to me. It's high time you realize that . . ." or "You can get away with that kind of stuff when you're in high school, but college is a different ball game. . . ."

Most of the time, he'd sit politely through these exercises in last-minute parenting, indulging my need to hang on to the job I'd been doing the past eighteen years. Then he'd acknowledge I was right and promise to do better.

Other times, he'd just smile and cut me off, saying something like, 'It's okay, Dad. I know what you're going to say and—well, I don't mean to be impolite or anything, but I really don't need to hear it. I'm going to be all right, really I am." He knew I needed to talk more than he needed the lecture, and he was right.

I thought it would be easy. At least, I tried hard to convince myself it would be. His mother was having a rough time of it because, I thought smugly, mothers have more difficulty with separation. Dads can handle this stuff. We encourage our kids' independence and look forward to their leaving home. We're tough.

Who was I fooling? Only me. I wasn't handling this any better than his mother, I was just better at hiding my feelings and kidding myself.

The truth is, I missed him terribly. The truth is, I worried about him. The truth is, there were times after he left when I walked into his almost-empty room expecting to find him there. And then there were times I went in, knowing he wasn't there, and just sat and tried to come to grips with the whole thing—that this was the way it should be and everything would work out and he'd be fine and so would I.

And we were.

Looking Back

On the afternoon of Friday, November 13, 1969, Willie and I, along with three other college friends, piled into a van lent us by her father and headed east out of Chicago. After driving all night, we arrived in Washington at daybreak, joined hands and spirits with nearly a million other intrepid travelers, and marched to protest the Vietnam War.

Thirty years later, Woodstock is better remembered, but the March on Washington, as it was called, was truly the most significant event of, by, and for our generation. Woodstock wasn't in the same league. In Washington, there was purpose and passion, commitment and risk. Woodstock was nothing but a party.

When it was over, when the last speech had been made and the last anthem sung, we ate and piled back into the van for the drive west. Arriving back in Chicago at noon Sunday, we showered, slept a few merciful hours, and drove downtown to see the Rolling Stones—the world's greatest rock 'n' roll band, as they had come to be known—in concert. It was a fitting climax to the most exhilarating weekend of my life.

Twenty years later, Willie and I, along with our two children, Eric—then in his third year of college—and Amy—a high school senior, and two of their young friends, made the trek from Charlotte to Carter-Finley Stadium in Raleigh to see the Stones hit the boards for their first tour in eight years.

I had looked forward to the concert for months and knew it was going to be good, but it exceeded my wildest expectations. Though I'd seen many rock 'n' roll shows, this one was *it*. From the stage (a futuristic industrial ruin that towered above the band) to the show (twenty-eight direct hits to the body), to the fireworks at the end of "Jumpin' Jack Flash," the night was perfection.

When Mick and the boys finally came on, there were dark storm clouds gathering to the west and the clean electric smell of rain in the air. From the opening chords of "Start Me Up," the Stones charged through a set that included familiar favorites, a few songs only die-hard Stones fans would know, and a few off their latest album. About a third of the way into the two-and-a-half-hour performance, the storm blew away and a full moon rose above the stadium as if to say, You didn't think I'd miss this, now, did you?

It was the best, but it was more than rock 'n' roll to me. As the band played, I looked at Eric and Amy and could tell that they too were transported. Looking around, I saw many other parents our age with their kids, all bouncing up and down to the Stones' infectious beat.

Watching my kids singing along with the band, it occurred to me that ours is a generation perhaps unlike any ever before, certainly unlike our parents'. Somehow, we have managed to bridge the so-called generation gap. The span may not always be in good repair, but it's there, always available for crossing.

I remembered with regret that in 1969 when my father heard I was going to Washington, he ceased all contact with me for three years. He not only didn't understand, he couldn't. After all, he'd gone to war. He'd been willing to lay down his life for a noble cause. To him, my politics were a slap in the face.

As the Stones started into "Two Thousand Light-Years from Home," I thought of the distance that had separated many of us from our parents then and said a silent prayer of thanks that we had somehow found the means of communicating with our kids through thick and thin, of understanding their trials and tribulations, of having patience with their determination to head down blind alleys, of tolerating their naive idealism.

And at the center of this reconciliation there was the music—the Beatles and the Stones and Led Zeppelin and Jimi Hendrix. A music for our time but a music for all time. A music we could share with our children. A music we could dance to with our children and sing with our children. And not just music but a culture with a heart of hope and healing.

It's only rock 'n' roll? Not in my life.

PART 3

So What's Your Problem?

As I TRAVEL AROUND the country eight months a year, giving talks and workshops, I collect questions from parents. Most of these are of the "What should I do when" variety, as in:

"What should I do when my five-year-old refuses to eat what I put in front of him?"

"What should we do when our children bicker with one another?"

"What should I do when my sixteen-year-old daughter says she hates the ground I walk on?"

Part 3 answers questions of this sort. My first aim is to help parents understand that most child-rearing problems are not psychological in nature. They don't mean anything, other than that the child is, as all children are and forever have been, strong-willed, rebellious, self-centered, and prone to all manner of antisocial behavior. When parents ask "What does it mean?" concerning a behavior problem, they paralyze their ability to deal with the problem successfully.

My second aim, therefore, is to give to parents practical, non-psychological, effective approaches to the very normal problems that arise in the course of raising children.

My third aim is to help people laugh at things they've been taking (or might otherwise take) all too seriously, like kids throwing up at the dinner table because you've served broccoli or letting the air out of your tires so you can't check up on them on Friday night.

I hope I've succeeded.

15

Toilet Training

Q: *My son is twenty-eight months old and not yet toilet-trained. My mother-in-law says he should no longer be wearing diapers, but on a recent talk show, a pediatrician said that parents should be in no hurry where "toilet teaching"—as he called it—is concerned, because children will begin using the toilet pretty much on their own when they are ready. Who's right, my mother-in-law or the doctor?*

A: Although I have no way of knowing whether she is on target concerning *your* son, your mother-in-law is more generally correct than the doctor.

Saying that children will teach themselves to use the toilet when they are ready is like saying children will teach themselves to read when they are ready. There are indeed children who teach themselves to read, but they are a small minority. The same is true of children who teach themselves to use the toilet at an appropriate time. In both areas, the majority of children require adults to initiate the learning process and guide them through it.

The idea that parents should adopt a come-what-may approach to teaching children to be civilized about their bodily wastes is an artifact of Freudian notions to the effect that pushing children in this area will cause psychic traumas that might take later form as debilitating adult neuroses. Suffice to say that Freud's theories, novel and fascinating as they were, have no predictive value; therefore, they are scientifically worthless.

The fact is, teaching a child to use the toilet is no more significant than teaching a child to eat with utensils, except that children generally make more of a mess learning to eat than learning how to dispose of their body wastes. Our cultural neurosis over this topic lingers on, however, fueled by well-intentioned professionals who regularly suggest that the term *toilet training* be changed to "toilet teaching" or "toilet facilitation" or something equally tedious. Their general skittishness over the use of the word *training* is a certain indication that their mothers traumatized *them* with premature toilet dogma.

The overwhelming majority of children—probably at least 90 percent—are ready to use the toilet sometime between twenty-four and thirty months of age. Parents should capitalize on this readiness not for their own sakes but because it is in the best interests of their child to take this most significant step toward self-reliance as early as is reasonable. Furthermore, if parents do not seize the opportunity to teach toilet use when a child is ready, the readiness may wane, resulting in a child who is indefinitely content with messy diapers. For proof of this, one need only talk to parents who, having missed the boat in this area, are now struggling with toilet-blasé three-year-olds. This increasingly commonplace state of affairs benefits only the manufacturers of disposable diapers and diaper rash cream and the professionals who charge parents large fees for advising them on how to get four-year-olds to put their tee-tee and poo-poo in the teetee pooper. It does not benefit children or their parents.

Children should not be rushed to grow up, but neither should they be denied opportunities to take charge of their own lives. Knowing when a child is ready to take charge of this particular area of his or her life is a simple matter, as is *training* the child (there, I said it and I feel much better, thank you!) to use the toilet. But before describing my simple and very successful method, which I originally called "Naked and $75," allow me to make several key points:

- It is *not* okay for parents to allow a child to remain in diapers past his or her third birthday. In fact, it's an insult to the child's intelligence.

- Early toilet training—between twenty and thirty months—is in a child's best interest for a number of reasons, not the least of which being that it represents a significant leap toward self-control, or what parenting is largely about.

- "Child-oriented" toilet training has profited manufacturers of disposable diapers. Period.

- Tabless diapers, which children can theoretically pull up and down themselves, are a scam. Lots of padding in the pelvic area is associated with permission to release at will, and diaper manufacturers must surely know this retards training rather than facilitates it.

So, on to toilet training by "Naked and $75." When you sense that your child is ready (in most cases, sometime between twenty and thirty months), buy a small potty and announce that the child is no longer going to wear diapers during the day. Instead, he or she is going to put (insert favorite euphemisms) in the potty, which you have strategically placed in that area of the home in which the child spends the most of time. Yes, even if it's the kitchen! Say, of course, that if he or she needs help just to call you. Then, until success is achieved, have your child wear no clothing—or, at most, something similar to a nightshirt—around the house. Why naked? Because, while they're perfectly content to release warm, gooshy stuff into their diapers, children do not like these same substances running down their legs. When that happens, they spread their legs, stand stock-still, and yell for help. When you hear this distress call, say that an accident is no big deal and remind the child to use the potty next time. During the week or so that this method typically takes, keep your distance. Nothing is more counterproductive to success than a hovering, anxious parent.

When your child is using the toilet regularly—with or without your help—call a carpet cleaner and spend $75—or whatever today's going rate—to have your carpets cleaned. Believe me, the stains are not permanent. From that point on, you can slowly but surely promote your child from naked to underpants (not training pants!) and, later, to full dress when at home.

There you have it: "Naked and $75." Nothing could be more hassle-free. Furthermore, unlike whatever method is in vogue, "Naked and $75" is truly child-oriented because it respects children's intelligence as well as their right to begin taking control of themselves and their lives as early as is reasonably possible. Naturally, this method is not for parents who are neurotic about cleanliness issues.

And despair not, working parents! If you initiate training on a Friday evening and focus on nothing else through the weekend, you'll probably be close to, if not over, the hump by bedtime on Sunday. If need be, take a couple of days off. In any case, this old-fashioned method will tolerate less-than-ideal circumstances. My daughter-in-law Nancy, for example, successfully trained her son Jack at thirty months in less than a week—the week before his brother was born!

Q: *A professional in the town we live in will come into your home and toilet-train your child for about $300. He uses a method that he claims virtually guarantees complete success in one day. We have a twenty-six-month-old daughter who seems ready to use the potty, and we want to know what your thoughts are on having him perform this service for us.*

A: Frankly, the whole idea is profoundly disturbing. I do not believe it is within the legitimate province of a professional to offer such a service.

Learning to use the toilet is a normal part of every child's socialization. Given time, the child's readiness, and gentle encouragement from the parents, it will happen without undue stress or any great investment of effort. In this respect, it is no more significant a skill than learning how to drink from a cup, use a fork, or get dressed.

Toilet training does, however, involve more of a mess than buttoning a shirt, and after two or more years of changing diapers, parents are usually eager to get it over with. It is this eagerness that your friendly neighborhood professional is capitalizing on by offering his service.

Any specialist in child development should be able to comment on the acquisition of this skill and identify, for instance, factors that facilitate the child's success. However, except in cases where either the child or the circumstance is exceptional, the firsthand on-site services of a specialist are not necessary for the actual learning. In fact, it is probably better for both parents and children that professionals keep a respectful distance from normal developmental processes of this nature.

There is more going on during toilet training than meets this professional's eye. Apparently, he has little appreciation for the transition that toilet training brings about in the parent–child relationship.

Not only is the child learning where to put BMs, he or she is learning to be less dependent on parents. This usually involves some ambivalence. Does the child really want to give up the creature comforts that come with being an infant in exchange for dry pants? This ambivalence, and the anxiety that accompanies it, can be resolved successfully *only* with the parents.

For parents, toilet training means readjusting their perceptions and their manner of relating to the child. It is crucial that parents and their children work through this transition together, in their own way and their own time.

You want your daughter to give up her diapers? Buy her a potty and some training pants and tell her where to put her business. Help at first with the details. Then stand well out of the way so she can experience this as an exercise in independence.

Simple, yes? You don't need a Ph.D. to do that. This professional probably has enough candy up his sleeve to persuade a toddler to use the potty, but most children are smart enough to go poop in the corner as soon as he leaves.

Q: *My almost-four-year-old shows no interest in using the toilet. When he was two, I decided I would let things be until he showed me he was good and ready. Now it's almost two years later and all he shows me is wet, messy training pants. When he was about three, I became panicky and upset at his lack of progress, but then I felt bad about having made such an issue of it and backed off entirely. When he has an accident (five or six times a day), he is very good about cleaning himself up and putting his wet clothes in the right place. At night, he still wears diapers. He goes to a day-care program (which he lives for) five mornings a week, and while he's with other children he controls himself. He has even used the toilet there on several occasions. But as soon as we get home, he floods. Don't tell me to withhold privileges, as there is nothing he cares enough about to make him cooperate. The nurse at our family doctor's told me that this is a sign of emotional problems and we need to make an appointment with a psychologist. Do you agree?*

A: Nope. He doesn't have emotional problems, he's a four-year-old who has never been given a straight message about using the toilet. He has probably never heard you say clearly, "I want you to put your wee-wee and BMs in the potty—and nowhere else."

There is a difference between making an issue of something and making a statement about it. Unfortunately, toilet training has become a major issue, full of myth, anxiety, and misinformation. Consequently, we have difficulty *thinking* effectively about it, much less making effective statements about it to our children.

Only in America, for instance, will you find entire books devoted to the subject. Several of them come complete with stories to read to the child. One has drawings showing a fireman, a policeman, and a teacher, all sitting merrily on toilets. What a production!

Only in America would someone think to write, for a public hungry to buy, a book entitled *Toilet Training in Less Than a Day*. Only in America will you find professionals with impressive credentials offering, for a fee, to come to your home and, with the aid of a doll that wets, toilet-train your child while you sip coffee and watch *As the World Burns.*

It's the twentieth-century medicine show: "Amazin', just amazin'. Yessiree, folks, step right up and watch as I demonstrate in front of your very eyes with a real live two-year-old just like the one you got at home how you too can toilet-train your child in one day! That's right! One day—count 'em—one! You heard me: No more poopy pants, no more ammonia smell piercing your nostrils, no more disposable diapers clogging up your septic tank, and all accomplished in one amazing short day!"

Amid all the hocus-pocus, confusion reigns. We have made a mystery out of something that is simply a practical, unamazing exercise in self-sufficiency—like learning how to eat with a spoon. Think about it. First, your son saw you using a spoon and experienced what it was like to be fed with the spoon. When you saw that he had developed enough manual dexterity to hold a spoon and guide it to his mouth, you gave him his own little spoon. Initially, he slopped his food everywhere—he had "accidents," which you patiently, and with words of encouragement, cleaned up. And lo and behold! In time he learned to eat with a spoon. Through this whole process of learning to use a spoon ran the message *You can feed yourself.* And so he did. And I have never heard of a child who was psychologically traumatized by spoon training.

Two years ago you could have shown your son how to use a potty his own size and said, "You can use the potty just like everyone else does." And he would have done his business there and everywhere else for a while. And you could have been patiently encouraging. And he would have learned.

But he never got the message. Then, a year later, he sensed your anxiety, heard conflicting statements, and said to himself, "Well, if *they* don't know what they want me to do, I don't know what I want me to do either."

So now? Now you gotta convince him. But first, convince yourself. Do you want him to use the potty like the rest of the world's four-year-olds, or do you want to continue acting confused and paralyzed by words like "emotional problems"?

Don't tell me there's nothing he cares enough about, because you also said, "He lives for day care."

So here's a four-year-old who knows what to do but won't. Convince him! Say to him, with no uncertainty, "I want you to put your wee-wee and BMs in the potty—and nowhere else."

Give him an "allowance" of one accident a day for the first two weeks. "If you have two accidents, you don't go to school the next day." At the end of two weeks, take away the "allowance."

During this time, keep an accident scorecard posted in a prominent place (such as the refrigerator). Put a check in the box-of-the-day for each accident.

And don't *ever* ask him, "Do you have to go to the bathroom!" Make *him* be responsible. And he will be.

The most delightful story I ever heard about toilet training was of a mother who gave her two-year-old son a set of training pants and a potty of his own and said, "Use it."

Well, the little fella just flat refused. *"No!"* he said. "I wanna poo in my didee!"

"Fine," his mother said, taking a diaper and laying it in the bottom of his potty. "Poo in your didee—right here."

It was all the convincing he needed.

Q: *Our bright, well-adjusted four-year-old son has a full bowel movement in his underwear four or five times a week. He knows how to use the toilet and is not, like some children, afraid to do so. Nor, according to his pediatrician, does he have a physical problem. He's just lazy. We've tried everything we can think of, from rewards to taking away special activities, but nothing has worked for long. Do you have any suggestions, including ideas as to what might be bothering him?*

A: At this distance, I'm able to offer no idea as to what might be bothering your son, if anything. Why some otherwise well-adjusted children soil themselves well beyond toddlerhood is a mystery. Psychological theories, of course, abound, all amounting to educated guesses. My experience with this problem, which—because today's parents are generally waiting far too long to toilet-train—is no longer all that uncommon, has been that self-soiling is usually a behavior problem, as opposed to an emotional one. In other words, there's probably nothing wrong with your son.

To reinforce what you've already done, any child who's passed the third birthday and has demonstrated bowel competence but continues to soil his or her pants should be evaluated by a pediatrician or family practitioner. Certain physical dysfunctions can cause diminished bowel control.

Once the possibility of a physical cause has been eliminated, one is left with the mystery: What could possibly be driving such obviously self-defeating behavior?

In the absence of outstanding family pathology, my general explanation would unfold as follows: The parents waited too long to toilet-train. By the time they initiated training, the child was perfectly content with messy diapers. The child's failure to catch on caused the parents' anxiety level to rise. They began making a very big deal of using the toilet. The child, being a typically obstinate human being, became less and less cooperative as the parents lost their cool.

My most successful "treatment" involves making sure the child becomes bothered—big time!—by this bowel laziness. Keep in mind you can't make a child use the toilet. You can, however, make the cost of *not* using the toilet so great that the child doesn't want to pay it.

Buy a large-diameter bucket or galvanized tub. Show your son how to wash stains out of his own clothing. If you still have him in diapers, even tabless ones, inform him that he will no longer wear anything but "big boy" underwear and that you will no longer, ever again, ask him if he has to use the toilet. From that point on, every time he messes his pants, his life stops. As soon as you discover his lapse, he must proceed to wash and rinse his soiled clothing until it's free of stain and smell. Then he takes either a bath or a shower, cleaning himself thoroughly. (Note: You are not to stand over him while he performs these tasks. You simply approve or disapprove of the outcome. In the latter case, he must try again.) Once clean and smelling as fresh as a flower, he gets in his pajamas and spends the remainder of the day in his room (yes, even if the "accident" occurs at nine o'clock in the morning) and goes to bed immediately after supper.

Parents who've followed this plan—consistently and dispassionately—have never reported anything other than success. Don't expect miracles, but if you're willing to make your child harmlessly miserable every time he has one of his lazy spells, this should—if history does indeed repeat itself—be over within a few weeks.

Q: *Our almost-three-year-old son absolutely refuses to use the toilet. He responds with a firm, amplified* no! *nearly every time I ask him if he would like to use the potty. If I try coaxing him, he wails. Actually, I have caught him off guard several times during the past six months, and he has shown me that he does know how to use it. Otherwise, he refuses to cooperate. I am looking forward to getting rid of diapers. Help!*

A: Why should he cooperate? Obviously, you have yet to tell him, in definite terms, exactly what it is you expect of him. As long as you continue to ask, in whatever way, "Won't you *please* use the potty instead of using your diapers?" he has your permission to say *no!*

Children spend nearly the first two years of their lives viewing the universe as though they sit at its center. Because of their obvious limitations, we wait on them hand and foot—we carry them, bathe them, powder them, comfort them, feed them, and dress them.

It should come as no surprise to any of us that almost every child emerges from this cocoon feeling as though he or she is the world's most significant person, rightfully in control of everything and everyone. This fantasy has obvious appeal, and most children are reluctant to give it up.

For parents to survive the terrible twos they must develop an uncanny ability to sense and avoid power struggles. Whenever we react to a two-year-old's natural inclination to oppose us by attempting to force cooperation (after all, from the child's point of view, *we* are the ones who are stepping out of line), the game is lost. The struggle itself is our undoing. A person in control has no need to struggle.

So far, so good. You are definitely *not* in a power struggle with your son over the use of the toilet. You say "Please?" he says *no!* and you back down. Under the circumstances, he has no need to struggle. He is in control.

Ah, but avoiding power struggles is only part of the picture. The real trick is to learn to maneuver around opposition, rather than retreat from it. In other words, you don't fight, but you don't run away either. Up to now, you have not taken an assertive stance on the question of whether your son uses the potty or not. Because of your indecision, your son has seized the opportunity to proclaim, I'm more powerful than you are.

For seven days, make no mention of the potty. Change his diapers on schedule, without protest or impatience. If he tells you he *wants* to sit on the toilet, give him an assist and then excuse yourself. If he calls you to see his accomplishment, acknowledge what he has done in a positive but matter-of-fact way: "That's very good. I'm going to put your diapers back on now."

During the week, purchase several pairs of heavy cotton training pants. On the morning of the eighth day, greet him with this announcement: "Today is a brand-new day! Today you begin to use the potty. You are not going to wear diapers anymore. You are going to wear these big-boy pants and learn how to keep them dry. Come with Mommy. I want to show you something."

Take him to the bathroom and show him an alarm clock you put there the night before (as an alternative, the timer on your stove will do).

"This clock has a bell that will tell you when you need to sit down and use the potty. It's called the potty bell. When you hear the potty bell, I want you to come in here and sit on the potty. The bell will ring four times today"—set it to ring in the morning, after lunch, before dinner, and before bed—"but you may use the potty any other time you need to. You aren't wearing diapers anymore. I *want you* to keep these big-boy pants dry."

Set the alarm to ring at the same times every day for the next few days. When it rings, tell your son, "It's time for you to use the potty. Call me if you need help." Don't become overly involved. Prompt him when the bell rings and then keep your distance.

If he tells you he doesn't want to sit right then, don't push, but gently remind him that he needs to keep his pants dry.

Respond to his successes with encouragement, but without unnecessary razzmatazz. Deal with accidents (and there will be some) in a calm, direct manner: "You forgot to use the potty. That's all right. You'll do better next time. I'll help you put dry pants on. Remember, I *want you* to keep these pants dry by using the potty."

By using an alarm to signal potty time, you are gently turning his resistance away from you. At the same time you are making clear authoritative statements that convey what you expect of him.

Instead of giving him permission to say I won't, you can give him an opportunity to grow. It's an offer he can't refuse.

Q: *My four-year-old daughter holds her bowel movements. Her pediatrician assures us that there is nothing physically wrong with her. She lets out only a little at a time and therefore is still in diapers. I have been playing it cool and not forcing the issue, but she has a young brother who is an infant, and the thrill of changing diapers is wearing thin.*

A: I would not hesitate, with a four-year-old, to communicate some firm expectations about where to put BMs. Young children are quite intuitive and can sense when their parents have a big investment in an issue. I suspect that your daughter has seized on this passive form of rebellion to keep attention focused on her rather than on her younger brother. In this way, she continues to get her importance confirmed. What you need is a method that will get her to use the toilet and at the same time reassure her that she is important.

Tape a sheet of paper daily to the refrigerator door or some equally visible place. Tell her firmly that she is not going to wear diapers anymore and that she will use the toilet for BMs. Inform her that when she has an accident, she will receive a large mark on her scorecard.

Now consider what privileges she enjoys daily. Playing outside after supper? Riding her tricycle? Going to a friend's house? Make a list of the three activities she values most. Tell her you will eliminate one activity for every accident, starting with the one that is most important to her.

Expect two to three weeks to pass before you see steady progress. Don't be discouraged by a relapse after a good start. Stay firm but gentle, and always be encouraging. Your confidence in her, combined with a steady attitude of authority, will make more of a difference to her than anything else.

Q: *Jimmy, our four-year-old, is not bowel trained. He holds his BMs and constipates himself for several days at a time, sometimes nearly a week. When he can't hold any longer, he usually releases them in his pants. Sometimes he tells us when he is about to go, and one of us literally runs him to the bathroom, but once we get there he usually loses the urge. Later he will have his inevitable accident. We have tried laxatives, and they made him somewhat more regular but no more cooperative. We have him clean himself with supervision after every mistake. He also needs help taking his pants down and getting up on the toilet. We've tried everything.*

A: Wow! I'm exhausted! Frankly, your son is not putting his BMs in the toilet because you are doing all the work. *He* may not be trained, but *you* certainly are. And by the way, he *is* cooperating—in creating the confusion.

You are investing a tremendous amount of energy in monitoring, supervising, and helping him with something he should be in charge of by the age of four. This long-term investment has created a climate of chaos and confusion concerning "Jimmy's BMs."

No one, including Jimmy, knows exactly what to do when he feels like having a BM. The statement "We've tried everything" probably means that over the years there has been an accumulation of inconsistent responses and messages in reaction to his gestures, requests, and mistakes.

Your son is confused. He is probably wondering, Who's having the BM, me or my parents? Is a BM something that should or shouldn't happen? Can I have one by myself? Who am I doing it for? Am I really four years old?" Because there are no clear definitions, the confusion has never been resolved. It is essential that you back out of the picture.

First, define the situation. Teach him, if he *really* does not know, how to pull his pants down or off and position himself on the toilet seat. If he has difficulty, dress him in elastic-waisted shorts. A wooden stool will give him any additional boost he needs.

Most four-year-olds are capable of cleaning themselves without supervision. Some initial guidance for Jimmy will help to define this as his responsibility. Take the time to teach him exactly what he should do when he soils himself. However, this lesson should take place *when he is clean.*

Organize the necessary equipment (washcloth, sponge, liquid soap, towels, clean underwear, and so on) in one specific accessible area of the bathroom, and put him through the paces of cleaning himself. Practice the sequence several times, in an encouraging and positive manner.

When he tells you he feels the pressure of a BM, tell him to go to the bathroom and sit on the toilet, "just like everyone else does." If he wants you to take him (after all, he hasn't had to do the work up until now), tell him, "I will not help you have a BM."

If he has an accident (count on it), send him to the bathroom to clean himself. If he comes out before either he or the room is clean, simply say, "You are not finished. Go back in and finish. Then you may come out."

During the day, do *not* ask him if he needs to go or provide him with reminders. A four-year-old no longer needs to be protected from the consequences of his own mistakes.

When he has success, keep your reactions low-key. After all, he's learning to accept this responsibility for *his* benefit, not yours. Furthermore, success is not a big deal—it's expected of him. "That's fine. No, I don't need to come see. You can do it all by yourself. You don't need Daddy to look."

Finally, give him plenty of time to adjust and expect some lapses along the way. If you stay with the program and roll with the initial ups and downs, he will eventually match the pace you set for him—just as he has all along.

16

Bed-Wetting

IF YOUR CHILD WETS THE BED almost every night, you undoubtedly know that none of the home remedies are much help. Punishment, restriction of liquids, getting the child up at intervals—none of these works. Some of these methods may provide temporary relief, but all of them together won't stop a child from wetting the bed. Somewhere along the line, most of us have been taught that wetting the bed is a symptom of laziness or insecurity and is a child's way of saying that things aren't going right at home. While it is true that many children who wet the bed do feel ashamed and are under a great deal of stress because of it, there is no reason to believe that bed-wetting is an expression of a damaged emotional condition.

Actually, bed-wetting happens, in most cases, because the child is an unusually deep sleeper. Deep sleep will prevent a child from waking when the bladder sends an I'm-full signal to the brain. The signal is too weak or the brain is too deeply asleep to "hear" it. In either case, the bladder does the natural thing, which is to empty itself. It's easy to see why home remedies will be no more useful than beating one's head against a brick wall.

However, there is a way to approach bed-wetting that requires nothing more than your patience and understanding. First, give the problem back to your child. Stop trying frantically to solve it. It's the child's body and the child's problem, and he or she can solve it only by taking possession of it.

Stop making "Did you wet the bed last night?" the first question of every day. Bed-wetting should not be a topic of family discussion. Say that, when the bed is wet to put on dry pajamas, lay a heavy towel across the wet spot, and go back to sleep without waking the family. In the morning, the child is to strip the bed and place the linens and wet pajamas in a pile just inside the bedroom door. After you have done the wash, put the folded linen back in the room. At bedtime, make the bed together, patiently leading the way and letting the child take over more and more of the chore until he or she is able to do it alone.

Give the child as much liquid as he or she wants all day. It's probably good to remind young children to use the bathroom just before bed, but do it casually.

Help your child understand this problem by providing some basic education. Say that there is a muscle just below the bladder (you can call it the doughnut muscle) that is normally closed. When we go to the bathroom, we relax this muscle and it opens (open and close your fist to demonstrate). Suggest that the child might want to make this muscle stronger by practicing tightening and holding it for several seconds off and on during the day. And when she goes to the bathroom, she can further strengthen it by turning the flow of urine off and on. Most children will cooperate willingly in this exercise.

A number of pediatricians now advise parents of children who wet the bed to eliminate all refined sugar from the child's diet. Substitute fruits, nuts, raw vegetables, or peanut butter and crackers along with a glass of unsweetened juice for bedtime snacks instead of sugar-sweetened goodies.

If, after doing these things for about six weeks, the bed-wetting has not stopped, I recommend that you purchase a bed-wetting alarm. A typical system consists of a set of pads arranged under the bottom sheet and an alarm connected to the pads that sounds immediately when the child begins to wet. Through repetition, this device eventually teaches the child to wake to the feeling of a full bladder. Then use of the alarm can be discontinued.

This alarm operates on low-voltage batteries, is completely safe, and when used properly it usually works. It is *not*, however, to be used with children younger than four, many of whom are still developing nightmare control. Nor is it to be used without the child's consent and a definite indication that he or she wants to stop wetting the bed.

Bed-wetting kids are not "bad" kids. However, you can bet that the more of an issue you make of the problem, the more overwhelmed the child will feel and the longer it will take for him or her solve it.

Q: *Our five-year-old, who has always been a bed-wetter, has recently started wetting his pants during the day. He doesn't tell us about it, but waits until one of us points out that he's damp and suggests that he change his clothes. We haven't criticized or reprimanded him for these accidents, and the bed-wetting is not a topic for discussion either. Do you think he could be wetting himself for attention? Do you have any suggestions?*

A: My first suggestion is that you break your vow of silence. Bed-wetting can become an increasingly burdensome handicap for your son as he grows older, one that will limit his social life and damage his self-concept.

Your decision not to discuss it, although motivated by good intentions, is actually preventing him from initiating any work toward a lasting solution. You seem to be giving tacit permission for the problem to linger indefinitely. This is not in anyone's best interest.

To begin with, I would wager that you *are* upset—about both the daytime accidents and the bed-wetting. Your frustration at having to change and wash smelly sheets, pajamas, and now clothes, nearly every day, needs to be acknowledged and accepted as legitimate. *How* you express that frustration, rather than *whether* you express it, is the central question.

You have probably succeeded admirably at suppressing your annoyance. But our children are more sensitive to us than we generally imagine. Although neither situation has been a topic for discussion, you probably cannot avoid sending subtle nonverbal cues that tell of your displeasure: an expression, a gesture, an exchanged look. Your silence itself is perhaps the most blatant message.

The topic needs clarification, but because no one has permission to talk about it, your son can't ask, "Are you mad?" So, in an attempt to resolve this ambiguity, he begins wetting his pants during the day, when you can't fail to notice. Will you say anything *now*? How much will it take to bring you out of hiding?

It is probably wrong to say he's doing this for attention. The fact that he waits for you to mention it strongly suggests he is trying to draw you out. It's time to show your hand.

Begin with a discussion of his bed-wetting. Define it as a problem for you. Tell him you don't enjoy changing and washing sheets and pajamas every day. Bring the problem out in the open, so you can begin helping him solve it.

Be careful, however, that you don't take responsibility for it. The responsibility must be his. He needs a clear, straightforward message from you regarding your feelings and a commitment of understanding and support.

"Son, we want to talk with you about wetting the bed. You are wetting your bed almost every night, and we both think it's time you began staying dry at night. We want to know how you feel about this. Do you want to continue wetting the bed, or do you want to stop?"

Some indication from him that *he* wants to stop wetting the bed is essential, but you cannot force this point of view upon him. However, it will be much easier for him to make that statement once he knows where you stand.

He also needs to hear a clear message concerning the daytime accidents: "We also want you to stop wetting during the day."

Once you have squarely faced the issue and settled your ambivalence, he will no longer need to wet his pants. The chances are also good that he will stop wetting the bed. If he doesn't, and he begins to express some frustration at not having the success he wants, I would recommend that you purchase a bed-wetting alarm.

I have heard these alarms criticized as an artificial, impersonal means of conditioning a child to stop bed-wetting. This is completely off the mark.

My son began wetting his bed when he was four and a half, shortly after we moved to North Carolina from Illinois. Nine months later, a friend and colleague told us about the bed-wetting alarm. We bought one and asked Eric if he would like to try it out. The first night, he wet the bed before he went to sleep just to hear the alarm go off.

Over the next three weeks, he alone triumphed over what all of us struggling together had managed to make worse. At the end of that three weeks, he informed us that he did not need the unit anymore. I'm certain he had never felt so proud of himself before. If that smacks of something impersonal, I must have missed something.

The manufacturer does not guarantee success, and it would be foolish of me to imply that it's foolproof. However, your child's self-esteem is worth the money it will cost you to give it a try.

Q: *Our son will be three in one week. He has been day and night potty-trained for several months. He started Montessori school last week. A month or so ago, before starting school, he wet the bed a couple of times. A friend with older children advised us to spank, and one spanking stopped it. After the start of school, he started to wake us up again, so at two A.M. I told him if he got up again he would get a spanking. He didn't get up, but he wet the bed. Now he has started school full time and is wetting the bed nearly every night. We want to nip this in the bud. We have a nephew who is almost four who wets the bed every night. His parents were told by a therapist that it was a way of controlling them. Could our son be wetting the bed as a way of controlling us? I would like a solution that will keep him dry and in the bed all night without causing him to act out in some other way.*

A: The friend who told you to spank gave you very bad advice. And the therapist who told your nephew's parents that bed-wetting is a control issue is wrong. Your nephew may be in control of the parent–child relationship (most kids are these days), but bed-wetting is *not* one of his weapons.

Wetting the bed at thirty-six months of age is no cause for concern. The mere fact that your son was dry at night for a few months after he was toilet-trained doesn't mean he can control his bed-wetting now. No one knows why, but boys have more of a struggle with this than girls. By age four, for every girl who is still wetting the bed, there are four boys. Furthermore, it's not unusual for a child—a boy, usually—to be dry at night until age five and suddenly, inexplicably, begin wetting the bed.

Punishing the problem will not correct it, and may well make matters worse—much worse, in fact!—over time. Bed-wetting is linked to deep sleep. The best explanation is that your son simply sleeps so deeply he can't sense that his bladder is full. Consequently, instead of "holding" or getting up and using the bathroom, the child wets the bed. And he may not even wake up even then! He may sleep through the night on sheets that are soaked.

A change in routine often precedes the start of bed-wetting. Our son, Eric, wet his bed for a short time after we moved. And your son started wetting, not coincidentally, shortly after he started school. Being in school during the day may wear him out. On one hand, that's good. On the other, he probably sleeps more deeply than before and has started wetting the bed as a consequence.

If you concern yourself with more important things and let time take its course, this little glitch will probably resolve itself within a year. On the other hand, if you want to help a solution along, you can purchase a bed-wetting alarm. The directions are clear and simple, although they don't tell you that the child usually sleeps too deeply to hear the alarm (signaling wetting) at first. For a few nights, at least, when the alarm goes off, the parents need to wake the child and go through the toileting paces. Your pediatrician may prefer or have access to a similar system, so check with him or her first. In any case, the least show of frustration or anger on your part and you may as well dig yourself in for the long haul, because a long haul it's probably going to be.

Q: *Our thirty-two-month-old daughter has been daytime toilet-trained for six months. Three months ago, she started getting up once a night to use the toilet even though she went to sleep with a diaper on. Shortly thereafter, we began putting her in panties at night. Now, however, instead of waking once a night, she wakes anywhere from two to three times a night. The good news is she's had only four accidents in the two months since the switch from diapers to panties. The bad news is she wants my help using the toilet two or three times a night. Will this eventually take care of itself or is there something I can do so I can begin getting a full night's sleep again?*

A: Okay, this is a new one on me, but I'll share a trick that works across a broad range of behavioral situations with toddlers. Tonight, before bed, tell your very intelligent daughter that you spoke with "the doctor" and he said when she wakes up in the middle of the night she should use the potty on her own, without waking anyone. Put a "totty potty" (I just made that up) in her room and walk her through the procedure. Appeal to her vivacious sense of imagination, beginning with "Pretend you're asleep and you need to use the potty." Or if she indicates that she'd rather use the big potty, fine and dandy; walk her through the procedure that way. Make an appeal to the big girl in her. Tell her the doctor is very proud of her for not needing diapers at night any longer and now he wants her to take the next step.

Then, if she still wakes you up, remind her what the doctor wants her to do. If, however, she resists, don't get into a conflict with her over this in the middle of the night. Just cooperate with her. The next night, remind her again of what the doctor wants her to do and walk her through the "let's pretend" of it again. This may take awhile to sink in, but it shouldn't take long—a year or two; no, just kidding—a few weeks, I'd guess. And be assured, this will continue to afford her a positive attitude toward her bodily functions.

P.S.: When dealing with toddlers, invoking the authority of the doctor often neutralizes potential conflict. The explanation that things are the way they are because that's the way the doctor says they should be is eminently satisfying to most toddlers, who have already intuited that even their parents defer to medical authority. And fear not, this does not cause children to grow up with warped attitudes toward physicians. They get over it, just like they get over discovering there is no Easter Bunny.

17

Head-Banging

Q: *We have a three-year-old who is a head-banger. At six months, she began banging on the bars of her crib, hard enough to cause bruises. When she was nearly two, the banging shifted from bedtime to an almost constant banging on the floor, a chair, and so on. There are two types of banging: one to soothe or put her to sleep; the other to express anger or frustration. She knows this gets to us, and we have been known to give in to her just to get her to stop. I know this is not a solution, but nothing else we do seems to have any effect. Our pediatrician insists she cannot hurt herself. He does, however, feel that she has a psychological problem. Friends and relatives are beginning to ask what's wrong with her. What can we do to stop her?*

A: To begin with, your pediatrician is correct: She is not likely to hurt herself. That certainly isn't her aim.

But head-banging isn't necessarily indicative of a psychological problem. While it *is* true that many emotionally disturbed and autistic children head-bang, it is also a fact that many normal children do the same thing.

Head-banging is fairly common among infants and toddlers. Generally speaking, it begins around the sixth month, shortly after the infant is first able to raise herself to a crawling position. At this stage, infants test their balance by rocking back and forth on their hands and knees, looking as though they're trying to build up enough momentum to take off. If a solid object, such as a wall or headboard, is immediately in front of them, they are likely to discover the untold pleasures of head-banging.

The monotonous combination of rhythm and self-stimulation is hypnotic, lulling the child into a blissful self-absorbed trance. In this respect, head-banging is no different from thumb-sucking or nuzzling a favorite blanket. All these behaviors are soothing, and your daughter has found an ingenious way of providing for herself some of the comfort she might otherwise be demanding of her parents. By banging her head, she is able to put herself to sleep, separate from her mother, occupy idle time, and even postpone the need to be held or fed. In one sense, then, it's a fortunate parent who has a head-banger.

But that's *not* the way most parents look at it. In the first place, good parents don't allow their children to hurt themselves. Furthermore, rocking and head-banging have been associated with severe emotional problems. The idea that they might be raising a child who is so disturbed that she actually enjoys pain is too much to deal with.

So they try to stop her. First, they give her something else to do. The distraction works—temporarily. A short while later, a *thud-thud* sound comes from the den. They rush in to find that she has crawled over to the wall and is steadily ramming her head into the baseboard. They pick her up, carry her into the kitchen, and offer her a cookie.

This goes on throughout the day, and eventually she puts things together: banging her head not only feels good but is a form of communication. When you want Mommy, just bang your head on something. It's like Morse code.

The more she bangs her forehead, the greater her threshold for pain in that area becomes, and the harder she must bang to feel anything at all. Bruises become discolored bumps, and people begin eyeing the parents suspiciously, their imaginations in high gear.

But the harder they work at getting her to stop, the more she bangs. When she reaches her terrible twos, the head-banging is absorbed into her tantrums, and, since she is already out of control, the banging becomes more violent. By this time, her parents will go to almost any length to stop her, and she learns that head-banging can get her just about anything she wants. What started as an irrelevant self-indulgence has become a focus of tension in the family. The entire family is obviously edging closer to the brink.

You must gain control of this situation. What should you do? Very little. The more fuel you funnel into this issue, the higher the flames will leap.

Find a time when the house is calm and running in tune for both parents to talk with her. "We have decided that you need a place to bang your head. Banging your head is okay with us, but we don't want to watch or listen. If you want to bang, go to your room. You can bang on anything you want in there. Mommy and I will help you remember the rule."

Keep it short and to the point. Don't expect her to remember. Every time she bangs, whether it's to soothe or express rage, say, "You forgot the rule. You may bang your head in your room. I'll help you get there." Whether she resists or not, take her there and leave her, saying, "When you finish banging, you may come out."

You may not see any results for several weeks. In fact, an upsurge may occur as she pits her will against yours. The more violent form should subside within six weeks, but she may continue to bang her head as a means of relaxing for several years to come.

After all, it still feels good.

18

Bedtime

A LONG, LONG TIME AGO, in a bedroom far away, there lay a three-year-old boy named Grumph Nadly, who would not sleep.

Every night at eight-thirty his mother would say, "Grumph Nadly, it's time for bed."

He would yell, "I don't want to!" and his mother would ask, "Why not?" and Grumph would reply, "Cuz."

He would scream, "I'm scared!" and his father would inquire, "Of what?" Grumph would earnestly answer, "Things."

His mother would say, "Let's go, Grumph, it's time for munchkins to be asleep," and Grumph would collapse in a heap on the floor. The heap would not move, but it would sob and moan piteously.

At last, Grumph's father would pick him up and carry him, shrieking, off to bed. Then, when Grumph was finally quiet and looking the other way, his parents would scurry off and hide. But it was no use. The sound would always find them.

It began softly. "Mommy?"

But if the sound got no answer it grew louder and louder until it fairly shook the rafters: *"Mommeeeee!"*

Then the sound would get an answer. "Yes, Grumph, what is it?"

Sometimes Grumph would say he was hungry or had to go to the "bafoom" or wanted to tell somebody "sump'n." Whatever it was, he would make all the noise he could until the whatever was seen to properly.

Grumph usually went to sleep around midnight and woke up with the sun. His parents had dark circles under their eyes and shuffled when they walked.

One day, Grumph Nadly's mother set out from home and shuffled deep into the woods, seeking peace and quiet. She had shuffled for several hours, and was passing a small pond alive with water lilies and butterflies, when she heard a small baritone voice ask, "Are you lost or what?"

"Who's there?" she asked, startled, and looked around.

"Me. Look down here, lady."

And sure enough, when she looked, there he was, a rather unremarkable frog. Unremarkable, that is, except for the fact that he talked, which is *quite* remarkable for frogs.

Before the startled woman could say anything, the frog spoke again, asking, "What brings you to my front yard?"

And Grumph's mother suddenly felt moved to tell the frog everything—about how Grumph would not sleep and the heap and the sound and the rest—until the frog, having heard quite enough, said, "Hold it! You wanna know how to get this Grumph child into bed and off to sleep?" With hardly a pause, he went right on. "I'll tell you. But first you have to promise *not* to kiss me when I'm done."

"Why on earth should I want to kiss you in the first place?" asked Grumph's mother.

"Mark my words, you'll want to, and if you manage to grab me and do it, I'll turn into the most handsome and charming prince you ever saw, which is the worst thing that could *ever* happen to a frog who wants to just spend the rest of his life sitting on water lilies, eating bugs."

"All right, I won't kiss you," promised the woman, who had never kissed a frog anyway. "Tell, tell!"

"Well," the frog began, "you make a book, see, called 'Grumph Nadly's Bedtime Book.' All you need is some sturdy paper, paste, a hole punch, and yarn.

"First, make a list of what's done to prepare the heap for bed.

"Then gather up several magazines and find pictures to go with each of the things on your list. Make sure you find one of a kid sleeping—draw one if you have to.

"Paste each picture on a separate sheet of paper, put them in order, with the picture of the kid sleeping last. Punch holes in the left-hand side, and tie a loose loop of yarn through the holes.

"Then write a story to go with the pictures, and read the story to Grumph every night, right before bed.

"For example, the book might begin, 'It's eight o'clock, and time for Grumph Nadly to begin getting ready for bed. The first thing he does is . . .' and you show him the picture of a child taking a bath. Together, you and Grumph say, 'Take a bath!' The next page reads, 'After his bath, Grumph dries himself and puts on his pajamas.' And Grumph sees a picture of a kid in pajamas. Keep going until the last page, which says something like, 'And when everything is done, Grumph's mommy and daddy tuck him in, kiss him good night, and Grumph Nadly goes to sleep like a good little tadpole."

When the frog finished his description, he looked at Grumph's mother, adding, "By the time you get to the end, Grumph should be so involved in his story that he'll take the cue and nod right off."

Grumph's mother thanked the frog profusely, being careful not to kiss him, and hurried home with nary a shuffle in her step. She did exactly as the frog had told her and, lo and behold, that night Grumph Nadly was asleep by eight forty-five.

Every night thereafter, Grumph and his mother would read the Bedtime Book together, and he would go quickly and quietly off to sleep—which is where our story should end, but it doesn't.

Several years later, Grumph's mother was skipping through the woods when she happened across the same pond. "Well?" a familiar baritone voice intoned. "Did it work?"

Grumph's mother stopped short and, looking down, saw the very same frog, looking not a year older. "Yes! Oh, yes! It worked, just like you said!" she replied. Then, remembering what the frog had said about being a handsome prince, she grabbed him and planted a big kiss on the middle of his head. Nothing happened.

She kissed him again, longer this time (with her eyes closed). Still nothing happened.

"Hey! What's wrong?" complained Grumph's mother, letting him go: "Turn into a prince already."

The frog just laughed as he hopped back onto his lily pad. "Sorry, lady, but I'm just a talking frog who likes to be kissed." And without even a goodbye, he jumped off his pad, landed in the center of the pond with a great splash, and was never seen again.

The moral, good reader, is simply this: Don't ever kiss a frog, no matter what he may have toad you.

Q: *Our first child is thirteen months old. For thirteen months, I have been rocking him to sleep at night and also for his daytime naps. I don't mind doing this—I'd rather rock him than listen to him cry, which he does if I put him in his crib before he's completely asleep. Although I'd like for him to be in bed by eight-thirty P.M., the actual time varies because there are nights when he just doesn't seem tired until nine or ten o'clock. But regardless of when I put him in bed, he always sleeps all night. Recently, my pediatrician told me to stop rocking him, put him in bed at the same time every night, and let him go off to sleep on his own, even if it means some crying. The doctor says Joey is learning that if he cries at bedtime, I'll pick him up. Do you agree with this?*

A: Almost. I definitely agree with your pediatrician that you need to stop rocking young Joey off to sleep, establish a definite bedtime (with allowances built in for occasional times when it isn't possible to keep him on schedule), and let him go to sleep on his own.

There's far more at stake here, however, than a relatively simple matter of learning to connect crying with being picked up. In fact, it's what Joey *isn't* learning that warrants the lion's share of attention and concern.

For instance, Joey isn't learning how to go to sleep by himself. Instead, he is becoming increasingly reliant on you. There's a strong possibility that he may eventually think that being next to you is essential to falling asleep. Having a thirteen-month-old cry for a while at bedtime is one thing; having a three-year-old *fight* you at bedtime is quite another.

Joey isn't learning how to predict when bedtime is at hand. It is important that there be some certainty about this, because a child's feelings of security rest, in large measure, on being able to read the environment for cues that certain events are about to happen. In a child's world, time needs to be as well organized as the furniture and other things. Confusion over where things are or when things happen encumbers your child's attempts to make sense of his surroundings. Establishing routines will help him develop a clear sense of cause and effect (logical thinking) and contribute to his feelings of competence and confidence.

Joey isn't learning that you control when things occur. Instead of deciding when Joey's bedtime is, you seem to be looking to *him* for a signal, a vague sign of some sort that he is ready. This puts him in the driver's seat before he has even learned to be a good passenger.

But the biggest problem of all is that Joey isn't learning how to let go of you when day is done. And you aren't learning how to let go of him comfortably either.

The importance of bedtime has little to do with when children get tired or how much sleep they need. But it has *everything* to do with parents, who need time together. Most of all, it has to do with teaching children that letting go is okay. Bedtime is really nothing more than a ritual of separation.

Virtually every important issue that comes up between parent and child involves, to some degree, questions of attachment versus nonattachment. To the extent that these questions are successfully resolved, a child becomes less dependent upon the parents. In other words, learning how to let go of parents, mother in particular, is learning how to grow up.

Bedtime problems often bring up this larger issue for the first time. How they are handled will set a precedent for dealing with future separations of many kinds, among which are staying with baby-sitters and going to school.

It's up to you, as Joey's parents, to take the lead and set a good precedent. If you are indecisive about letting go at bedtime, he may interpret your hesitation or reluctance as a signal that something is wrong with separating. And, believe me, few things are more stressful to a family than a clinging child.

If you want Joey in bed at eight-thirty P.M., first establish a routine that begins at eight P.M. and lets him know that bedtime is coming. Cap the routine with a tucking-in ceremony; then leave the room.

If he cries (as he almost surely will), you and your husband should take turns going back into his room every five or ten minutes to calm him and reassure him that you are still there, taking care of him. Don't pick him up and don't hang around. (See Bedlam at Bedtime in chapter 8.)

Q: *We have a three-year-old son who is afraid of the dark and will not go to bed unless one of us stays with him until he is asleep. This started about a year ago, but he was okay at bedtime as long as the hall light was on. Now that's not enough. When we put him to bed (at eight-thirty P.M.), he screams about being afraid of the dark until one of us goes back in to stay with him. If we do that, he usually stays up until eleven and sometimes twelve o'clock; then he sleeps until six-thirty A.M. and is rarin' to go. I don't see how he could be getting enough sleep. We have tried spanking him and keeping him up later to make him sleepy, to no avail. My doctor said to let him scream, but the first night we tried that, he went on for three hours. We are all about to go crazy. Can you offer any suggestions or hope for the future?*

A: I'll take a stab at both.

To begin with, let's get this whole reason-for-bedtime business straightened out. Once we do that, I believe everything else will fall right into place. It is my sworn professional obligation to inform you that bedtimes do not exist because children need sleep. You've been hoodwinked. Rumor has it that three-year-olds need ten to twelve hours of sleep each night. Hogwash. Except in the most unusual of circumstances, children get all the sleep they need, *regardless* of when they fall asleep or how long they stay that way.

Generally speaking, children will let you know when they're tired, and if they need twelve hours of sleep, they'll get it. On the other hand, there are some three-year-olds who need only eight hours of sleep a night, and some need even less.

In other words, every child's need for sleep is different. That makes sense, doesn't it? Why should we expect that two children who have different appetites, dispositions, and activity levels will both need ten hours of sleep each night?

You may not understand how your son can get up at the crack of dawn all bright-eyed and bushy-tailed while you feel like leftovers, but that's the way it is. I assure you, he is getting all the sleep he needs.

But that has nothing to do with bedtime because, I repeat, bedtimes are not set because of a child's need for sleep. A bedtime is for the *parents'* benefit.

Only after the children are in bed can parents renew their acquaintance with one another without being interrupted for *feed me* or *hold me* or whatever the latest *me* may be." What difference does it make if the children aren't asleep? Who cares if they want the lights on? Not I.

When my daughter Amy was three and a half, she absolutely refused to go quietly off to sleep at her appointed time (also eight-thirty P.M.). She pulled the old cry-awhile-and-then-come-downstairs-for-one-last-look routine.

"Yes, Amy, what is it?"

"Uhhhh . . . I wanna as' you sump'n."

"Well, what is it?"

"Uhhhh . . ."

"Come on, Amy, let's hear it!"

"When's my birfday?"

And so it went, night after night, until we realized that sleep wasn't what she needed and wasn't necessarily why we were putting her to bed in the first place. We put her to bed because of lust!

At that point, we simply told her she had to go to her room at eight-thirty P.M. and stay there. But she didn't have to sleep if she didn't want to. After we tucked her in, kissed her night-night, and closed her door, she could turn on her light and play to her heart's content while we relaxed and renewed our relationship.

By the time we were ready for bed, she was usually asleep on the floor, surrounded by her playthings, and we would pick her up and tuck her in again.

Q: *Our two-and-a-half-year-old usually goes to bed at eight-thirty without a fuss and sleeps through the night. My husband's job takes him out of town one or two nights a week. Within the last few months, Brian has had difficulty going to bed by himself when his daddy isn't home.*

Instead of going quietly to sleep, he cries and says he wants to sleep with me. I don't feel right about letting him sleep in our bed because I don't want this to become a habit, but I must admit I've given in to him until now. My mother and several friends have told me to let Brian cry it out and never let him sleep with me. I'm confused.

A: I have a hard time with words like *never* and *always*. More often than not, they're used to transform generally true statements into complete falsehoods.

In this case, the generally true statement is "Children belong in their own beds." The complete falsehood is "Children should *never* be allowed to sleep with their parents."

Putting children in their own beds reaffirms their individuality and defines them as separate from the marriage. It also defines the marriage as a separate entity—part of the family in which children do not participate but benefit from nonetheless.

There are, however, rare occasions when allowing a child to sleep with one or both parents is harmless and perhaps even appropriate.

A sick child, for instance, may need the added security and tender loving care of the parents' bed. (I would hesitate to extend this arrangement on a regular basis to a chronically ill child.) And letting a child sleep with parents the first few nights after a move may help in making the adjustment to new surroundings.

The exception could be invoked during *any* family crisis, especially those involving loss or transition—a death in the family, a parent or sibling hospitalized—or a major trauma such as after a house fire.

There is no harm, either, in letting children climb in bed with parents in the morning for a few minutes. (I found this particularly stimulating on Mondays. It may have something to do with being kicked repeatedly in the side, but nothing so completely motivated me to leave the bed as a child who had just crawled in with me.)

In Brian's case, I see no reason why he shouldn't be allowed to sleep with his mother when Dad's out of town. Brian is seeking additional closeness with you as a way of calming his anxiety over his father's absence. The more reassurance he is given, the easier it will become for Brian to deal with these interruptions in the family routine.

I caution his parents not to extend this practice to nights when Daddy is home. But not necessarily *never*.

Q: *Our four-year-old son did something the other night that literally freaked us out. About one in the morning, we heard him in the den, talking to himself. I got up, went down the hall, and found him on the sofa. When he saw me, he became agitated and acted like he didn't recognize me. I sat down next to him to try and calm him, but when I put my arm around him he began hitting me and screaming for me to let him go. By this time, his father had joined us and, seeing that Brian was delirious, tried to pick him up and hold him. Instead of relaxing, Brian became stiff, pushed away, and made this absolutely awful face: his teeth were clenched, his eyes were wide open and rolling around, and he was breathing rapidly. Then he started screaming again. This went on for about ten minutes, although it seemed like an hour. Finally, my husband lay down with him and Brian went back to sleep. In the morning he remembered nothing of the incident. What was that all about?*

A: Brian had what's known as a "night terror," which is different in character from the more common nightmare. During a nightmare, the child awakens, becomes fully conscious quickly, and is able to remember the context of the bad dream. Nightmares, especially recurrent or frequent ones, may be related to emotional stress.

Night terrors are to nightmares what Ghengis Khan was to Al Capone. An episode usually begins suddenly, with the child sitting up and screaming in terror. He is confused, incoherent, disoriented, and possibly hallucinating. Signs of intense physical stress are present, including a rapid heartbeat, sweating, and dilated pupils. During the terror, which may last from ten to thirty minutes, any attempt to console the child will generally fail and may even elevate his agitation. When the child finally calms down, he'll fall back to sleep quickly. In the morning, he will probably not have any memory of the episode.

Most pediatricians and psychologists agree that night terrors are developmental phenomena, unrelated to stress or trauma in the child's waking life. They occur most often with children between three and eight but may persist into early adolescence.

I conducted extensive research into night terrors for eight years. My motivation was my daughter, Amy, who had her first night terror at three and her last at eleven. Initially, an episode always began with her sleepwalking into the upstairs bathroom, after which we would find her and the freak-out would commence. The first few years, she had one about every four months as well as every time she ran a fever. As time wore on, they occurred less often and she became able to recognize and exercise more conscious control over them. On the last occasion, she just came into our bedroom and announced, "I'm feeling weird," whereupon she got in bed with us until she felt better.

I asked Amy a few questions concerning her feelings and perceptions during an episode. Her description gives some insight into the altered state of consciousness characteristic of a terror.

"When I'm having a freak-out, I feel weird, especially in my stomach. It's like everything gets all crumpled up and then it gets straight and then it gets crumpled up again. When things are crumpled up, I feel crazy and scared and I feel like knocking things over and tearing things up. When they get straight again, I feel okay. It's kind of like I'm lost in a maze and can't find my way out. I also see things that aren't really there, but I can't describe them. It's more like a feeling than really seeing something. Everything, even stuff I see every day, seems different and scary."

The next time Brian has a night terror, and the likelihood is that he will, hold him on your lap and rock him until he calms down. As you do, talk softly to him. Tell him who you are and say that everything's all right. If he suddenly acts rational but wants to go somewhere, like into another room of the house, be firm but gentle in telling him he has to stay put with you. After the episode is over, remain with him until he's fallen back to sleep.

Q: *Our four-year-old goes to bed easily but wants us to leave his bedside lamp on until he falls asleep. We've tried making Scott go to sleep with his lamp off, his door open, and the hall light on, but he acts afraid, calls us back into his room repeatedly, and takes much longer to fall asleep. Nine out of ten times, if he has trouble falling asleep, he wakes up in the middle of the night and calls for us. The obvious solution is simply to leave his lamp on, but we're both concerned that Scott may develop the habit of always needing a light on his room at night. Also, by catering to his fears in this way, won't we be reinforcing them?*

A: To begin with, it's unlikely that Scott will develop a lifelong dependency on bright lights at bedtime just because you let him go to sleep with a lamp on when he's four.

Fears, especially ones associated with the dark, are common to four-year-olds. Imagination, which begins emerging around age three, is in full bloom by this time. Understandably, children are not in complete control of the imaginative process, and sometimes it gets away from them. To top it off, preschool children don't understand how there can be a word for something that doesn't exist. For example, the phrase "witches aren't real" is contradictory. In the mind of a four-year-old, there wouldn't be a word for them if there weren't witches.

One way a child of this age deals with fears is to form attachments to transitional objects like teddy bears and bedside lights. These provide imagined protection against imagined things that go bump in the night. By indulging your child in this respect, you are not catering to the fear, nor will the transitional object become a lifelong fixation. How many adults do you know who still cuddle up with teddy bears?

On his own, Scott has come up with a solution to his fearfulness, a way of controlling it that is, after all, more desirable than screaming or demanding to sleep with you. By allowing him his bedside lamp, you will reinforce not the fear but rather his ingenuity, self-sufficiency, independence, and creative intelligence, not to mention his courage. Furthermore, he will go to sleep quickly and quietly, a joy for which many parents would gladly turn on every light in the house.

Q: *Our five-year-old daughter, who just started kindergarten, is afraid to go upstairs by herself. She will not climb the stairs, day or night, without one of us in front of her, and she demands that we check her bedroom, and the closet in particular, for monsters. If we balk or insist she go by herself, she becomes hysterical. I'm afraid this may be the beginning of a serious emotional problem that, handled wrong, could have a permanent effect. What should we do? We have another child, who is fourteen months old.*

A: There's a monster in your closet, too. It's the Something-horrible-will-happen-to-my-child's-mind-if-I-do-the-wrong-thing monster. This foul creature lives wherever there are parents who believe that children are little Humpty-Dumptys in life's biggest egg-toss game: one wrong move and they'll be broken forever.

This monster in the parental closet haunts our relationships with our children, jumping out at us when we least expect it, zapping our common sense and paralyzing our spontaneity. it lurches through our waking nightmares, hissing, "Your children have emotional problems, and it's all because of you."

Well, I'm afraid I bring you bad news. *All* children grow up with emotional problems. Emotions *are* a problem, especially for children. Emotions are powerful, unpredictable, violent, stormy, confusing, and often painful. Most of a person's growing years are spent learning how to tame these beasts within.

For the first twenty years of life, a human being stumbles through one emotional upheaval after another: birth (the all-time champ), separation, being two, learning to share, going off to school, puberty, sexuality, and leaving home.

Just as one crisis begins to subside, another comes along to knock children over, turn them upside down, and shake all the change out of their pockets. That's enough to put monsters in anybody's closet.

Being a parent, however, can be just as frustrating and confusing and emotionally painful as being a child. The important difference is that, while children have little control over how rough their lives are, parenthood is only as rough as *we* make it. One way of making it rough is to feed the monster that waits in *our* closets.

Most children have monsters of one sort or another lurking about. But the only ones that hang around for long live in homes where the parents have a pet monster too. By itself, a child's monster is impotent. But put it in league with a parent's monster, and pandemonium is guaranteed to break loose.

Banish *your* monster first. Children aren't fragile little eggs that can't be put together again. If they were, they'd never survive past their third birthdays. Children are tough, resilient, flexible little people who rebound extremely well from hardship, frustration, trauma, and all the other slings and arrows of their truly outrageous fortunes. With a little support from us, they also do quite well at chasing their monsters.

Sure, your daughter's fears are probably an indication that her world is suddenly a bit more scary than it ever was before. She has to go to school all alone and watch all that attention go to baby sister, who is home with Mommy all day long just as big sister used to be. Ah, well, that's life, right?

So get in there and do what you already know you have to do. Refuse to scout the way to her room. Tuck her in as usual at bedtime, and if she screams for you stay, say, "I'm sorry. I won't stay. *You* put the monster in your closet by pretending it's there. Now you must pretend it's gone."

Once you chase *your* monster off, hers will waste away in no time. It's lonely being the only monster in the house.

19

Food Fights

PARENTS ASK ME A LOT OF QUESTIONS about children who refuse to eat the food put in front of them, generally at the evening meal. The generic form of all these questions is, "How can you make a child eat?"

Answer: You can't. You can't *make*—as in *force*—a child do anything, at least not without creating more of a problem than you solve. Force once, and you'll have to force again. Force enough, and you'll find yourself always forcing. In the final analysis, obedience is a choice, whether we're talking about a child who is deciding whether or not to eat or an adult who's deciding whether or not to drive the speed limit. You can't *make* someone observe the speed limit. Likewise, you can't *make* a twelve-year-old do homework, you can't *make* an eight-year-old pick up toys, you can't *make* a two-year-old use the potty, you can't *make* a four-year-old go to sleep, and you can't *make* a child of any age eat the food put on his or her plate. You can, however, employ consequences such that a child is *persuaded* to do the right thing, but persuading and making are two very different things.

Here are some kernels of advice for parents of children who are ungrateful concerning the food put in front of them.

- Do not make a child's dislike of certain foods a topic of dinner conversation. The more attention paid to the issue, the worse it's going to get.

- It's generally okay to cater to food neuroses at breakfast and lunch but not at the evening meal or any other special meal. On those occasions, present the child in question with a plate on which sits a sample of each of the foods prepared. This says, in effect, You are not a privileged member of this family; therefore, you don't get a specially prepared plate.

- Don't try to coerce, bribe, or talk a child into eating something. It is impossible to reason with the unreasonable, and again, the more talking parents do, the more the child's resolve strengthens.

- Don't worry that a picky eater isn't getting enough to eat. A child who "doesn't eat anything" is always eating *something*, after all. Peanut butter on crackers, American cheese on white bread, or French fries (from a single fast-food outlet and no other), perhaps, but *something*. Believe it or not these children make it to adulthood, at which time they get married, become parents, and have children who "don't eat anything." Payback time!

- Don't require a child to sit at the table until everything on the plate is finished. This only invites a power struggle that parents will lose. Besides, young children are remarkably adept at passing food under the table to the family pet.

- Present the young food neurotic with small portions and cover and save whatever is refused. When, later that evening, the child asks for a snack (almost inevitable), simply reheat the dinner plate and put it back on the table. If the child eats what's left on the plate, he or she gets a snack. If not, fine, but no snack.

- To the child who cries piteously at this turn of events, simply say, "Things could be worse. I could be feeding you sushi."

- Remember, the child will live. If you don't believe me, call your pediatrician.

Q: *We have one child, a two-and-a-half-year-old daughter. She was breast-fed until she was ten months old. When she was five months old, our pediatrician told me to begin giving her solid foods. I was reluctant to do that since she seemed to be getting enough nourishment from me, but he told me bluntly that my attitude was irresponsible. She refused to cooperate with her new diet, spitting out food, turning her head, screaming, and so on. At the pediatrician's insistence, I began virtually force-feeding her. To make a long story short, the same situation exists today. My daughter will not eat anything resembling a meal. She eats cereal and toast in the morning and cheese, potato chips, popcorn, peanut butter and crackers, and celery slices for snacks. Lunch is a sandwich—maybe. Supper always turns into a scene. We have made her sit at the table, spanked her, bribed her, and literally forced food into her mouth to make her eat. But if we make her eat something she doesn't like, she throws it up later. As a result, every aspect of our relationship is strained. What can we do?*

A: Food has the potential of acquiring tremendous significance within a family, involving issues completely unrelated to its nutritional value.

The transfer of food from parent to child during the first year of life entails lots of physical closeness and stimulation, so that the infant receiving nourishment is also being nurtured.

As the child toddles into the second year of life, the parental role of keeper of the cupboard can easily become a central issue in the almost inevitable power struggles that develop as the second birthday approaches.

The almost-two-year-old, growing increasingly verbal, is likely to begin asserting definite likes and dislikes for particular foods and demand to be fed on a schedule that runs counter to family custom.

In addition, these toddlers are no longer wholly dependent on their parents for food and will further test their independence by experimenting with ways of obtaining food for themselves. They discover how to climb on the counter, open the refrigerator, and take the lid off the pickle jar.

In short, the giving of food from parent to child can, under certain stressful circumstances, become confused with the quality or quantity of affection in the relationship, the question of who is in control of the family, and how much autonomy the child is permitted.

When food assumes this significance, it begins to mediate the relationship. It becomes the substance through which (or over which) parent and child attempt to resolve certain issues.

Everyone can easily forget that the reason for sitting down to a meal is *not* to consume food. Eating is secondary to the social and ritual aspects of mealtime. Meals, and the evening meal in particular, bring the family together. They are a setting in which the values of sharing and unity are reaffirmed. It matters little *what* people eat or *how much,* good conversation and the feeling that "we are all of one family" are what count. So the idea is not to persuade your daughter to eat. She is eating enough and her diet is adequately balanced. The goal is to involve her in the ritual of unification at the dinner table.

During the day, you can cater to her preference to a reasonable extent, but retain control over *when* food is served (two-year-olds usually need a midmorning and a midafternoon snack).

At the evening meal, prepare your daughter's plate with small portions of the same food that the rest of the family is eating. If she mentions her distaste for any of the items on her plate, ignore the content of her statement but take the opportunity to involve her in conversation by responding with something like "Tell Daddy what we did today." Encourage her participation in conversation, although there should be times when the talk between adults does not involve her except as a listener.

Any comments that adults make about the meal should be brief and complimentary. Require her to remain at the table until everyone is excused, but do not at any time ask her to eat even a single bite.

Don't serve dessert as an extension of the meal. If something special is on the menu, serve it one or two hours later, before her bedtime perhaps. Don't use dessert as an enticement for eating. Nor should her right to share in late-evening treats be made conditional on how much she eats for supper.

One last word: For your next child, find a pediatrician who is supportive of breast-feeding and more knowledgeable about infant nutritional needs.

Q: *This may sound trivial, but my daughter, who is four, asks for food almost constantly throughout the day. The rule is that she may have one small snack midway through the afternoon, but she can't seem to understand and won't accept that limit. I'm tired of her demands and whining and am counting on you for an idea.*

A: Have I got an idea for you! But first, let's clear up one thing. This is not a trivial question. Any question involving food is important. After all, what's more essential than food?

For that reason, food can acquire potent symbolic character within a family, and disputes regarding *what* people eat, *when,* and *how much* can generate lots of conflict among family members. Food takes on even more significance in the relationship between parent and child.

Certainly one of the strongest and most enduring associations formed during the child's first year is that of food with parent (usually mother). As the child grows, parents retain the role of food givers. From this perspective, it's easy to comprehend why food so often becomes the issue of choice in power struggles between parents and children. The conflict can take many forms, but the basic issue remains, Who controls the food? In a broader sense, the overriding issue is, "Who controls the family?"

Therefore, it is as essential as food itself that parents exercise absolute and unquestionable control of the distribution of food in the family. This is not to say that the system cannot be flexible enough to allow children some freedom to serve themselves, but the final authority must rest with parents. If parents cannot demonstrate their authority in this area, how can they claim to be authorities at all?

It is a legitimate and necessary exercise of their responsibility and authority for parents to restrict the *when* of eating to certain set times of the day. Most children require a midmorning and a midafternoon snack, so plan for one or both, depending on the age of the child and the mealtime schedule.

There is a hassle-free field-tested way of announcing snack time while at the same time communicating your authority as keeper of the pantry. I assume there is a relatively large clock face somewhere in your house, probably in the kitchen. Take a piece of paper and make an identical clock face, minus the hands. Now, decide when snack time will take place and draw the hands at that time. Tape the paper clock next to the real clock, call your daughter in, and tell her, "When the hands on the real clock look like the hands on the paper clock, I will give you a snack. Now you can tell when snack time is!"

It is unlikely that any preschooler will grasp the connection immediately, so expect her requests to be off the mark for several days. When they are, simply show her the two clocks, point out that they are not the same, and reassure her that when they are, she will get her snack as promised. Be sure you remember to show her what you mean by "the same" when the magic time arrives.

Techniques such as this are especially effective when you want to establish routines with a young child. Children often need some visible reminder of rules, times, and other boundaries that are otherwise invisible.

Q: *We have tried various approaches to getting our four-year-old daughter to eat vegetables, but nothing has worked. Do you have a solution?*

A: I might. First, I'll tell you what doesn't work. Young children care nothing about the benefits of vitamins. Don't waste your time saying vegetables are good for them.

Talking about how wonderful vegetables taste as you shove them in your mouth doesn't work either. It's true that children learn by example. But in this case, your daughter will simply learn never to believe anything you say. In addition, she will begin to suspect your sanity.

Trying to scare the child with stories of malnutrition and rickets won't work either. Not only will she continue to refuse to eat vegetables, she'll also start having nightmares, which will keep you up all night, every night, eventually making *you* look as if you have some bizarre nutritional deficiency.

Making the child sit at the table until she's eaten her vegetables will only result in a power struggle no one can win. You will lose because getting into power struggles with children indicates to them that you really have very little power. They will lose because when children don't have confidence in their parents' power, they feel insecure.

When my daughter, Amy, was four years old, she complained bitterly about the presence of green things on her plate. She not only wouldn't eat them, she didn't even want them there, ruining the presentation and polluting the taste of the other foods.

The first thing we did was make a rule: The same foods will be served to everybody. No one in the family will get a special plate. Next we told Amy she didn't *ever* have to eat green things. We made no attempt to persuade and frighten. We didn't simulate a religious experience when we were eating vegetables, nor did we tell her she would have to sit at the table until she ate her green things.

"But," we said, "you must eat everything on the first plate we give you in order to receive a second helping of anything on the plate that you particularly like."

From that day forward, we put only slightly more than a tablespoon of each of the foods served at dinner, including a vegetable, on her plate. This virtually guaranteed that after she finished eating those foods that she liked—roast "beast" and mashed potatoes, for example—she'd still be hungry. At that point, she had a choice: Did she want to go hungry, or did she eat her veggie and receive seconds of the things she liked?

We predicted that, at least initially, Amy would choose not to eat her veggies. She didn't let us down. We allowed her to leave the table whenever she chose but covered any food remaining on her plate with plastic wrap. If, later in the evening, Amy said she was hungry and requested something to eat, we simply pointed to her dinner plate and said, "We'll be glad to warm the rest of your dinner for you in the microwave. When you've eaten the rest of what's on your plate, you may have just about any snack you want."

She struggled with the dilemma we laid before her for several weeks before she began eating her veggies at first sitting, grudgingly but without complaint. Not always, mind you, but more often than not.

Q: *Our seven-year-old will not eat. I don't think he has ever finished a plate of food, regardless of how little it held. I have gone so far as to play Restaurant. No good. His "favorite" food is only his favorite until I put it in front of him. Then come the excuses: "I'm not hungry anymore," "It doesn't taste good," "This isn't the way so-and-so fixes it," "I have a stomachache."*

At the evening meal, he dawdles, complains, nibbles, and picks— everything except eat. I am nearly out of my mind. We've tried making him eat, taking privileges away, sending him to bed early, even bribing him. No change.

Two hours after the dishes have been done and my chest pains have nearly stopped, he wants potato chips or popcorn or ice cream; as he puts it, "I'm hungry now." To keep from wringing his neck, I'm wringing my hands. Help me.

A: The urgent and anguished tone of your letter moved me to seek the counsel of the famous sage Juan Hoo Nose, whose ability to sniff out solutions to riddles such as these has become legend. I persuaded him to meditate on your problem. Here are his remarks:

Tell the belle to stop wringing. Juan Hoo Nose to the rescue. *Ta-da!* No wonder her son will not eat. She has told him, in effect, that the most wonderful thing he can do for her is eat the food she prepares. When he refuses, her self-esteem suffers more than his belly. Why should he be responsible for making her feel like a good mother?

She hands him a whip and then complains when he uses it. Any child worth his weight in Legos will seize the slightest opportunity to face off with parents in a power struggle. It's only natural. Unfortunately, there are no winners in such a struggle. In the long run, this mother will feel bad about herself and resentful of her son. In turn, the son will learn distorted and untrue things about women, and his ability to establish successful relationships with them will suffer.

Without realizing it, this mother has subscribed to the old adage, "The way to a man's heart is through his stomach." This saying was invented by men who wanted to keep women enslaved in the kitchen. To solve the problem, she must stop basing her opinion of herself on whether or not her child eats and concentrate on improving his manners instead of his appetite.

First, she must never play Restaurant again, particularly at family meals. His plate should have small amounts of the same foods everyone else is having, not special orders.

Second, no attempt should be made to persuade or force him to eat, but every attempt must be made to improve his decorum at the table. His parents should tell him that he is not required to eat, but he is required to sit at the table and behave properly. A list of his bad manners should be made, including all the complaints he makes concerning food. If he does or says something on the list, he should be sent from the table to spend the rest of the meal in an isolated part of the house, like the bathroom.

During the meal, parents should avoid long conversations about food. Table talk should be about pleasant subjects only. This changes the meal from an exercise in eating to an exercise in togetherness. The child should be encouraged to enter the conversation but not allowed to dominate it.

If food remains on his plate after he has been excused from the table, it should be covered in plastic wrap and set aside. Later, when he complains of hunger, unwrap the plate, warm it, and give it to him, saying, "When you finish your supper, you may have potato chips or whatever else you want before bed."

If he yells and screams, send him to his room until he is calm. Parents shouldn't compromise. The child must eat the food on his plate before any other food is given to him, including seconds of any one item.

If this mother wants to be reassured that her son will not waste away because of her stubbornness, she can call her pediatrician. He will appreciate the comic relief.

It may take several weeks or several months before the child regains a normal appetite and begins behaving himself at the table. But it will happen. The Nose knows.

Q: *When we sit down to eat, our ten-year-old complains about the food on her plate. Trying to persuade her to take even one bite of something she doesn't like is worse than pulling teeth. On several occasions, after we insisted that she eat something, she ran to the bathroom and threw up. We have made her sit at the table until she finishes everything on her plate—she sits and sits but still refuses to eat. I know it's wrong, but guilt-ridden Mom here has sometimes given up and fixed her something she* would *eat, in the name of peace. Do you have a better way?*

A: Sure. But first, let's untangle the situation. The overriding issue has nothing to do with nutrition. It's a matter of manners and your daughter's proper place in the family.

It is rude to complain about food that someone else has prepared. It is equally rude to refuse to eat it because of some neurotic prejudice. Do you want your daughter going to someone else's home and complaining about food her hosts prepare for her? Then don't allow her to complain about the food you prepare.

With regard to her place in the family, must I remind you that she is a child? By allowing her to disrupt family meals with her complaints, by pleading with her to eat, by fixing her special food, you are, in effect, aiding and abetting her push for prominence within the family. As long as she can control the family by whining and complaining at the dinner table, she will.

Stop catering to her! From now on, serve her plate with ridiculously small portions of the same foods everyone else in the family is eating—two or three forkfuls of each item. As time goes on, and the problem is nearing solution, gradually increase her portions until they are reasonable for her age and appetite.

Inform her that she doesn't have to eat anything that is not to her liking, but that she may not, under any circumstances, complain. If she violates this rule, either verbally or facially, take away whatever privileges she usually enjoys after dinner and move her bedtime up one hour.

Refuse to let her have seconds of anything, and certainly not dessert, until she cleans her plate. Do not make any remarks about what she eats or doesn't eat and don't make any attempt to persuade her to eat. In fact, pay no more attention to her than you do to anyone else at the table. If she eats everything, allow her seconds of anything. If she acts as if she's going to throw up after eating something, simply tell her to go to the bathroom. When she returns, inform her that throwing up or acting as if she has to is tantamount to a nonverbal complaint and earns the same punishment.

When the meal is over, clear her place along with everyone else's. If any food remains, cover it and set it aside. Later, when she complains of hunger and asks for food, show her her plate and tell her that when she finishes what remains, she may have whatever snacks you normally allow. If she happens to take you up on your offer, however, and cleans her plate, do not then cook for her or fix her any special foods.

Initially, she will test the new rules. She will complain, she will throw up, she will refuse to eat, and then later she will complain of hunger pains. In other words, you ain't seen nothin' yet. Take heart! Two or three weeks of hurling herself upon the barricades, and she will become convinced and cooperate.

Take your choice: Three weeks or eight more years?

20

Security Blankets

BIG PEOPLE REALLY DON'T KNOW much about children. We like to think we know it all, but nothing belies that more quickly than the things we get *ourselves* upset about.

Take little Sammy, for instance. He's going to be five years old next week, and he still carries a blanket with him wherever he goes. At least, that torn ragged piece of cloth *used* to be a blanket. Once upon a time, it was the blanket that kept him warm in his bassinet. Then it moved with him to his crib, and then to his bed, and then. . . . As Sammy goes, so goes the used-to-be-a-blanket.

"What's the matter with Sammy?" ask his parents. Something *must* be wrong. Children aren't supposed to carry blankets around for five years. Sure, Linus carries a blanket, but that's just in the funny pages, so you think Linus is cute. When it's your own little Sammy it's not so funny.

Maybe Sammy is insecure. This means nervous, doesn't it? "Oh my gosh!" exclaim his nervous parents. "We must have done something awful to Sammy to make him so nervous!"

Maybe they took his bottle away too quickly. Or perhaps they toilet-trained him too early. The parents' separation—yes, that must be it—when they had that big argument and separated for three months when Sammy was only twenty months old. He missed his daddy so much. "What have we done? Maybe we should take him to a psychologist!"

Something must be done to make Sammy more secure so he will give up that blanket. He goes to kindergarten next fall, and his teacher will know what fiends his parents are if he walks in waving that blanket around for the whole world to see.

"C'mon, Sammy, give us the blanket. You're a big boy now. You don't need that smelly old blanket anymore. If you give us the blanket, we will buy you a new bicycle. . . . Why not, Sammy?"

Take the blanket while he's sleeping? Say that Santa Claus took it? How about having the blanket fairy come and leave him some money for it in exchange? No, we musn't take it by force; that might make him *more* insecure. Then he might start sucking his thumb. On and on go Sammy's parents.

But the problem with Sammy is not Sammy at all. The issue is with his parents. Big people must have answers for everything. The more complicated the answer, the more blind faith we invest in it. In the process of becoming big, many of us forget how simple life can be. Big people become upset, and even frightened, by things they do not understand, such as children.

When big people do not understand something, they weave security blankets out of words and call them explanations. Sometimes these explanations get ponderous and cumbersome. When they get sufficiently complicated, they become fantasies.

This is what happened to Sammy's big people. They do not comprehend the insignificance of the blanket, because they no longer see the world in simple terms. They have learned too many words. They do not understand why Sammy wants his blanket with him wherever he goes, and this is upsetting. The four-year-old down the street doesn't carry a blanket around. Sammy is different. Sammy's parents think that something is wrong, so they invent a fantasy filled with dragons and demons, and in no time the blanket becomes the most important thing in the house. The issue of the blanket grows to such proportions that it suffocates everyone's common sense.

"Hey, Sammy! Just between you and me, tell me about your blanket."

"I jus' like it."

That sounds simple enough. On the other hand, maybe Sammy *is* a bit insecure. After all, everyone's trying to take his blanket.

21

Thumb-Sucking

WHEN SHE WAS A CHILD, my daughter, Amy, would park her thumb in her mouth when she was bored, tired, cranky, or just plain laid back. And that was fine with me. She began perfecting her technique the day she was born.

Not everyone feels the way I do. Quite a few people believe that something is wrong with the Amys of the world. Thumb-sucking defies convention, and this makes adults uncomfortable. As long as adults have "reasons" for things, they feel okay. So, they have invented some to explain why an occasional thumb is where it shouldn't be. Take your pick.

The "Bad Nerves Theory" says that thumb-sucking is a sign of insecurity. To parents who buy this idea, a thumb-sucking child is a constant reminder of what monsters the parents are. They become especially distraught when their child sucks in public, thus broadcasting this miserable condition to the world.

Another theory, attributed by some to a certain Sigmund Fraud, says that children suck their thumbs because during infancy they experienced some trauma associated with breast- or bottle-feeding. These poor kids grow up sucking on one substitute nipple after another—cigarettes, straws, siphon tubes, Life Savers, anything. As adults, they are the perverts who prefer to drink their beer straight from the bottle.

Sometimes it's easier for little girls to get away with sucking their thumbs than it is for little boys. There are even people who think a girl who sucks her thumb is "cute" (until she goes to school). A thumb-sucking boy is in mortal danger of growing up to be effeminate, or so the story goes. The solution? Paint the offending digit with colorless yuk. That'll make a man out of him.

Then there are the horror stories, Bedtime Tales for Thumb-suckers: "There once was a frog prince who sucked his thumb. When he grew up, his teeth were crooked, his eyes were crossed, his ears stuck out and flapped in the wind, he caught a dread disease, his cheeks dimpled, and the princess would not marry him." The part about the dimples gets 'em every time.

I have my own theory. Because of thumbs, people can build the things they dream of, like rocket ships and time machines. A child who sucks her thumb is saying, "I love my thumb. I love being human." Now isn't that nicer than bad nerves and a face like Alfred E. Newman?

As far as I can tell, children suck their thumbs simply because it feels good. Thumb-sucking is calming and relaxing to a child. It is a portable source of pleasure, always right on hand. The answer to why some children suck their thumbs and others don't is simply, "Because." It's no more significant than liking or not liking spinach.

So, the big fuss is over something rather insignificant. Children are not going to stop sucking their thumbs because of ridicule, threats, criticism, demands, or punishment. These "persuasive" measures can, in fact, create a problem where there was none to begin with.

Children cannot separate the feelings we communicate to them about thumb-sucking from the feelings they have about themselves as little people. If they are harassed about sucking their thumbs, it is a good bet they will begin to feel bad about themselves. They may withdraw and spend more time alone so they can suck in private, often seeking relief from their growing insecurity by sucking more and more. Where there was once a healthy child who sucked for pleasure, there is now a child who sucks to relieve the anxiety and discomfort of feeling that there's something wrong with him or her.

If your daughter sucks her thumb like mine did, leave her alone. If you must mention it, say something like, "Hey, there! I see your thumb in your mouth. I'll bet that feels pretty good. You know something? I love you."

One of these days, when she feels like it and has developed other interests, she will stop—but it will be in her own time, not yours.

22

Discipline in Public Places

Mommy took me to the store
To shop and spend the day,
But I had other things in mind
Like, for instance, play!

While she was looking for a dress
I ran away and hid;
I went under a table
And found another kid.

Mom found me in the makeup,
Playing with this child.
Together we were having fun;
Mom said that I was wild.

I cried for her to carry me,
I said I hurt my feet.
I cried 'cause I was hungry
And then I wouldn't eat.

I asked for toys but she said "no!"
And so I threw a fit.
I screamed and kicked and pulled my hair;
When she bought a toy, I quit.

I took my shoes off in the store
But can't remember where.
Mom got all red and shook a lot
And bought another pair.

We're home now; Mommy's resting.
I'm playing with her pen.
When she wakes up I'll ask her,
"When can we go again?"

Controlling children in public places is a sticky problem, to be sure. If you scream at them or spank them, everybody looks at you and you feel lower than a rattlesnake. If you look the other way, children play Hide and Seek (guess who does the seeking?), or they break something, or they help themselves to some candy or something horrible like that. If you hold their hands, they fight you. If you don't, they run wild. Shopping can be loads of fun.

Here's an idea. First make a list of rules for public places. It could read something like this:

1. You walk with me and stay with me. I will not hold your hand unless you want me to.

2. You are quiet in the stores. You do not scream, yell, or have a tantrum.

3. You walk. You do not run.

Those three are enough to cover most of the child's favorite public pastimes. Besides, three are probably all the child can remember.

Next, cut five or six tickets out of stiff colored cardboard. When that's done, you are prepared to meet with your youngster. You are the chairperson (chairparent?) at this conference. Begin by saying, "Moe, you are probably wondering why we are having this little talk, so I'm going to tell you. We are going to talk about going to the store, and after we talk about it, we are going to get in the car and go there. When we go to the store, I get mad because you run in the store, and you scream, and you yell, and you throw tantrums when you want toys, and you run away from me. I'm not laughing, Moe.

"I'm going to tell you what the rules are before we go to the store. The first rule is: You will walk with me and stay with me while I am shopping. I am not going to hold your hand unless you want me to. The second rule . . ." and so on.

When you finish going over the rules, pull out the tickets and say, "Before we go to the store, I am going to give you these tickets. The tickets are yours, so don't lose them. Every time you break a rule I'm going to take away a ticket. If you lose all your tickets in the store today, I will not let you go outside to play after supper [or some other such desirable activity]. You must have at least *one* ticket left in order to play outside tonight. Do you understand? Good. Then let's go practice the rules at the store."

The number of tickets should vary according to the time you expect to be shopping. Start by estimating how many hours you are going to be gone, add one to this number, and give that many tickets. In other words, if you think it's going to be a two-hour trip, give three tickets.

When you get to the store, review the rules in the parking lot, give Moe the tickets, repeat what the deal is, and proceed. If Moe breaks a rule, say, "You were running. The rule says you will walk. Give me a ticket for breaking the rule." If you must take the last ticket, do so without any big fuss, but gently remind Moe what the consequences are, in case the child "forgot."

Try to remember when you were small and what torture shopping was. When children are bored or tired, they are more likely to misbehave, so don't expect a preschool child to tag along with you cheerfully for more than an hour. Bring a stroller or take the time to hunt one when you get to the store (many stores provide them).

The deal made with the tickets should involve some privilege that the child would normally look forward to doing at home that same day. Do not offer bribes such as ice cream or minibikes for good behavior. Several years ago, I was waiting in the customer service area of a large department store when a young couple came in with their son, who was about two and a half. The father held the child as the mother talked with the clerk. But this two-year-old had obviously had enough of being carried, because he immediately began squirming and pushing away from Dad, wanting to get down. Dad held on and tried to distract him, but to no avail.

The child, a typical two-year-old, continued to struggle and protest, becoming increasingly agitated and vocal.

Finally Dad sat him on the counter and said, "Hey, Frankie, how about if you and I go look at the toys and pick one out for you to take home, okay?" That must have sounded good to Frankie, because he stopped crying and, still sniffling, nodded assent. Dad told Mom they'd meet her in the toy department, and off they went. Frankie's parents inevitably wound up paying for that little trip to the toy department for months, maybe years, to come.

For many reasons, children are far more difficult to handle in public places than in the relative quiet and privacy of home. Anyone looking for a quick and easy way of dispensing forever with public shenanigans is going to be disappointed, however, because there isn't any. There are, however, things parents can do to contain even the worst situation imaginable and gradually bring a child's public behavior under control. A few suggestions are:

- Announce the purpose of the outing in advance, so the child knows what to expect.

- Do not make promises of "If you're good, we'll buy you a so-and-so." Deals like this teach a child to expect compensation for appropriate behavior. A child so taught may never learn that good behavior is its own reward.

- You can save yourself a lot of grief if you do not teach your young'un to expect a goodie every time the family goes shopping. In fact, I advise just the opposite—teach children to expect nothing but basic necessities. Not only will they never acquire the obnoxious habit of constantly pleading for toys during shopping trips, but they will be surprised and appreciative when you do present them with something special.

- Just before going into the shopping center or restaurant, remind the child of a few simple rules, such as "Stay in your stroller, talk quietly, and touch things only with your eyes."

- When rules are broken or need to be created on the spot, take the child aside immediately and either remind or inform.

- Stay away from places where toys or candy are sold. Don't even walk through them if you can avoid it.

- Take the child who starts screaming or acting out of control quickly into a remote area of the store and sit there until the tantrum subsides or control is reestablished. The quicker you stop the momentum of the child's misbehavior, the better. If things don't improve, you might consider going outside the store for a while or even straight home.

- A spanking administered at the scene rarely accomplishes anything except louder screams and lots of disapproving looks. On those infrequent occasions when I felt spanking was appropriate, I would remove myself and my child to a private place (a corridor, a bathroom, outside) and, with no warning, give the spanking there. Intended only as a slight shock to terminate the tantrum and remind the child of my authority, it was usually effective.

- Abandoning a shopping cart of groceries or a table of restaurant food to reestablish control over a child may seem drastic and self-defeating, but I know from personal experience that it pays off in the long run. I recall, on one occasion, getting up in the midst of a meal, taking my younger child outside, and sitting in the car with her while the rest of the family finished eating. The minor inconvenience was well worth the lesson it taught Amy.

For extreme emergencies, each parent might carry a fake-nose-and-glasses set, so that if all else fails they can beat a hasty retreat into anonymity.

23

How to Survive a Trip

A FRIEND OF MINE has a recurring nightmare in which he is handcuffed to the steering wheel of a car traveling down a deserted stretch of four-lane highway. There are two young children in the backseat, both gorging on junk food. In his dream, the highway has no exits. The children are bouncing up and down in the backseat, screaming about needing to use the bathroom, fighting over toys, crying, and constantly asking, "When are we going to get there?"

My friend should be thankful that this is just a nightmare. I know a lot of parents for whom this scenario is all too real. Backseats were not designed with children in mind. They are confining and boring, and it's asking a great deal of a child (or any human being) to sit peacefully in one for an extended time.

The mood of an entire vacation is set during the trip, but there is no reason the tone of the ride must be one of anger and frustration. Parents can spare themselves and their children a lot of misery by planning thoughtfully for everyone's needs during the journey.

To begin with, pack a small cooler chockful of a variety of healthy sugar-free snacks. These can include raisins, carrot and celery sticks, dry roasted peanuts, crackers, peanut-butter sandwiches, fruit, and such good old-fashioned drinks as apple and orange juice.

Let the children eat freely; just the act of eating will help them stay calm. Keep junk food off the menu. The refined sugar (and often caffeine) in soft drinks doses children with an oversupply of quick energy, turning a car into a pressure cooker. And when you eliminate all sugar-sweetened foods and drinks from the trip menu, the children probably won't have to use the bathroom as often. How about that? Two birds with one stone.

Pack a cloth bag or box with books, coloring books, colored pencils (crayons melt on the back shelf), and other trip toys to hold the children's attention and interest. Keep this inventory in the front seat, with an adult acting as toy librarian. When you sense that a child is losing interest in one toy, take it away and provide another in its place.

It also helps to vary the seating arrangement during the trip. For instance, the adults can switch back and forth between driving and sitting in the back with one of the children. Keeping children separated in this way, at least part of the time, is often a good idea. An older child can ride in the front with the driver, while another adult keeps younger children occupied in the back by reading stories or carrying on a quiet conversation.

Word games are fun, and even the driver can play. Rhyming games (What rhymes with *cat*?), guessing games (I see something that is green, what is it?), and name games (I am an animal with a long neck who eats leaves from trees, who am I?) are just some ideas for keeping everyone in a positive frame of mind.

Plan regular stops so people can stretch and empty their bladders. Trying to travel more than six or eight hours in a day with children can easily backfire. By leaving in the middle of the night, however, my family could manage to drive a straight twelve hours without turning into a bunch of blithering idiots. Blithering maybe, but not yet to the idiot stage.

There is even a creative answer to the question, "What do we do when they misbehave in the car?" What else but Tickets? All you need to play are those pocket-sized rectangles of colored cardboard.

Before anyone gets into the car, explain to the children the rules governing behavior during the ride. Keep the list brief. Some suggestions: seat belts must be buckled, no fighting or arguing, no yelling or screaming, no throwing, and each child is allowed to ask, "When are we gonna be there?" just once.

Remind the children that they have a special event waiting for them at the end of the trip (swimming, exploring, playing with cousins, whatever). Now comes the clincher: "I am giving the same number of tickets to each of you. Each time you break a car rule, I will take a ticket away. If you fight, I will take a ticket from each of you, regardless of who started it. When we get to the beach, you must have at least one ticket left to go swimming. If you don't have a ticket, you must sit on the beach with me for thirty minutes."

It works, believe me (see A Trip to the Beach in chapter 3). Take careful note of the punishment; it is quite enough that you promise to withhold the special event for a brief time. Vacations are not for suffering. Besides, if one suffers, all will suffer. The number of tickets can vary with the anticipated length of the trip—one ticket per hour, perhaps, up to a maximum of five or six.

Have an enjoyable vacation. Plan ahead, drive carefully, and don't forget the sunscreen.

24

Miscellaneous Disciplinary Disorders

Q: *I am writing to you out of sheer desperation. My problem may seem trivial, but it is driving me absolutely up the wall. Both my husband and I work, and it is necessary that we leave the house by seven forty-five every morning. On the way to work, I drop our Jamie, who is four and a half, at his day-care center. The problem is that every morning Jamie plays and stalls and everything else you can think of—except getting dressed.*

I lay out his clothes when we all get up at six-thirty, and the fight begins. I start by telling him calmly to get dressed, but I always end up yelling at him and often putting the last few pieces on him myself. The only thing he can't do alone is tie his shoes. We all end up angry, and everybody's day begins on this miserable note. The problem is not that Jamie is tired. He goes to bed (no problems here) at eight-thirty (after a bedtime story— his favorite thing) and is alert in the mornings. He just finds all kinds of reasons for not putting his clothes on. Can you help us?

A: Come down off the wall. Your problems are almost over. It's quite clear that Jamie is a clever little fellow. Clever enough to figure out that when Mom and Dad are busy and in a hurry, one surefire way of getting everybody's attention is *not* to cooperate. After all, what's the rush? Who wants to hurry up and be without Mom and Dad all day long?

You made two very important statements. First, Jamie *can* dress himself. Second, Jamie likes being read to in the evening. If you will purchase a kitchen timer, we will have all the ingredients for our recipe.

With the timer in hand, Mom and Dad sit down with Jamie and say, "Hey, big guy, we aren't going to yell at you about getting dressed in the morning anymore. Instead, we are going to play a game called Put Your Clothes On. Here's how the game is played. When we wake you up, we will put your clothes on the chair in your room. Then we will set the timer for fifteen minutes and put it on your dresser.

"When we set the timer, it will begin ticking like a clock, and in fifteen minutes, a bell will ring like this [demonstrate the bell ringing]. If you have all your clothes on before the bell rings, then you win the game. The prize for winning is that you get to pick your bedtime story that night.

"If the bell rings and you don't have your clothes on, Mom and Dad will do it. But you don't win the game, so you cannot have a bedtime story."

Then do exactly that. If he wins, make a big deal about it, letting him know how nicely he dresses himself and so on. Maybe there is time to read him a short story before school. If he doesn't win the game, dress him yourself. If you have to do this and he protests, simply tell him those are the rules, and you want him to win tomorrow. He *will* start to win, believe me.

You can gradually shorten the time until he can put his clothes on at a comfortable pace. A star chart taped to the refrigerator is an additional way to reward him when he wins. It's the no-more-foot-prints-on-the-wall method of child-rearing.

Q: *My seven-year-old is the sloppiest child you ever saw. He never puts anything where it belongs. His coat is never hung up, his bike is always parked dead center in the driveway, his dirty clothes are piled where he took them off, his book bag lands on the sofa when he comes home from school . . . need I go on? It seems as though I yell at him all the time, but nothing changes. Help keep me from tearing out my hair!*

A: Yelling is a trap fraught with paradox. The more you yell, the less you accomplish. A yell is threatening; and the sheer volume may prompt a child to follow instructions, but once the shock wave passes, it's generally back to business as usual. Yelling is also a waste of energy. You invest a tremendous amount of yourself and get nothing of lasting value in return. The more you yell, the more of yourself you exhaust, until finally you're bankrupt. And your seven-year-old is ready to cash in all the chips.

A yell is aggressive but not assertive. It's an expression of frustration and an admission of powerlessness. In fact, the yell transfers control of the issue to the child, who is all too willing to be the center of the storm, in control of the family. It is essential that you do something more constructive than yelling, before the entire family gets hooked into behaving as though a seven-year-old sits in the driver's seat!

Take a piece of paper and, down the left-hand side, make a list of all the things your son "misplaces"—bicycle, coat, schoolbooks, dirty clothes, shoes, and so on. Be very specific, so there is no room for misunderstandings. ("It only says *coat;* I didn't know you meant my *raincoat* too!")

Then, to the right of your first list, make a second that tells *exactly* where each item belongs. Coat . . . on a hanger in the hall closet. Bicycle . . . parked against the side wall of the carport. Dirty clothes . . . in the hamper in the upstairs bathroom.

Find a quiet time to sit down with your son and go over the list of things and places. "You and I have not been working together very well, so I have made this list to help both of us know what the rules are for putting things away."

After your discussion, post the list on the refrigerator door or some other equally visible place. Beside it, post a score card, a sheet with seven boxes in a row, representing seven days.

"For the next seven days, we are going to keep score on how well you are learning the rules. If you leave something out of place, I will call it to your attention. You must mark a check in the box for that day and then put the item where it belongs. In return, I promise *not* to yell."

During the week, monitor his compliance but don't crowd him. If he refuses to put his own check in the box, make it for him. Be sure to call his attention not only to things *out* of place but to things that are *in* place as well, letting him know you appreciate his help. As the days go by, discuss his progress or lack of it in optimistic matter-of-fact terms.

Don't offer him any goodies for a certain level of performance, but if you are so moved you might reward several days of improvement (or a "perfect" day) with some spontaneous show of affection and gratitude: "You have done so well, how would you like to go with me to McArnold's for a Crabapple Swizzle?"

On the other hand, the week may not produce any measurable change in his willingness to abide by the rules. He may not be quite ready to stop fighting with you. In that case, at the end of the week, be prepared to make him a deal.

Put up another scorecard. Write a large number "four" at the top. Arrange a second summit conference. Inform him that he will be confined to his room for thirty minutes when he receives his fourth check of the day, and that any additional checks will immediately earn him another thirty minutes apiece.

Then you simply enforce the rules. In the end, it's largely a matter of trust. You trust him to abide by the rules, and he learns to trust that you will enforce them.

By following this plan or a variation of it, you will make significant changes in the way you handle the situation. You will define the nature of the problem in clear, precise terms. You will give accurate nonjudgmental feedback on his compliance with the rules. And finally, you will take an authoritative position on the issue, letting your son see you stand firmly but gently in one place.

He can be expected to test the system for weaknesses. That is his right. If you hold firm, he will eventually accept that you are no longer willing to participate in a struggle over where things belong.

Q: *Our eighteen-month-old son is forever pulling our cat's tail or picking it up by the neck. Punishing him and talking to him have not worked. How can we teach him not to do this?*

A: At this age, your son is driven to touch, feel, and squeeze everything in sight. Every squeeze, every poke, is a way of asking the question, "What are you and what do you do?" You should child-proof your toddler's environment so he can interact freely and safely with his surroundings. Child-proofing also improves the mental health of the parents, who might otherwise struggle constantly to keep the child out of places where he shouldn't be.

When a pet is a part of the child's world, decide how to deal with the child's curiosity about the animal. One way to prevent frustration or harm is to keep the child and the pet completely separated, but this may be incompatible with the place the pet occupies in the family.

Another option is to hold the child's hand and patiently teach him how to stroke and handle the pet. Don't, however, bank on seeing any immediate results. Teaching a toddler restraint, tenderness, and sensitivity requires lots of patience.

Another way of handling the child's interest in the pet is to let them interact freely (which usually means as often as the pet will allow). Personal experience tells me that when the pet is familiar with the child and the child means no harm, no harm is likely to come to either.

When my son was this age, we had a cat named Roy that Eric would maul every time their paths crossed. At first we were concerned that perhaps Eric was hurting Roy or that Roy might scratch him. Whenever Eric had Roy in his grip, we talked to him about being gentle or became mildly excited and pried them apart. Eventually we noticed that whenever Eric grabbed him, Roy went limp and endured the assault looking like last year's dishrag. After seeing how well Roy handled it, we stopped paying attention to the situation. Roy was obviously surviving the attacks and seemed to "know" that Eric meant no harm.

Lo and behold! After we stopped making it an issue, Eric stopped chasing Roy around the house.

To satisfy my own curiosity, I asked the opinion of several veterinarians. They all said they thought separation was the best solution if the parents were concerned about the child's handling of the pet. However, they knew of few pets injured by toddlers. The smaller the pet (kittens and puppies), the more vulnerable it is to innocent abuse. These veterinarians also thought that the family pet was not likely to retaliate against a child and that the pet could, in most cases, take care of itself.

A supervising emergency room nurse told me that although emergency room personnel see many children who have been hurt by animals, almost all the injuries involve older children or animals that are either strays or belong to another family. It is very rare, she said, to see a serious injury inflicted on a toddler by a family pet. In fact, she was unable to recall any incident of that nature in her many years of experience.

Young children require supervision, pet or no pet. For the sake of the animal, it is probably unwise to raise toddlers and kittens or puppies at the same time. For safety reasons, keep toddlers away from pets with a history of belligerence, strays, and other families' pets that may not be tolerant of strange probing hands.

All these approaches have drawbacks. If parents choose to take the path of least resistance and let Mother Nature take care of the situation, however, harm is unlikely to come to either child or pet. That the child will ever become intentionally cruel and abusive to animals is even more unlikely. Most important in determining a child's permanent attitude toward animals is the example *we* set.

Q: *Being a first-time mother, I have difficulty knowing how much one-to-one attention my three-year-old daughter needs. It seems the more we give, the more she demands. What are some general guidelines? I interact with her all day long during housework and shopping as I answer questions, tie bibs on dolls, and so on. We try to have a story at bedtime and some time during the morning to play as she directs, but it's never enough. Any suggestions?*

A: With the first child, parents are prone to confuse what is actually *needed* with what is simply *wanted*. It's an easy trap to stumble into for several reasons, not the least of which is our anxiety about dealing with a relatively unfamiliar set of demands and responsibilities. Hand in hand goes a desire to do everything just right, which further blurs the already faint line between what is necessary for the child's well-being and those things that are simply whimsy.

Don't count on children to clarify matters. They are just as likely to scream for a toy fire truck as they are for something to eat when they are hungry.

Children *need* nutritious food and water and warmth and room to explore and stimulation and people who talk softly and loving relationships and routines that organize their lives and cuddles and kisses and praise. They need parents who set limits and enforce rules—and give lots of warm, accepting strokes.

On the other hand, children *want* parents who will be at their beck and call and solve all their problems and carry them everywhere and make them the center of attention and let them do and have whatever they demand—and give lots of warm, accepting strokes.

It's not difficult to see why many children come to believe that parents are for anything and everything. From the moment children arrive in the world, parents bathe and feed and carry and hold and rock and wait on them hand and foot. From a young child's point of view, parents are servants. Mom is a lady-in-waiting and Dad is a valet.

Ah, but good domestic help isn't easy to find these days. Sometimes the servants get uppity and refuse to follow instructions.

That's usually no problem for a child with a healthy set of lungs. Servants are easily intimidated by tantrums.

Many parents interpret tantrums as screams of genuine pain, a symptom of needs that have gone abused and neglected, so they perform whatever peculiar act the scream demands. By-and-by the child learns that tantrums push all the right buttons. In the long run, then, children get the lesser part of what they need and the greater part of what they want, some of which they don't need at all. How confusing!

The solution? The same one that solves most other problems of raising children: establish predictable guidelines, set firm limits, and enforce them consistently. Set aside several times during the day—say, once in the morning, afternoon, and evening—when you will devote thirty minutes to nothing but your daughter. Give each period a name, such as "playtime," "doll time," and "story time." A child of three and a half has no concept of what thirty minutes means, so use a timer. At the beginning of each period, set the timer for thirty minutes and say, "Mommy will read stories until the bell rings, and then I am going to do my own work [be specific]." When the bell rings, you then excuse yourself, saying how much fun you had, and leave the little one alone with a suggestion for occupying her time.

If you stay with the routine and let her know how determined you are, things will settle into place quickly. Children may *want* servants, but they *need* parents.

Q: *My son is almost four years old, and he is driving me crazy. He will hardly do anything I ask until I become upset enough to spank him. And this is the child I promised myself I would* never *spank. When I ask him to do something, he gives me this "you gotta be kidding!" look and turns away. It's maddening! Sometimes he just says no, as coolly as you please. If he knows he is going to get a spanking (and he almost always does) why does he do these things?*

A: Your almost-four-year-old is only doing what every young child must eventually do—he is challenging your authority. He demands to know, "By what right do *you* tell *me* what to do?"

As long as the question is unanswered, he is free to engage in a power struggle with you. After all, no one told him the rules before he got here. It is your responsibility to describe the rules to him, not his to figure them out. If you aren't clear on what they are, he is free to make up his own game and his own rules. And he has. It's called Betcha!

In Betcha! the parent starts the play by asking the child to perform some task, however small. The child counters by refusing to cooperate. Parent then responds, "Oh, yes, you will!" The child says, "Betcha!" and the game is on.

Betcha! isn't much fun, however, because no one ever wins. In fact, both players always end up losers. How monotonous! But maybe it's the only game in town.

"But he almost always gets a spanking," you say. So what? Who pays *that* price? You do.

The game repeats itself because it has never been resolved. And it will not be resolved until you stop expecting him to change. He's not going to stop inviting you to play Betcha! until you stop accepting the invitation. In fact, he doesn't even know *how* to stop.

To begin the end of playing Betcha! stop *asking* your son for his cooperation and start *telling* him exactly what you want him to do. Begin every request with the phrase, "I want you to . . ." and then fill in the blank with a clear, concise description of the task. Stop apologizing for having brought him into a less-than-perfect world.

Here are two of many possible approaches you can take to bring Betcha! to a close. Choose the one that suits you better, or use them as models for devising a solution of your own.

Plan A: Instead of spanking as a last resort, spank as a *first* resort. I have no problems with spankings per se, as long as they are used effectively, to accomplish something. Up until now, your spankings have been an expression of frustration and defeat. Use your hand to emphasize your authority and stop the game before it has a chance to get started. Tell him what you want from him. If he signals his refusal, immediately reach around and clap him firmly on the rear (*do not* announce what is coming with warnings or threats). Then, face him and repeat what you want. Remember in the movie *The Godfather* when Marlon Brando made someone an offer he couldn't refuse? Use that tone of voice. If he still refuses (and he probably will, the first few times), take him to a chair and have him sit until he's ready to comply. Meanwhile, you go some other place and busy yourself.

If that sounds too mean, try Plan B: Buy a kitchen timer if you don't have one. Sit down with almost-four son and say, "Yesterday"—all things in the past happened *yesterday* to an almost-four— "when I told you to [use an example], you said *no*! I got mad and yelled and spanked. I don't like that. Today, if you say *no*, I'm going to put you in your room for five minutes. When I put you in the room, I'll set this timer, and when five minutes is over, it will ring, like this. Then you can come out and do what I told you to do. Understand?"

He will nod his head, which means that he doesn't understand but knows when to nod his head. You are letting him know that you are changing the game. You must then show him what kind of change you're talking about.

Now it's *your* move.

Q: *We have a four-and-a-half-year-old daughter and an eighteen-month-old son. Our problem is other people—neighbors, friends, even grandparents—who pay lots of attention to the baby and very little to the older child, to the point of virtually ignoring her. When other people come over, my daughter begins "performing," interrupting conversations and misbehaving in other ways to get attention. How can I get other people to understand that she needs attention too?*

A: I'm sorry, but your daughter's plight fails to evoke my sympathy. It seems obvious that the real problem is her misbehavior when you have guests in your home.

This problem involves other people only to the extent that they have become *her* audience and *your* excuse for failing to control her.

You have unintentionally given her permission to misbehave when there is company, and she has seized on the opportunity to command as much attention as possible.

I suspect she would get more attention if her behavior were appropriate to her age and the situation. She is probably being ignored because of her performance, not because your guests are insensitive.

One disappointment in being an eldest child occurs when the spotlight moves to the second born. Babies attract lots of attention. That's a fact of life your daughter is capable of living with. But she won't make a comfortable adjustment to her slightly diminished status unless you stop trying to protect her from the hardship of having a younger sibling. Take a quiet moment to sit and talk with her. Tell her you understand how difficult it is to share things, including attention from other people. Point out that she must nonetheless learn to share and promise to help her.

Make a list of the inappropriate things she does in front of guests: cartwheels, Ed Sullivan impressions, and so on. Make it clear that you will no longer accept this behavior, and let her know how you *do* expect her to act. When she entertains company with one of the items on the list, put her in her room for a time-out, perhaps with a kitchen timer set for five minutes. Make sure you give her a hug and a kiss when she manages to control her enthusiasm in front of visitors.

The world may be a stage, but your daughter is a bit young for a leading role.

Q: *I take care of a nearly four-year-old boy whose parents both work. For reasons his parents cannot explain, he has developed a habit of cursing when he becomes upset. He does not say anything vulgar yet but will burst forth with "damn!" or "hell!" when something doesn't go his way. His parents say they have talked to him about his language, but it keeps getting worse. They have given me permission to punish him, but I'm not sure of the best approach. Any suggestions?*

A: As you are well aware, a child does not acquire a vocabulary of this sort in a vacuum. This child is mimicking an adult, an older child, or a character on some television program he is allowed to watch. If the nefarious influence is not in *your* home (and I don't think you would have asked this question if it was), it is something his parents are capable of identifying and eliminating. Methinks they are not being completely forthright with you, in which case whatever you do to curb this language in your home will be undone when this little fellow is not in your care. Perhaps you can suggest to the parents, without implying that they themselves are the influence in question, that they make an all-out effort to determine where this language is coming from and eliminate it at its source.

On days when he *is* in your care, I would recommend a variation on my ticket technique, which is actually a modification of the old Boy Scout demerit system. Using a magnetic clip, affix three tickets—rectangles of colored cardboard—to the refrigerator. On any given day, the first time this little guy curses, he loses a ticket and must sit in an isolated time-out area for ten minutes. The second time, he loses a second ticket and sits for twenty minutes. The third such incident results in the loss of the third and last ticket, as well as a thirty-minute period of time-out.

But that's not all! With his parents' cooperation, each ticket lost represents a privilege at home, something he looks forward to doing in the late afternoon or early evening. When he loses the first ticket, he might lose the privilege of being able to play outside when he gets home. The second ticket might represent watching television, and the third might represent his normal bedtime. So, if he loses all three tickets at your house (which he's likely to do for several days at least), when he arrives home he cannot play outside or watch television, and he would be put to bed at least one hour early. The combination of a punishment at your house (ever-increasing periods of time-out), and corresponding punishments at home (loss of privilege) builds a bridge of communication and consequences between the two environments. If both you and his parents manage the system properly, meaning consistently and dispassionately, I would predict that he will quickly learn to contain his exclamatory outbursts.

Again, however, while a reactive approach of this sort may serve as an effective deterrent, actually correcting the problem will require that his parents ferret out and eliminate whatever disreputable influence has caused it in the first place. Perhaps a mirror would help in their search.

Q: *My seven-year-old is a poor sport, gloating when he wins a game and crying when he loses. My husband's entire family shares this trait with him, so it's more than just his age. Games and competitive sports with his peers are especially problematic. When we play board games at home, he cries when he loses and makes fun of us when he wins, just like he does with his peers. By the way, my husband is coming to grips with this about himself, but he's still got a way to go.*

A: If by "so it's more than just his age" you mean your son inherited this tendency, I doubt it. Unbeknownst to the general public, the search for genetic explanations of human behavior has not panned out. In fact, studies of identical twins reared apart have debunked the notion that specific behavioral traits are passed from generation to generation through any reliable genetic mechanisms.

You're right to be concerned. His peers will not tolerate your son's poor sportsmanship much longer. The older he becomes, the more social problems this will cause, and for good reason. Poor sportsmanship is, after all, a show of self-centered disrespect for others. Whereas seven-year-olds may tolerate it, ten-year-olds will not. Likewise, adults who are presently likely to regard this as simple immaturity will view it as a much more serious problem in a few years.

In short, you cannot afford to waste time. Assuming your husband shares your concerns, he should join you in a full-scale curative effort. In fact, I'd venture to say that if your son doesn't begin hearing a strong message of disapproval from his father, unilateral efforts on your part to remedy this problem will not succeed.

In my experience, there's just one effective way to handle this. As soon as your son begins to gloat or get upset during a game, he should be *immediately* removed and not allowed to continue unless he apologizes to everyone—the coaches, his teammates, and the kids on the other team. If he refuses to do this, you must take him home immediately and confine him to his room for the rest of the day. Needless to say, his coaches must also be completely supportive. If it's not convenient for the game to stop so he can apologize, you should immediately take him home. Under those circumstances, before he can join the team for the next practice or game, he must apologize for his previous bad behavior.

You may be asking yourself, "Won't that embarrass him?" The answer is "Absolutely!" That, in fact, is the point. He must be required to experience a negative emotional consequence powerful enough to cause him to begin controlling his antisocial behavior on the field.

When he displays the same sort of behavior during games with either or both of you, you should stop the game immediately and send him to his room. He stays in his room until he produces a written apology to the two of you. This apology should be no less than one page in length and should contain an explanation of why it is wrong to gloat or get upset during games.

Apologies are good for the soul, and what's good for the soul helps children change their behavior.

Q: *Two years ago, we adopted an intelligent, creative, outgoing four-year-old girl whose birth parents had been neglectful and often homeless. The one and only problem we're having with Shelly is she steals from us. Jewelry, money, you name it, whatever she can lay her hands on disappears. When we confront her, she always denies having taken the item in question. When it shows up later among her possessions, as it always does, she claims not to know how it got there. A therapist we consulted said the problem was symptomatic of "unresolved security issues" and that punishing her would only make matters worse. What do you think?*

A: The notion that Shelly's stealing stems from "unresolved security issues" can be neither proved nor disproved. Neither, therefore, can the statement that punishing her will make matters worse. For all we know, furthermore, therapeutic attempts to resolve issues that may or may not be involved might be counterproductive.

Stealing is antisocial. That's a fact, not a theory. And so far, well-intentioned social liberals have yet to come up with a response to antisocial behavior that's more generally effective than punishment. Therefore, I'm going to recommend that you punish your daughter for stealing, but benignly so. Since stealing deprives people of privilege and property, it makes perfect sense to deprive Shelly of privilege and property when she steals.

I'll just bet that whenever Shelly steals something, a family soap opera—call it *Uproar*—ensues in which she becomes the focus of lots of attention and energy. Whether or not this explains her stealing is moot; regardless, you need to begin responding to the problem so that *Uproar* is canceled and stealing causes Shelly more problems than it does the two of you.

Put a MISSING THINGS list on the refrigerator. When you discover something missing, act nonchalant. Don't even ask Shelly if she has it, just put it on the list. Then make a rule: As long as there's even one item on the list, Shelly can't participate in any after-school activities, go to friend's houses, or have friends over, and you, furthermore, can't buy her anything except what is absolutely essential. Put a RETURNS box in the back hall or some other relatively inconspicuous place and inform Shelly that when the item, or items, on the list shows up in the box, her privileges will be restored. This allows her to atone without a big and potentially humiliating deal being made of it.

It's of the utmost importance that you deprive the problem of the energy off which it feeds. If, while her life is "suspended," Shelly protests her innocence, just say, "We're not going to talk about it. The rule is the rule." Likewise, when a missing something shows up in the box, just cross it off the list without fanfare. This is not, mind you, a quick fix. Nonetheless, my experience has been that this method slowly but surely causes (or allows) a child's stealing to die a natural death. The operative word is *slowly*. The good news is that you should be able to contain the problem before it spills out of the family and into the social arena.

The logical question becomes, "What if an item is missing, but it turns out that Shelly didn't take it." In that case, of course, the child would be punished for something she didn't do. Under the circumstances, are the parents obligated to make up for the injustice in some way? My answer is *no*. They should apologize, indeed, but the apology should not imply they are seeking forgiveness. Perhaps they can lighten the moment by telling the child a story about a similar injustice that happened to one of them as children. Anyone who does not suffer from chronic I Take Myself Too Seriously syndrome can come up with something along those lines and make it funny.

Actually, a mistake of this sort gives the parents an ideal opportunity to instruct the child as to the meaning and significance of a reputation: to wit, if you develop a reputation for doing something improper and then something occurs, people are likely to decide that you did it.

Someone might protest that while the preceding is certainly true, to assume guilt without hard evidence of proof is not only un-American but also might cause psychological trauma. In fact, it is very American to hold someone who is suspected of committing a crime in custody until guilt or innocence is proven. That's the way our legal system works. Please keep in mind that I'm not suggesting the child be beaten or locked in a crawl space, but simply grounded until the missing item or items are restored: a quite painless procedure, although not to the typical child's liking. At the very least, if Shelly did not commit the deed, she will be highly motivated to help find the missing property.

As to the matter of psychological trauma, everyone, at some time or another, is held responsible for something he or she did not actually do. While being tortured for a crime you didn't commit would probably be psychologically traumatic, being restricted to your home at age four for a theft you didn't perpetrate is unlikely to leave any scars. It behooves parents to keep in mind that this is not a perfect pain-free world. In fact, a case could be made that growing up in an artificially "perfect" world created by one's parents might cause great psychological trauma when the person in question, as an adult, discovers the truth.

So the next time you hold your child responsible for something you later discover he or she did not do, by all means apologize but please don't grovel, weep, compensate the child with a new toy, or otherwise make a big deal of it, because it isn't. It's just the way the cookie crumbles sometimes. Sweep up the crumbs and go forward to your next mistake.

Q: *I have a friend whose five-year-old daughter is an only child. My children adore the ground she walks on even though she's a spoiled brat. She screams at her parents when she doesn't get her way, always has to be first at everything, is bossy, and cheats at games so she can always win. I limit the time my children are allowed to play with her. Are there other ways I can discourage the friendship? To be honest, I can't understand why my kids even like her!*

A: When our daughter, Amy, was in elementary school, she had a friend who was absolutely obnoxious toward her parents. She sassed them, openly defied them, and even called them names. The parents did nothing but act dramatically exasperated. Willie and I quickly noticed it was difficult for Amy to play with this child without becoming infected. We decided not to interfere with the relationship, feeling Amy needed to learn to resist negative peer influence, and the earlier the better. We told her she could play with her friend all she wanted, but the minute we saw her imitate the child's misbehavior and disrespect, we were going to punish her by sending her to her room for the remainder of the day. As I recall, it only took two or three such confinements before Amy was able to play with this child without becoming her twin. As a general rule, I recommend that parents not interfere with their children's friendships unless those friendships constitute some real and present danger. Your children will probably always have friends you don't particularly like. You need to get used to it.

Q: *How should I deal with my children's friends who are often rude and ill mannered to my children, husband, and myself? Recently, for example,* *my nine-year-old daughter hosted a sleepover with six girls, one of whom made rude comments throughout the evening ("I hate cake," "You are copying that from my birthday," "I don't like that game"), threw gifts on the floor, and left without a thank-you. This child tells my daughter we are mean because we insist on good manners. Is it proper for me to correct a child who is a guest in my home?*

A: It is, but if you do so, you had better prepare yourself for an angry call from one of the child's parents, a permanent cold shoulder from both of the child's parents, the rumor that you are mean to children who come into your home, or all of the above.

Unfortunately, all too many of today's parents—the overwhelming majority, I sense—seem to think that such things as learning how to play soccer or a musical instrument and acquiring a "martial art" are more vital to a child's development than learning good manners. I happen to be a hopeless, albeit contented, throwback who believes good manners are more important even than good grades. Good manners are a usually reliable sign of good character, and while I have known of people with good grades who, as adults, made messes of their lives, I have never known a person of good character who did likewise.

Today's parents tend to think child-rearing is all about the individual child, as opposed to culture building. This extreme focus on the child—tunnel vision, if you will—causes the typical parent to become extremely defensive when someone implies his or her child is not immaculate. Gone are the days, unfortunately, when it was safe for an adult to correct any child and there was a sense of community where child-rearing was concerned.

The risks aside, I think it is right and proper, under certain circumstances, for a responsible adult to correct someone else's child. Those circumstances are when the child's parent is present but obviously not aware of the child's misbehavior or when the child is in someone else's home. In the latter instance, it is appropriate for the host to correct a child even when the child's parent is present and aware of the child's behavior, if the parent is obviously not going to do the correcting in person (which is all too likely these days). The lord and lady of the manor have every right to define and insist upon proper behavior in their domain.

To take your example of the boorish six-year-old, it would have been perfectly appropriate for you to say, "It is impolite to come into someone else's home and complain about the food or anything else the hosts provide for you. I don't think your mother and father would approve of your behavior, and neither do I. When you are in my home, I insist that you be well behaved and polite. Do I hear an apology?" If the child refused to apologize, I would call her parents and ask that they come and take her home, explaining that she is "not having a good behavior day."

If the child's parent was present but "choked" on correcting the child, a brief, but straightforward reprimand, as in, "We do not behave that way in our home, and I want you to obey our rules while you are our guest" should suffice. That gives the child's parent the opportunity to support you, which is the likelihood. But then again, one never knows anymore.

If, as a child, I had caused my host to reprimand me in front of my parents, they would have punished me later. Today, a reprimanded boy's parents might buy him ice cream on the way home in order to soothe the injury to his self-esteem. After all, Dare to Discipline Disorder (with a nod to my friend and colleague, Dr. James Dobson) is rampant these days.

Q: *Our eight-year-old smacks horribly when he is eating. We have tried nagging, threatening, and sending him away from the table. We obviously are not doing something right. It's driving us slowly insane, not to mention ruining the atmosphere of our meals together.*

A: When Eric, our thirtysomething married corporate pilot son, was about your son's age, he drove us crazy at every meal by slurping his drink. He'd pick up his glass, hold it horizontally to his mouth, and then try to suck the liquid up the side. That's what it looked and sounded like, anyway. Our family meals would be interrupted, every few minutes, with this loud, wet *"slurrrrrrrrrrrrrrp!"*

that sounded like that suction thing the dentist uses to keep your mouth free of fluid while you're pinned in the chair.

As you're doing with your young smacker-in-residence, Willie and I nagged, threatened, sent Eric away from the table, and even offered to buy him expensive things if he'd stop torturing us. Nothing worked.

Around that time that I came up with my "three strikes, you're out" method of curtailing behavior problems with tickets, a variation of the old Boy Scout demerit system. After identifying a specific behavior problem—be it tantrums, whining, ignoring instructions, interrupting conversations, whatever—the parents would cut three rectangular tickets from colored cardboard and clip them to the refrigerator. The child in question began each day with the same three tickets. Every time the specified misbehavior occurred, the parents took a ticket and (this is optional) sent the child to time-out for ten minutes or so. When, on any given day, the child lost the third ticket, he or she spent the rest of the day in the bedroom and went to bed immediately after supper.

The success parents in my practice were having with this simple technique caused me to think that maybe a modified version would help Eric become more aware of his slurping and, therefore, control it. So I made three tickets and put them at the top of Eric's place setting, explaining that when he slurped, I'd no longer nag or even mention it. Instead, I'd just reach over and take a ticket. Each ticket represented thirty minutes off his normal bedtime of nine o'clock. If he lost one ticket, his bedtime became eight-thirty; two tickets, eight; and so on.

Several early bedtimes later, Eric was no longer slurping. We kept the tickets on the table for a while, just to make sure he didn't have a relapse, and then let him go "ticket free." Every once in a while, he'd slip, but a brief "Do you need your tickets at tonight's meal?" would straighten him right out.

This method can be modified to deal with a variety of discipline issues, helping children become aware of what they are doing and providing them with a consequence that motivates them to bring it under control. Remember, folks, you can't talk, nag, cajole, or threaten a child into controlling misbehavior. The only thing that persuades is a *consequence*, and the more matter-of-factly the consequence is delivered, the more effective it will be.

Q: *Do you have any ideas on how to stop two children, ages ten and eight, from bickering constantly with each other?*

A: If you have more than one child, a certain amount of bickering is inevitable, but when clashes between the kids become the rule rather than the exception, it's time to take action. Not the action of trying to determine who started it, either, because nothing fuels this kind of family feud like a parent who decides the kids need a referee. The secret to keeping sibling conflict to a minimum lies in making the two (or more) children involved equally responsible for the problem. Here's how to do just that.

On a sheet of paper, draw a large rectangle and divide it into ten smaller boxes (two rows of five). Starting with the upper left box, number the boxes from 10 down to 1 (in the lower right box). Then, select five privileges the children enjoy and write the name of the privilege in each of boxes 5 through 1. For example, you might put RIDING BIKE in box 5, PLAYING OUTSIDE in box 4, HAVING FRIENDS OVER in box 3, WATCHING TV in box 2, and REGULAR BEDTIME in box 1.

Show the chart to the children and say, "Your bickering and arguing is disturbing the peace of the family. This chart will help you learn to solve your differences quietly and without involving us. Every Monday morning, we will put it on the refrigerator door, where it will stay for the next week. Every time you let your bickering disturb one or both of us—and that includes when one of you complains to us about the other—we will mark off a number, beginning with ten. The first five numbers, ten through six, are free, meaning there is no penalty for losing them. But the last five boxes have things you like to do written in them. When you lose one of these numbers, you also lose the privilege that goes with it for the rest of the week. For example, when you lose number five, you both lose riding your bikes. When you lose number four, neither of you can play outside, and so on. Every Monday, a new chart goes up, you have your privileges back, and we start fresh."

Be sure to point out to the children that they are held equally responsible for bickering that violates your new disturbing-the-peace ordinance. Rather than trying to determine who started what, you penalize them both. Remember that you aren't forbidding arguing, just noisy arguing.

Once the chart is up, if they shatter your peace by yelling at one another or asking you to referee, simply say, "Because you can't seem to solve this problem without disturbing me, I'm marking off [the next number]. Now, I suggest you find a quiet way to handle your differences before you lose another one."

Suddenly, the children have cause for cooperation, and within a couple of weeks you should notice a distinct change for the better. In subsequent charts, the number of freebies can, and should, be reduced to an eventual minimum of two. Keep the chart in force for a few months, because it takes at least that long for behavior change to become permanent.

Q: *My eight-year-old son, Smitty, has been enrolled in Suzuki violin lessons since kindergarten. He likes his teacher and the opportunities for performing and seems to take pride in playing well. What he doesn't like is practice. He hates it, and has from day one. From reading your book, I know how you approached the piano practice problem with your daughter, Amy. I'm unwilling to take that path because, to my way of thinking, a music education is not optional.*

Suzuki method stresses parent participation. Consequently, I supervise Smitty's practice, during which he unfailingly act cross and ugly. In response, I feel angry and resentful, and practice becomes an ordeal for us both. I've tried various rewards and punishments, including having him pay for his own lessons, to encourage a better attitude on his part, but nothing has worked. What I need from you is some way to help Smitty be more pleasant, so I can be pleasant, and we can enjoy this thirty or so minutes together.

A: Since receiving your letter, I've talked to several others parents whose children are enrolled in Suzuki violin and also to a former Suzuki teacher. The parents all confirmed that, yes, parents are practically required to supervise practice. The former teacher, however, shook her head in dismay and told me that parent involvement was not as much stressed when the Suzuki method was first introduced to this country.

Who made the decision that Smitty should take violin? If it was you, why should Smitty take responsibility for that decision? If it was Smitty, and he likes his lessons and likes his teacher, why not let the teacher deal with whether he practices or not? I suspect that if you weren't involved, and Smitty could approach his practice with complete autonomy, he would practice somewhat less but enjoy it more. In the long run, he would probably make more progress. In the event he decides he doesn't want to practice, and the teacher won't continue with him unless he does, one can only conclude that the violin is not for Smitty. Maybe he's destined to become a rock 'n' roll star.

The tone of your letter says you've made your son's violin practice some sort of test. Of your authority? Of your parenting skills, perhaps? If so, you're bound to lose, sooner or later. I guarantee that with enough strategically applied force you can push violin practice down Smitty's throat. I also guarantee that, should you succeed, you'd better prepare yourself for future power struggles that are bigger and far more disruptive than this one.

If I were you, I'd stop being my own worst enemy. This Suzuki violin thing, in the grander scheme of a lifetime, just isn't worth it. I'd tell Smitty that learning an instrument is part of his education, but that whether he does his homework or not is his business, to be dealt with by his teacher. If he decides to practice, fine. If not, so be it. If he decides to practice and needs your help, let him ask for it. If he asks for it and then seems to resent it, get the message and get going.

25

Divorce

EVEN THOUGH AMERICA'S rate of divorce has slowed within recent years, it's estimated that nearly half of all children born in the 1990s will spend some time in a single-parent household. Early research into the effects of divorce on children tended to characterize them as victims of "broken homes." It was taken for granted that these children would suffer psychologically.

Newer research has shed additional light on the impact of divorce on children. We now know that the divorce experience is profoundly different from one child to another and is influenced by such things as age, gender, birth order, and socioeconomic status.

Looking closely at the various stresses affecting divorced families, researchers now conclude that the risk to children stems more from stressful family situations than the act of divorce. They find that the level of discord between parents is a more accurate predictor of later problems than the separation itself.

Although divorce is almost always painful for children, it creates fewer problems than does continuing to live in the midst of a bad marriage. It's been shown that the lower the level of parental conflict before and after a separation, the better the children's overall adjustment. When conflict continues following a separation, it's almost inevitable that children will become embroiled, if not as pawns then as mediators. Either role puts the child's emotional health at great risk.

Regarding the often hotly contested issue of custody, children whose parents perpetuate bitter conflict after a divorce are probably not going to benefit psychologically from joint custody. Not surprisingly, children whose parents work out a relatively amicable divorce are relatively unaffected by the specifics of the custody arrangement.

In cases where one parent has primary custody (usually the mother), the child's successful adjustment is very much a function of how successfully the custodial parent adjusts.

In general, however, boys have greater difficulty adjusting to divorce than do girls. In particular, boys are more likely than girls to react to the stresses of divorce with inappropriate social behavior or depressed school performance or both.

Since only 10 percent of children in single-parent households live primarily with their fathers, many psychologists believe that boys have more problems because they lack the consistent influence of a male role model. This explanation is supported by the finding that girls living primarily with their fathers tend to experience comparable adjustment difficulties.

These gender-specific findings have caused psychologists to question the traditional assumption that mothers should be given the benefit of the doubt where custody is concerned. It appears that the standard arrangement wherein mothers retain primary custody may not be generally best for boys, but more research is needed to determine whether this is more of a factor at certain ages than at others.

Speaking of age, divorce tends to be hardest on kids between the ages of seven and thirteen. Some researchers think this is because young school-age children are old enough to understand the concept of divorce, but not old enough to understand and deal with the emotional issues involved. In addition, a preschool child tends to invest security in the primary caregiver, usually the mother, whereas an older child's security is more invested in the family as a *unit*. For both reasons, young school-age children are more vulnerable to the stresses of divorce.

It's interesting to note, however, that teens in single-parent households often show more independence, responsibility, and maturity than their peers. It appears that divorce can, in some cases, be a strengthening experience for a child, especially if the child can make a successful adjustment to adolescence.

In summary, the evidence overwhelmingly suggests that divorcing parents should avoid prolonged legal battles and make every effort to resolve their anger and establish reasonably good communication with each other. Otherwise, a complicated and stressful time in a child's life will be made even more difficult.

Q: *My wife and I have decided to separate and divorce. What's the best way to tell the kids, ages seven and five?*

A: Telling children that you've decided to separate is never easy, and reaching agreement on what to tell them can be especially difficult when you haven't been able to agree on much of anything lately. Nevertheless, this is a time for parents to set their animosities aside and work together. It's one of the most important conversations parents can ever have with their children, so it's vital that it be done properly.

With that in mind, here are some guidelines for parents to follow when telling children about the decision to separate or divorce.

- Tell them together. Neither parent should be excused or excluded from this important conversation. Even if it wasn't exactly a joint decision, you should inform the children jointly.

- Don't inform the children until your decision is final. Telling children "We're thinking of separating," or words to that effect, will only upset them and make them tremendously anxious. Don't ask the children their opinions about the decision, either. Inform, don't ask permission.

- Wait until a day or two before the actual separation to tell the children. Make your decision, make your arrangements, then tell the children and go through with it. The more time there is between breaking the news to the kids and the separation, the harder they will work to try to keep the two of you together.

- Ideally, the day you tell them should be a nonschool day, but if that's not possible or convenient, keep them out of school. One of the worst things you can do is tell the children and then send them off to worry for the rest of the day at school or day care.

- Don't improvise! Decide beforehand exactly what you're going to tell the children and stick to the program. The more you stumble over or surprise each other, the more confused and upset both you and the children will become. It's a good idea to outline the conversation. Decide what topics you're going to cover, what you're going to say, and who's going to say it. After preparing your outline, rehearse the conversation. This minimizes the likelihood of surprises.

- Anticipate what questions the kids may ask and have your answers ready. Careful planning of this sort demonstrates to the children that you're confident of the decision and helps them feel more secure about it as well.

- Keep the actual conversation short and to the point. There's really no reason to let it last longer than a few minutes, five at the most. And no speeches, please! As Detective Joe Friday of *Dragnet* used to say, "Just the facts, ma'am." Give the children time to ask questions, but don't hesitate to call *time* if their questions become repetitive or too personal.

- Don't editorialize. Tell the children "what," but keep your explanations simple and brief. The best explanation of all is simply, "Things haven't worked out the way we planned, and we think it's best we no longer live together." The children should also hear that you believe it's a good decision that will, in the long run, work out well for everyone. Under no circumstances should you say things like "We don't love each other anymore." Nor should one parent make the other out to be the villain, as in "Your mother has decided she doesn't love me anymore and wants me to move out."

- Be prepared for the worst possible reaction. Sometimes children take these things well, sometimes they don't. If a child becomes hysterical, you must be prepared to step in with authority and restore control.

- Reassure the children that nothing has changed about your love for them. In this time of upheaval, it's important for children to know that certain things aren't changing and never will. In other words, help them understand that even though you are no longer going to be husband and wife, you're still going to be Mom and Dad.

- Let them know what custody and visitation arrangements you've decided upon. This is one area where the children may want to have some input. Regardless, this is neither the time nor the place for a discussion of such a sensitive subject. Later, when things have calmed down, you can solicit their opinions about custody and visitation issues, but this is the wrong time to let them have the floor where such things are concerned. The children should also know that although the parent with primary custody is going to be making the everyday decisions, major decisions will still be made jointly.

Q: *After twelve years of marriage, my husband and I are separating with every intention of making it final. We bear no ill will toward one another, however, and want to do what's best for our two boys, ages seven and four. Since both of us will continue to live in the same town, and since the kids have good relationships with both of us, we have talked about joint custody. Neither of us feels comfortable with depriving the other of time with them, so we will probably settle upon an arrangement that gives us both equal time with them. We want your advice on how to split the kids' time as well as how visitation should be handled.*

A: You're probably going to regret asking me, because I am generally opposed to custody arrangements of the type you two are considering.

The matter of child custody is one that should be resolved solely in terms of the best interests of the children. Split-custody agreements, however, are usually drawn with the interests of the parents uppermost in mind.

In my experience, the parents are wanting either to be "fair" to one another, to avoid conflict over the issue of custody, or to minimize feelings of guilt over having broken up the family. From this perspective, split custody is mistakenly viewed as the most rational and democratic of all custody options, when in fact it is potentially the most unstable and disruptive.

A broken home is an imperfect solution to an imperfect situation. Likewise, there are no perfect custody arrangements, but some are better than others. Before I proceed any further, I should say that I'm sure there are some split-custody situations out there that are the best of all possible arrangements for everyone involved. But show me one that was arrived at by putting children's interests first, and I'll show you ten that were arrived at by parents seeking to protect their own interests.

I must also acknowledge the danger inherent to speaking in generalities. In the final analysis, the answer to "What's the best custody arrangement for us, and especially the children?" is an individual matter. What's best for the Smiths may not be best for the Joneses. So when I say that, in general, split custody is not a desirable situation, I mean exactly that—in general.

What's so undesirable about it? More often than not, split-custody agreements interfere with the formation of stable peer relationships, reduce discretionary time, disrupt academics, and result in a lack of continuity with respect to discipline, routines, and responsibilities. As such, they are destabilizing, stressful, and harmful to a child's sense of security. I call it the Suitcase Kid syndrome.

Divorce is unsettling and uprooting enough for a child without the additional uprootedness of split custody. The alternative is a traditional custody arrangement, involving a primary parent and a primary place of residence. As for visitation with the noncustodial parent, it should be regular and predictable.

When your children are old enough to participate in and accept responsibility for a decision to split custody, discuss the option among yourselves. Until then, I encourage you to put the children's interests before your own when deciding the custody terms.

Q: *My husband and I separated several months ago. Ever since then, our usually outgoing happy four-year-old daughter has been clinging and whiny. She wants to be with me all the time, which can be extremely annoying, but if I tell her to stop following me around, she begins to cry. Almost every day, she asks if her daddy is coming back. He's not, and that's my choice, but I'm worried that the truth will upset her even more. What should I be doing to help her through this crisis?*

A: Following a separation, young children will often cling almost desperately to the remaining parent. Preschoolers—boys as well as girls—tend to be more dependent upon their mothers than their fathers. Nevertheless, your husband's presence in the home was essential to your daughter's picture of the family as a constant, unchanging unit. His departure altered this picture, disrupting her sense of how the world works. To reduce her anxiety, she clings to you, her remaining parent, as if to say, Don't you leave me too!

This is no doubt an extremely vulnerable time for you as well. Your security has been turned upside down, and your emotional resources are stretched to their limits. Under the circumstances, it may be difficult for you to respond patiently to your daughter's intense, often overpowering need for reassurance. So, if it hasn't already, a vicious circle may be developing: The more anxious you are, the more anxious your daughter becomes. The more insecure she acts, the more anxious you become, and so on.

If you feel yourself to be caught up in this circle, it may be wise for you to see an experienced family counselor. A competent professional can help stabilize your new family situation.

Under the circumstances, it isn't unusual for a child to regress to behaviors typical of earlier stages of growth, behaviors associated with safety and security. Your daughter's clinging is one example of this. She's asking for reassurance that you alone are capable of meeting her needs. And whether you realize it or not, you are.

Let your daughter know that there are times for closeness and times when both of you need to be in different places, doing different things. If you don't want her sitting on your lap or following you around, be clear and firm about it. If she cries, show her a comfortable place to do her crying in. Giving her unlimited access to you, while it's what she wants, isn't what she needs and will only make matters worse.

Answer her questions clearly and honestly. By no means should you editorialize about the separation. Just stick to the facts. Tell her that Daddy isn't coming back to live with you, but make no attempt to explain the reasons why. Tell her what role her daddy will continue to play in her life, and remember that he will continue to play a role in your life as well. In the long run, the best thing for your daughter is two parents who do their best to put aside the animosities that contributed to their breakup and make every effort to communicate often and well.

Q: *Three years ago, my husband and I divorced. Our son, six, sees his daddy two weekends a month and during holidays. The problem is that whenever I discipline Kevin or tell him he can't have something he wants, he becomes furious with me. He tells me he hates me and wants to live with his daddy. Several friends have said this is just a manipulation and not to let it bother me, but I don't understand why he says it so much.*

A: He says it because you believe it. When you stop believing a six-year-old knows which parent is best suited to meeting his needs, he will stop saying it. Relax. Nearly all children say things of this sort sometime. In my years on the front lines, I've heard them all, ranging from that timeless standard "I hate you!" (played in the key of screech) to the slightly more up-tempo "You're the meanest daddy in the world" (sho-bop-sho-bop). So what? Nothing, that's what.

Children are masters of exaggeration. Under the influence of frustration, they can blow the most insignificant event completely out of proportion. Why take "I hate you" any more seriously than "I hate Rusty!" ("He pushed me!") What makes the former more final, more meaningful, than the latter?

Children are mountain makers. They can't control their emotions any better than they can control their lives. And for these reasons, they need parents in control of their *own* emotions and circumstances. The mountains children build crumble quickly—unless adults seem impressed by them. You're making too much of Kevin's threats. Your anxiety has put power in his hands, too much power for a six-year-old to handle.

Far from his manipulating *you*, you are inadvertently manipulating *him* into believing he really rather would be with his daddy. If the words are powerful enough to make Mom cringe, perhaps they are true.

The next time Kevin says he wants to live with his daddy, look him in the eye and say, "You live with *me*, and you will do what I tell you to do." If he persists in his fury, send him to his room immediately, with instructions not to come out until he's calm and ready to cooperate.

Parenthood is not a popularity contest.

Q: *I am a divorced father and have visitation time with my six-year-old daughter every other weekend. For the first year or so after her mother and I separated, Angie always seemed excited to see me when I picked her up. During our time together, she usually stayed close to me, wanting and giving lots of affection. Within the last few months, however, she seems to want more attention from women we're around than from me. If we're over at my parents' house, for instance, Angie sticks close to her grandmother and wants to be included in everything she's doing. If she has a hurt or needs help with something, to Grandmother she goes. She's much the same way if we're with my girlfriend. This probably sounds ridiculous, and I feel ridiculous saying it, but I'm jealous. Is Angie's behavior normal or does it mean I'm doing something wrong? If I am, how can I correct it?*

A: You're not doing anything wrong.

Sometime around age three or four, children realize that boys and girls are different. A year or so later, they further realize that boys grow up to be men and girls grow up to be women. These revelations define a new stage in the development of self-concept for a child, because implicit in all this learning is the understanding that boys and girls not only look different but *act* different as well.

Consequently, boys begin looking more toward their fathers and other men for tips on proper boy behavior, and girls to their mothers and other women for tips on proper girl behavior. The amount of attention a child formerly gave to and wanted from any particular parent was defined by a number of factors, including the time that parent spent in the home and whether the child perceived him or her as primarily nurturing or punitive. Now, however, children clearly begin expressing more interest in the same-sex parent.

This process is known as *identification* and lasts for upward of two years. During this time, children pay close attention to the parent who is more "like" them. In addition, at this age the boy will be more interested in men in general and the girl will be more interested in women.

Angie is nothing but normal. If anything, she must feel very secure in her relationship with you to be able to give attention so freely to other adults in your presence.

My advice is to let the situation run its course, as it will in a couple of years' time. If you express your jealousy, it will only confuse her and make it difficult for her to be open with and close to you. As Angie nears adolescence, she will begin seeking more attention from you as a means of testing her newly acquired femininity.

Having a daughter who went through these stages, I can assure you it's well worth the wait.

Q: *I have been divorced from my ex-husband for nearly ten years. We've both remarried but I have custody of our son, who is now thirteen. His visits with his dad, which occur fairly often, are like a vacation. He has* *very few responsibilities, and because there are no children in his father's second marriage, he is treated like royalty by father and stepmother alike. Now he tells me he wants to go live with his father, which is like a slap in the face after ten years of being the responsible parent. Sooner or later, he's bound to become disillusioned at discovering some of his father's faults, which include a bad temper and a tendency to blame the closest person when something goes wrong. Both my mother and my husband say I should let him go, but I'm not so sure. What do you say?*

A: I'm not going to attempt to tell you what to do, because I don't know enough facts even to arrive at an opinion. But I'll tell you a story, for what it's worth.

Once upon a time, there was a boy whose parents were divorced when he was four years old. When he was six, his mother remarried and they moved to a big city more than a thousand miles away from his father, who had also remarried.

From that time on, until he was fourteen, his only visits with his father occurred during the summer. Compared with living with his mother and stepfather, his visits with his father were like heaven. He did pretty much what he pleased, and his father bought him just about anything he wanted. The older he got, the more he believed that his father could do no wrong and all his problems would be solved if he could only live with him all the time.

You see, at his mother's, there were rules and he had lots of chores and he didn't get along with his stepfather well at all. He began to think of himself as a boy Cinderella—"Cinder-fella," if you will. The more he thought about it, life with Mom looked worse and worse while his imagined life with Dad got better and better.

When he was fourteen and at his father's for the summer, the boy told his dad he wanted to live with him all the time. His dad said that was okay with him. Whoopee! Now all the boy's troubles were over!

He wrote his mom a letter, telling her of his decision. He expected her to call out the National Guard to try and get him back. Instead, he got a letter from her:

Dear Son:

I think I can understand why you've decided to live with your father. I'm not mad and I don't think you're making a mistake. In fact, I think you're at the age when you need to spend more time with your father. We will all miss you and we hope you will come visit us during the summer, but if you don't want to for a while, that's all right. We love you and want you to know that if you ever want to come home, you can, no questions asked. Be good.

Love,
Mom

To make a long story short, the year the boy lived with his dad was not all he had imagined it would be. Things were different but, when everything was tallied, no better. At the end of the year, the boy decided it would be best if he went back to live with his mother and stepfather. Just like they promised, they asked him no questions, which was probably best, because he wouldn't have known the answers.

I was the boy in the story. I didn't know it then, but I do now, that letting me go was the hardest thing my mother ever did. Of all the sacrifices she made for me, that was the biggest and the one for which I respect her the most. Had she not been so understanding, had she let go with anger instead of love, I would never have been able to change my mind and go back home.

You obviously harbor animosity toward your ex-husband, perhaps for good reason, but the fact that you don't like him doesn't mean he isn't or won't be a good parent. Given your son's intense desire to go live with his dad, it may be best for all concerned if you don't stand in his way. Letting go will be one of the most difficult things you've ever done. If you do it like a winner, however, no one will lose, and *that's* what's really important.

Q: *I am the divorced and remarried mother of a five-year-old boy who spends every other weekend with his father. Until recently, Paul has looked forward to these visits. Lately, though, he's been telling us he doesn't want* *to go and has thrown extremely dramatic temper tantrums when we have forced him.*

According to his father, however, Paul stops crying shortly after they pull away from the house and is acting his normal, happy self by the time they get on the road.

When he returns, he seems fine, although he doesn't volunteer much information about the visit or seem eager to talk about it. What little he does say tells us that the visits are not very exciting—most of the weekend is spent watching television, with an occasional trip to the park.

Asked why he doesn't want to go, Paul shrugs and says, "I just don't want to." We are certain that nothing inappropriate is happening during the visits but are worried that we may be damaging him psychologically by forcing him to go.

Should we continue to force, or should we let him make this decision? If he's not old enough to decide, please tell us how to handle his resistance. You probably need to know that Paul has formed an excellent relationship with my new husband and seems to be growing increasingly attached to him.

A: If there were any indication that Paul were being subjected to anything inappropriate during his visits, I would advise you to suspend them until you could look more closely at the situation. In this case, that doesn't sound necessary. The explanation for Paul's behavior is probably as simple as this: His visits with Dad are boring. Increasingly, your new husband is meeting Paul's need for a male role model and father figure.

And so, given the choice between staying where his heart is, as opposed to going where the action isn't, Paul makes the logical one. He can't articulate his feelings, he just doesn't want to go. When you won't let him have his way, he becomes upset. In turn, you become unsure of yourself and begin to waver. Paul senses your indecision and his tantrum escalates, which is what tantrums do when they are not handled firmly.

You should not allow Paul the privilege of this decision. He is hardly old enough to appreciate the importance of spending time with his father on a regular basis.

In advance of his next visit with his dad, sit down with your son and tell him something to this effect: "Paul, you have been telling us you don't want to visit your dad. When we make you go, you throw a tantrum. We think it's important for you to spend time with him, and the decision of whether you go or stay is up to us. We have decided that you must go. If there is something you don't like about the visits, you can tell us and we will talk about it. But you are going with your dad, whether you throw a tantrum or not." Short, direct, and authoritative, which is just what Paul needs, no more and no less.

When Dad comes to get him, if Paul starts to complain, remind him of the conversation and tell him firmly that he must go, no matter what. Then follow through, even if that means carrying him kicking and screaming to the car. I believe his tantrums will stop as soon as you take the bull by the horns.

I don't think your role should stop there, however. Someone needs to tell Paul's father that the visits are probably boring and give him guidance concerning his responsibilities. Maybe he doesn't know what Paul likes and doesn't like and needs you to tell him.

In other words, the father–son relationship needs a little shove, and it sounds like you're in the best position to give it.

Q: *I am a divorced single mother. My daughter is fourteen years old. Occasionally things come up with which I feel I need my ex-husband's support.*

In the past, when I have felt she needed discipline from him, I have called and asked him to incorporate that into one of their visitation weekends. This has happened several times. The last time I asked him for his support he refused, saying he wasn't going to be the heavy anymore.

My ex-husband feels that when a discipline problem comes up in my home, I should handle it. Likewise, when a discipline problem comes up in his home, he said he would handle it. I disagreed with him, pointing out that she is just as much his daughter as mine, but I couldn't change his mind.

What is your opinion?

A: I agree with each of you to a certain extent. For the most part, you should each handle the day-to-day discipline of your daughter in your own homes. There will also be times, however, when you should both be involved in whatever discipline the situation demands. But when those occasions arise, I agree with your ex-husband that you shouldn't ask him to be the main disciplinarian.

It's completely appropriate for you to request his support (and vice versa) when you feel your daughter needs to be confronted by both of you. After all, you're no longer husband and wife, but you're still father and mother. Even though you don't live together, you should still work together where your daughter's upbringing is concerned. This is especially necessary when major decisions need to be made, including major decisions concerning discipline. And the more your daughter sees the two of you working together, the more secure she'll feel and the less chance there will be of her trying to work both sides of the fence to her advantage.

When a serious situation arises concerning her behavior, instead of asking your ex-husband to handle it during his next visitation, request that he join you in confronting your daughter with the problem. First, arrange a time when just the two of you can get together to discuss the problem, either face-to-face or over the phone. Then, once you've decided how you're going to handle it, arrange a second time when the two of you can discuss the situation with your daughter.

Let her see that where discipline is concerned, the two of you are on the same wavelength. This approach provides you with the support you will sometimes need from your ex-husband but relieves him of having to play the heavy.

Q: *After twelve years of marriage, we have decided to get a divorce. We recently read an article that said that children from broken homes are at great risk for developing emotional problems. Now we're not so sure about our plans. Even though we both know we would be happier apart than living together, we aren't willing to do anything for ourselves that would permanently damage our children, ages ten, seven, and four. Can you help us solve our dilemma?*

A: What you read is true, as far as it goes. Children of divorce are at increased risk for emotional, social, and academic difficulties. Two of your children are within the range of highest risk, which lies between seven and thirteen.

What the research doesn't tell us, however—and, in fact, will never be able to tell us—is how these children would have fared had their parents stayed together. That's the "children of parents who probably should have gotten a divorce but didn't" group. Although we will never be certain how these kids are affected, we can base a certain amount of speculation on the findings of research into the lives of adults who, as children, grew up in dysfunctional families. This includes adult children of alcoholics.

Preliminary findings suggest that, as adults, these kids do even less well than children whose parents divorced. They are likely to enter into codependent relationships themselves, and it is highly likely that they will develop emotional problems. In this way, the seeds of dysfunctionality get handed down from generation to generation.

Keep in mind that for a given individual, research can never tell us what *will* happen. It can only tell us what *has* happened. Whether might becomes fact depends on the interplay of more variables than researchers will ever be able to identify, much less allow for as control factors.

Research also generates dilemmas of its own. For example, it finds that boys generally do better academically and otherwise in the custody of their fathers. However, to routinely give fathers custody of their male children would mean, in many cases, that male and female siblings would be separated. While this might solve one problem, it would create a host of others.

I have always maintained that what is in the best interest of parents is also most likely in the best interest of the children. My parents divorced when I was four years old. Both parents remarried, and with the exception of one year during high school spent with my father, I lived with my mother and stepfather. As a child, I was never aware of suffering as the result of my parents' decision, and as an adult I am absolutely certain they did the right thing for themselves and that I was better off for it.

This is certain: The negative effects of divorce are significantly mitigated when children have regular contact with the noncustodial parent and when parents continue to communicate well concerning the children. While there are no guarantees, the fact that you were concerned enough by what you read to reconsider your decision, that you took time to seek a professional opinion, and that you were willing to make a personal sacrifice suggests that if you go ahead with your original plans, your children will be fine.

Q: *I am divorced and the mother of a five-year-old girl. My ex-husband sees our daughter every other weekend. He has money to do things for her that I simply can't afford, so her time with Daddy is generally very exciting, and I have problems settling her down after every visit. For a day or two, she is moody, irritable, very active, and wants to talk constantly about what "Daddy and I did," which is the last thing I want to hear. She has recently started screaming things like, "I like my daddy better'n you!" and "I wanna live with my daddy!" when she's upset with me. This tears me up, and I don't know how to handle her at these times. I've tried talking calmly, but she can probably tell I'm upset. What do you suggest?*

A: The problems and frustrations you describe are all part of "single-mother syndrome."

You resent the freedom and the range of options your ex-husband enjoys in his relationship with your daughter. You resent the fact that he can afford to fill their weekends together with goodies but doesn't have to invest any of his time toward the day-to-day responsibilities required of a full-time parent. The arrangement seems to guarantee that you get all the work while he gets most of the rewards.

So naturally the last thing you want to hear from your daughter is what fun time she has with Daddy. But you will hear it anyway, because she comes back with her batteries fully charged, already looking forward to next time. You may feel like somebody who just fills the gaps between one "holiday" and the next.

It would help if you developed more understanding of your daughter's point of view. For instance, it is common for a child whose parents are divorced to put the absent parent (usually the father) on a pedestal. In the child's eyes, Daddy becomes a heroic figure without fault or blemish. The ideal quickly becomes a substitute for the real. The child appoints herself keeper of the image, which she polishes and keeps spotless from one visit to the next.

This hero worship is quite enough to push any single mother's tolerance over the line. After all, you probably remember Daddy as a genuine unmentionable.

Unfortunately, the more irritated you are with the talk about Daddy and the marvelous things he does, the more defensive and protective your daughter will become about her relationship with him. Furthermore, she will sense the power that Daddy's name commands in her behalf. When things don't go her way, she will let fly with, "I like my daddy better'n you!"

The best thing you could do for yourself is *listen* when your daughter wants to describe her weekend adventures. In fact, don't just listen—ask questions and probe for details. Take control of the conversation so you will be in a position to say, after an appropriate length of time, "Well, that's all very exciting to talk about, and I'm glad you have fun with your daddy. Mommy is going to stop talking now and go finish my magazine, and I want you to go play in your room." In this way, you begin to redefine the terms of your relationship as soon as she comes home.

Accept that she has a glorious time with Daddy. That's the way it should be. You wouldn't wish her a rotten time every two weeks, would you? Furthermore, Dad has a right to take her higher than a kite every time he sees her. Her joy and enthusiasm make being a once-every-two-weeks daddy almost meaningful for him.

The trouble you have managing her after she comes home is not Dad's fault. Your resentment is your own undoing. It incapacitates your authority, drives a wedge between the two of you, and sets up confrontations.

Everything rests on your willingness to lay down the sword and listen. By listening and talking, you invite her to become reinvolved with you and make it less likely that she will carry Daddy's banner around the house. The more interest you show in her, the easier it will be to reestablish control and the more she will appreciate and look forward to the low-key, secure predictability you provide. After all, there really is no place like home, and she knows it.

Q: *My husband and I separated about three months ago but have remained on fairly good terms. The older of our two children, ages eight and four, recently started complaining of things that make us worry that he might be depressed.*

Every so often, for instance, he tells us he thinks "bad thoughts" about one of us getting hurt. He says these thoughts just "pop into his head" without warning. He's a very active, imaginative child who does well in school.

Both he and his brother, who seems oblivious to our separation, spend plenty of time with each of us. Can you give us some idea of what's going on and what we can do to help him?

A: To begin with, there's a distinct difference between an adjustment reaction and depression. When parents separate, children are likely to experience a temporary loss of security.

In this case, your son is probably experiencing fears and anxieties around the issues of loss and abandonment. He may not be able to put his feelings into words, so they take the form of "bad thoughts" that may seem to him almost nightmarish, in terms of both content and his inability to control them. They may indicate a need for him to do more talking about the separation, if not with you, then perhaps with a professional counselor. Up to this point, however, we're talking about an adjustment reaction.

Depression presents a far more serious clinical picture. Typically, a depressed child will exhibit one or more of the following symptoms:

- Deteriorating school performance

- A dramatic personality change, usually marked by moodiness, irritability, fatigue, and withdrawal

- A retreat from social activities

- The relatively sudden onset of provocative attention-seeking behaviors

- Prolonged loss of appetite or sleeplessness

It's impossible, of course, for me to make a diagnosis, but the information provided leads me to believe your son probably isn't depressed. If you have any doubts, however, you should seek a formal evaluation from a psychologist or psychiatrist who specializes in children's mental health issues.

There are two reasons why your eight-year-old has reacted more dramatically to the separation than your four-year-old.

First, the oldest child in a family is almost always the one hardest hit by separation and divorce. This is the child who feels the greatest sense of responsibility for the overall well-being of the family. In this regard it may be helpful, if you haven't done so already, to reassure your son that he had nothing to do with the decision to separate and that he couldn't have done anything to prevent it.

Second, a four-year-old child usually attaches more security to one parent than the other. If that parent is available and meeting the child's security needs in an adequate manner, a four-year-old may not experience any significant loss of security when parents separate. By age six or seven, however, a child will have attached a great deal of security to the fact of parents being together. For this reason, a separation is more likely to hit a child of this age harder than it would have earlier.

26

Adoption

IN THE YEARS SINCE *Parent Power!* was first published, I've become increasingly interested in adoption issues. My interest was first piqued by a mid-1980s *Charlotte Observer* feature story about a woman who had found the son she'd given up for adoption some twenty years earlier. The story gushed about how wonderful it was that these two people had finally been reunited, that their lives were now truly complete, and so on. Little was made of the fact that the birth mother had hired a "search consultant" (aka private detective) to find her child and, that accomplished, simply called him one day to announce, "Hi. I'm your mother." This was, I felt, completely irresponsible. I also felt that the manner in which the story was written cast birth mother and long-since-adopted son as victims of an insensitive system that had conspired to keep them apart from each other.

I began asking questions and discovered that there is a movement afoot to reunite birth parents with their adopted children; that the organizations behind this movement are lobbying for legislation that would force all adoptions to be "open," meaning that the birth parent(s) know the adoptive parents' identities and vice versa; that these organizations are encouraging birth parents to believe and act as if their "rights" supersede those of the child's legal parents. The media give these folks a platform and treat them as victims. Talk-show hosts stage tearful "reunions" on their shows, to the applause of their studio audiences. As a result, adoptive parents are beginning to feel as if they are under siege, that their privacy is threatened, that their children may someday be claimed by someone else and the courts will support the claim.

I wrote a series of articles attacking the philosophy, practices, and motives of the birth-parent movement. As a result, my name showed up on a hit list published by a group calling itself Concerned United Birth parents. I was, they asserted, one of a number of scoundrels who were in need of "education." On the contrary. It is these birth parents who are in need of lessons—in manners, respect, and reality. The children they are so bold as to call "theirs" are not theirs at all. Whatever the circumstances, they gave those children up for adoption, thus relinquishing all parental rights. Those children have but one set of parents—the people who raised them.

Q: *My husband and I have been married for seven years and have a five-year-old daughter. Our original plan was to have two children, but physical problems prevent my getting pregnant again.*

We are thinking about adopting an older, hard-to-place child, perhaps as old as ten. Our reasons for wanting an older child include not only wanting to provide one of these kids with a much-needed home, but also the fact that the waiting period is considerably shorter, by as much as several years.

If we didn't have anyone else to think of but ourselves, we would adopt as soon as possible, but we are somewhat concerned about how this might affect our daughter. She is extremely well adjusted, and we wouldn't want to do anything at this point that would jeopardize her self-esteem.

We have talked with her about it, and she has expressed excitement at the idea, but we aren't convinced that she knows what would be involved. We would appreciate any advice you can give us.

A: I see no problem with the idea of adopting a second child. However, I would definitely advise against adopting a child older than your daughter. One can't help but appreciate your reasons for wanting an older child, but I think things would work out much better in the long run if you bit the bullet and put yourselves on the waiting list for an infant or toddler.

Bringing an older child into your family would, in effect, displace your daughter's status as firstborn. This displacement could be potentially devastating to her security and self-esteem.

A child's personality and self-concept develop, to a significant degree, in response to position in the family. In fact, it's possible to make predictions about personality characteristics on the basis of birth order; firstborn children, for instance, tend to be more responsible and achievement-oriented than children born second or third in the family.

In turn, a child's sense of security is firmly rooted in his or her perception of self and the world, which we've established is intimately related to the child's birth order. So to tamper with a child's position in the family is also to tamper with that child's personality, self-concept, and security. Since a child's self-concept is fairly well established between ages three and four, I would recommend to parents who are considering adopting an older child that they not do so if an already existing child is four or older.

You're right in saying that your daughter cannot possibly understand the consequences to her of suddenly having an older sibling. To her, the idea of having a brother or sister, regardless of age, sounds wonderful. Little does she realize how important being the first and forever oldest child in the family is to her.

The consequences to the older adopted child would not be desirable, either. If the adoption proved disruptive to the life of the family, the adopted child might very well feel responsible. In that case, which is quite likely, the adopted child's self-esteem would also suffer.

Please don't misunderstand me. I'm not saying people shouldn't adopt older children, but simply that, before doing so, they carefully consider not only the needs of existing children in the family but also the needs of the to-be-adopted child.

Q: *We recently adopted a baby boy. The social worker at the agency told us we should make this adoption part of "normal everyday conversation" from day one. She said we should talk to him about adoption long before he understands what it means, so that it won't come as a shock later. She insisted this approach will prevent problems, but common sense tells us to be more low-key. What's your opinion?*

A: Chalk up another one for common sense.

The social worker's advice is considered "conventional wisdom" among adoption professionals. An adoption professional once even told me that, from infancy onward, parents should frequently insert the word *adopted* into bedtime stories and make up songs and nursery rhymes about adoption!

This philosophy springs from a 1964 study done by sociologist H. David Kirk, the author of *Shared Fate*, a book on adoptive relationships. Kirk identified two approaches used by adoptive parents, "acknowledgments of differences" and "rejection of differences." His support of the *acknowledgment* style led to a simplistic belief in the adoption field that adoptive parents who do not regularly proclaim the differences between adoptive and biological parenting are in a perpetual state of denial and are inadvertently hurting their children.

A 1988 study by family therapist Dr. Kenneth Kaye of Northwestern University Medical School offered refreshingly sensible advice to parents of adoptive children: Take a relaxed, middle-of-the-road approach to the adoption issue. Kaye concluded that too much acknowledgment can cause as many problems as rejection. He also found that overacknowledgment can result in the child's eventually feeling *too* different and therefore inferior.

Granted, parents should tell children they are adopted. The best time to introduce the subject is between ages four and five. This is when children begin to realize that life has a definite beginning and a definite end. As a result, they begin asking questions about where babies come from. Children of this age are not only curious but also intellectually capable of understanding the difference between being born into a family and being adopted.

However, talking about the adoption nearly every day and incorporating the word into story and song is as unnecessary as making a daily effort to remind a child that you are his or her birth parents. Making a mountain out of the adoption molehill also enlarges the possibility of what I term the "adoption myth": the mistaken belief that all problems that arise in the parent–child relationship are related in some way to the adoption.

I once saw an adoptive family in which a young teenage girl was experiencing conflict with her parents. Although the problems were typical of the girl's age, her parents were convinced they were due to "unresolved anger" concerning the adoption. They wanted me to talk with their daughter and help her "work through her feelings."

Although fairly certain the girl was not in need of counseling, I did have one talk with her. I discovered that, while she wasn't angry at having been adopted, she was tired of her parents' constant references to it.

"They want to talk about it all the time," she said, "like it's something weird, you know? Adopted, adopted, adopted! It's all I've heard ever since I can remember. I'm so sick of hearing it I could scream!"

Her parents later told me they were only following advice given them by the adoption agency caseworkers. "Well, you're lucky," I told them.

"How's that?" they asked.

"Because," I said, "despite the fact that you were encouraged to blow the adoption out of proportion, your daughter has managed to keep straight in her own mind that it really isn't any big deal at all."

Q: *Seven years ago, I became pregnant out of wedlock and gave birth to a son. When he was fifteen months old, I married a wonderful man who adopted my son and has a fantastic relationship with him. We now have another son who is three years old. We have not yet told the older boy the facts of his birth but feel that he ought to know. However, several people (friends and relatives) have advised us against telling him, saying it will hurt him or he's still too young. We want to be honest with him, but we're confused. What is your opinion?*

A: He needs to know, he has a right to know, he needs to hear it from you before he figures it out or hears it from someone else, and now is an excellent time to tell him.

A seven-year-old will be able to grasp the subtle complexities of the situation. A child of this age can think more flexibly than a child even two years younger; therefore, he stands less of a chance of becoming confused. A seven-year-old's emotional character is more clearly established and less vulnerable than a younger child's. He is more capable of dealing successfully with emotional conflicts that might temporarily surface when the circumstances of his background are presented to him.

An excellent case can be made for not waiting any longer. Unless old power struggles are still begging for resolution, the early elementary years are relatively calm. There is, however, an upsurge in rebelliousness beginning at nine or ten and building to a peak sometime during early adolescence.

Your child's reaction to finding out he was adopted by one or both parents is likely to be more extreme if you wait until the rebellious period to tell him. He could interpret the delay as an indication of a lack of trust in the relationship. That might be all the excuse he would need to escalate his rebelliousness to an inappropriate and perhaps even deviant extent.

So, having established this as an opportune time to give him the information, I have a few suggestions that might help prevent everyone's going into a tailspin.

First, make sure your son understands the basic facts of conception, pregnancy, and birth and that he knows what *adoption* means. If he isn't clear on these concepts, you need to give him a mini-course in sex education, with an explanation of the different kinds of families (natural, single-parent, blended) and the difference between natural, step, and adoptive parents. Give him examples of people he knows to bring all this into sharper focus and allow several weeks for it to sink in.

Anticipate that he may react by becoming temporarily sullen and withdrawn. There's also a chance that he will exhibit mood swings in which he becomes suddenly angry, accusatory, and more easily frustrated.

It's a good bet that he will throw a few curves into the system to test how well it holds up under any stress he might apply to it. To him it may seem that a lot has changed, including his definition of who he is and how he fits into the family. The news may create some temporary disruptions. If so, acting through the strength and solidarity of your marriage, you must demonstrate to him that nothing has changed. He is the *same* person, in the *same* family, living by the *same* rules, sharing the *same* love as before.

Schedule a family vacation to begin several days after you explain things to him. Use this time together to reaffirm your bonds. The vacation will make it possible for both parents to be available to each other at nearly all times, thus preventing the child from cornering either of you. Any clarifying, disciplining, or comforting that needs to be done can be handled immediately by both of you.

He may have questions about his biological father, including "When can I meet him?" Answer everything in a straightforward and honest way. It is not wise to allow the child to meet the third party immediately. Explain that his biological father has a life, and perhaps even a family, of his own, and that uninvited contacts would invade his privacy.

If your son persists, assure him that you will share the identity of the biological parent later, perhaps after he graduates from high school. By then, he will be old enough to make a reasonably well-thought-out decision about using that information.

Above all else, let him know that *you* are his real parents, *both* of you. Remember, almost anyone can be a mother or father, but only very special people can be mommies and daddies.

27

Classroom Misbehavior

HERE'S AN INTERESTING TALE: A four-year-old—I'll call him Bluto—has a habit of hitting other children in his preschool program. Bluto's teachers try various approaches, none of which work. Their latest attempt involved rewarding him with something special on days when he didn't hit. That didn't work either, which came as no surprise to yours truly. Extending rewards to a child who is misbehaving not only sends the wrong message but may also make matters worse.

At her wits' end, Bluto's mom asks my advice, which I give as follows: When Bluto hits, his teachers should immediately remove him from class, take him to a neutral holding zone, and call her. As soon as she is able, Mom should retrieve Bluto from school and take him home. There, she should confine him to his room for the remainder of the day and put him to bed immediately after supper. During Bluto's rehab, his room should be cleansed of all toys except two (of his choosing) and all electronic entertainment. Mom says she'd do it and get back to me with a progress report.

Several weeks later, I receive an e-mail from Mom, who reports great improvement. Reminding me that Bluto had been hitting on a daily basis, she tells me she's only had to confine Bluto to his room three times in three weeks. She's made a slight change in the plan, however, because when she told Bluto's teachers what I had originally recommended, they expressed disapproval, saying they were sure he didn't *mean* to hit other children. His hitting was "impulsive," they said, "not deliberate," and he should not be punished. So instead of calling Mom when he hits, they inform her of any incidents at pickup. If Bluto has hit, Mom takes him home, confines him to his room, and puts him to bed immediately after supper. The teachers don't know what Mom is doing because she is convinced, and probably rightly so, that if they knew he was being confined to his room they would not give her accurate information.

Actually, I accept the teachers' assertion that most of Bluto's hitting is impulsive. Nonetheless, they are wrong to think he should not be punished. The only way a child learns impulse control is to be punished when the lack thereof produces antisocial behavior—and let's face it, there is nothing more antisocial than hitting. The punishment, furthermore, must be discomforting, because discomfort is motivating. Nothing less will cause Bluto to exert the effort necessary to master his impulses.

Toddlers are antisocial behavior factories. They hit, bite, scream, openly defy authority, snatch things out of other children's hands, and so on. It could be argued that in a toddler this sort of behavior is impulsive, not deliberate. Imagine, however, what the world would be like if adults failed to punish these antisocial outbursts because toddlers "didn't mean it." Come to think of it, the reason many older children today are still behaving like toddlers is because many of today's adults are reluctant to nip antisocial toddler behavior in the bud through the application of firm punishment.

Bluto is just one of an epidemic of children who are suffering from extended toddlerhood syndrome. Instead of supporting his rehabilitation, Bluto's well-intentioned teachers made excuses for him. Had their point of view prevailed, he would have been denied the opportunity to develop self-discipline and improve his social relationships. He might still be hitting five years from now. Good for Bluto's mom that she went ahead and did what was necessary to bring his antisocial outbursts to a halt.

Q: *My son is four years old. He has never been a perfect child and I don't want him to be, but he has always been easy to raise. He misbehaves sometimes, but my husband and I enforce the rules and nothing ever gets out of hand.*

But he gives his teachers at the day-care center a hard time. I don't work, but I put him in a center so he can be with other children. He goes there only in the mornings. Every time I pick him up, his teacher has another story of what he has done. It all seems like such little stuff to us, but she gets upset because it happens so often. For instance, the other day he pulled down his pants on the playground. Last week, he stuck his tongue out at the teacher and then laughed while she chased him around the room.

What I don't understand is why he isn't like this at home. Is he rebelling so he can spend more time with me? Is he not getting enough attention at home? Please tell me what you think I should do.

A: To begin with, children always manage to get enough attention, wherever they are. Some of the attention is positive (praise, interest, enthusiasm, and encouragement) and some is negative (criticism, punishment, reprimands). Children need more positive strokes than negative, but they will work for whatever kind they can get.

It sounds as though you are sensitive to your child's needs. You put him in day care so he can be with other children, and you enforce rules. I would guess he gets many more positive than negative strokes from you and your husband.

Sometimes, however, it's more *fun* to work for negative attention. For instance, wouldn't it be fun to drop your pants and listen to everyone howl and scream? And wouldn't it be fun to have the teacher chase you around the room? This doesn't work out well with every grown-up, but some will go for the bait every time. Your son is not doing anything malicious, he isn't hurting anyone, and he's having loads of fun doing what all the other children (and most adults as well) wish they had the nerve to do.

Call it the class clown syndrome. Once the bug strikes, it's almost impossible to cure. In fact, I doubt this is something that we even *want* to cure. The class clown is blessed with an irrepressible sense of humor, a flair for the absurd, and an imagination that defies convention.

What this all adds up to is a happy and extremely creative child. Happy creative children, if not given enough opportunity to use their talents constructively, will use them any way they can. What is more exciting and creative than to entice a grown-up into your game and then beat her at it? The problem is that some grown-ups can't stand being outdone by a child.

Your son's behavior may be an indication that he is with the wrong age group at the center. Perhaps he would fare better with five-year-olds. Or the program at the center may be too structured for him. Generally speaking, creative children need less structure and more open-ended opportunities to explore, discover, and experiment with the environment. Perhaps a different program is the answer. Shop around and see what other centers have to offer. Or perhaps a day-care program is not the answer to his needs. Look into other possibilities, such as swimming, dancing, gymnastics (tumbling), or art classes.

There is one small point to consider. Dropping your trousers and sticking your tongue out at grown-ups are fun and get everyone's attention; nonetheless, this is not desirable public behavior.

The teacher could ignore the behavior. Unfortunately, ignoring behavior such as this simply doesn't work. There is no way a classroom of four-year-olds isn't going to laugh and squeal when someone's pants come down. Forget about ignoring.

The teacher could put your son in isolation for five minutes whenever this kind of behavior occurs. In this case, however, I doubt whether this alone will work. If your son is bored, he needs more stimulation, and the teacher needs to provide it before he provides it for himself by dropping his pants again. If the teacher cannot give him more opportunity to earn positive strokes, my suggestions about another age group or program should be considered.

If you feel the program is what you want for him and wish to leave him there, ask his teacher to give you a brief daily summary of his misbehavior. Take privileges away at home based on the number of incidents that occur at school. For instance, one incident at school and he can't ride his bike that day. Two incidents, and he can't play his CDs in the evening. But whatever you do, don't offer him any special rewards for being "good." Just hug and kiss him and tell him you're pleased that he's found other ways to have fun. Talk about what those other ways are. After all, what's more special than a parent's love and attention?

A second-grade teacher once asked my advice about one of her students, a seven-year-old girl who, within six weeks of the beginning of school, had managed to walk away with the Outstanding Nuisance of the Second Grade Award by—believe it or not—asking questions.

Indeed, blue-eyed Julia asked, according to the teacher's first estimates, close to a hundred questions a day. This usually patient veteran of thirteen second-grade campaigns was showing all the classic symptoms of a sudden midyear retirement as we stood talking in the hall. She apologized profusely for taking my time with such trivia, but her hands were fluttering in and out of the pockets of her smock like a pair of lunatic hummingbirds.

Just then the classroom door opened and out walked (as I quickly learned) the infamous blue-eyed Julia herself.

"Mrs. Boulderdam?"

Immediately, hands fluttering madly, Mrs. Boulderdam's eyes darted down the hall, measuring, I'm now sure, the distance between where we stood and the front door. For several moments her eyes jumped back and forth between Julia and freedom, finally coming to rest on the child's upturned face.

"Why, yes, Julia, what do you want?" Her lips were stretched into a tight smile over clenched teeth.

"Is this the way to write my name?"

Mrs. Boulderdam tensed, and I thought I saw her hands fluttering toward the child and then quickly back into her smock, but it happened too fast to be sure.

"Yes, Julia," she stammered, "that's the spell you write—make your name"—and then, with great effort—"the way you write your name now go back into the room I'll be there in a minute."

As Julia disappeared through the door, Mrs. Boulderdam looked at me with one of the most pitiful expressions I've ever seen on a grown-up. "Help."

A rough count through the remainder of the day showed Julie was asking between six and ten questions an hour, and her pace never slackened. The really amazing thing was that Mrs. Boulderdam had lasted six days, much less six weeks.

Almost all of Julia's questions were unnecessary, in that she probably knew the answer or could have figured it out. Intelligence, or the lack of it, was definitely *not* the problem. Actually, Julia's only question, asked in various ways throughout the day, was, "Will you reassure me that I'm an important person around here?" The trick involved getting her to ask fewer questions and feel better about herself.

To begin with, I advised Mrs. Boulderdam to draw a large question mark on each of twelve index cards. Sometime later, she took Julia aside and told her how much she liked her—she really did, too—but that Julia needed to begin thinking through answers to her own questions. Mrs. Boulderdam offered to help Julie practice "thinking without help" by giving her the cards as "reminders."

Every time Julia came to Mrs. Boulderdam with a question, she had to give up one of her cards in exchange for an answer. When Julia's twelve cards were gone, Mrs. Boulderdam would refuse to answer any more questions for that day.

Julia started each new day with the twelve cards in her possession. When she had a question, Mrs. Boulderdam would ask her, "Have you thought about it, Julia?" and then, "Do you want to give me a card for the answer?"

Julia caught on very quickly. After a week, she was asking fewer than ten questions a day, most of them necessary.

Julie felt important because Mrs. Boulderdam had done something special—just for her. She also learned something valuable about independence. Mrs. Boulderdam's hands stopped fluttering, and she finished out the year in fine form.

Q: *At least twice a week, my son's first-grade teacher sends home assignments he should have finished in class but didn't because of dawdling. It's obvious the teacher doesn't and won't penalize him for this. I feel we should penalize him at home. Do you agree?*

A: Yes, I agree. If he finishes some class assignments and doesn't finish others, he can obviously finish them all. You have an opportunity here to nip in the bud a problem that will only get worse over time if left unchecked. I'd recommend making it a rule that if he brings unfinished work home one day of the school week, he'll be restricted one weekend day—confined to the house with no television and no visitors. If he brings unfinished work home two or more days through the week, he'll be restricted through the entire weekend. That should constitute an offer he can't refuse (but because he's a child, he will, for a while).

Q: *I am a new third-grade teacher who seems to have inherited a group of children with a superhuman proclivity for tattling on one another. How should I handle this?*

A: When children have conflicts, the easiest solution is often to appeal to the nearest adult to come bail them out. Because it is the easiest thing to do, it also takes the least amount of thought and effort on the part of the tattler. Therefore, when we respond to a tattletale, we encourage children not to think.

Tattling is senseless and destructive. Not only does it often prove unfair to the child who is tattled on, it is equally harmful to the child who does the tattling. The tattletale is usually the child least liked by siblings, shunned by peers, and held in disfavor by adults.

We adults inadvertently create the problem. The unfortunate victim of our actions is the "tattletale," because the child who tattles will have trouble being trusted and accepted by peers.

Tattling should be discouraged. When a child comes to you with a tale of woe, wanting to play informer, say, "I'm sorry that happened, Ashley, but I will not be able to come and help. This sounds like something you and Bruce can work out peacefully on your own."

If tattling is a habit with the child, be more definite about your feelings. "You are tattling again. You and I have talked about this before, and you know I will not settle your problems for you. You must solve this one for yourself."

Don't make the mistake of saying, "I don't like tattling," and then rushing to the scene anyway. Children learn more by what we do than what we say.

If the problem occurs frequently in a certain group of children, take the time to talk to everyone in the group about proper ways of solving problems. Help children make the distinction between what you *want* to know about (cuts, falls, and so on) and what you don't want to hear.

Tattling is the beginning of a long string of yarn that, unless cut early, grows larger and larger, becoming a burden for the child who must carry it around.

Q: *Two years ago, my daughter, now four and a half, could recite her ABCs and numbers through ten. She has been printing her name since she was three and correctly identifies every letter of the alphabet. Now I am having a problem with her and don't know what to make of it. Every day, we sit down for at least thirty minutes and work on her letters, name, and so on. For the past few months, however, she either refuses to work with me, complains that it's too hard, or acts as though she has forgotten much of what I taught her. I am becoming quite frustrated. Could she really be forgetting? What do you think?*

A: I think she is trying to tell you something. The games she once enjoyed playing with you have ceased to be fun. Something about the way Mom plays the game has changed. The rules are different.

As that first day of school inches steadily closer, you have become increasingly determined to ensure that, when the dash to the head of the class begins, she will be in the pole position. And she, in turn, has grown increasingly confused and uncomfortable with your expectations. This is no longer a game, this is serious business, the make-it-or-break-it stuff of real life. What began as a playful adventure two years ago has evolved into a repetitiously boring demand that shouldn't be made on a child her age.

Where on earth did you get the idea that knowing letters and numbers is essential for a four-and-a-half-year-old? Never mind, I know the answer. I've been there too. Parenthood is an uncertain undertaking. No one comes around saying, "Good job, Mom!" The standards are vague and indefinite, making it virtually impossible to assess how well you are doing. Somewhere along the line we begin measuring our own adequacy against how well, or quickly, our children "perform" the normal process of growth and development. Christy, who talked at twelve months, is "smarter" than sixteen-month-old Jody, who still says "goo-gaa." Therefore, Christy's parents must be creating a better environment than Jody's parents.

This absurd concern with who has the most advanced kid on the block is all too common. Whose lives are our children living, theirs or ours? Any developmentally healthy child can be taught to recite and even recognize the letters of the alphabet by the age of four. The same is true for numbers. But it doesn't mean a thing. Learning how to say *ef* when shown this shape—F—is no more outstanding an accomplishment than learning to say *dog,* when a furry four-legged creature runs up and licks your face. The crucial difference, however, is that the meaning of *dog* can be experienced directly, while the meaning of *ef* is completely abstract. It doesn't mean a thing to a four-year-old.

Furthermore, the head start you hope to provide your daughter is unlikely to give her any enduring advantage. The little girl who enters school already armed with her ABCs (and so on) may enjoy a brief stint as valedictorian of her kindergarten or first grade, but within two years she will, in all likelihood, be performing at about the same level she would have been without the push.

Take the cue and stop working so hard. You aren't a teacher, you're her mother, remember? And she's just four and a half. If she has what it takes to excel, all she needs from you is the opportunity and your support and confidence.

Instead of the daily drill, take a walk together around the neighborhood. Go to a park. Feed the ducks. She's only four and a half once—for a very short time.

Q: *Our four children have been in parochial school up until this year, when we put our three youngest into public school. In no time, I found myself becoming more and more stressed out as I ran between two different schools trying to keep up with their schedules. Quite frankly, I had a meltdown. My husband took the bull by the horns and immediately reenrolled the kids in parochial school. They were upset but have since made a good adjustment. I'm the one who's coming apart. Now that they've had a positive public school experience, I'm worried they will lose their enthusiasm for learning in the more regimented parochial atmosphere. I feel guilty about causing them insecurity and am also afraid they've learned it's okay to cave and run in the face of adversity. If we ultimately decide that public school is better, how should we tell the kids? I view this whole episode as the biggest mistake I've ever made as a parent. It's tearing me apart so much I feel I need professional help.*

A: If this is the biggest mistake you've ever made as a parent, you're doing just fine—better than most, in fact.

The problem is that like most moms you think it's your job to engineer the Perfect Everything for your children—the perfect school experience, the perfect after-school activities, the perfect social life, the perfect birthday party, the perfectly balanced nutritional regimen, perfect medical care, and so on. In short, you have assigned yourself the task of being the Perfect Mother who always makes Perfect Decisions. Since you apparently have some regard for Christian scripture, I will point out to you that you are bordering on blasphemy here.

Seek professional help if you want, but I am a professional, and herein is my help: You have ruined nothing. Your children are four of the luckiest children in the world, not just in the material sense but also in the sense of having parents who are so darned concerned about their welfare. Given the chance, no less than 60 percent of the world's kids would change places with them in a heartbeat. Your husband saw you agonizing over something and unable to think straight, so he did the thinking for the both of you. Thank him profusely for being such a good husband and doing what a good spouse should do in such situations.

You are thinking apocalyptically about the effect of this whole brouhaha on your kids. This isn't going to make them apathetic toward learning or lifelong losers. Nor will it cause them, as adults, to have to go into therapy to resolve "childhood issues" around the "insecurity" caused when their parents flip-flopped on a school placement decision when they were kids. As you pointed out, they seem to be adjusting well. You're not giving your children enough credit here. Furthermore, this will not be significant to anything in five years, at most.

You're too wrapped up in your kids. You need to stop using all your energy and time to engineer the Perfect Everything for them and do some things for yourself. Join an exercise class. Enroll in a watercolor painting class through your local junior college or YWCA. Most of all, pay more attention to your marriage. Sounds like you have a winner for a hubby. Count your lucky stars!

Last, if you decide to put them back in public school (wait until next school year, please!), just sit down and tell them, "Well, kids, if you've learned one thing about us by now, it's that we like variety and are fairly unpredictable. So, we've decided you're going to public school this year. Any questions?" Mind you, not, "How do you feel about that?" but, rather, "Any questions?"

Afterword

HAVING BEGUN THIS BOOK by talking about my children, I think it appropriate to end that way as well.

As I write these final lines, Eric is almost thirty-three years old. He is married to Nancy, with whom he has three children: Jack, Patrick, and Thomas, ages six, three, and three months, respectively. They tell us that's it. We'll see. Eric and Nancy and the boys live two doors down from us, which is either a blessing or a curse, depending on whom you ask and on what day. Actually, it's been nothing but a blessing for Willie and me, who thoroughly enjoy having the grandkids in our home, where we have set up a bedroom playroom just for them and which they visit on an almost daily basis. Eric is a commercial pilot for a major national bank. Nancy is a homemaker, and a fine one at that.

Amy is twenty-eight. She and her husband, Marshall, live in Texas with their sixteen-month-old son, Connor. Amy informed us recently that she is newly pregnant with grandchild number five, who will arrive before my fifty-fourth birthday. What a bunch of blessings! Marshall works for a corporation without which the Internet would not work. Amy is also a fine homemaker.

The grandchildren are all well behaved, in case you are wondering. Naturally, they are more well behaved when their parents are not with them, but that's normal. It must be galling—in fact, I remember the gall quite well—to have grandparents say, "They're absolutely no trouble when they're with us," but it's the truth. Grandparents are not inclined to worry about whether their grandchildren will continue to love them if they discipline them. They know discipline and love cannot be separated and that children intuitively know the difference between discipline that is loving and discipline that is not—and which, therefore, is not discipline at all. Parents are worried about such things, so they tend to pull their disciplinary punches. Grandparents tend to tell their grandchildren what to do and what not to do. Parents tend to ask, cajole, wheedle, bribe, bargain, plead, threaten, and so on.

I love being a grandfather. I also love being a husband, a father, and a father-in-law. Nothing beats family. Family can be one's greatest challenge, but it can also be one's greatest blessing. It has been both for me, and I wouldn't have it any other way. Family has been the cause of my growing up; it has also been the source of my perpetual childhood. Family has been the cause of much pain; it has also been the source of untold pleasure. Family has been the source of much strength; it has also been the context within which many of my weaknesses have been acted out on the way to being worked out. Family has been the source of everything I have learned about children and child-rearing, and I have learned it all the hard way. Family has been my journey, which I have shared with you in this book.

I hope I've accomplished what I set out to do: to liberate your thinking from the very confining box of "psychological correctness" and, in so doing, helped you create a more rewarding family life.

I have two final thoughts to pass along.

First, raise your children *your* way. Understand that people like me, people who write "parenting" books, articles, and newspaper columns, have suggestions, ideas, and guidelines. They do not have the final word when it comes to your kids. You do. If you disagree with an expert on a child-rearing matter, give yourself the benefit of the doubt.

Second and last, but by no means least, something we all tend to lose sight of when the milk is spilled and the children are sending us up the wall . . .

Enjoy!

Index